MONOGRAPHS OF THE HEBREW UNION COLLEGE · 35

A Great Voice that Did Not Cease

The Growth of the Rabbinic Canon and Its Interpretation

I. EDWARD KIEV LIBRARY FOUNDATION VOLUMES

In loving memory of Dr. I. Edward Kiev, distinguished Rabbi, Chaplain, and Librarian of the Hebrew Union College-Jewish Institute of Religion in New York, his family and friends established a Library Foundation in September 1976 to support and encourage scholarship in Judaica and Hebraica. The Hebrew Union College Press is proud to add this work by Michael Chernick to the growing list of scholarly works supported by the Kiev Foundation.

Benny Kraut *From Reform Judaism to Ethical Culture*
The Religious Evolution of Felix Adler

Alan Mendelson *Secular Education in Philo of Alexandria*

Raphael Jospe *Torah and Sophia*
The Life and Thought of Shem Tov ibn Falaquera

Richard Kalmin *The Redaction of the Babylonian Talmud*

Shuly Rubin Schwartz *The Emergence of Jewish Scholarship in American*
The Publication of the Jewish Encyclopedia

Philip Miller *Karaite Separatism in Nineteenth-Century Russia*

Warren Bargad *To Write the Lips of Sleepers*
The Poetry of Amir Gilboa

Marc Saperstein *Your Voice LIke a Ram's Horn*
Themes and Texts in Traditional Jewish Preaching

Eric L. Friedland *"Were Our Mouths Filled with Song"*
Studies in Liberal Jewish Liturgy

Edward Fram *Ideals Face Reality*
Jewish Law and Life in Poland, 1550–1665

Ruth Langer *To Worship God Properly*
Tensions Between Liturgical Custom and Halakhah in Judaism

Carole Balin *To Reveal Our Hearts: Jewish Women Writers in Tsarist Russia*

Shaul Bar *A Letter That Has Not Been Read*
Dreams in the Hebrew Bible

Eric Caplan *From Ideology to Liturgy*
Reconstructionist Worship and American Liberal Judaism

Zafrira Lidovsky Cohen *"Loosen the Fetters of Thy Tongue, Woman"*
A Study of the Poetry and Poetics of Yona Wallach

Marc Saperstein *Exile in Amsterdam*
Saul Levi Morteira's Sermons to a Congregation of "New Jews"

Gershon Shaked *The New Tradition*
Essays on Modern Hebrew Literature

Edward Fram *My Dear Daughter*
Rabbi Benjamin Slonik and the Education of Jewish Women in Sixteenth-Century Poland

Michael Chernick *"A Great Voice that Did Not Cease"*
The Growth of the Rabbinic Canon and Its Interpretation

A Great Voice that Did Not Cease

The Growth of the Rabbinic Canon and Its Interpretation

Michael Chernick

Hebrew Union College Press
Cincinnati

For Miriam

Hebrew Union College – Jewish Institute of Religion

Library of Congress Cataloging-in-Publication Data

Chernick, Michael L.

"A great voice that did not cease": the growth of the rabbinic canon and its interpretation / Michael Chernick.

ISBN 0-87820-461-8; 978-0-87820-461-8 (alk. paper)

1. Rabbinical literature — History and criticism — Theory, etc. 2. Jewish law Interpretation and construction. 3. Bible. O.T. Pentateuch — Criticism, interpretation, etc. 4. Hermeneutics — Religious aspects — Judaism. I. Title.

BM496.6 C48 2009
296.1'20601–dc22 2009004536

Printed on acid-free paper in the United States of America
Typography and design by Kelby Bowers
Distributed by Wayne State University Press
4809 Woodward Avenue, Detroit, Michigan 48201
Toll free: 800-978-7323

Contents

Acknowledgments

באדם יש שותפין הרבה. Many people collaborate with an author in bringing a work of research and ideas to fruition. I am indebted to many "partners," and I take this opportunity to acknowledge their support and assistance.

I am especially indebted to Richard Sarason, Professor of Rabbinic Literature and Thought at Hebrew Union College-Jewish Institute of Religion, for taking the time to look at the earliest version of my manuscript. His rigorous reading and wisdom were invaluable in determining the direction that this work has taken.

Along with Professor Sarason, I am indebted to the many colleagues whose suggestions, interest, and encouragement have contributed to this work. All of them provided important and positive feedback, and whatever shortcomings this book contains are entirely my own.

My association with the Hebrew Union College-Jewish Institute of Religion has provided me with the privilege of being a teacher of Torah. The College-Institute has also generously made it possible for me to have the most up-to-date tools necessary for contemporary research in my field. Its support of travel to scholarly conferences where ideas can be exchanged and sharpened has also been invaluable. It is with gratitude for all of this that I thank the institution that has so greatly contributed to my wonderfully varied and interesting Jewish life.

My thanks also to the Publications Committee of the Hebrew Union College Press and its chair, Professor Michael A. Meyer, for the confidence they have shown in my work. Barbara Selya, the press's managing editor, and her staff have given my book meticulous care and have made its production a true pleasure. For that and for so much more, I thank all of my aforementioned "partners" for their contributions toward the creation of this book and the making of this author. Finally, I am grateful to the I. Edward Kiev Library Foundation for its generous support of this volume and other scholarly publications of the Hebrew Union College Press.

General and Methodological Introduction

The Pentateuch's description of the Sinaitic revelation speaks of how God communicated with the Israelite community. As Deuteronomy 5:19 portrays the event, God spoke to the assembled people with a קול גדול ולא יסף. This phrase does not yield easily to translation. Recent attempts have suggested that it means that God revealed "those words – those and no more . . . with a mighty voice."[1] The "words," of course, refer to the famous "Ten Pronouncements," better known as the Ten Commandments. Traditional Jewish *targumim* (Aramaic translations) and commentaries did not accept this translation or understanding of the verse. The standard *targum*, traditionally called *Targum Onqelos*, translates the phrase as קל רב ולא פסק, "a great voice that did not cease," and the so-called *Targum Yonatan* translates it the same way. Rashi, the famous eleventh-century Bible and Talmud commentator, follows the *targumim*, though he adds a comment and provides an alternative thought. His comment is revealing. He writes, "And we translate 'and it did not cease' for God's Voice was strong and it exists forever. . . ."[2]

This study proceeds from the views expressed by the *targumim* and in the first part of Rashi's comment. As I understand those views, they propose that the Sinaitic revelation was produced by a voice that spoke at that moment and did not cease to speak to the Jewish people throughout history. This view, I believe, is at the core of rabbinic Judaism, the Judaism that interpreted and claimed to hear that voice through the medium of interpretation. This study will take us even further than that claim. It seems that at certain points in time the canon that starts with the Pentateuch seems to grow and extend, or to put it in a formulation attributed to R. Elazar b. Azariah, "The words of the Torah are fruitful and multiply." Our study proposes that each extension views the next canonical text as part of the divine revelation, as part of the "great voice that did not cease."

Hermeneutics and *Midrash*

In order to trace the development of the ideas stated above, this work focuses upon several examples of rabbinic hermeneutics, which in this study are

1 *TaNaKh* (Philadelphia: Jewish Publication Society, 1985), p. 283. The *English Standard Version of the Bible* (2001) and several other English translations translate the verse along the same lines.

2 See also Nachmanides' Commentary, Deut 5:19. For a traditional commentator whose thinking is more in line with more recent translations, see Rashi's second comment and RaShbaM, Deut 5:19.

methodologies of interpretation applied by the Rabbis to the texts they regarded as scriptural. In rabbinic praxis, hermeneutics and *midrash* go hand in hand.[3] The first generally produces the second. *Midrash* is by definition a form of interpretation of Scripture that goes beyond the text's most obvious meaning. Indeed, the Hebrew root of the word (*d-r-š*) means "to seek, to search," and clearly one need not search for that which is obvious and immediately accessible. This study, then, is on one level a standard academic rabbinics exploration of six interpretational methods: "even though there is no proof for this matter, there is a prooftext for it" (אף על פי שאין ראיה לדבר, זכר לדבר), "the resolution of two contradictory verses" (שני כתובים המכחישים זה את זה), "transferral of the rules of one pentateuchal rubric to another" (אם אינו ענין), "two verses that teach a single principle" (שני כתובים הבאים כאחד), "two restrictions" (תרי מיעוטי), and "these scriptural passages are necessary" (צריכי). Consistent with that type of study, we analyze developments in the form, logic, and results of the interpretational methods under analysis. If there is chronological development, we chart it Though this aspect of the study is mainly directed toward those in the field of historical-critical rabbinics, I have tried to make it accessible to those who are interested in the history of biblical interpretation, the development of rabbinic Judaism, or early rabbinic Jewish theology, all of which are also among the major concerns of this study.

Midrash and the Constitutional Status of the Torah

It is impossible to explain the etiology of midrashic interpretation without a word about the status of the Torah as a constitutional document for the Jewish people. For our purposes a constitution is either a document or oral tradition that a society uses to define its fundamental laws, establish the basic

3 In Hebrew, the hermeneutical methods are called *middot* (מדות), literally "measures." There is the possibility that the Greek term κανων (lit., straight rod) influences this choice of terminology for the rabbinic hermeneutical methods. Metaphorically, the Greek term has the meaning "rule," "standard," or in regard to grammar, a "general rule" about grammatical usage. We might reasonably extend any of these meanings to mean the (general) rules or standard methods for the reading of a text, in the case of the Rabbis' exegesis, the Torah. See H. G. Liddel and R. Scott, *Greek-English Lexicon* (Oxford: Clarendon Press, 1996), p. 875, s.v. κανων. See D. Z. Hoffman, "לחקר מדרש התנאים" (German, *Zur Einleitung in die halachischen Midraschim*, p. 37), מסילות לתורת התנאים: trans. A. S. Rabinowitz (Tel-Aviv: n.p., 1928, reprinted, Jerusalem: Carmiel, 1970), p. 3:

> מדרש הלכה יליף מהכתוב על פי כללים ידועים, שנקראים מדות. פעמים רבות המדרש בעצמו נקרא מטעם זה „מדות" (בארמית – מכילתא).

> Halakhic *midrash* is learned from Scripture by means of known general principles, which are called *middot*. Often the *midrash* (collection) itself, for this reason, is called *middot* (in Aramaic, *mekhilta*).

See also Hoffman, chap. 1, n. 11.

institutions of its government, and delineate the obligations and rights of its individual constituents. Equally important is the actual application of the constitution to the inevitable vicissitudes a society undergoes. The sign of a group's faithfulness to its constitution is not the lip service it pays it, but the practical use the group makes of it to confront the legal, religious, ethical, and social issues that inevitably arise as a society changes.

The history of the Torah as the constitution of the Jewish people is not linear. Though there is conjecture and debate in academic circles about how much of the Pentateuch was available to Israel at various times, one point seems clear: it took considerable time for Israel to accept the Torah as its constitution. It certainly was not its constitution during the earliest periods of Israelite life as the *TaNaKh* itself attests. The pre-Exilic period made markedly less constitutional use of the Torah, though various institutions of the Law were observed even when wholehearted loyalty to it was not present.

The first time in Jewish history that the Torah was widely accepted as a constitutional document was in the period of the "Return to Zion," especially under Ezra and Nehemiah and the Prophets of the Return – Haggai, Zechariah, and Malachi. Thus the post-Exilic Jewish community ultimately chose the Torah as a societal constitution and used it to guide the community's re-establishment. From that point on, the trajectory of Jewish legal history reveals that the Torah increasingly became Israel's Law *par excellence*, though even during the Second Commonwealth there were moments of backsliding and outright rebellion such as when a Hellenized Jewish ruling class sought to convert Jerusalem into a *polis*.

Though the Torah became the agreed-upon source for defining what Jewish religio-national life and observance was,[4] different Jewish sects, movements, and ideologies like the Maccabeans, Hasidim, Sadducees, Pharisees, Essenes, Apocalyptics, Rabbis, and Jewish-Christians had quite different ideas about how the Torah-constitution should be interpreted and lived. All these groups faced the question of how to apply the Torah to the most significant and pressing temporal issues facing them. Therefore, each group developed its own hermeneutical approach to the Torah's text and with it its own means of exegesis. Some allowed for expansive interpretation of the Torah, while others were what today we would call strict constructionists. Some groups occasionally skirted the exegetical process and resorted to creating "new" Torah revelations in order to extend or amend the Torah-constitution, as sections of the Apocrypha, Pseudepigrapha, and Qumran documents show. Others created alternative Torahs, which had for them the same status as the Mosaic

4 For an excellent example of this phenomenon, see E. P. Sanders, *Judaism: Practice and Belief 63 B.C.E.–66 C.E.* (London and Philadelphia: SCM and Trinity, 1992), pp. 222–29.

Torah, as is the case regarding the Samaritan Pentateuch, the Septuagint, or the Gospels. Indeed, it might be argued that even rabbinic Jews eventually accepted an additional Torah, the Oral Torah, which its later adherents considered equal to the Mosaic Torah.

The following essays focus upon the world of the Rabbis and their methods of Torah interpretation. I have chosen to analyze the Rabbis' hermeneutical methods because the midrashic results they produced are part of the largest Jewish textual corpus that has survived from antiquity and because what started as rabbinic Judaism became over time simply Judaism. While other Second Commonwealth Judaisms have left little or no trace except in the remnants of ancient documents and other artifacts from archeological digs, rabbinic Judaism still significantly influences the practices and thinking even of those modern Jews who no longer grant the Torah the kind of constitutional authority it had in pre-modern Jewish communities.

Translating the Bible according to its *Midrash*

There are various schools of midrashic interpretation, some more radical in their approach to the biblical text than others. The school identified by some as the Akiban school tends to interpret even the finest grammatical parts of the biblical text, while what they call the school of R. Ishmael tends to be more restrained in its approach.[5] Nevertheless, both types of *midrash* produce results at some remove from the basic meaning of the biblical text that generates them. This lack of "plain meaning" orientation sometimes makes reading *midrash* somewhat of a mystery. Since this work is directed to both those in the

5 See Azzan Yadin, *Scripture as Logos*, chaps. 2 and 4 and pp. 120–21. For views regarding the division of the halakhic *midrashim* into Akiban and Ishmael school *midrashim* see D. Z. Hoffman, לחקר מדרשי התנאים, pp. 5–7; H. S. Horovitz, "Einleitung," ספרי דבי רב (Leipzig, Gustav Fock, G.m.b.H, 1917), v–xvii; J. N. Epstein, מבואות לספרות התנאים (Jerusalem and Tel Aviv: Magnes and Dvir Press, 1957; second edition 1978), pp. 521–36. Other scholars deny that there are truly Akiban and Ishmael schools, but they do admit that there are different methods of *midrash* employed in various midrashic works. See, for example, Ch. Albeck, *Untersuchungen über die Halakischen Midraschim* (Berlin: Akademie Verlag, 1927), pp. 84–86. For more recent contributions to the debate on the side of there being Akiban and Ishmael *midrashim*, see Azzan Yadin, *Scripture as Logos*, pp. x–xii, Menahem Kahana, "The Tannaitic Midrashim," *The Cambridge Genizah Collection, Their Content and Significance*, ed. Stefen Reif (Cambridge: Cambridge University Press, 2002), 61, 64–66 and idem., ספרי זוטא דברים (Jerusalem: Hebrew University, 2002), pp. 51; 82–84; 109–10; Abraham Goldberg, "דבי ר' עקיבא ור' ישמעאל בספרי דברים פיס' א-נד," תעודה (Ramat Aviv: Tel Aviv University, 1983), 3:9–16. Regarding those who have taken a position closer to Albeck, see Jay Harris, *How Do We Know This?* (Albany: State University of New York Press, 1995), pp. 51–72; Gary Porton, *The Traditions of Rabbi Ishmael,* part 2 (Leiden: E. J. Brill, 1977) p. 7; ibid., part 4 (Leiden: E. J. Brill, 1982), pp. 55f.; 65f. 67, and 191; see also Stemberger's conclusions about this issue in H. L. Strack and Günther Stemberger, *Introduction to the Talmud and Midrash* (Minneapolis: Fortress Press, 1996), pp. 249–50.

field of rabbinics and those who wish to understand that field better, I have often translated scriptural verses or passages in light of their midrashic interpretation rather than according to the accepted and more typical contemporary Jewish and Christian translations of the Hebrew Bible. It is my hope that these translations will provide insight into the rabbinic midrashists' style of "translation/traduction" of Scripture. I cannot, at this distance of centuries, be sure that my translations reflect what was actually on the minds of the original rabbinic midrashists as they did their interpretive work. Nevertheless, I hope these translations will orient the readers to the midrashic reading of Scripture and make them more sympathetic to it.

I have also included commentary – mostly my own, though often based on more traditional rabbinic commentaries – as a part of the analysis of the many midrashic citations in this work in order to clarify what may have prompted the midrashists to interpret Scripture as they did. I hope this commentary will help the reader follow the midrashic arguments and understand the relationship between the scriptural verse and its midrashic interpretation.

Theoretical Issues of Significance to this Study

A number of theoretical issues are germane to my research. The most important of these are: the question of the trustworthiness of attributions of dicta in rabbinic sources; the nature of talmudic material cited as tannaitica; and the dating of the anonymous stratum of the Talmud (סתם, *stam* or סתמא דגמרא, *stama di-gemara*).

The first issue is of serious consequence. The names of tradents are temporal markers. If it is impossible to state with some confidence that the attribution of an idea to a tradent or his circle is accurate, then we cannot make the case that an halakhic, aggadic, or midrashic dictum emerged during a particular time within the various formative rabbinic periods (tannaitic, amoraic, post-amoraic but pre-geonic).

The second issue is important because if the Palestinian Talmud (henceforth, PT) or the Babylonian Talmud (henceforth, BT) cites something as a tannaitic source, we need to know whether the source is actually tannaitic if we are to do an historically accurate analysis of the hermeneutics involved. This is especially true in this study, which deals with a plethora of midrashic sources, many of which the *Talmudim* present as tannaitic *midrashim*. We cannot proceed to analyze hermeneutical development without knowing whether these claims are true.

The period of the anonymous stratum of the Talmud is also of consequence to this study. Like the issue of the accuracy of attributions, anonymity also raises the question of dating. By its very nature, anonymity seems to preclude dating. However, BT, and to a lesser degree, PT include anonymous strata that appear in a variety of relationships to attributed material. To an extent, these relationships open the door to hypothesizing about the date of the *stam*. Therefore, to a degree this issue and the issue of accuracy of attributions cohere. Certainly, if we could date the *stam*, even generally, this would help to provide a more complete picture of how and when hermeneutical methods developed and at what moments their forms and "logic" changed.[6]

The Accuracy of Attributions and Biographies of the Sages

There was a time when it was a given that attributions of dicta to tannaitic and amoraic Sages were accurate. Historians of the Jewish people and of the development of Judaism were confident as well in the accuracy of reports about individuals and events in formative rabbinic literature. Those who engaged in the general study of Jewish history, the biographies of the Sages, or the intellectual history of Judaism felt that they could pursue their research without many difficulties. After all, they could refer to a considerable body of accurate tannaitic and amoraic records that came directly from the periods they were studying. Their most difficult theoretical problems came from those so-called historical or biographical sources in which there were miraculous or supernatural elements. In such cases, the historians I speak of developed the "kernel of truth" hypothesis. That is, they agreed that they had to dismiss the miraculous and supernatural elements of a story and focus on those elements that could reasonably provide a modicum of historical truth. Such sources provided historians with what they considered to be usable records for historiographical purposes.

The above methodology informs the work of writers of "modern" Jewish histories from the nineteenth century until the 1980s. These writers represent some of the best known figures in Jewish historiography and the study of the development of rabbinic Judaism, which they generally defined simply as

6 While some *middot* function according to reasoned argument (e.g., קל וחומר, *a fortiori*), many have what I call a "literary logic." For example, analogies formed by word comparison called *gezerah shavah* are predicated on the repetition of the same word or of the same or similar phrases in the Pentateuch. A rule attached to the context of the rubric in which one of the repeated words or phrases appears, for example the use of "in its fixed time" (במועדו, see Num 28:2), referring to the daily offering, is used to shed light on a question of a rule related to the Passover offering, where the term במועדו is also used (Num 9:2–3) in an undefined manner. The connection established by the use of במועדו allows for a comparison of a rule regarding the daily offering – namely that it may be brought even on the Sabbath (Num 28:10) – to the Passover offering, even though the Passover is different from the daily offering in many ways. There is no basis in this *midrash* for an analogy of a truly logical type. The "logic" is based on literary formulation and intertextual connections.

Judaism or "normative Judaism" when they wrote about the period of the development of the Mishnah and Talmud.[7]

To a greater or lesser degree, unquestioning acceptance of attributions also characterized the works of non-Jewish writers who wrote about Jewish history, the "historical Jesus," Christianity and its Jewish origins, or about Paul's Jewish roots and his relationship to first-century Palestinian Judaism. This approach typified works such as Emil Schürer's *Geschichte des jüdischen Volkes im Zeitalter Jesu Christi* (1886–1890), especially the sections on life in the Jewish territory of Palestine during the period he describes and the institutions of Jewish life such as the Sanhedrin, priesthood and Temple, and the work and teachings of the "Scribes." Ernest Renan's rather distasteful treatment of rabbinic Judaism in his *Histoire du peuple d'Israël* (vol. 5, 1893) also accepts statements attributed to Hillel and Shammai and stories about them as absolutely factual. In his history of Judaism, George Foote Moore dealt in a more descriptive fashion with the tannaitic material that is at the heart of his work.[8] His approach does not necessarily make any claims for the accuracy of attributions or for the historical truth of any story about a tannaitic figure. Moore, however, included a historical introduction. It is there that he takes tannaitic and amoraic descriptions of institutions, reports about rabbinic masters, and accounts of events more or less at face value. Most importantly, Moore created the sense that early Palestinian rabbinic Judaism vanquished all other contending expressions of Judaism and became the normative and orthodox form of Judaism. Hence, rabbinic literature's statements about legal matters were in his opinion statements about how Jewish life was actually lived in the Palestinian and Babylonian Jewish communities of late antiquity.

The form of historiography I have just described characterized Jewish historical scholarship until Jacob Neusner began his work on the rabbinic cor-

7 This approach characterizes the works of Heinrich Graetz, the 19th-century father of Jewish historiography and author of *Geschichte der Juden* (1853–1875); Salo Baron, the author of the twenty-seven volume work *The Social and Religious History of the Jews* (1952–1983); and Louis Finkelstein in works like *Akiba: Scholar, Saint and Martyr* (1936) and *The Pharisees* (1938). Among the Israeli historians, we find that historians like Michael Avi-Yonah, author of *History of Israel and the Holy Land* (1963, reprinted with additions 2003) and *The Jews Under Roman and Byzantine Rule* (first Hebrew edition, 1946; English, 1976 and 1984) and Gedaliah Alon, author of *The Jews in their Land in the Talmudic Age* (in Hebrew, 1953–1956; in English 1980, 1984, 1994) and *Meḥqarim be-Toledot Yisrael bimei Bayit Sheni uve-Tequfat ha-Mishnah ve-ha-Talmud* (1957–1958) followed this approach. Similarly, in his attempt to create a history of the ideas and beliefs of the Sages in his *Ḥazal: Emunot ve-De'ot* (first edition, 1969; second edition, 1971; third edition, 1975), Ephraim E. Urbach accepted statements and some "biographical" *aggadot* about the Sages at face value.

8 *Judaism in the First Centuries of the Christian Era: The Teachings of the Tannaim*, 1927–1930, second edition, 1966, reprinted in 1971.

pus. At the outset, Neusner himself proceeded according to the canons we outlined above (see his *A History of the Jews in Babylonia*, 1965–1970). But in his introduction to the 1984 reprinted edition of that work he retracts the methodology he originally pursued. The more his work progressed, the more he expressed skepticism about "historicism" in the study of rabbinic works. One can find one of Neusner's most pointed expressions of this skepticism in *Reading and Believing: Ancient Judaism and Contemporary Gullibility* (1986). His attack on what he considered naïve and gullible methodology brought into question much of modern scholarship in the areas of the history of the Jewish people and Judaism during the late Second Commonwealth, especially for the formative period of rabbinic Judaism.[9] William Scott Green, one of Neusner's students, wrote a much cited article, "What's in a Name? The Problematic of Rabbinic Biography,'" which dealt with whether or not it is really possible to write biographies of the tannaitic teachers.[10] His conclusions were similar to those of his teacher: attributions are not reliable, and one cannot trust stories about the Sages to be historical records.[11]

These positions are not, as Green puts it, "... the result of excessive skepticism." As he notes, manuscripts occasionally attribute tannaitic halakhic dicta to different tradents. Even when there is a unified manuscript tradition, the names of tradents often differ in different works, and later tradents sometimes provide double attributions for a lemma, or admit that attributions are confused or reversed. Pseudepigraphy is also a factor that makes attributions suspect.[12]

In regard to biographies of the Sages, those who attempt to construct them do so mostly on the basis of *aggadot*. But are *aggadot* containing what appears to be historical information actually reliable historical sources? Green believes they are not. He bases his view partly on the scholarship of Fischel and A. A. Halevy, who compare the rabbinic "Sage story" to the *chreia* that portray Greek sages in a form that might be described as "sophos-sapiens-hakham" and on the studies of the folklorists Noy and Ben-Amos.[13] More recent studies of the literary art of *aggadot*, especially the case of the "Sage story" and the changes in such stories from their Palestinian origins to their Babylo-

9 The following hold similar views regarding the reliability of attributions: W. S. Towner, *The Rabbinic "Enumeration of Scriptural Examples"* (Leiden: E. J. Brill, 1973), p. 34; S. Stern, "Attribution and Authorship in the Babylonian Talmud," *Journal of Jewish Studies* 45 (1994): 28–51.

10 W. S. Green, "What's in a Name – The Problematic of Rabbinic 'Biography,'" *Approaches to Ancient Judaism: Theory and Practice* (Missoula: Scholars Press, 1978), pp. 77–96.

11 Ibid., pp. 80–84 (regarding attributions); from 85–96, the author deals with rabbinic biography.

12 Ibid., p. 84 and nn. 32–33. See also, H. L. Strack and Günther Stemberger, *Introduction to the Talmud and Midrash* (Minneapolis: Fortress Press, second printing, 1996), pp. 58–59.

13 Ibid., p. 86, and n. 45.

nian form, add to the data that suggest that skepticism about the creation of accurate rabbinic biographies is warranted.[14]

According to Neusner, a further issue undermines the search for certainty regarding attributions: the nature of the redaction of formative rabbinic works. He has taken the position that the "documents" of early rabbinic Judaism reflect only the views of their redactors. They alone controlled the traditional material that came down to them, and they chose from that pool of material that which reflected their own agenda. Hence there was a leveling of the received material in favor of the redactional point of view. This leveling destroyed the historical value the material may have possessed before it was subjected to the redactors' considerations.

These skeptical attitudes toward attributions in early rabbinic literature and the reliability of *aggadot* as sources for rabbinic biographies has engendered a literature of response. The respondents indicate that what was at stake for them was the continued feasibility of writing the history of the Jews or of Judaism and its development in late antiquity.[15] They claim they have the methodological means to re-establish the possibility of writing histories of Judaism and the Jewish people, though many if not most of these scholars accept the fact that reliable rabbinic biographies are irretrievable.[16] The basic principles of their methodologies, then, are as follows:

1. Dicta that refer to realia, institutions, or practices in early rabbinic literature may be considered accurate when they pass the test of external verification.[17]

14 For recent studies of *aggadah* as literature, see Yonah Frankel, *Midrash ve-Aggadah*, vol. 2 (Tel Aviv: Everyman's University, 1997); Jeffrey Rubenstein, *Talmudic Stories: Narrative Art, Composition, and Culture* (Baltimore: Johns Hopkins University Press, 1999).

15 This concern is explicit in David Kraemer, "On the Reliability of Attributions in the Babylonian Talmud," *HUCA* 60:175–89 and in David Goodblatt, "Toward the Rehabilitation of Talmudic History," *History of Judaism – The Next Ten Years*, Brown Judaic Series 21, ed. Baruch Bokser (Chico: Scholars Press, 1980), pp. 36–38 and 38–42. Implicitly, this is what motivates Lee I. Levine's comments in his introduction to *The Rabbinic Class of Roman Palestine in Late Antiquity* (Jerusalem and New York: Yad Ben Zvi Press and Jewish Theological Seminary, 1989), pp. 16–21. To a degree this is an interest of Richard Kalmin in *Sages, Stories, Authors and Editors in Rabbinic Babylonia*, Brown Judaic Studies 300 (Atlanta: Scholars Press, 1994). See his Introduction, pp. 1–3 and 15.

16 Goodblatt, "Toward the Rehabilitation of Talmudic History," p. 34; Kraemer, "On the Reliability of Attributions," p. 189; Kalmin is somewhat more sanguine about making occasional and tentative biographical claims, see *Sages, Stories*, p. 14.

17 Lee I. Levine, *The Rabbinic Class of Roman Palestine in Late Antiquity*, pp. 17–18 and nn. 11–15, but see pp. 18–19. Datable archeological evidence or the testimony of non-Jewish sources to a reality described in a *tanna's* or *amora's* dictum often adds to the reliability of a particular statement and to the attribution of it to a particular Sage, his circle, or generation. The same sorts of material, however, can show that the claims of the Sages were biased or a description of "reality" as the

2. Dicta attributed to particular Rabbis are reliable when they appear in independent corpora of rabbinic literature. For example, the attribution of a statement by Rabbi X may be considered verified if it appears in both PT and BT, since in general these works are independent of one another.[18]

3. A rabbinic dictum or idea may be assigned with a high degree of accuracy to a particular tradent, his circle, or generation if it can be shown that specific patterns of expression and thinking characterize the generation to which that tradent belongs.[19] Similarly, if a tradent of a later generation assumes or elaborates on a statement of a teacher of a previous generation, or if he revises or comments on the dictum of an earlier teacher, the attribution may be considered verified.[20]

4. Uniformity of attribution throughout the text witnesses (manuscripts and incunabula), especially if these do not come from a single "family" of manuscripts or if the manuscripts come from widely separated geographical areas, increases certainty about the accuracy of the attribution. If the attributed dictum appears in several early rabbinic sources – for example, Tosefta, PT, and BT, without any change in attribution and minimal or no changes in formulation – this provides further evidence that the attribution is accurate.[21]

I believe that the accuracy of an attribution can no longer be assumed and that a degree of skepticism is warranted. But a degree of skepticism does not mean total denial of the possibility that Rabbi X or Y did in fact say, though probably not in the exact words ascribed to him, that which is attributed to him.

Rabbis would have wished it to be, but not as it was. See H. L. Strack and Günther Stemberger, *Introduction to the Talmud and Midrash* (Minneapolis: Fortress Press, second printing, 1996), p. 48.

18 For more details regarding the independence of the *Talmudim*, see David Kraemer, "On the Reliability of Attributions," pp. 179–81; and idem., *The Mind of the Talmud* (Oxford: Oxford University Press, 1990), pp. 22–23.

19 For a detailed discussion of this criterion for the verification of an attribution, see David Kraemer, "On the Reliability of Attributions," pp. 182–86 and Goodblatt, "Toward the Rehabilitation," pp. 37–38; Kalmin, *Sages, Stories*, especially chaps. 2, 3, and 7.

20 Green, "What's in a Name?" p. 83; Jacob Neusner, *The History of the Mishnaic Law of Purities* (Leiden: E. J. Brill, 1974–1977), 8:206–20.

21 William Scott Green suggests that manuscript evidence is not probative regarding the accuracy of an attribution because the attribution traditions in them *not uncommonly* (emphasis mine – MC) differ. He also reminds us that attributions *occasionally* change (my emphasis – MC) from document to document among the early rabbinic literary sources. He rightly notes that *sometimes* (my emphasis – MC) later tradents cite traditions with double attributions, or admit that the attributions are confused or reversed. Stemberger enumerates other problems that arise when one tries to verify the accuracy of an attribution. See above, n. 8. By inference, however, where none of Green's and Stemberger's cautions about determining the accuracy of an attribution are applicable, one may consider an attribution verified.

The works of Kraemer and Kalmin are exacting in their use of statistics that are based on hundreds, and sometimes thousands, of cases. As they examine phenomena, they follow the very criteria suggested by Neusner himself for the verification of attributions. In this way, they make a case against the leveling of sources in at least BT and to some extent in PT. They accomplish this by showing that different generations of the *amoraim* exhibit different characteristics that are peculiar to them, but not blatantly obvious. Consequently, these authors claim that there is a way to know that a dictum has its roots in a specific generation. Using other criteria, as mentioned above, even more specificity about the authorship of a statement may be achieved.

I am more persuaded by the work of Kalmin and Kraemer than I am by the work of Neusner and those of his students who continue to use his methods. This does not mean that he and they have contributed little to the study of rabbinic literature. Quite the contrary. They have raised questions of singular import. Yet skepticism regarding the accuracy and verifiability of attributions based on phenomena that occur "not uncommonly," "sometimes," or "occasionally" makes that skepticism less compelling. Careful use of the criteria for assessing the accuracy of attributions that Neusner and his students accept, together with the evidence that Kalmin and Kraemer have amassed and the methodology they have employed in gathering it, provide useful tools for my work.

Furthermore, my work on כלל ופרט וכלל, ריבוי ומיעוט and גזירה שווה shows that the formal characteristics of these hermeneutics changed from one major era to another in the formative rabbinic period. These formal developments allowed for a general dating of tannaitic *derashot*, amoraic *memrot* containing *midrash*, and *sugyot* in which the hermeneutic that I analyzed appeared. There was no indication that the material that contained distinct forms of these *middot* had been "levelled" or that the *derashot* based on them served the interests of the redactors. The proof of this was the fact that the late *amoraim* and the *stam* recognized only certain forms of the *middot* I studied and rejected those that earlier *amoraim* had accepted. The same is true in regard to the earlier *amoraim* and the *tannaim*. The formal patterns the *tannaim* demanded in order for a *middah*'s use to be considered legitimate were rejected and replaced by their amoraic successors. Further, specific developments in the forms of these hermeneutics occurred at specific moments within the amoraic period – for example, during the fourth and seventh amoraic generations. This meant that one could frequently verify the accuracy of attributions of *derashot* and *memrot* with a degree of specificity if the midrashist used a particular form of a hermeneutic.[22]

22 Michael Chernick, לחקר המידות „כלל ופרט וכלל" ו„ריבוי ומיעוט" במדרשים ובתלמודים (Lod: Haber-

For these reasons, I generally accept attributions based on the criteria listed above. Since this work is not about the accuracy of attributions nor about rabbinic biography, I do not repeatedly test the accuracy of attributions unless correct attribution is crucial to dating a hermeneutic phenomenon or to making use of an especially significant rabbinic dictum that is central to this study's subject matter. I make no reference to rabbinic biographical information since it is usually impossible to determine whether a story about a Sage and his relations with characters whom we presume are his colleagues, teachers, or family members is historically factual. Nevertheless, *aggadot* do tell us something about the world views of the Sages. And if we can assign them in a general way to eras within the formative rabbinic period – for example, to the tannaitic or amoraic periods – we still may have valuable information about views that circulated during the eras of formative early rabbinic Judaism.[23]

The Problem of the Tannaitic Status of Talmudic *Baraitot*

1. Talmudic *Baraitot* are Authentically Tannaitic

As was the case regarding attributions and rabbinic biography, there were traditional and academic Talmudists who considered the *Talmudim* and other post-tannaitic documents of the formative rabbinic period as reliable sources of tannaitica. Even if the source had no parallel in the classical tannaitic collections like Tosefta and the halakhic *midrashim* or in other early rabbinic works, if it was presented as a *baraita*, it was one.[24] Rather than questioning this material's status, these scholars were grateful for its preservation, which, from their point of view, provided them with access to material that otherwise might have been lost. Rashi adopted this position, as his comments in several places in the Talmud indicate.[25] Among modern scholars, Arthur Spanier (1889–1944)[26] took this position as well, and, generally speaking, Yaakov

mann Institute, 1984), p. 127; מידת גזירה שווה: צורותיה במדרשים ובתלמודים (Lod: Habermann Institute, 1994), chaps. 7–8.

23 Goodblatt, "Toward the Rehabilitation," pp. 36–38; Kalmin, *Sages, Stories*, pp. 14–15. For examples of the kind of use I will make of aggadic material, see Kraemer, *The Mind of the Talmud*, pp. 141–46 and 156–58.

24 A *baraita* (Aram., ברייתא) is a tannaitic source that is not part of the Mishnah. The word means "outside," that is, "outside of the Mishnah."

25 See, for example, Rashi, bBeẓah 29a, s.v. תנא דבי שמואל; bZebaḥim 41b, s.v. תנא דבי ר' ישמעאל; bḤullin 141b, s.v. ר' חייא ור' אושעיא.

26 His works on Tosefta include *Die Toseftaperiode in der tannaitischen Literatur* (Berlin: C. A. Schwetschke, 1922, Schocken, 1936) and *Zur Frage des literarischen Verhältnisses zwischen Mischnah und Tosefta* (1931). His views about Babylonian talmudic *baraitot* appear in the first work, especially on pp. 52–65.

Elman adopts this approach, noting certain exceptions to the rule.[27]

If this position had stood undisputed, a chronology of the development of the midrashic hermeneutics would be fairly easy to construct. We could simply assign all *baraitot*, wherever they appeared, whether paralleled or unparalleled in the literature, to the tannaitic era. If a talmudic *baraita* contained a midrashic hermeneutic with certain formal and logical features, we could claim with certainty that we possessed a tannaitic paradigm for this variety of hermeneutic. The matter, however, is not that simple.

2. Some Talmudic *Baraitot* as Amoraic *Memrot* or Amoraic Fabrications

In this matter, as in the matter of the reliability of attributions, there have been those who have suggested that at least some talmudic *baraitot* are either forgeries or post-tannaitic sources. Yizḥak Eizik Halevi (1847–1914), despite his basic traditionalism, held the post-mishnaic collections attributed to R. Ḥiyya, R. Oshaya, Levi, and other late tannaitic-early amoraic Sages to be simply amoraic works. According to him, their collections represent the thinking of their authors based on the traditions of the *tannaim*, but not works that contained the *bona fide* teachings of the tannaitic Sages.[28] Thus, the contents of these collections had the status and authority of *memrot* (amoraic dicta).[29] Hence, if one of the *Talmudim* cited this sort of material preceded by a rhetorical formula that indicated a *baraita*, it did not grant the status of a tannaitic source to it. In *Dor Dor ve-Doreshav*, Isaac Hirsch Weiss (1815–1905) exhibited an even higher degree of skepticism about the tannaitic origins of some talmudic *baraitot*. According to him, there were *amoraim* who fabricated *baraitot* in order to have their views accepted or to challenge a fellow *amora*.[30]

If these scholars' views were irrefutably correct and lacking in further nuance, then any study that aimed at creating a chronology of the development of any of the midrashic hermeneutics would be doomed from the outset. Lacking any criteria for the identification of an amoraic or fabricated *baraita*, writers of the history of rabbinic ideas, including ideas about how the Rabbis interpreted scriptural texts, could not proceed. Fortunately, Halevi's view

27 Yaakov Elman, *Authority and Tradition* (New York: Yeshiva University Press, 1994), see pp. 134–35 and idem., "Babylonian Baraitot in the Tosefta and the 'Dialectology' of Middle Hebrew," *AJS Review* 16 (1991): 26–27 and n. 101.

28 Yitzḥak Eizik Halevi, *Dorot ha-Rishonim* (Frankfurt A. M.: M. Slobotzky, 1901), 5:129–31 and 142.

29 According to Halevi, this explains the fact that some of this material appears as a *baraita* in one of the *Talmudim* and as a *memra* in the other. This, however, does not explain the same phenomenon when it occurs in a toseftan or midrashic *baraita*. These issues will be important at several points in the coming chapters, especially in Chapter Three.

30 I. H. Weiss, *Dor Dor ve-Doreshav* (Jerusalem and Tel Aviv: reprinted, Ziv, n.d.), 2:215–16.

is mostly based on assertion rather than proof, and the evidence for Weiss's position comes from a few important examples. Overall, Weiss was willing to accept that most talmudic *baraitot* were in fact tannaitic. Nevertheless, his view regarding fabricated amoraic *baraitot* cautions us about naive use of talmudic *baraitot* as infallible chronological markers.

3. Talmudic *Baraitot* as Tannaitic Sources Reworked or Added to by *Amoraim*

The view that most medieval, *Wissenschaft*, and modern scholars held or presently hold is that talmudic *baraitot*, especially those without parallels in what are generally held to be tannaitic sources, have a good chance of having a tannaitic core. Nevertheless, the core may have either been added to or changed for a variety of reasons that we will discuss below.

Among the medieval commentators who held the view that talmudic *baraitot* often contain amoraic additions are R. Abraham b. David of Posquieres (1125–1198), Nachmanides (1194–1270) and members of his school, and more sporadically the Tosafists.[31] We find the roots of a literature that tried to produce *kelalim* (general principles) describing the literary characteristics and methodologies of the basic genres of rabbinic literature in the medieval period. But this literature truly began to flourish starting with the fifteenth century.

Two of the major *ba^calei ha-kelalim* are R. Joseph Karo (1488–1575), author of *Kelalei ha-Gemara*, and R. Ya'akov Ḥagiz (1620–1574), author of *Teḥilat Ḥokhmah*. In his *Kelalei ha-Gemara*, R. Joseph Karo notes that an *amora* may occasionally reformulate a *baraita* so that it will not contradict his view.[32] In his description of the methods of the Mishnah and *baraita*, Ḥagiz notes that Tosafot identified the possibility of a later addition into a talmudic *baraita* in order to make it conform to normative *halakhah*.[33] In another case, the Talmud attributes to an *amora* an admission that he added a word into a *baraita*. He did so, it is claimed, in order to use the *baraita* as a challenge to and a test of another *amora*'s view.[34] In each case, the *baraita* appears as if it were a typical tannaitic source.

31 Nachmanides, תורת האדם – ענין האבילות, ed. Chavel (Jerusalem: Mossad ha-Rav Kook, 1963), p. רכז, s.v. חידושי הרמב״ן ואם תאמר וכו׳; b^cAvodah Zarah 37a, s.v. מדקאמרינן מסתמיך. See also the references to the *rishonim* in Shamma Friedman, "הברייתות בתלמוד הבבלי ויחסן למקבילותיהן שבתוספתא," עטרה לחיים (Jerusalem: Jewish Theological Seminary, 2000), pp. 199–200. Regarding the Tosafists, see Rabbenu Tam, ספר הישר, ed. Schlesinger (Jerusalem, n.p., 1959), p. 10 and R. Samson of Sens, תוספות – בכורות כז ב׳, s.v. וכי. R. Samson speaks of *mishnayyot* rather than *baraitot*, but if his statement is true regarding the Mishnah, we might argue it is certainly so for *baraitot*, to which the *amoraim* did not generally grant the same level of authority.

32 R. Joseph Karo, כללי הגמרא, printed with הליכות עולם (Warsaw: 1883), p. 134, s.v. מצינו שאמורא מגיה וכו׳.

33 R. Ya'akov Ḥagiz, תחילת חכמה (Warsaw: Isaac Goldman, 1884), p. 37, #סו.

34 Ibid., p. 47, #כז.

Rabbinics, the modern study of the major documents produced by the Rabbis, also produced studies of *baraita* collections – for example, Tosefta, *ʾAvot de-R. Natan*, and the halakhic *midrashim* – as well as studies of the relationship between these collections and the *baraitot* of BT and PT. Many of those who have engaged in these studies find themselves in agreement with the medieval commentators: talmudic *baraitot* are fundamentally tannaitic sources, but post-tannaitic Sages have reworked and added to them. The difference between the modern rabbinics scholars and the medieval talmudic commentators is the difference between viewing this phenomenon as an occasional occurrence and viewing it as a more pervasive one.

Those who are substantially in agreement with the idea that talmudic *baraitot* generally have a tannaitic nucleus that has sometimes been reworked or added to are Zacharias Frankel (1801–1875), J. N. Epstein (1878–1852), Ch. Albeck (1890–1972), and more recently, Judith Hauptman and Shamma Friedman.[35]

4. A Methodology for the Analysis of Talmudic *Baraitot*

The views of the *rishonim*, *baʿalei ha-kelalim*, and modern scholars tend to support the idea that *baraitot* in the *Talmudim* may have been reworked or enhanced in other ways. There are also some scholars who believe that some of the talmudic *baraitot* are "fictitious."[36] This demands that as we work with talmudic *baraitot*, we exercise care when we claim that they are tannaitic sources. What criteria can we use in trying to make this determination?

First, we have at our disposal critical editions and greater access to manuscripts of the Tosefta and the halakhic *midrashim* than ever before. Some of these manuscripts have been digitalized by Bar-Ilan University under the direction of Shamma Friedman and Leib Moscovitz. This allows us to compare the talmudic *baraitot* to texts that are more reliably tannaitic ones, though caution is demanded even here because of the occasional harmonization of some of these texts with BT.[37] Where there are differences between the more

35 Zacharias Frankel, מבוא הירושלמי (Breslau: Schletter, 1870, reprinted, Jerusalem: n. p., 1967), pp. כו א–ב'. J. N. Epstein, מבואות לספרות התנאים (Jerusalem and Tel Aviv: Magnes and Dvir Presses, 1957), pp. 246 and 666, for example; idem., מבוא לנוסח המשנה (Jerusalem and Tel Aviv: Magnes and Dvir Presses, 2nd edition, 1964), pp. 677–81. Ch. Albeck, מחקרים בברייתא ובתוספתא (Jerusalem: Mossad ha-Rav Kook, 1969), pp. 23, 26–28, and 31. Judith Hauptman, *Development of the Talmudic Sugya* (Lanham, New York, and London: University Press of America, 1988), pp. 214–17. Shamma Friedman, "הברייתות בתלמוד הבבלי ויחסן למקבילותיהן שבתוספתא," pp. 195–96 and 199–200 and idem., "Uncovering Literary Dependencies in the Talmudic Literary Corpus," *The Synoptic Problem in Rabbinic Literature*, ed. Shaye J. D. Cohen, Brown Judaic Studies 326 (Providence: Brown Judaic Studies, 2000), pp. 35–57.

36 See n. 25, and more recently, Louis Jacobs, "Are There Fictitious Baraitot in the Babylonian Talmud?" *HUCA* 42 (1971): 185–96.

37 Yaakov Elman, *Authority and Tradition*, p. 17, n. 21 regarding Ms. Erfurt of the Tosefta.

original texts and the *Bavli*, careful examination may reveal a post-tannaitic addition or element within a *baraita* that in our case may affect the chronological data it yields.[38]

Second, the two *Talmudim* themselves may be useful sources of comparison for *baraitot* where no tannaitic collections are available. For that purpose, the availability of what amount to critical editions of BT – for example, Rabbinovicz's *Diqduqe Soferim* and Makhon ha-Talmud ha-Yisraeli's *Talmud Bavli ᶜim Shinuyei Nusḥa'ot*, works like *Synopse zum Talmud Yerushalmi*, eds. Peter Schäfer and Hans-Jürgen Becker, and the Academy for the Hebrew Language's edition of MS Leiden for PT – are invaluable. We also have at our disposal the excellent collection of text witnesses for BT that the Saul Lieberman Institute has assembled under the direction of Shamma Friedman. Sometimes comparisons between *baraitot* in the two Talmuds confirm that we are dealing with a tannaitic *baraita*. Under other circumstances the comparison reveals a matter that arouses suspicion and must be taken into account when considering the chronology of the development of a midrashic hermeneutic.[39] One of the best examples of such a matter is the appearance of a source as a *baraita* in one Talmud and as a *memra* in another.[40]

On the basis of the above considerations, I would consider a talmudic *baraita* with an exact or approximate parallel in a tannaitic collection or collections to be tannaitic. In the case of an approximate parallel, the content of the two *baraitot* would have to be the same. This would also hold true for sources cited as *baraitot* in the two *Talmudim*. The appearance of a source as a *baraita* in one Talmud and as a *memra* in another would raise serious doubts about the tannaitic status of the source. Similarly, I would be suspicious about the tannaitic status of a talmudic *baraita* without a parallel in any tannaitic collection or in its fellow Talmud.

The Dating of the Anonymous Stratum of the Talmud

As early as the period of the *rishonim*, there was a recognition that the anonymous stratum of the Talmud represented a separate entity from the tannaitic

38 For examples of the application of this methodology see Judith Hauptman, *Development of the Talmudic Sugya*, chap. 4; Shamma Friedman, "הברייתות בתלמוד הבבלי ויחסן למקבילותיהן שבתוספתא," pp. 167–83, especially p. 172, regarding the influence of an amoraic *memra* on the formulation of a toseftan *baraita*. Their concerns are different from mine, but their methodology is important for the issues with which I deal.

39 H. L. Strack and Günter Stemberger, *Introduction to the Talmud and Midrash*, pp. 198–99.

40 There is an entire literature that tries to explain this phenomenon. Among the works that deal with it are I. H. Weiss, דור דור ודורשיו, 2:215–16; Zacharias Frankel, מבוא הירושלמי, pp. כד א׳–ב׳; Arthur Spanier, *Die Tosefta Periode* (Berlin: C. A. Schwetschke, 1922; reprinted, Schocken, 1936), pp. 142–43; Abraham Weiss, לחקר התלמוד (New York: Feldheim, 1954), pp. 48–49 and 59–60; and Judith Hauptman, *Development of the Talmudic Sugya*, pp. 216–17.

and amoraic elements in BT (and perhaps PT as well). The *stam* again became the subject of intense investigation starting with the *Wissenschaft des Judentums* scholars and continuing apace throughout the twentieth century. The matters of dating and the relationship of the *stam* to other strata of the Talmud continue to exercise scholars to this day.

At issue is whether the *stam* represents the latest stratum of the Talmud, one that comments on and connects earlier tannaitic and amoraic teachings, or whether the *stam* is mostly or at least occasionally part of the amoraic stratum of the Talmud. Shamma Friedman organized a review of the medieval and early twentieth-century scholars and literature that propose a late dating for the *stam*. Among those he mentions are Maimonides, Nachmanides, R. Yom Tov b. Abraham of Seville, Rashi, Tosafot, Zacharias Frankel, B. M. Lewin, Julius Kaplan, Abraham Weiss, Hyman Klein, Meyer S. Feldblum, and David Weiss Halivni.[41] At the end of this review Friedman includes himself among those who take this position, and he provides criteria for identifying the latest strata of the Talmud.[42] He also notes that one late stratum of the Talmud may be assigned to the *stam*, but both medieval commentators and modern scholars have recognized that there are even later additions by the *geonim*.[43]

To a great extent the view that the *stam* is late – barring blatant evidence to the contrary – informs the work of contemporary American rabbinics scholars such as Yaakov Elman, Judith Hauptman, Richard Kalmin, David Kraemer, and Jeffrey Rubenstein. This list also includes many of their Israeli compatriots, such as Moshe Benovitz, Avinoam Cohen, Leib Moscovitz, and Pinchas Hayman, though there tends to be more reservation about the lateness of the *stam* among the Israeli group.[44]

41 See Shamma Friedman, "על דרך חקר הסוגיא," מחקרים ומקורות (New York: Jewish Theological Seminary, 1977), pp. 283–300 and Friedman's notes ad loc. See especially pp. 293–94, nn. 41 and 42. It should be noted that David Weiss Halivni presently takes the most vigorous stance on behalf of the theory of the lateness of the *stam*. His views developed over time, but his first statement that virtually all the *stamot* are post-Ravina and R. Ashi, the last *amoraim*, appears in his Introduction to *Meqorot u-Mesorot* – Yoma to *Ḥagigah* (Heb., Jerusalem: Jewish Theological Seminary, 1975), pp. 1–11. He later declared the period of the *stam* even later than he did in 1975. See the Introduction to *Meqorot u-Mesorot* – Baba Meẓiᶜaᵓ (Jerusalem:-Tel Magnes Press, 2003), pp. 11–13. There he states his conviction to be stronger than ever that all the *stamot* post-dated the time of the last *amoraim*. He adds that he is now convinced that the work of the *stam* does not begin before the second half of the sixth century. Because he holds that the *saboraim* represent another, very insignificant stratum of the Talmud, and one that begins only at the outset of the geonic period, we may infer that he would set the end of the period of the *stam* in the latter part of the seventh century or the first half of the eighth century.

42 Ibid., pp. 301–8. Other Israeli academic Talmudists who are in basic agreement with Friedman are Zvi Arieh Steinfeld and Noah Aminoah.

43 Op. cit., p. 301.

44 Elman, *Authority and Tradition*, pp. 10–11; 15 and n. 14; 184–85 and n. 86; idem., "Righteousness as its Own Reward: An Inquiry into the Theologies of the Stam," *PAAJR* (1991): 36–39. In the PAAJR

This view, though widely held, has not gone unchallenged in the past, and resistance to it has recently resurfaced. The most vociferous opponent of the idea of the lateness of the *stam* was Chanoch Albeck, who put forth his arguments for this position in his *Mevo ha-Talmudim*, chapter 10.[45] Albeck presents citations from the Talmud in which various *amoraim* appear to respond to the *stam*, and in some cases his evidence is very convincing.[46] Others have taken the position that the most straightforward approach to the situation of

---

article Elman uses the term "stam" to refer to the final redactional level of a *sugya*. He notes, "... this layer will often reflect earlier stages of the *sugya*'s history. Since we are far from establishing absolute dates for these stages of redaction, the duration of this redactional period is still an open question." Hauptman, *Development of the Talmudic Sugya*, pp. 1–2; 217–18. Kalmin, *The Redaction of the Babylonian Talmud: Amoraic or Saboraic?* (Cincinnati: Hebrew Union College Press, 1989), pp. 66–94, especially pp. 90–94, but see pp. 10–11. Recently, Kalmin has expressed continued lack of certainty about a late chronology for the *stam*. See *Sages, Stories*, p. 45, n. 2, where Kalmin raises the possibility of early *stamot*, though he ultimately rejects this in regard to the sources he cites; chap. 6, especially 137–40; 166–67; and 172. Kraemer, *The Mind of the Talmud* (Oxford: Oxford University Press, 1990), chap. 4. Jeffrey Rubenstein, *Talmudic Stories: Narrative Art, Composition and Culture* (Baltimore and London: Johns Hopkins University Press, 1999, pp. 15–21; idem., *The Culture of the Babylonian Talmud* (Baltimore and London: Johns Hopkins University Press, 2003), pp. 1–5. Moshe Benovitz, תלמוד בבלי מסכת שבועות – פרק שבועות שתים בתרא (Jerusalem: Jewish Theological Seminary, 2003), pp. 8–11. Avinoam Cohen, "על מיקום הבלתי-כרונולוגי של דברי מר בר רב אשי," *Sidra* 2 (1986), 65–66, n. 67. Leib Moscovitz, *Talmudic Reasoning* (Tübingen: Mohr-Siebeck), pp. 303–13, 350–51. Pinchas Hayman, "On the Teaching of Talmud: Toward a Methodological Basis for a Curriculum in Oral-Tradition Studies," *Religious Education* (Atlanta: Religious Education Association, 1997), 92:1:61–76; "Implications of the Academic Study of the Babylonian Talmud for Student Beliefs and Religious Attitudes," *Abiding Challenges*, eds., Yisrael Rich and Michael Rosenak (London: Freund and Ramat Gan: Bar Ilan University, 1999) pp. 375–99. Hayman is also the director of *Revadim*, which is an on-line project for the teaching and dissemination of the historical-critical method, which generally speaking assumes the lateness of the *stam*. Whether the anonymous material (*stam*) is in fact late in all cases or not, the *Revadim* methodology demands drawing a distinction between named talmudic statements and anonymous ones.

45 Chanoch Albeck, מבוא התלמודים (Tel Aviv: Dvir, 1969), pp. 576–96.

46 See, for example, p. 585. Albeck's citations are from bBaba Qamma 39a and bBerakhot 3b–4a. Many of his other examples are refutable. For example, his citation from b^cAvodah Zarah 44b on p. 589. Albeck claims that all the *amoraim* in the *sugya* respond to the *stam*'s question, "מאי גנובתיה?" and what Albeck understands as the the *stam*'s response to his own question. What Albeck takes to be the *stam*'s response is probably R. Ḥama b. Jose (be-Rabbi's) explanation of his own position. R. Ḥama is a second generation Palestinian *amora*. His explanation is framed by the *stam*'s question and interrupted by an anonymous question based on a view of Rava (Babylonia, fourth generation) raised about a point in R. Ḥama's explanantion of R. Oshaya's view. R. Ḥama would have been totally unaware of this question since he was separated from Rava by time (he was probably not alive by Rava's time) and space. In contrast, see Abraham Weiss, על היצירה הספרותית של האמוראים (New York: Horeb-Yeshiva University, 1962), pp. 24–16 and 33–50. Weiss agrees with Albeck in some cases despite his tendency to view anonymous *sugyot* and comments as late, see pp. 49–50; 295–307.

a named *amora* apparently responding to a question or comment of the *stam* is to accept the situation as it is.[47]

Most recently, Robert Brody of Hebrew University has again raised the issue of the existence of an early anonymous talmudic stratum. He delivered a challenge to the growing consensus regarding the general lateness of the *stam* at the Fourteenth World Congress of Jewish Studies (2005).[48] Among his criticisms of David Weiss Halivni and Shamma Friedman, the most outstanding contemporary champions of the lateness theory, is that they tend to generalize from specific examples and from what Brody considers to be a relatively small sampling of talmudic data, even though the phenomena it contains proves Halivni's or Friedman's point.

Beyond the historical and logical challenges that Brody marshals against proponents of the theory of the lateness of the *stam*,[49] he also provides sixteen examples from bKetubot of a named *amora* responding to an anonymous comment or question.[50] Brody claims that in these examples there is no choice

47 Zacharias Frankel, מבוא הירושלמי, pp. מז א׳-ב׳; Yizḥak Eizik Halevi, דורות הראשונים, 5:551–62 and 6:116–21; J. N. Epstein, מבוא לנוסח השמנה (Jerusalem and Tel Aviv: Magnes Press and Dvir, 1948), p. 440; מבואות לספרות האמוראים (Jerusalem and Tel Aviv: Magnes Press and Dvir, 1962), p. 50, #6. Epstein is aware of the contribution of the Saboraim, with whom he sometimes connects what he calls "*stam ha-Bavli*," the anonymous voice of BT. See idem., pp. 37; 49–50, #2. Epstein proposes even later additions, ibid., p. 137. David Rosenthal in his article "פירקא דאביי," *Tarbiẓ* 46 (1977): 97–109. Rosenthal accepts that there are additions onto earlier strata by the *stam*, even ones that make it appear that an *amora* responds to the *stam*, but he does not assign these additions to any specific date. Shamma Friedman cites the doctoral thesis of Y. Sussman as another example of a scholar who accepts the idea of early *stamot*. Sussman, סוגיות בבליות לסדרים זרעים וטהרות (Hebrew University, 1969), pp. 30ב–30ג. See more recently, Y. Sussman, "ושוב לירושלמי נזיקין" *Meḥqerei Talmud* 1, eds. D. Rosenthal and Y. Zussman (1990): 109, n. 204.

48 I take this opportunity to thank Prof. Brody for his presentation at the Jewish Theological Seminary of America and for his willingness to share his paper from the Congress and the Jewish Theological Seminary lecture with me.

49 For example, there are those who claim that removal of the *stam* from a BT *sugya* results in something that looks closer to its PT parallel. This suggests that BT added *stam* material to an earlier Palestinian *sugya* at a date later than the final formation of the Palestinian *sugya*. Brody's response to this is that one has to consider how much anonymous material there is in PT itself. Hence, anonymous formulation may be more a matter of the style of certain comments than a sign that material is post-amoraic. After all, there is general agreement that PT and Palestinian *sugyot* are amoraic.

Some have pointed to a high degree of textual variants within anonymous passages as a sign of their lateness. This is based on the view that late, post-amoraic traditions were more complicated in formulation and less authoritative than apodictic amoraic sources. Hence, they could be transmitted in a looser fashion. Brody would respond that if anything, a greater amount of textual variants would argue for an early date. The more a tradition is transmitted – especially if this is done orally – the more it would be subject to variation.

50 His sources are bKetubot 4b; 16a; 21b; 26b; 30b; 31b; 33a-b; 37b; 47a; 56b; 66a; 69a; 70b; 77b; 80b; and 90b.

but to accept that the *amora* addressed the *stam*.

After a careful study of the examples in his Congress paper, it appears that most of Brody's conclusions are correct, especially when one compares them to the views of the earliest commentators – for example, R. Ḥananel. Only two categories of phenomena are problematic: 1) amoraic remarks that appear to be responses to short anonymous questions and 2) *memrot* that in their present place look like responses to the *stam* but might be responses to a *mishnah* or *baraita*. The latter usually take the form "ר' פלוני אומר: ב....," "R. X said, (it) is speaking of (the case of). . . ."[51]

As mentioned above, Brody's work covers a very small sampling of the many *stamot* that constitute the major portion of the Talmud. He himself cautions against making generalizations out of individual cases, and, therefore, he carefully refrains from declaring all *stamot* either amoraic or early. His careful work and Leib Moscovitz's critique of the criteria used by scholars committed to the theory of the lateness of the *stam* are important cautions against assuming that anonymity automatically means late provenance.[52]

The same may be said of the recent work of Alyssa Gray. Gray's study of p^{c}Avodah Zarah and b^{c}Avodah Zarah militates against immediately assigning a late date to the anonymous material in PT or BT. As she notes, some of what appears as anonymous in BT can be shown to be Palestinian amoraic, Palestinian *stam*, or purely Babylonian anonymous material. Until one understands the relationship between these three categories, one must maintain an open attitude to the lateness of anonymous talmudic material.[53]

Overall, I am convinced that much of the *stam* is in fact late. Those who accept this view have never claimed that there are no early *stamot*, nor do I. This means that cases that appear to contradict the theory of the lateness of the *stam* must not be brushed aside or tortured into conformity with the theory. If it is more reasonable to decide in favor of a particular anonymous statement or detailed give-and-take being amoraic, then integrity demands that reason prevail. If, however, there is reason to believe that the *stam* chronologically postdates the amoraic layer of a *sugya* – for example, when the *stam* explains a tannaitic or amoraic statement – I will consider it late and post-amoraic, even if the commentary precedes the statement.[54] The cautionary

51 See Appendix A.

52 These critiques were delivered in a paper at the 14th World Congress of Jewish Studies (2005) entitled "בין אמוראים לעורכים: הרהורים מתודולוגיים." This was at the same session at which Brody spoke.

53 Alyssa Gray, *A Talmud in Exile: the Influence of Yerushalmi Avodah Zara on the Formation of Bavli Avodah Zarah*, Brown Judaic Studies 342 (Providence: Brown University, 2005), chap. 5.

54 See Judith Hauptman on non-linear entry of comments into the *sugya* in *The Development of the Talmudic Sugya*, pp. 214–16 and nn. 4–5. That explanatory material entered from the margins of manuscripts into the main text of the Talmud was a phenomonon of which the *geonim* were

views of Brody, Moscovitz, and Gray and their methodological suggestions as to how to make decisions about the dating of the *stam* will be taken into consideration in our work.

The Use of *Aggadah* in this Study

In this study I will make use of certain genres of aggadic material. These include rabbinic statements about what was included in the revelation at Sinai and stories about the relationship of God to "rabbinic Torah." As I make use of these aggadic dicta, I will try to provide a general date for them based on the tradents to whom they are attributed. My purpose in using this material is to assess what different generations of Sages thought about what was revealed at Sinai and, therefore, what they considered to be part of the sacred canon. For strata without aggadic information about what that strata's Rabbis thought about the canon, I will try to infer the Rabbis' views from their hermeneutical practices and from the sources to which they applied them.

Rabbinic Theological Views of Scripture and Midrashic Methods

This study grapples with a basic theoretical question: What is the relationship between what the talmudic period's Rabbis considered the scriptural canon, the methods they employed in interpreting it, and their theology of revelation? Throughout the work, I assume this relationship existed, and I try to document it as I move from hermeneutic to hermeneutic or from form to form within a given hermeneutic. Thus, I claim that a Rabbi's theology of Torah and revelation inevitably impacted and determined the strategy or strategies he employed in reading a scriptural text that he sought to interpret.

In view of such considerations, the degree to which *midrash* is rooted in what appears to be a rabbinic sensitivity to rhetoric is a matter of singular interest. Most if not all of the Sages of the rabbinic world were highly sensitive to stylistic matters like superfluity, repetition, contradictions, and oddities of syntax in canonical works.[55] It appears that the Rabbis could not accept the idea that something as important as the obligations and prohibitions that

---

aware. It is possible that this later material may have ocasionally been placed before older sources either by accident or in order to frame it and provide it with the meaning the commentator believed it had. See B. M. Lewin, אוצר הגאונים – בבא מציעא, חלק הפירושים (n.p., n.d.), pp. 3–4, #ג and similarly, אוצר הגאונים – בבא קמא, חלק התשובות (Jerusalem: Mossad ha-Rav Kook, 1943), p. 37, #ק.

55 Some of these phenomena appear to have something in common with Greek and Roman rhetorical considerations about style. See, for example, Aristotle's views on superfluous verbosity in his *Rhetoric*, trans., W. Rhys. Roberts, p. 1406a. There is, however, little evidence from the rabbinic hermeneutics that I analyze that indicates a direct connection to these rhetorical considerations.

formed the terms required of Israel for participation in the covenant with God could be formulated in a haphazard fashion. This left the interpreters of these works no choice but to explain these stylistic "quirks" as meaningful and intended expressions of the Divine Will. The interpreter's task was to tease this meaning and intention from the canonical work being interpreted. When the source dealt with praxis, the interpreter's duty was to explain the practical ramifications implied in the work.

What the entire rabbinic world shared was the belief that God was the Author of what became the scriptural canon of twenty-four biblical books. What changed over time was what various rabbinic Sages included in the sacred canon of their Judaism, a matter that seems to have been determined by what those Sages considered to be expressions of God's revealed word. Thus, we discover that later rabbinic figures eventually applied midrashic interpretation even to post-biblical rabbinic works like the Mishnah, using hermeneutics once applied only to canonized Scripture. It is a fact that they did this to a lesser degree in regard to what we would call rabbinic works than they did in relation to Scripture,[56] but the mere fact that they did so at all is worthy of study.

In sum, this study undertakes the analysis of six midrashic hermeneutics: אף על פי שאין ראיה לדבר, זכר לדבר (a midrashic method that draws a distinction between what constitutes scriptural proof and what is merely a prooftext), שני כתובים הכחישים זה את זה (midrashic resolutions of contradictions in Scripture), אם אינו עניין (a midrashic hermeneutic that transfers the rules of one rubric to another), שני כתובים אין מלמדין and תרי ריבויי (hermeneutics that limit interpretive extensions of *halakhot*), and צריכי (a claim that two redundant pentateuchal rubrics are needed to ward off incorrect analogies). Midrashic interpreters applied the first of these midrashic hermeneutics only to scriptural texts. It appears mostly, though not exclusively, in tannaitic sources. The second hermeneutic appears only in tannaitic sources and disappears from the amoraic and post-amoraic strata of the Talmuds. The third appears in every level of rabbinic literature starting with the halakhic *midrashim* through the redactional level of BT. The last three hermeneutics appear only in the late amoraic period and in the *stam*.

In analyzing these midrashic methods, this work attempts to chart the interface between the rabbinic view of revelation and rabbinic *midrash*. I posit that because the *tannaim* connected the issue of revelation and canonicity primarily to the text of the Pentateuch, that text was with rare exception the exclusive source for their halakhic *midrash*. Similarly, I hold that because the early *amoraim* extended equal canonical authority to the entire *TaNaKh*, they

56 This is both a quantitative and qualitative judgment. See Yaakov Elman, "Prospective *Derash* and Retrospective *Peshat*," in *Modern Scholarship in the Study of Torah*, The Orthodox Forum Series, ed. Shalom Carmy (Northvale and Jerusalem: Jason Aronson, 1996), pp. 229–32.

applied halakhic *midrash* to the entire scriptural canon. Finally, because the late *amoraim* and BT's redactors viewed rabbinic corpora as divine revelation, they applied midrashic methods to them as well. Since, however, their tannaitic and amoraic forbears' legacy was for them equivalent to Sinaitic Torah, their interpretations no longer extended the borders of *halakhah* but only maintained them. As Martin Jaffee has proposed, the idea of Oral Torah was hardly existent in the tannaitic period, but it grew into a more defined ideology because of the requirement in amoraic rabbinic circles that a student study under a teacher in order to become a recognized Torah scholar.[57] I would now add to this view that by the end of the period of the formation of the Babylonian Talmud, Oral Torah came to mean the entire legacy of those Rabbis whose views tradition had preserved. This rabbinic legacy, along with Scripture, was deemed to have been revealed by God and therefore to be canonical and, ironically enough, "scriptural" itself in some sense.

Let us now turn to the analysis of the individual hermeneutics cursorily described above. This analysis traces these hermeneutics' formal and logical developments and shows how their application was extended to include rabbinic sources as well as Scripture.[58] Once we have traced this history, we will endeavor to show that there is a correlation between it and the periodic developments in rabbinic theories of what was included in the Sinaitic revelation.

57 Martin Jaffee, *Torah in the Mouth* (Oxford: Oxford University Press, 2001), pp. 151–52.

58 See Elizabeth Shanks Alexander, *Transmitting the Mishnah* (Cambridge: Cambridge University Press, 2006) p. 78, n. 3. My work goes beyond the "*midrash*" of the Mishnah to include other early rabbinic sources. My work also provides a theory for the extension of midrashic methods to rabbinic dicta from a variety of periods.

1

Pentateuchal Narratives and Non-Pentateuchal Sources as Prooftexts for Halakhic Legislation

No form of ancient Judaism could reasonably dissociate itself from Scripture[1] and still call itself Judaism. Therefore, it is undeniable that Scripture, especially the Pentateuch, had a profound influence on rabbinic *halakhah*. The *tannaim*, however, recognized an authoritative Jewish *nomos* that went beyond Scripture. Sometimes they viewed that *nomos* as rooted in or licensed by Scripture, but other times they acknowledged that it was entirely of their own making.[2] The fact that a certain *halakhah* was of rabbinic origin did not stop the tannaitic Sages from supporting it with scriptural citations. Yet, once this happened, how could one tell whether the Sages thought that the *halakhah*'s authority was scriptural or rabbinic? Further, why was it necessary to distinguish between one type of law and the other? After all, a committed rabbinic Jew would punctiliously observe both.

Though the tannaitic Sages believed they had wide latitude regarding scriptural interpretation and legislation, it does not seem that they believed their words and those of God were equivalent. Indeed, the Torah itself prohibited adding or subtracting from its laws (Deut 13:1). It is for this reason that the Sages drew a distinction between "the words of the Torah" (דברי תורה) and "the words of the Scribes" (דברי סופרים).[3] In terms of rabbinic thought, it could

1 I use the term "Scripture" guardedly because it is not clear whether all groups, including the *tannaim*, considered the various writings we know of as authoritative Scripture. I believe we stand on firm ground when we say that all Second Commonwealth Jewish groups acknowledged the authority of the Pentateuch. What constituted Scripture beyond that for various Jewish groups is hard to say.

2 The term in tannaitic literature designating the source of a law as rabbinic is דברי סופרים or מדברי סופרים. It appears in m^{c}Orlah 3:9; mYebamot 2:4 and 9:3; mSanhedrin 11:3; mParah 11:5–6; mTahorot 4:7 and 11; mYadayyim 3:2; tTaanit (Lieberman) 2:6; tYebamot (Lieberman) 2:4; ibid. 3:1; t^{c}Eduyyot (Zuckermandel, all following Tosefta citations are ed. Zuckermandel) 1:1 and 5; tKelim 7:7; tParah 11:8; tNiddah 9:14; tMiqva$^{\supset}$ot 5:4; tTebul Yom 1:10; *Mek. de-RSBY*, Exod 19:5; *Sifra Shemini* 2:11 and par. 8:5; *Sifra Zabim* 2:12; *Sifra $^{\supset}$Emor*, par. 10:11; *Sifra Behar*, 4:5; *Sifre Num.* 73, 75; *Sifre Deut.* 115, 154; *Midrash Tannaim*, Deut 12:22; 14:22, 17:11, 19:15, and 22:10.

3 There are cases where the term דברי תורה is not contrasted with דברי סופרים and its meaning appears to include rabbinic Torah. Some examples from tannaitic literature bear this out. This usage is, however, restricted to aggadic passages, e.g., six cases in m$^{\supset}$Avot. The one time that דברי

not be otherwise. After all, "the (written) Law of the Eternal is perfect," and therefore immutable,[4] even though change is an integral part of formative rabbinic legislation.[5] Thus, the tannaitic Rabbis probably would have accepted a distinction between *mizvah* and *halakhah*. *Mizvah* would be that which appeared as law or regulation in the Torah itself; *halakhah* would be the rabbinic program for the observance of a *mizvah* of the Torah or a purely rabbinic en-

---

תורה appears with no comparison to דברי סופרים is in Mishnah, mParah 11:4, but there the term actually refers only to pentateuchal law. In all other halakhic contexts the Mishnah contrasts דברי תורה with דברי סופרים. The same arrangement characterizes Tosefta. See tSotah 7:11 and tḤullin 2:24, in which דברי תורה seems to refer to both written and rabbinic Torah, but both are cases of *aggadah*; tDemai 2:4 is a possible exception to this rule, but see ibid. 2:5 (R. Joseh). In the halakhic *midrashim*'s aggadic sections, of which there are about 150 examples (I have excluded *Midrash Tannaim* and *Sifre Zuta*), the meaning of דברי תורה can extend to both written and rabbinic Torah. Very few examples are exceptions, e.g., *Mek. Baḥodesh* 8, ed. Horovitz, p.232, lines 10–11. This appears in a legal section of the Torah, though the idea expressed in the *derashah* seems to be aggadic. There the term means "written Torah," given the context of the *derashah*. The same is true of *Sifre Deut.* 160, p. 211, lines 3–5. See the interesting variants in the critical apparatus there to line 5. Context also dictates that דברי תורה means the written Torah in *Sifre Deut.* 218, p. 251, lines 6–7. See Finkelstein's commentary to line 5. There are four cases in which דברי תורה and דברי סופרים are juxtaposed: *Sifra Behar*, 4:5; *Sifre Num.* 73 (2x); and *Sifre Deut.* 115.

4 See Deut 4:2 and 13:1. *Sifra Beḥuqotai* 13:6 indicates this idea as well: „אלה המצוות" (ויקרא כז, לד) – אין נביא רשאי לחדש דבר מעתה, "These are the commandments"– (therefore,) no prophet may create anything new from this point on.

Apparent rabbinic changes in what appear to be clear obligations imposed by the written Torah appear to require tannaitic midrashic justification. The well known example of the *prosbul* is instructive. See, regarding *prosbul*, which effectively eliminated the cancellation of debts as a result of the sabbatical year, *Sifre Deut.* 113, ed. Finkelstein, p. 173, lines 14–15; *Midrash Tannaim*, *Deuteronomy*, ed. Hoffman, 15:3, p. 80. See also pShevi^cit, end of 10:1 and beginning of 10:2 (39c). There PT argues that even if Hillel simply enacted the *prosbul* on the basis of his personal authority, the Sages felt it necessary to justify this and base it on the interpretation of the Torah itself. This act of midrashic support indicates that the *tannaim* considered the written Torah's requirements basically immutable. In essence, they required that the Torah's text provide them with a legal loophole that would license Hillel's enactment. Even the Mishnah, which does not use midrashic support for Hillel's enactment of the *prosbul*, still states that this enactment's goal was to prevent the violation of the Torah's prohibition against refusing to make loans in the sixth year for fear of their being cancelled by the sabbatical year (Deut 15:9). This mishnaic justification for Hillel's enactment seems to indicate that one can only abolish a Torah law if another Torah law, perhaps a weightier one, is being violated. Again, the Mishnah's position is that if the Torah's law is to be abrogated, its abrogation must be based on a license provided by the Torah itself. This suggests again that the Torah is essentially immutable unless it sanctioned its own mutability. Though of much later vintage, see Ibn Ezra's and Nachmanides' comments on Deut 4:2, which capture the basic meaning of this verse.

5 All the sources in Mishnah and Tosefta that include the formula בראשונה ... התקינ[ו], "at the outset," prove this to be the case. This phenomenon describes how abuses or other problems that existed "at the outset" were corrected by rabbinic enactment. See mShebi^cit 4:1; Bikkurim 3:7; Sheqalim 1:2 and 7:5; Sukkah 3:12; Rosh ha-Shanah 2:1, 2:2, 2:5 and 4:3–4; Gittin 4:2; tShebi^cit (Lieberman) 3:8; Ketubot 9:6, 12:1; Baba Mezi^ca^ɔ 2:16–17 and Zebaḥim (Zuckermandel) 11:16.

actment that the Sages legislated for the proper ordering of their society. If their *halakhah* was the rabbinic program for the observance of a *mizvah*, the *tannaim* probably deemed the *halakhah* itself as in some sense pentateuchal. If the law was purely a matter of their own legislation for "the good of society and the need of the hour," to use Maimonides' phrase, then the *tannaim* probably regarded it as completely "the words of the Scribes."

As we will see, this thinking led the tannaitic Rabbis to read some biblical sources in a "constitutional" fashion – that is, with the assumption that their interpretation of these sources would lead to halakhic legislation, which in their view would fulfill the Torah's commands. The tannaitic Rabbis read other biblical sources, however, not as proof for their *halakhah* from the Torah's text, but as a זכר לדבר. This led to the development of a hermeneutic called אף על פי שאין ראיה לדבר, זכר לדבר, "Though there is no (solid biblical) proof for the matter (under consideration), there is a (less than solid) support for it (in the biblical text)." By saying this, the interpreters tell us that we are dealing with something they are not able to derive in any direct sense from the authoritative word of God.

ראיה לדבר simply means a full proof for a matter. זכר לדבר is somewhat more elusive in terms of its definition. Literally, it may be translated as "a reminder of the matter," much as זכר למקדש means "a reminder of the Temple" and the practices that took place there. These nuances appear to have led Marcus Jastrow, the author of the *Dictionary of Talmud Babli, Yerushalmi, Midrashic Literature and Targumim* (1903), to define זכר לדבר as a "mnemonical allusion" (1:400).[6]

Jastrow's definition implies a certain view of the tannaitic Sages' activity in creating a זכר לדבר – namely, that most of the tannaitic Sages, especially those whose metier was midrashic interpretation, knew the *TaNaKH* thoroughly enough to choose scriptural verses that could function as mnemonic allusions. These allusions would help them and their students recall the *halakhah*. On the basis of my studies on כלל ופרט וכלל and גזירה שווה, it is evident that the midrashists' knowledge of the Torah was immense. Their exhaustive familiarity with the text enabled them, for example, to recall or locate those places in the Pentateuch where a verse or neighboring verses included an initial כלל (general clause), followed by a פרט (a list of particulars), followed by a second כלל, which was more inclusive than the initial one. This arrangement of general and particular clauses allowed a midrashist to construct a כלל ופרט וכלל interpretation. In the case of גזירה שווה, the midrashists had to know

6 See also ערוך השלם (R. Nathan b. Yehiel of Rome), ed. Kohut (no publication information; the edition, however, is a reprint of the edition printed in Vienna and New York from 1878–1894). The only definitions provided for זכר are "die Erinnerung, das Andenken," both related to memory. אף על פי שאין ראיה לדבר זכר לדבר appears under this entry on p. רצ ע"ב.

that a word or phrase appeared only twice in the entire Pentateuch in order to construct a גזירה שווה. If this knowledge extended to the entire *TaNaKH*,[7] it is possible that where tannaitic midrashists did not find a sufficiently authoritative source from the Torah to support their *halakhah* or their aggadic interpretations, a matter we will discuss below, they chose a verse that at least provided a mnemonic to help them recall their teachings.

Other somewhat more contemporary scholars have chosen to define זכר לדבר differently than Jastrow. According to them, the juxtaposition of ראיה (proof) to זכר לדבר suggests that זכר לדבר should be defined as a "hint" (רמז) that suggests or gives support to rabbinic legislation or aggadic interpretation.[8] ראיה, by comparison, would be full-fledged proof for an interpretation or for halakhic legislation based on the Torah.

It seems to me that it is not at all clear that זכר לדבר means a mnemonic. There is no way to prove that the midrashist or midrashists who used this hermeneutic intended the verse that serves as a זכר לדבר to function as an aid to memory. The idea that a זכר לדבר is a "hint" in support of halakhic legislation or rabbinic interpretation also does not seem to account for זכר לדבר being the opposite of ראיה לדבר. Further, a separate formulation uses the term רמז in pointing out "hints" in the Torah to a law or a matter of rabbinic Jewish belief, namely, רמז ל-.[9] This raises some question as to whether זכר לדבר and רמז ל- ought to be viewed as equivalent terms. I would therefore suggest that a זכר לדבר is simply a prooftext for an *halakhah* or an aggadic interpretation but not true proof for it. This is because זכר לדבר lacks either sufficient authority to act as a full proof for a law or sufficient contextual connection to a scriptural narrative or poetic passage to prove the accuracy of an aggadic interpretation.

We will see that rabbinic thinking shifted in the amoraic period, when it appears that the entire biblical canon came to be regarded as a single divinely revealed entity. The Pentateuch was, of course, central, but the Prophets and Writings (נ"ך), and especially those sections dealing with laws, functioned in the amoraic view as commentary to the Mosaic Torah. Consequently, the *amoraim* and those who followed them considered the entire *TaNaKh* equally authoritative for the support or derivation of halakhic legislation or aggadic ideas. Therefore, there are no אף על פי שאין ראיה לדבר interpretations from

7 See *Introduction to the Talmud and Midrash*, p. 40, par. 2.

8 See Ch. Albeck, ששה סדרי משנה – מפורשים ומנוקדים, סדר מועד (Jerusalem and Tel Aviv: Bialik Institute and Dvir, 6th printing, 1987), p. 39, s.v. אין ראיה; Avraham Goldberg, פירוש למשנת שבת (Jerusalem: JTSA, 1986), p. 187, commentary, s.v. אף על פי שאין ראייה לדבר וכו׳. Goldberg describes the cases of זכר לדבר in chaps. 8–9 of mShabbat as שורה של רמזים מן המקרא. Again, the meaning of זכר לדבר for this modern commentator is "hint," suggesting or supporting a certain law.

9 See *Sifre Num.* 116, ed, Horovitz, pp. 131–32; *Sifre Deut.* 329, ed. Finkelstein, p. 379; *Midrash Tannaim*, ed. Hoffman, Deut 21:23, p. 132; ibid., Deut 24:13, p. 158.

the amoraic period. Such changes in thinking about the biblical text and its authority suggest different and evolving considerations about the levels and content of revelation.

It seems that the *tannaim* limited the source of their halakhic programs for *mizṿah* observance to the Torah itself, based on their sense that once the revelation of the Torah had taken place, no prophet could innovate anything.[10] As a result, rules derived from the Prophets and Writings had lesser standing because they were not rooted in truly legislative prophecy. In contrast, some of the *amoraim* appear to have subscribed to a view articulated early in the amoraic period that God revealed the entire canon of written and oral tradition at Sinai and that nothing was actually new.[11] That being the case, the entire canon could be used for the creation of *halakhah*, and all of the *halakhah* might be viewed as having "pentateuchal" standing unless the amoraic Rabbis indicated otherwise.

With this background in mind, let us analyze some of the tannaitic examples of the "prooftext" interpretations, their sources, and method.

The Midrashic Sources of זכר לדבר Interpretations

As noted above, a rhetorical phrase that appears in the tannaitic halakhic *midrashim* and is embedded in later sources is אף על פי שאין ראיה לדבר, זכר לדבר – that is, "Though there is no (solid biblical) proof for the matter (under consideration), there is a prooftext for it (in the biblical text)." The following example illustrates how this hermeneutical action operates in an actual midrashic context:

מכילתא דרבי ישמעאל בא – מס' דפסחא בא פרשה א ד"ה פרשה א

החדש הזה זה ניסן אתה אומר זה ניסן או אינו אלא אחד מחדשי השנה כשהוא אומר חג האסיף בצאת השנה (שמות כג, טז) וחג האסיף תקופת השנה (שמות לד, כב) אמרת צא וראה אי זה חדש שיש בו אסיף ותקופה ושנה יוצאה בו וקרוי שביעי אי אתה מוצא אלא תשרי לאחר שלמדת ששביעי זה תשרי ראשון זה ניסן ואף על פי שאין ראיה לדבר זכר לדבר בחדש הראשון הוא חדש ניסן (אסתר ג, ז).

"This month (shall be for you the beginning of months)" (Exod 12:1) – This means (the month of) Nisan. You say it is Nisan, but perhaps it is some other month of the year? When (Scripture) says (referring to the observance of Sukkot), ". . . and the Feast of the Ingathering at the end of the year" (Exod 23:16) and "the Feast of Ingathering at the turn of the

10 See n. 4 above.

11 See pPeʾah 2:4 (17a) רבי יהושע בן לוי אמר: ... מקרא, משנה, תלמוד, ואגדה, אפילו מה שתלמיד ותיק עתיד להורות לפני רבו נאמר למשה בסיני....: "R. Joshua b. Levi said, '. . . Scripture, Mishnah, Talmud, and *aggadah*, even that which an experienced student will teach before his master, was said to Moses at Sinai. . . .'"

> year" (ibid. 34:22), you must say: Go and see which month has within it crop ingathering, a "turn" (i.e., the beginning of a season determined by the solar calendar), and a (new) year and yet is called the seventh (month). You will find only Tishri (fitting this description). Once you have learned that Tishri is the seventh (month), then the first (month) is Nisan. And though there is no solid proof for this matter, there is a prooftext for it, "In the first (month), which is the month of Nisan" (Esth 3:7).[12]

When one analyzes this midrashic interpretation, one wonders why the highly explicit citation from Esther does not constitute "solid proof" that Nisan is the first month of the Jewish calendar year, especially in comparison to the convoluted, highly inferential "proof" about Nisan's status that opens the exposition. While not every example of אף על פי שאין ראיה לדבר זכר לדבר is equally high in its quality of proof as this citation from Esther, many are. It is this fact that generates the talmudic question "Why do the midrashic interpreters regard the biblical citations that follow the phrase, 'though there is no proof for the matter, etc.,' as mere prooftexts and not as solid proof?"

The Biblical Sources of אף על פי שאין ראיה לדבר זכר לדבר Expositions

Biblical sources found in midrashic passages including אף על פי שאין ראיה לדבר זכר לדבר are not considered full proofs for the laws under discussion in the halakhic *midrashim* because they are either pentateuchal narrative passages or non-pentateuchal biblical sources. The following list of אף על פי שאין ראיה לדבר זכר לדבר midrashic expositions in tannaitic sources and their biblical prooftexts shows this to be so:

Mishnah. Shabbat 8:7 (Isa 30:14). Shabbat 9:4 (Ps 109:18). Sanhedrin 8:2 (Prov 23:20).

Tosefta. Berakhot 1:1 (Neh 4:15). Shevi^{c}it 4:2 (Jer 32:14). ibid. 7:11 (1 Kgs 10:27, 2 Chr 1:15; 9:27). ibid. 7:12 (Gen 49:27). Shabbat 7:4 (Hos 4:12). ibid. 7:10 (Job 21:14). Pesaḥim 1:1 (Zeph 1:12). ibid. 10:5 (Jer 4:3). Yebamot 8:5 (Gen 16:3). Sotah 1:2 (Prov 10:6). Ḥullin 3:21 (Ps 69:32). ^{c}Arakhin 3:2 (Isa 7:21) ibid. 4:27 (Ezek 23:20). Temurah 4:8 (Ezek 17:16). Niddah 1:7 (Isa 26:18).

Mekhilta. Pisḥa 5 (Jer 6:4). 7 (Cant 2:8). 17 (Isa 48:13). ibid. (Gen 48:14).

12 The verse in Esther describes the month in which Haman cast lots to determine when he would destroy the Jews of the Persian Empire.

Baḥodesh 11 (1 Kgs 2:28). Nezikin 1=4 (Exod 5:3 and Gen 14:13). 5=13 (Num 21:26). 8 (Gen 42:38). 16 (Amos 3:12). Kaspa 20 (Gen 37:15).

Sifra Shemini, par. 3 (1 Sam 17:5). Qedoshim, par. 10:11 (Jer 22:30). *ʾEmor*, par. 9:11 (Jer 6:4);

Sifre Numbers. 8 (Dan 4:24–26). 11 (2 Sam 13:19). 45 (Isa 66:20). 112 (Jer 8:1). 126 (Num 25:3). 128 (Gen 26:19).

Sifre Deuteronomy. 35 (Isa 45:13). 36 (Jer 36:18). 43 (Jer 31:11). 219 (Prov 23:20).

R. Joseph Karo had already come to this conclusion when he pointed out two views regarding אף על פי שאין ראיה לדבר זכר לדבר in his treatise on talmudic phenomenology, כללי הגמרא (*The General Principles of the Talmud*, 57a). He writes:

> אע״פ שאין ראיה לדבר זכר לדבר: כתב ה״ר יונה בריש ברכות מפני שאינו מוכיח לגמרי אומר כן. ורש״י והר״ן בפ״ק דפסחים כתבו דמשום הכי אמרו אע״פ שאין ראיה לדבר משום דדברי תורה מדברי קבלה לא ילפינן.

> "Though there is no (solid biblical) proof for the matter (under discussion), there is a prooftext for the matter": R. Jonah wrote regarding the discussion at the beginning of Berakhot that the Talmud says this because the verse does not fully prove (the matter).[13] Rashi and R. Nissim (Gerondi) wrote that they (i.e., the Sages) said this (i.e., "though there is no proof, etc.") because we do not derive pentateuchal matters from non-pentateuchal biblical sources.[14]

This formulation, though seminal, does not in fact cover the entire range of "prooftext" interpretations. The commentators Karo mentions deal only with the immediate phenomena they confronted in bBerakhot and bPesaḥim and did not generalize beyond them. Therefore, their "conclusions" did not cover the entire spectrum of אף על פי שאין ראיה לדבר *midrashim*, nor were they intended to. It is Karo who implicitly generalizes their views. Consequently, cases in which purely rabbinic ordinances are connected to a midrashic exposition containing the formula "though there is no (solid biblical) proof, etc." do not fit into Rashi's and R. Nissim's phenomenology. They are not cases of deriving pentateuchal law from non-pentateuchal biblical sources. Similarly, Rashi's and R. Nissim's phenomenology does not cover cases of the use of a prooftext to more clearly define a pentateuchal law based either on the Torah itself or on a halakhic *midrash* of it. In such a case, the prooftext provides a

13 This is not always the case. See the first example we analyzed, *Pisḥa Bo* 1.

14 See R. Jonah, Berakhot 1b (Alfasi), s.v. גמ׳ ואע״פ שאין ראיה לדבר וכו׳; Rashi, bPesaḥim 7b, s.v. זכר לדבר and R. Nissim, Pesaḥim 4a (Alfasi), s.v. אף על פי שאין ראיה לדבר.

clearer summary of the *halakhah*. If, however, we simply conclude that the halakhic midrashic use of non-legal pentateuchal sources (for example, narratives) and non-pentateuchal sources always produces "scriptural prooftext" interpretations, then we have solved the problem of why such sources are not full proofs: they are not legal sources; hence, according to the *tannaim* they cannot produce law. Rather, they merely provide a clarifying connection between the Bible and the *halakhah*. Clearly, this points to the literary sensitivity of the *tannaim*, who determined that the function of identifiable and distinct genres of biblical literature was to impart different kinds of "messages." The *tannaim*'s division of scriptural literature into genres, each with its own distinct literary purpose, shares this methodology with those engaged in contemporary literary criticism of the Bible.[15] Since categorization of literature into genres engaged Greek philosophers and Greek and Latin rhetors,[16] these Greek and Roman activities may have influenced the thinking and behavior of the *tannaim*.

15 In this case, their form of literary criticism would have been closest to reader response criticism and literary form criticism. I.e., does the average reader or listener find legislative intent in a story or poem? Not if the author has used the forms and language appropriate to narratives and poems. This is because the forms and language specific to poetry address the emotions more than the mind; narrative seeks to instruct or entertain by creating a literature of empathy; legal literature organizes itself in its particularly logical way in order to help communities and individuals live orderly lives.

For the interest of modern literary criticism of the Bible in genres and forms, see Steven L. McKenzie, *How to Read the Bible* (Oxford: Oxford University Press, 2005), pp. 13–20. For a recognition of the midrashic interpreters' capabilities as literary readers of the Bible, see Robert Alter, *The Art of Biblical Narrative* (New York: Basic Books, Inc., 1981), pp. 11–12. Alter, however, distinguishes there between rabbinic midrashic methods of reading and those of the contemporary literary critics of the Bible.

16 Regarding the different functions of various literary genres according to some Greek and Roman philosophers and rhetors, see, for example, Aristotle, *Rhetoric*, trans. W. Rhys Robert (New York: The Modern Library, 1984), 1:3–7, pp. 1358a–1365b, where Aristotle lists the various genres of rhetorical speech, their uses, the style appropriate to them, and the kind of information the speaker must have when he addresses his audience. See Quintillian, *Institutio Oratoria*, trans. John Watson (Cambridge and London: Loeb Classics, 1922), 10:1:27–36, who categorizes the genres of poetry, history, and philosophy and some of the stylistic qualities and literary goals of each that are useful to the orator. Though not directed to the issue of how the Hellenistic rhetors classified literature by genres, see Henry A. Fischel, *Rabbinic Literature and Greco-Roman Philosophy* (Leiden: Brill, 1973), chaps. 2–3 and pp. 90–98. Fischel's work, though limited in scope, shows the relationship and influence of Greco-Roman philosophy and rhetoric on rabbinic literature and thought, especially for ben Azzai's thinking and image in rabbinic literature. For some of Fischel's methodological considerations in his comparisons of Greek and Roman rhetoric and rabbinic sources, see p. 90, n. 1. As Fischel notes in his introduction, the issue of Hellenistic influence on rabbinic (tannaitic) sources can be taken for granted. Even if Fischel's critics are right in claiming that he overstates his case, the works of Lieberman (*Greek in Jewish Palestine* and *Hellenism in Jewish Palestine*), Daube (for example, "Alexandrian Methods of Interpretation and the Rabbis," "*Con-*

אף על פי שאין ראיה לדבר זכר לדבר
Verses Lacking Sufficient Probative Content

The case we analyzed above is one in which there was actual halakhic content – namely, that the law was that Nisan was the first month of the calendar for certain purposes, especially for setting the order of the festivals and new months. From the point of view of the *Mekhilta*, this was actually established by the *midrash* of Exod 23:16 and 34:22, which determined that the seventh month of the Israelite calendar was Tishri, thereby making Nisan the first month by default. The citation of Esther was, according to the *Mekhilta*, of no probative significance because it lacked the authority of a legal source. It only served to state more succinctly and clearly what the *midrash* of the Pentateuch's legal verse had already determined, thereby lending that conclusion more support.

There are, however, cases in which a verse supports an *halakhah* related to a pentateuchal issue but can only do so obliquely because it lacks probative content. Aside from its non-legal source of origin, the nature of the verse's content may also contribute to its being a prooftext but not what the *tannaim* would consider proof. The following example provides a sense of the workings of this form of אף על פי שאין ראיה לדבר. The *midrash* concerns one of the qualifications for a child to be considered a rebellious son – namely, that he eats meat and drinks wine to excess.[17] This requirement is based on an intertextual reading of Deut 21:20, where the parents of a rebellious child describe him as זולל וסובא, and Prov 23:20, which cautions people not to be among those who are guzzlers of wine (סובאי יין) and gluttonous meat eaters (זוללי בשר). These terms as they appear in the Deuteronomy verse are unclear. Therefore, *Sifra Deut.* 219 alludes to Prov 23:20. The Proverbs verse connects ס-ב-א with wine and ז-ל-ל with meat, but this connection does not actually define these terms; nor does it mean that these terms are always connected with these foods. Because of the lack of a complete and indisputable definition of these terms, the verse from Proverbs is at best a prooftext for the *halakhah* that the "rebellious son" must consume excessive amounts of wine and meat to be culpable. Further, it cannot establish the halakhic perameters of the pentateuchal law of the "rebellious son" because it is a non-pentateuchal source. These two factors combine to prevent the Proverbs verse from being "proof" for some of the halakhic aspects of the Torah's law of the "rebellious son."

sortium in Roman and Hebrew Law," "Rabbinic Interpretation and Hellenistic Rhetoric," "Texts and Interpretations in Roman and Jewish Law," and "*Derelictio* and *Traditio*: Romans and Rabbis"), and recently, Martin Jaffee (*Torah in the Mouth*, chap. 7) suggest that we not ignore the possible influence of Greco-Roman and Hellenistic culture on Palestinian Jewish life in general and on the Rabbis in particular.

17 cf. mSanhedrin 8:2.

The midrashic interpretation of Exod 21:23 is similar. The verse appears in the context of a case of two men fighting. In the midst of their physical quarrel, one of them strikes a pregnant woman. She miscarries as a result. The Torah then declares that if she does not die, the one who struck her pays damages for the loss of the fetus. If, however, the woman dies, then *lex talonis* applies. The phrase that appears to indicate the pregnant woman's death is elusive: אם יהיה אסון. What does אסון mean? In response, *Mek. Nezikin* 8 states: „ואם אסון יהיה" – אין אסון אלא מיתה. ואף על פי שאין ראיה לדבר זכר לדבר: „וקראהו אסון". That is, אסון means "death." The support for this is Jacob's statement of concern for Benjamin when his brothers take him down to Joseph in Egypt (Gen 42:47–48). He expresses the concern that וקראהו אסון, "a disaster may befall him." There, אסון is not particularly more defined than it is in Exodus, but we know that when Jacob says that Joseph is lost, he believes that Joseph is dead. The Genesis verse can only obliquely support the Exodus verse because, in reality, אסון can mean any kind of disaster or serious accident. Also, Jacob refers to the loss of his son Simeon, who is still alive, though imprisoned or detained in Egypt, so the Genesis context cannot define אסון absolutely as "death." It is this lack of clear meaning – along with the fact that it is derived from a narrative section of the Pentateuch – that makes this verse only a זכר, a prooftext for the definition of the pentateuchal word אסון, but not a proof that it means death.

אף על פי שאין ראיה לדבר זכר לדבר in Tannaitic Aggadic *Midrash*

Other cases of support verses have no impact on halakhic matters at all. Their point is purely aggadic, but since the verse usually deals with a pentateuchal narrative, there is an interest in how things happened though that interest cannot be described as literally historical. In that case, the phrase "though there is no proof for the matter, there is a (poetic) prooftext for it" is a simple statement of fact. The verse cited could only function as an allusion to the aggadic matter by means of highly poetic interpretation. The case in *Mek. Pisḥa*, 7 (H-R, 22) exemplifies this. There several Rabbis interpret the verse, "... you shall eat it hurriedly (בחפזון)" (Exod 12:11), which describes how the Egyptian Passover offering should be eaten. Abba Ḥanan, citing R. Eliezer, claimed that the hurry was that of God seeking to redeem the Israelites:

> אבא חנן משום ר׳ אליעזר אומר: זה חפזון שכינה. אף על פי שאין ראיה לדבר, זכר לדבר. „קול דודי הנה זה בא מדלג על ההרים מקפץ על הגבעות."

Abba Hanan cited R. Eliezer: The (hurry mentioned in Scripture) is the hurrying of the Divine Presence. Even though there is no proof for this,

> there is a (poetic) prooftext for the matter: "The voice of my beloved, behold, he comes, skipping over the mountains, bounding over the hills" (Cant 2:8).

The verse from Canticles does not speak in any obvious way about the Exodus. Only a poetic leap of imagination could turn the verse into a reference to that event. Once one takes that leap, the description of God's speed as He skipped over the mountains and hills might be used to express His will to redeem Israel speedily from Egypt. The verse on its own is certainly no proof. At most it lends poetic support to R. Eliezer's teaching.

"But this is a Substantial Proof!..." Talmudic Responses to אף על פי שאין ראיה לדבר

As noted above, midrashic interpretations containing the phrase אף על פי שאין ראיה לדבר זכר לדבר originate exclusively in tannaitic sources. Though there are anonymous examples cited in BT, they are identified as *baraitot*.[18] Though the amoraic and post-amoraic worlds did not continue to use this form of midrashic rhetoric, they did comment on the אף על פי שאין ראיה לדבר זכר לדבר expositions they inherited.

Several times in the Babylonian Talmud we find that the statement אף על פי שאין ראיה לדבר זכר לדבר is challenged. For example:

> תלמוד בבלי מסכת יומא דף פג עמוד ב
>
> תנו רבנן: מי שאחזו בולמוס מאכילין אותו דבש וכל מיני מתיקה, שהדבש וכל מיני מתיקה מאירין מאור עיניו של אדם. ואף על פי שאין ראיה לדבר זכר לדבר – +שמואל א׳ יד+ ראו נא כי ארו עיני כי טעמתי מעט דבש הזה. ומאי אף על פי שאין ראיה לדבר–דהתם לאו בולמוס אחזיה.
>
> Our Rabbis taught (in a *baraita*): One suffering from (a dangerous degree of) hunger[19] should be fed honey and sweets, because honey and sweets restore the light to one's eyes.[20] Though there is no solid proof for this rule, there is a prooftext for it: "(Jonathan answered, '. . . behold how my eyes lit up when I tasted that bit of honey'" (1 Sam 14:29).[21]

18 Some of these *baraitot* appear only in BT. Others with parallels in the halakhic *midrashim*, Mishnah, or Tosefta appear as similar but not exact parallels. This is a common feature of Babylonian *baraitot*. We will discuss the phenomenon of Palestinian and Babylonian *baraitot* in greater depth later in this chapter.

19 Hypoglycemia or malnutrition.

20 Honey and sweets restore energy and nutritional balance.

21 The context is Jonathan's unwitting violation of his father's prohibition on the reserve troops' eat-

> Why (does the *baraita* say) "Though there is no proof for this rule" (given that the verse seems to provide excellent proof). Because there (in Jonathan's situation) he was not afflicted with dangerous hunger. (bYoma 83b)

Clearly, the Talmud does not simply reply, "The biblical citation is not solid proof for a law because it is a narrative, poetic, or non-pentateuchal source." More than likely this response was not provided because those who might have made it no longer knew that these sorts of citations never constituted "proofs" for laws or aggadic ideas according to tannaitic standards. Therefore, they sought some factor related to the biblical citation that would undermine its status as full biblical proof.[22]

Who is responsible for the attempts to discredit these citations as proofs? When did he or they live? And what factors caused the loss of the tradition that biblical narrative and poetic sources could not serve as underpinnings for an halakhic or aggadic proposition?

All these issues are intertwined. In all cases it is the anonymous voice of the Talmud, the סתם, that raises the questions of why these citations are not proofs, and then provides a reason for their status as only "support verses." Many if not most contemporary scholars agree that the סתם is late, barring indications to the contrary.[23] Generally speaking, this means this anonymous material is post-amoraic, probably dating from the first quarter of the sixth century and thereafter until perhaps the mid-seventh century. But why didn't the anonymous redactors of the Talmud know that these citations were not viewed as solid biblical proof for a law's authority since they were narrative or poetic citations?

As noted above, study of all the cases in which midrashic sources include the formula אף על פי שאין ראיה לדבר זכר לדבר shows that they are tannaitic or based on tannaitic sources. There are no amoraic examples of this midrashic form used in an halakhic or aggadic context.[24] This is because the *amoraim* generally used biblical narrative and poetic citations from the entire

---

ing on the day of the battle of Bet-Aven. Jonathan had not been present to hear his father, Saul, adjure the troops to fast that day.A soldier who saw Jonathan eating honey told him about Saul's prohibition.

22 This form of talmudic dialectic attempting to test the soundness of the prooftext in אף על פי שאין ראיה לדבר זכר לדבר does not appear in every case of אף על פי שאין ראיה לדבר זכר לדבר in BT. This is probably because certain citations worked perfectly as proofs, while others were transparently supports but not proof. In the first case, there would have been no reasonable way to undermine the prooftext as a substantiation for a law, an aspect of a law, or for an aggadic proposition. In the second instance, no one needed to raise the question of why the prooftext did not constitute "proof." It was obvious. See bShabbat 134b; Sotah 21a; Niddah 8b (2 examples).

23 See the Introduction, pp. 25–27.

24 The following is a list of all the examples of אף על פי שאין ראיה לדבר זכר לדבר sources embedded in the *Talmudim*:

TaNaKh as bases for laws, and they did not hedge this activity by saying, "This is no (actual) proof, but it is a prooftext." The following example regarding the source for Jewish courts to exercise the right of eminent domain is useful in demonstrating how typical amoraic *midrash halakhah* functions:

תלמוד בבלי יבמות פט עמוד ב

אמר ר' יצחק: מנין שהפקר ב"ד היה הפקר? שנא': כל אשר לא יבא לשלשת הימים כעצת השרים והזקנים יחרם כל רכושו והוא יבדל מקהל הגולה (עזרא י, ח). ר' אלעזר אמר, מהכא: אלה הנחלות אשר נחלו אלעזר הכהן ויהושע בן נון וראשי האבות למטות בני ישראל (יהושע יט, נא) וכי מה ענין ראשים אצל אבות? אלא לומר לך: מה אבות מנחילין בניהם כל מה שירצו, אף ראשים מנחילין את העם כל מה שירצו.

R.Isaac said: Whence (do we know) that the court has the right of eminent domain? As it is said, "Anyone who does not come in three days (to the

---

Babylonian Talmud. Berakhot 2b (=part of Tosefta Berakhot 1:1). Shabbat 20a (R. Judah b. Batyra, but no parallels). Ibid. 82a (R. Jose in Mishnah). Ibid. 86a (Mishnah). Ibid. 134b (R. Elazar b. Azariah, no parallels). Pesaḥim 7b–8a cf. tPesaḥim 1:1; the Toseftan *baraita* appears to have been subject to additions from amoraic constructions of the *midrash.* See bPesaḥim 7b the *memra* R. Ḥisda and the *Tanna de-be R. Ishmael* citation. Ibid. 53a (R. Simeon b. Gamaliel, ||R. Simeon b. Gamaliel, ||last clause in tShebiᶜit 7:11. There are slight variations between BT.). Ibid. 107b (*baraita* – תניא נמי הכי, ||tPesaḥim 10:5, slight difference of wording between Tosefta and BT). Yoma 76b (Mishnah). Ibid. 83b (*baraita* – תנו רבנן, cf. tShabbat 8:30, similar in content, but not parallel). Moᶜed Qatan 17a (*baraita* – תנו רבנן, cf. *Sifre Zuta, Num.* 12:14, but not actually parallel). Ibid. 26b (no parallel, most mss. and Pisaro do not have an introduction indicating a *baraita*; MSS Vatican 108 and 134 have תנו רבנן). Yebamot 64a (*baraita* – תנו רבנן, ||tYebamot 8:5). Nedarim 49a (R. Josiah, cf. *Mek. Pisḥa* 7, similar in content, no mention of אף על פי שאין ראיה לדבר in *Mekhilta*). Sotah 4a (Plimo||*Sifre Zuta*, 5:13, cf. tSotah 1:2. BT is basically parallel to *Sifre Zuta* with very slight differences. BT differs considerbaly in attributions and wording from Tosefta.). Ibid. 20b (R. Ishmael||*Sifre Num.* 8, ed. Horovitz, p. 15, see critical apparatus to lines 6–10. BT differs slightly from *Sifre Num.*). Baba Batra 9a (*baraita* – תנו רבנן, no parallel in tannaitic literature or PT). Sanhedrin 70a and 71a (Mishnah, cf. Mishnah in PT). ᶜArakhin 19b (*baraita* – תנו רבנן, ||tᶜArakhin 3:2, BT varies slightly from Tosefta until the end of the Toseftan *baraita*, which varies considerably from BT). Temurah 29b (Rabbi [Judah ha-Nasi], partially ||tTosefta 4:6 with many differences between Tosefta and BT). Niddah 8b [2x] (Symmachus citing R. Meir, ||tNiddah 1:7 with slight differences. First citation without אף על פי שאין ראיה לדבר וכו', second citation includes it.)

Palestinian Talmud. Berakhot 1:1 (2b) (*baraita*||last clause of tBerkahot 1:1 with additional scriptural citation in PT). Shebiᶜit 9:2 (38d) (R. Simeon b. Gamaliel, ||last clause in tShebiᶜit 7:11 with slight variations between PT and Tosefta.). Shabbat 8:7 (11a) (R. Meir, Mishnah). Ibid. 9:4 (11c) (Mishnah). Pesaḥim 1:1 (27a) (based on tPesaḥim 1:1 or *Mek. de-RSBY*, Exod 12:17. PT diverges considerably from both.). Ibid. 5:1 (31c) (based on *Mek. Pisḥa* 5||*Sifra ᵓEmor*, par. 9., 11:1. PT differs considerably from the midrashic *baraitot*). Moᶜed Qatan 1:4 (80c) (PT *baraita*, no parallels in the tannaitic literature or BT). Yebamot 4:11(6a)=Niddah 1:3 (49a) (Symmachus citing R. Meir; R. Yudan. ||tNiddah 1:7. In the Symmachus's citation we find אף על פי שאין ראיה לדבר וכו', but not in R. Yudan's. R. Yudan is not in T.

> convocation called by Ezra), by the decision of the officers and elders shall have all his property confiscated, and he shall be excluded from the congregation of (the returnees) from the exile" (Ezra 10:8). R. Elazar said: (It may be derived) from here: "These are the portions that Elazar the Priest, Joshua son of Nun, and the chiefs of the patriarchs (i.e., the chiefs of the patriarchal groups of the Israelite tribes) apportioned to the tribes of the House of Israel" (Josh 19:51). What is the relationship between "chiefs" and "patriarchs?" Just as fathers bequeath whatever they wish to their children, so the chiefs bequeath whatever they wish to the people. (bYebamot 89b)

Note that though there is an argument about what biblical text constitutes the source for the courts' right of eminent domain, both derivations are from narrative, non-pentateuchal sources. Another excellent example is R. Hamnuna's derivation of the laws of prayer from Hannah's behavior when she prayed for a son at Shiloh :

תלמוד בבלי ברכות עמוד לא עמוד א–ב

> אמר רב המנונא:[25] כמה הלכתא גברוותא איכא למשמע מהני קראי דחנה: +שמואל א' א'+ וחנה היא מדברת על לבה – מכאן למתפלל צריך שיכוין לבו. רק שפתיה נעות – מכאן למתפלל שיחתוך בשפתיו. וקולה לא ישמע – מכאן, שאסור להגביה קולו בתפלתו. ויחשבה עלי לשכרה – מכאן, ששכור אסור להתפלל....

> R. Hamnuna (some mss.: R. Huna) said: How many major *halakhot* can be derived from the verses of Hannah's prayer. "Now Hannah was praying in her heart"– from this (we learn that) one who prays must do so with intention; "only her lips moved"– from this (we learn that) one who prays must articulate (the prayer's words). "but her voice was not audible"– from this (we learn that) one who prays must not raise his/her voice; "Eli thought she was drunk"– from this (we learn that) it is forbidden for one who is inebriated to pray.... (bBerakhot 31a–b)

The formula אף על פי שאין ראיה לדבר זכר לדבר does not appear in the Berakhot citation. So again there is no hint that R. Hamnuna or R. Huna, either a second or third-generation Babylonian *amora*, regarded his prooftext as a mere support for the *halakhah* rather than "solid proof." These examples indicate a change in the stance of the *amoraim* toward the use of pentateuchal and non-pentateuchal narrative and poetic texts as sources of Jewish law.

It seems that this change in midrashic method represents a change of amoraic thinking about the authority of the scriptural canon. The tannaitic claim

25 ר' המנונא: כ"ה בכ"י אוקס' בבה"ג ובריי"ף ובפסקי הריי"ד. בכ"י פירנצה II 7–9 ופריז 671: ר' הונא.

that once the *mizvot* had been revealed, no prophet could add anything new to the Torah[26] meant for the tannaitic world that the Pentateuch's legislation was the only authoritative source for Jewish law. In contrast, the *amoraim* thought *halakhah* could be derived from the entire canon because all of it was from Sinai. Their position was that since no prophet could add to the Torah's legislation, the Prophets and Writings were somehow included in the Pentateuch and therefore possessed its authority.[27] In a sense, the Prophets and Writings constituted a commentary to the pentateuchal text and therefore could be used as it was for the derivation of laws.

The anonymous redactors of the *Bavli* (the סתם), who did not accept that the *amoraim* were permitted to contradict their tannaitic predecessors, were now given different criteria for what constituted biblical "proof" for halakhic regulations. Therefore, the anonymous redactors took upon themselves the task of resolving this problem by showing that wherever the *tannaim* said, "Though there is no (solid biblical) proof for the matter, there is a prooftext for the matter," they had good reason for doing so. By showing this to be the case, the *stam* could simultaneously explain why the *amoraim* did not consider these biblical texts as proof for various *halakhot*. The *stam*, however, raised no objections to similar sorts of amoraic "proofs" because their basic tradition was that these were, in fact, proof enough. It was the more distant tannaitic position that was puzzling and which, therefore, needed explanation.

Tannaitic Sources without the Formula אף על פי שאין ראיה לדבר זכר לדבר that Cite Non-Pentateuchal Prooftexts

Mishnah Shabbat 9:1–3. In the last section I argued that the *tannaim* never considered narrative, poetic, or non-pentateuchal biblical citations as full substantiation for halakhic rules or aggadic lore. Several tannaitic sources seem to stand in contradiction to this general rule. As we shall see, these

26 *Sifra Beḥuqotai*, 13:6.

27 The amoraic story of the preservation of the Book of Ezekiel by Ḥananiah b. Ḥezekiah is a good example of how at least some *amoraim* thought the relationship of Torah to prophetic material operated. The two had to agree with each other. If so, derivation of law from one source or the other made no difference. After all, all the scriptural sources agreed. See bShabbat 13a. See also pMegillah 1:5 (70d) where Rav, R. Ḥanina, R. Jonathan, Bar Kappara, and R. Joshua b. Levi declare that the Book of Esther was revealed to Moses at Sinai, but that there is no chronological order in the Torah. The *midrash* prior to this statement justifies the status of the Book of Esther as canonical because its canonicity was written in the Torah, Prophets, and Writings. Each seems to strengthen Esther's claim and each seems to have its own authority. See a parallel to the latter *midrash* in bMegillah 7a.

contradictions are, however, more a matter of appearance than of fact.

The largest collection of sources in which non-pentateuchal narrative and poetic biblical citation is used to provide prooftexts for halakhic positions is found in mShabbat, chapter 9. Practically the entire chapter consists of such proofs:

משנה שבת פרק ט

משנה א. אמר ר׳ עקיבא מנין לעבודת כוכבים שמטמאה במשא כנדה שנאמר (ישעיה ל, כב) תזרם כמו דוה צא תאמר לו מה נדה מטמאה במשא אף עבודת כוכבים מטמאה במשא:

משנה ב. מנין לספינה שהיא טהורה שנאמר (משלי ל, יט) דרך אניה בלב ים מנין לערוגה שהיא ששה על ששה טפחים שזורעין בתוכה חמשה זרעונין ארבעה בארבע רוחות הערוגה ואחד באמצע שנאמר (ישעיה סא, יא) כי כארץ תוציא צמחה וכגנה זרועיה תצמיח זרעה לא נאמר אלא זרועיה:

משנה ג. מנין לפולטת שכבת זרע ביום השלישי שהיא טמאה שנאמר (שמות יט, טו) היו נכונים לשלשת ימים מניין שמרחיצין את המילה ביום השלישי שחל להיות בשבת שנאמר (בראשית לד, כה) ויהי ביום השלישי בהיותם כואבים מנין שקושרין לשון של זהורית בראש שעיר המשתלח שנאמר (ישעיה א, יח) אם יהיו חטאיכם כשנים כשלג ילבינו:

משנה ד. מנין לסיכה שהיא כשתיה ביום הכפורים? אף אל פי שאין ראיה לדבר, זכר לדבר, שנאמר: „ותבא כמים בקרבו וכשמן בעצמותיו" (תהילים קט, יח).

Mishnah 1. Rabbi Akiba said: Whence (do we know that) an idol causes ritual contamination through carrying (or lifting) similar to that of a menstruant? As it says, "(And you will treat as unclean the silver overlay of your images and the golden plating of your idols;) you will cast them away like a menstruous woman; "Out!" you will call to them" (Isa 30:22) – just as a menstruous woman ritually contaminates through carrying (or lifting), so does an idol.

Mishnah 2. Whence (do we know that) a ship is (always considered ritually) pure? As it says, "[how] a ship makes its way in the sea" (Prov 30:19).[28] Whence (do we know that it is permissible) to plant five different kinds of seeds at the four corners and middle of a patch that is six by six handsbreadths (without violating the prohibition of כלאים, mixed seeds). As it says, "For as the earth brings forth its growth, and a garden makes its

28 The traditional commentators explain that just as the sea is always pure, so a ship is always pure. They say this is based on the midrashic principle called סמוכין. According to this principle, if several matters are juxtaposed in a single sentence, then the rules applicable to one issue are applicable to the other.

plantings to sprout (so the Eternal God will make victory and renown sprout forth. . . .)" (Isa 61:11)[29]

Mishnah 3. Whence (do we know that) a woman who expels semen on the third day (after intercourse) is ritually impure?[30] As it is said, "Be ready by the third day: do not approach a woman" (Exod 19:15)[31] Whence (do we know that) we may wash the circumcision wound on the third day if it falls on the Sabbath? As it says, "And it came to pass on the third day, when they were in great pain. . . ." (Gen 34:25). Whence (do we know that) we tie a crimson strap on the head of the scapegoat? As it is said, "(Even) if your sins are as crimson, they shall become white as snow. . . ." (Isa 1:18).

Mishnah 4. Whence (do we know that) anointing (oneself on Yom Kippur) is equivalent to drinking on Yom Kippur? Though there is no (solid) proof for the matter, there is a prooftext for it, as it says, "It shall go as water into his innards and like oil into his bones (Ps 109:18).

It is noteworthy that none of these sources contains the phrase אף על פי שאין ראיה לדבר, זכר לדבר except the last (mShabbat 9:4) though most of the traditional commentators claim that these *mishnayyot* appear in tractate Shabbat only because of their association with mShabbat 8:7 in which אף על פי שאין ראיה לדבר זכר לדבר appears.[32] It is these traditional commentators' view that despite the lack of the use of the phrase, "even though this is not proof for the

29 See bShabbat 45a, cited below, for an explanation of how this verse indicates that five types of vegetables may be planted in a 6 x 6 handbreadths patch. The most significant word in the *midrash* of the Isaian verse is "garden," which implies "patch" (ערוגה) to the midrashist.

30 Several mss. have שהיא טהורה, "that she is pure."

31 As Rashi explains the verse: Do not approach a woman for sexual purposes so that on the third day she may undergo immersion and be pure to receive the Torah. See Rashi, Exod 19:15, s.v. אל תגשו אל אשה.

32 mShabbat 8:7 states:

> חרס כדי ליתן בין פצים לחברו, דברי ר׳ יהודה. ר׳ מאיר אומר: כדי לחתות בו האור. ר׳ יוסי אומר: כדי לקבל בו רביעית. אמר ר׳ מאיר: אף על פי שאין ראיה לדבר זכר לדבר: „ולא ימצא במכתתו חרש לחתות אש מיקוד" (ישעיה ל, יד). אמר לו ר׳ יוסי: משם ראיה? „ולחשוף מים מגבא" (שם).
>
> (In regard to) an earthenware shard, (transporting the amount) sufficient to place between one board and another (in a door frame violates the prohibition of "carrying" on the Sabbath), these are R. Judah's words. R. Meir said: (the amount) sufficient to scoop coals. R. Jose said: (the amount) sufficient to hold a quarter of a *log* (of liquid). Said R. Meir: Though there is no (solid scriptural) proof (for my view), there is a prooftext (for it): "[t]here shall not be found among its breakage a shard to scoop coals from a brazier" (Isa 30:14). R. Jose responded: (You bring) proof from there?! (look at the verse's end:) "or ladle water from a puddle" (ibid.).

matter, there is a prooftext for it," all of the biblical citations in mShabbat 9:1–3 are אסמכתות, supports or mnemonic devices to recall these mishnaic *halakhot*, but not proofs that substantiate them. If so, why is there the singular lack of אף על פי שאין ראיה לדבר זכר לדבר in these *mishnayyot* when in every other tannaitic source this formula appears when a citation from narrative, poetic, or non-pentateuchal sources is used as a prooftext for some halakhic rule?

Abraham Goldberg, in his contemporary academic commentary to Mishnah *Shabbat*, explains that the appearance of the אף על פי שאין ראיה לדבר זכר לדבר rhetorical phrase at the beginning of the collection of these cases (mShabbat 8:7) and at its end (mShabbat 9:4) indicates that all the other *mishnayyot* should have included this formula, but they were abbreviated.[33] If we accept Goldberg's view, then we have solved the problem of these *mishnayyot*: they are really just truncated אף על פי שאין ראיה לדבר זכר לדבר sources. Even the repetition of R. Akiba's rule at m^cAvodah Zarah 3:6 without the אף על פי שאין ראיה לדבר זכר לדבר formula does not prove that R. Akiba's view was an exception. A close reading of the mᶜAvodah Zarah will show this to be so.

משנה עבודה זרה פרק ג משנה ו

מי שהיה ביתו סמוך לעבודה זרה ונפל אסור לבנותו כיצד יעשה כונס בתוך שלו ארבע אמות ובונה היה שלו ושל ע"ז נדון מחצה על מחצה אבניו עציו ועפרו מטמאין כשרץ שנאמר (דברים ז׳, כו) שקץ תשקצנו רבי עקיבא אומר כנדה שנאמר (ישעיה ל, כב) תזרם כמו דוה צא תאמר לו מה נדה מטמאה במשא אף ע"ז מטמאה במשא:

One who had a house close to (a place of) idolatry,[34] and it (the house) collapsed – it is prohibited to rebuild it. What should he do? He should withdraw four cubits into his own (property) and build.[35] If (the wall) belongs to him and the (place of) idolatry (in partnership), the wall is judged as half (his) and half (the idolatrous temple's).[36] Its stones, wood, and dust (i.e., of the idolatrous temple) ritually contaminates like a dead creeping thing, as it says: "You shall surely regard it as abhorrent. . . ." (Deut 7:26)[37]

33 Abraham Goldberg, פירוש למשנה – מסכת שבת (Jerusalem: Jewish Theological Seminary of America, 1976), p. 187.

34 "Close to a place of idolatry" means that one of the house's walls also serves the idolatrous temple.

35 That is, he should withdraw the wall away from the idolatrous temple four cubits and build. The temple will have to build its own wall.

36 This means that the Jewish owner may have full benefit from half the wall. The fact that it adjoins a place of idolatry does not prohibit the entire wall.

37 In Leviticus 11:43 the term שקץ is used to mean a creeping creature that should be viewed as abhorrent. The phrase, "You shall surely regard it (the spoils of idolatry) as abhorrent (שקץ תשקצנו)," employs the Hebrew radical ש-ק-ץ. Thus, a connection is drawn between שקץ תשקצנו and שקץ/שרץ.

> R. Akiba said: (Idolatry contaminates like) a menstruant, as it says: "You shall cast them away like a menstruous woman; 'Out!' you will call to them" (Isa 30:22) – just as a menstruous woman ritually contaminates by carrying, so does an idol. (m^{c}Avodah Zarah 3:6)

As one can see, the redactor of the Mishnah has changed R. Akiba's formulation as it appeared in mShabbat. There the issue was what form of contact is necessary for idolatrous material to convey rabbinically imposed ritual impurity. R. Akiba held that carrying or lifting was that form, and he derived it from an Isaian verse that compared idolatrous matter to a menstruous woman who contaminates by carrying or lifting.

How ritual contamination occurs is not m^{c}Avodah Zarah's central concern. Rather, it seeks to place idolatrous material into some category of ritual contamination. The category it chooses at first is that of a dead creeping thing, which it supports with a citation from a legal section of the Pentateuch found in Deut 7:26. In making use of R. Akiba's material from mShabbat, note how the redactor has reformulated that original material:

> רבי עקיבא אומר כנדה שנאמר...מה נדה מטמאה במשא אף ע״ז מטמאה במשא:
>
> R. Akiba says, (Idolatrous material contaminates) like a menstruant, as it says.... Just as a menstruant contaminates by carrying, so idolatrous material contaminates by carrying.

The redactor has made categorization central to R. Akiba: idolatrous material is like the menstruous woman, just as the first view opined that idolatrous material was like a dead creeping thing. The issue of the means by which idolatrous material contaminates, the center of Akiba's view in mShabbat, has been shunted aside until it arises again at the end of his statement cited in m^{c}Avodah Zarah. In short, the redactor did not feel he could totally eliminate the essential element in Akiba's thought as expressed in mShabbat, but he did rearrange R. Akiba's view enough to bring it into line with his own major concerns.

The appearance of R. Akiba's view in m^{c}Avodah Zarah without the requisite formula, אף על פי שאין ראיה לדבר זכר לדבר, is not an oversight or exception that undermines our thesis. It is merely the use of R. Akiba's source as it appeared in mShabbat without consideration of whether אף על פי שאין ראיה לדבר זכר לדבר should appear with it or not. Since the first opinion in the *mishnah* in ^{c}Avodah Zarah rested on a pentateuchal legal verse, no special introduction beyond שנאמר was necessary, and it appears that the editor simply continued this rhetorical pattern when he cited R. Akiba's view.

In view of this analysis, Goldberg's position seems to be substantially correct. The use of אף על פי שאין ראיה לדבר זכר לדבר beginning with mShabbat 8:7 and its repetition at the end of the mishnaic series at mShabbat 9:4 indicates that all the prooftexts in these *mishnayyot* originally included the אם אינו ענין formula. In their present form they have been abbreviated.

Additional proof for this thesis exists. For example, the Mishnah pericope on washing the circumcision wound has a parallel in bShabbat 134b:

תלמוד בבלי שבת דף קלד עמוד ב

...רבי אלעזר בן עזריה אומר מרחיצין את הקטן ביום השלישי שחל להיות בשבת ואף על פי שאין ראיה לדבר זכר לדבר שנאמר ויהי ביום השלישי בהיותם כאבים.

R. Elazar b. Azariah said: We wash (the circumcision wound of) a baby on the third day that falls on the Sabbath. And even though there is no (solid biblical) proof (for this rule), there is a prooftext for this matter: "And it came to pass on third day when they were in great pain" (Gen 34:25).

While it is clear that this *baraita* deals with a baby as opposed to any male, including an adult,[38] who underwent circumcision, its relationship in form and content to the material in mShabbat 9:3 is clear, but in the *baraita* we see that the citation from Genesis is properly designated "no solid scriptural proof" but rather a prooftext. This would indicate that the *mishnah*, too, would likely have had the אף על פי שאינו ראיה לדבר formula were it not for its truncation.

אף על פי שאינו ראיה לדבר זכר לדבר
The Phenomenon of Palestinian and Babylonian *Baraitot*

bShabbat 134b. The BT *baraita* in bShabbat 134b is a good starting point for the discussion of the phenomenon of *baraitot* that appear in the Palestinian and Babylonian *Talmudim*. This issue is not confined to the question of the relationship of these *baraitot* to the extant Tosefta and halakhic *midrashim*, a matter raised in depth early in the twentieth century by Chanoch Albeck and J. N. Epstein and more recently by Yaakov Elman and Shamma Friedman.[39]

38 Cf. mShabbat 19:3 and pShabbat 19:3 (17a) for the genesis of מרחיצין את הקטן and מרחיצין את המילה.

39 Albeck denies that our *Talmudim* knew the extant Tosefta and halakhic *midrashim*. See his מחקרים בברייתא ובתוספתא (Jerusalem: Mossad Ha-Rav Kook, 1969), pp. 90–137; מבוא התלמודים (Tel Aviv: Dvir, 1969), pp. 102–33; *Untersuchungen über die Halachischen Midraschim* (Berlin: Akadamie Verlag, 1927), chap. 3. J. N. Epstein accepts that the Talmuds knew our Tosefta and halakhic *midrashim* but often altered them by shortening, paraphrasing, glossing, and adding to them. He admits that in some instances the Talmud or an *amora* was unaware of a Toseftan or midrashic *baraita* that was germane to an issue under discussion. See מבואות לספרות התנאים (Jerusalem and Tel Aviv: Magnes Press and Dvir, 1957), pp. 249–51; 254–55; 551–62; 589–90, and

Rather, it extends to the question of whether these *baraitot* are actually purely tannaitic sources.[40]

Returning to the example of the *baraita* in bShabbat 134b, it is important to note and consider the fact that it does not have an exact parallel in tannaitic sources or in PT. This certainly raises the question of whether it is, in fact, a tannaitic source or not. The most we can say, it seems, is that the source is based on and interprets the *mishnah*, most likely the one in mShabbat 9:3, but possibly its parallel in mShabbat 19:3 as well.[41] That is, if we accept Abraham Goldberg's view cited above, we may be seeing phenomena described by Shamma Friedman in his article on Babylonian talmudic *baraitot* and their relationship to Tosefta.

Friedman believes that it is likely that BT knew tannaitic works like Tosefta and Sifra among others and that differences in formulation may be easily attributed to one of three factors: 1) new linguistic usages replacing older ones; 2) commentary that takes the form of harmonization of *baraitot* with Mishnah, with a nearby amoraic *memra*, or clarification of an issue by use of additional language or different terminology; or 3) reworking of older *baraitot* to reflect newer conceptions of the Sages.

594; 663–81. Yaakov Elman deals with the question of Babylonian *baraitot* and their relationship to Tosefta in his *Authority and Tradition* (New York: Yeshiva University Press, 1994). See chap. 11 for his view that the Tosefta as such was not known in amoraic Babylonia and that when BT cites material that is similar to or exactly the same as a toseftan *baraita* it knows it as a "singleton" or as a limited cluster of toseftan *baraitot*. For a review of the modern literature dealing with BT *baraitot* and Tosefta, see *Authority and Tradition*, chap. 2. We will discuss Shamma Friedman, "הברייתות בתלמוד הבבלי ויחסן למקבילותיהן בתוספתא," עטרה לחיים – מחקרים בספרות התלמודית והרבנית (Jerusalem 2000) on pp. 163–66 below. The question of the relationship of the *baraitot* in PT and BT to the Tosefta and halakhic *midrashim* elicited opinions even among the geonic and medieval authorities. See, for example, Saul Lieberman, "תשלום תוספתא," תוספתא – הוצאת צוקרמדל (Jerusalem: Wahrman, 1970), pp. 6–9. *Wissenschaft* scholars also dealt with this question, e.g., Joseph Zvi Hirsch Dünner in *Die Theorien über Wesen und Ursprung der Tosephta* (Amsterdam, 1874) and Arthur Spanier in *Die Toseftaperiode in der tannaitischen Literatur* (Berlin: 1922, reprinted, 1936) among others.

Regarding this issue as it relates to the halakhic *midrashim*, see also J. Z. Lauterbach, *Mekhilta de-Rabbi Ishmael* (Philadelphia: Jewish Publication Society, 1933–1935), 1:xxiii and E. Z. Melamed, מבואות לספרות התלמוד (Jerusalem: 1973), pp. 258–70 and 288–94. See more recently Menahem I. Kahana, ספרי זוטא דברים (Jerusalem: Magnes Press, 2003), pp. 108 and nn. 8–14.

40 Shamma Friedman, "הברייתות בתלמוד הבבלי ויחסן למקבילותיהן שבתוספתא," עטרה ליחיים (Jerusalem: Magnes Press, 2000) pp. 190–98; David Goodblatt, "Babylonian Talmud" in *The Study of Ancient Judaism*, ed., Jacob Neusner (New York: Ktav, 1981), pp. 277–78; 286–88 where Goodblatt points out some of the criteria for identifying Babylonian *baraitot*. Louis Jacobs, "Are there Fictitious Baraitot in the Babylonian Talmud?" *HUCA* 42, pp. 185–96; H. Strack and G. Stemberger, *Introduction to the Talmud and Midrash*, 177–79; 198–200, for a discussion of the nature and provenance of *baraitot* in PT and BT.

41 See above, n. 38.

The *baraita* in bShabbat 134b appears to fall into the second category of reformulations. That is, the *baraita* reworks the *mishnah* in mShabbat 9:3, but possibly the *mishnah* in mShabbat 19:3 as well, in order to make manifest that the scriptural verse in it (them) is a זכר לדבר but not a ראיה לדבר. That point needs clarification because, as we noted above, the *mishnayyot* in that chapter were abbreviated.

Another example among the *baraitot* in BT that include the phrase אף על פי שאין ראיה לדבר זכר לדבר is a *baraita* in bPesaḥim 107b. That *baraita* has a parallel in tPesaḥim 10:5:

תוספתא פסחים

השמש מכביש בבני מעים ונותן לפני האורחין. אע״ף שאין ראיה לדבר, זכר לדבר: נירו לכם ניר ואל תזרעו אל קוצים.

The servant presses into the entrails and places (them) before the guests. Even though there is no proof for (this) matter, there is support for it: "Break up the untilled ground, and do not sow among thorns" (Jer 4:3).

בבלי פסחים קז ב'

השמש מטביל בבני מעיין ונותנן לפני האורחים. ואע״פ שאין ראיה לדבר, זכר לדבר: נירו לכם ניר ואל תזרעו אל קצים.

The servant dips into the entrails and places (them) before the guests. Even though there is no proof for (this) matter, there is support for it: "Break up the untilled ground, and do not sow among thorns" (Jer 4:3).[42]

As we can easily see, the two texts differ by a single word, מכביש, which appears in Tosefta and is rarely used in formative rabbinic literature,[43] and מטביל, which appears in BT. Given the formulation of these two *baraitot* there is reason to believe that they are in fact the same source. A likely explanation for the one word difference between them is that BT replaced the less known, and therefore less comprehensible מכביש, with the better known and frequently used term מטביל.[44] This would conform to Friedman's first reason for differ-

42 Rashi explains this verse as applicable to the situation in the following manner: When you labor, you should have benefit from your labor. (Similarly,) if the servant dealing with the meal and the kitchen does not derive benefit (from the food being prepared and served), he suffers.

43 What looks like the *hiph'il* of כ-ב-ש is used six times in formative rabbinic sources, though in two cases in Tosefta it is actually the noun מכבש. In the halakhic *midrashim* it has the more regular meaning of "conquer." Once in Tosefta (above) and once in the halakhic *midrashim* (*Mek. de-RSBY*, Exod 14:30) its meaning seems to be "press down" or "squeeze."

44 A search of just the infinitive for and the present, past, and future tenses of the *hiph'il* of ט-ב-ל generates about 125 cases.

ences between Babylonian *baraitot* and Tosefta. There are no examples that I can discern of Babylonian *baraitot* containing the אף על פי שאין ראיה לדבר וכו' formula that have been reformulated to conform to new conceptions and concerns of the Sages.

Palestinian *Baraita* Parallels

pPesaḥim 1:1. Though I maintain that there are no amoraic cases of אף על פי שאין ראיה לדבר in the *Talmudim*, there are what appear to be *baraita* parallels attributed to amoraic Sages. How are we to explain this phenomenon?[45] Let us begin with an analysis of pPesaḥim 1:1 (27a):

> ר' ירמיה אמר רב שמואל בר רב יצחק[46] בעי מהו לבדוק לאור האבוקות. מה צריכה ליה מפני שאורן מבליח. ר' שמואל בר רב יצחק כדעתיה דר' שמואל בר רב יצחק אמר מפני שהנר בודק כל שהוא [אף על פי שאין ראיה לדבר זכר לדבר. והיה ביום ההוא אחפש את ירושלם בנרות. ואית דבעי מימר] נישמעינה מן הדא נר ה' נשמת אדם חופש כל חדרי בטן.

> R. Jeremiah said, "R. Samuel b. R. Isaac asked, 'What is the law regarding searching (for leaven) by the light of a torch?[46] Why need he ask?[47] Because its light flickers. R. Samuel b. R. Isaac (asked) according to his own view, for R. Samuel b. R. Isaac says, "Because a lamp searches out even the minutest thing. [Though there is no proof for the matter, there is prooftext for the matter: "It will come to pass that on that day I will search out Jerusalem with lamps" (Zeph 1:12). There are those who wish to say that] we derive it from this: "The soul of man is the lamp of God, which searches out all the recesses of his heart" (Prov 20:27).

45 The question of talmudic material that appears as a *baraita* and as an amoraic *memra* has been the subject of much discussion in *Wissenchaft* and contemporary critical-historical literature. See, for example, Zechariah Frankel, מבוא הירושלמי (Breslau: Schletter, 1870; reprinted, Jerusalem: no publisher, 1967), pp. כה א'-כז ב'; I. H. Weiss, דור ודור ודורשיו (Vilna: no publisher, 1871–1873; reprinted, Vilna 1904; reprinted, Jerusalem and Tel Aviv: Ziv Publishers, n.d.), pp. 2:195 and 215 and 3:207–8; J. N. Epstein, מבוא לספרות התנאים, pp. 252–53; 615 and nn. 161–62; Chanoch Albeck, מחקרים בברייתא ותוספת, pp. 52–53; Abraham Weiss, לחקר התלמוד (New York: Feldheim, 1955), pp. 35–63; Judith Hauptman, *Development of the Talmudic Sugya: Relationship Between Tannaitic and Amoraic Sources* (Lanham, New York, and London: University of America Press, 1988), chaps. 3–5; and Yaakov Elman, *Authority and Tradition* (New York: Yeshiva University Press, 1994), pp. 134–37. Given the wealth of material on the subject of *baraitot* that appear as *memrot*, I will limit my conclusions regarding each case to the theory that explains it best.

46 ר' ירמיה אמר ר' שמואל בר רב יצחק: דפוס קושטא: אמר רשב"י. ואיתא רשב"י בכל מקום שנזכר ר' שמואל בר רב יצחק. [] : תוספת הסופר של כ"י ליידן. R. Jeremiah said, "R. Samuel b. R. Isaac asked, 'What is the law regarding searching (for leaven) by the light of a torch?'": Ed. Constantinople has "RSB"Y" in all places where R. Samuel b. R. Isaac is mentioned in Ed. Venice and MS Leiden.

47 Isn't it obvious that a torch, which gives more light than a lamp, would be permitted?

According to the reading in the Leiden manuscript and the *editio princeps* Venice based on it, the אף על פי שאין ראיה לדבר *midrash* appears as if it is attributed to R. Samuel b. R. Isaac, a third generation *amora* who emigrated from Babylonia to Palestine. His *derashah*, though different in wording, seems related in content to *baraitot* in *Mek. de-RSBY* and tPesaḥim 1:1 as these citations show:

Tosefta Pesaḥim 1.1

אור לארבעה עשר בודקין את החמץ לאור הנר אין בודקין לא לאור החמה ולא לאור הלבנה אלא לאור הנר לפי שבדיקת הנר יפה מרובה. אע״פ שאין ראיה לדבר זכר לדבר: והיה בעת ההיא אחפש את ירושלים בנרות ואומר נר אלהים נשמת אדם.

On the eve of the fourteenth (of Nisan), we search out the *hameẓ* by the light of a lamp. We do not search by the light of the sun or the moon, but by the light of a lamp, because the searching ability of a lamp is exceptionally good. Even though there is no proof for the matter, there is a prooftext for the matter: "It shall come to pass at that time that I will search Jerusalem with lamps," and it (also) says, "The lamp of God is the soul of man (searching out all the inner recesses [of the soul])."

Mek. de-RSBY

ושמרתם את היום הזה: שמריהו מלפניו <מאור ארבעה עשר>. מכאן אמרו: אור ארבעה עשר בודקין את החמץ לאור הנר ואין בודקין לא לאור חמה ולא לאור לבנה <ולא לאור האבוקה> אלא לאור הנר. אע״פ שאין ראיה לדבר זכר לדבר: והיה בעת ההיא אחפש את ירושלים בנרות.

"And you shall observe this day"– observe it before it (occurs) <from the eve of the fourteenth>. From this they (the Sages) said: On the eve of the fourteenth (of Nisan) we search out the *hameẓ* by the light of a lamp. We do not search by the light of the sun or the moon <or a torch>, but by the light of a lamp. Even though there is no proof for the matter, there is a prooftext for the matter: "It shall come to pass at that time that I will search Jerusalem with lamps."

By way of comparison, small but significant details divide the different sources we have cited. For example, Tosefta gives a reason for requiring the use of a lamp for the search for *hameẓ*: a lamp searches out things in a superior fashion. It also prohibits the use of sunlight and moonlight. *Mek. de-RSBY* does not state that the lamp provides superior light for a search. It simply requires the use of a lamp and prohibits the use of sunlight or moonlight, and according to some formulations, the light of a torch. R. Samuel b. R. Isaac, somewhat like the Tosefta, speaks of the special quality of a lamp as an instrument for searching: a lamp searches out the smallest entity. However, in a departure from both Tosefta and *Mek. de-RSBY*, he does not clearly rule out the use of other instruments for the search, which may lead to his halakhic inquiry about the use of a torch. The end result of that inquiry is that a torch is prohibited because the benefits of its greater light are outweighed by the fact that it flickers.

Regarding the אף על פי שאינו ראיה section of these three sources, Tosefta stands alone in citing both the Zephaniah and Proverbs sources. *Mek.de-RSBY* and R. Samuel b. R. Isaac seem to cite only Zephaniah. Other amoraic authorities mentioned in the *sugya* in its present form point to Proverbs as the source of the idea that a lamp must be used for the search for *hameẓ*.

Though the formulation in the critical apparatus of the *Talmud Yerushalmi* published by the Academy for the Hebrew Language does not necessarily obviate the issue of *baraitot* appearing as *memrot* in this PT *sugya*, it does remove the connection between R. Samuel b. R. Isaac's *memra* and the prooftext for it. This is because the section containing אף על פי שאינו ראיה is a "correction" of MS Leiden added in by editor 1.[48] Hence, R. Samuel b. R. Isaac's *memra* appears to stand alone here as it did earlier in this PT *sugya*. In an attempt to provide the scriptural basis for using lamplight to search out *hameẓ*, an unnamed interlocutor suggests Prov 20:2.[49]

As just noted, though, this distances R. Samuel b. R. Isaac from the *derashah* whose source is in a *baraita*, it does not necessarily resolve the problem of how what looks like an amoraic citation also appears as a *baraita*. In our case, whoever said, "Let us learn this (R. Samuel b. R. Isaac's view) from this (Prov 20:27)," still may have known a *baraita* tradition that used this verse either from the Tosefta or from some source similar to it. If so, one explanation of the phenomenon we are analyzing is that at least in this case the Palestinian *amoraim* had a general knowledge of the content of a source somehow related to Tosefta. The Palestinian *amoraim* reconstructed this vague tradition as best they could. Since, however, they were not sure that their reconstruction properly reflected the original source, they did not transmit it as a *baraita*.[50]

It is also possible that PT independently thought of and provided a prooftext

48 See Binyamin Elizur, "הקדמה," תלמוד ירושלמי יוצא לאור ע"י האקדמיה ללשון העברית, p. מא. This "correction" is most likely based on sources in bPesaḥim 7b. Ibid., p. כא, n. 129.

49 See Saul Lieberman, ירושלמי כפשוטו (New York and Jerusalem: Jewish Theological Seminary of America, reprint 1995), p. 369, s.v. ... אף על פי שאין ראיה.

50 David Weiss-Halivni, מקורות ומסורות – נשים, p. תרמה and idem., מועד, p. פא. See also Michael Chernick, "לחקר המידות „כלל ופרט וכלל" ו„ריבוי ומיעוט", pp. 125 and 127. I prefer the theory of "vague traditions" to other theories regarding *baraitot* that appear as *memrot* because other theories deal with *memrot* with similar wording to *baraitot*. Here the wording is very different from the Toseftan and *Mek. de-RSBY baraitot*, though, as I have noted, the content is similar to tPesaḥim 1:1.

for R. Samuel b. R. Isaac's view. The *amoraim* certainly were expert enough in the *TaNaKh* to connect a "lamp that searches out the innermost recesses. . . ." (Prov 20:27) to a lamp that searches out the minutest entity, in this case the smallest piece of *hameẓ*. Also, the absence of the אף על פי שאין ראיה לדבר formula in the original part of the Leiden manuscript version of this PT *sugya* leaves us with a formulation reflective of the amoraic style of deriving or supporting *halakhah* from non-legal passages in the *TaNaKh*. If this is the case, the *sugya* does not refer to a *baraita* at all.

Pesaḥim 5:1. There is another PT passage in which there appears to be an anonymous amoraic interlocutor speaking within a text that is similar in content to the אף על פי שאינו ראיה לדבר clause in *Mek. Pisḥa* 5||*Sifra ᵓEmor*, par. 9., 11:1.[51] The full PT source reads as follows:

> כתיב וזה אשר תעשה על המזבח וגו׳ הייתי אומר יקרבו שניהן בשחרית ושניהן בין הערבים ת״ל את הכבש אחד תעשה בבקר. הייתי אומר יקרב של שחר עם הנץ החמה ושל בין הערבים עם דמדומי החמה ת״ל בין הערבים. נאמר כאן בין הערבים ונאמר להלן בין הערבים מה בין הערבים שנאמר להלן משש שעות ולמעלן אף בין הערבים שנא׳ כאן משש שעות ולמעלן.
>
> מה חמית מימר בין הערבים משש שעות ולמעלן? [אף על פי שאין ראיה לדבר זכר לדבר] אוי לנו כי פנה היום כי ינטו צללי ערב. מה ערב שנאמר להלן משש שעות ולמעלן אף ערב שנאמר כאן משש שעות ולמעלן.

51 *Mek. Pisḥa* 5 states:

> ...ר׳ נתן אומר מנין ראיה לבין הערבים שהוא משש שעות ולמעלה? אף על פי שאין ראיה לדבר זכר לדבר: (ירמיה ו, ד) קדשו עליה מלחמה קומו ונעלה בצהרים אוי לנו כי פנה היום כי ינטו צללי ערב.

> . . . R. Nathan says: Whence do we derive a proof that afternoon (begins) from six hours and a half (after midday)? Even though there is no solid proof for the matter, there is a prooftext for the matter: "Prepare for battle against her: 'Up! we will attack at noon.' 'Alas for us! for day is declining, The shadows of evening grow long.'"

The following is the formulation in Sifra:

> ובחודש הראשון בארבעה עשר יום לחודש בין הערבים. יכול משתחשך תלמוד לומר יום. אי יום יכול משתי שעות תלמוד לומר בין הערבים. מה בין הערבים מיוחד משפנה יום. אף יום משפנה יום משש שעות ולמעלה ואע״פ שאין ראייה לדבר זכר לדבר. אוי לנו כי פנה יום כי נטו צללי ערב.

> "In the first month on the fourteenth day of the month in the afternoon"– I might have thought when it becomes dark. Therefore, the Torah says, "Day." If (during) the day, I might have thought from the second hour (of the day). Therefore the Torah said, "in the afternoon." Just as afternoon is specifically from when the day wanes, so the day (mentioned here) is from when the day wanes, (which is) from the sixth and a half hour (of the day) and onward. Even though there is no proof for this matter, there is a prooftext for it: "Alas for us! for day is declining, The shadows of evening grow long."

> It is written: "This is what you shall offer on the altar, (two yearling lambs each day, regularly)" (Exod 29:38). I might have said that two should be brought in the morning and two in the afternoon. Therefore the Torah says, "You should offer one lamb in the morning, (and the second lamb in the afternoon)" (ibid. 29:39). I might have said the morning sacrifice should be offered at sunrise and the afternoon sacrifice at twilight. Therefore the Torah says, "in the afternoon" (lit., "between the two sunsets." That is, between the time the sun passes the zenith and the time it actually sets.) It says here (in Exod 29) "in the afternoon" and it says there (regarding the Passover offering) "in the afternoon." Just as the afternoon there is from the sixth and a half hour (of the day) and onward,[52] so the afternoon here is from the sixth and a half hour (of the day) and onward.
>
> What did you see that makes you say that afternoon means from the sixth and a half hour of the day? [Though there is no proof for the matter, there is support for the matter:] ". . . Woe to us for the day is passing, the shadows of evening are lengthening" (Jer 6:4). Just as evening that is mentioned there (in Jeremiah) is from the sixth and a half hour (of the day) and onward, so evening that is mentioned here (regarding Passover) is from the sixth and a half hour (of the day) and onward.

I have separated the PT *sugya* into two paragraphs in order to discuss them in an orderly fashion. The first paragraph contains a *midrash* about the daily offering that appears only in PT, which suggests it may be either a pseudepigraphic PT *baraita*-like *midrash* or a *baraita* from a collection unknown to us. The second paragraph cites a source that is similar in content to R. Nathan's view in *Mek. Pisḥa* 5 and an anonymous *baraita* in *Sifra ᵓEmor*. The extension of the *baraita* material that appears in the formulation, "Just as evening that is mentioned there is from the sixth and a half hour (of the day) and onward, so evening that is mentioned here is from the sixth and a half hour (of the day) and onward," may be borrowed from the end of the *midrash* in the first paragraph.

If this is so, PT may have introduced the *baraita* material with the formula *מה חמית מימר בין הערבים משש שעות ולמעלן?* ("What did you see that makes you say that afternoon means from the sixth and a half hour of the day?") because it wanted to use the *midrash* attributed to R. Nathan or the anonymous *Sifra midrash* in relation to the daily offering. The application of this *midrash* to the daily offering deviates from the classical halakhic *midrashim*'s application of it to the Passover offering. Hence, it is basically an העברה, a source

52 The verse in Jeremiah begins, "Prepare for battle against her: 'Up! we will attack at noon.'" Hence, according to the midrashist, "the shadows of evening are lengthening" indicates the first period after noon in which the shadows noticeably lengthen. He considers this to be a half hour after the midway point between dawn and night.

transferred from one context to another. It may be that the *amora* who made use of this source did not identify it as a *baraita* because he used it in his own novel manner. On the other hand, the presentation of *baraita* material without formulary introductions and in shortened form are commonplaces in PT.

Despite the fact that אף על פי שאין ראיה לדבר זכר לדבר in this PT passage is an editorial gloss in MS Leiden, it is probably an accurate "correction."[53] Unlike the *midrash* in pPesaḥim 1:1 where the *amoraim* themselves might have independently made the connection between the Proverbs verse and the use of a lamp for intense searching, the connection between the Jeremiah verse and the sixth and a half hour of the day is more tenuous. This is not to say that in a literary world like that of the *amoraim*,[54] one in which orality and memorization also played significant roles,[55] it was impossible for them to recreate this *midrash* on their own. Nevertheless, it seems more plausible that some tannaitic halakhic midrashic collection provided the anonymous Palestinian interlocutor with the source for his comment.

Summary
Babylonian and Palestinian *Baraitot* and אף על פי שאין ראיה לדבר זכר לדבר *Midrashim*

In my short analysis of a minute sampling of Babylonian *baraita* sources and Palestinian *baraita* parallels, I did not intend to answer the major questions about the relationship of such sources to Tosefta and the halakhic *midrashim*. Rather, I have sought to strengthen my contention that the *amoraim* did not use the אף על פי שאין ראיה לדבר זכר לדבר hermeneutic. My analysis of a Babylonian *baraita* in bShabbat 134b, closely related in formulation to mShabbat 9:3, suggested that it was tannaitic. The appearance of אף על פי שאין ראיה לדבר זכר לדבר in the *baraita* in bShabbat 134b is therefore expected.

I found that the Palestinian *baraita* parallels presented a more challenging and less clear picture. These appeared in pPesaḥim 1:1 and 5:1. In both cases an unnamed, presumably amoraic interlocutor introduced the *baraita* parallels. This raised the complicated question of *baraitot* that appear as amoraic *memrot*. Use of the Academy of the Hebrew Language's critical edition of MS Leiden indicated that the אף על פי שאין ראיה לדבר זכר לדבר that apparently introduced a scriptural prooftext was, in fact, Editor 1's editorial correction of the original MS Leiden text. It is possible that the *amoraim* themselves made the connection between the scriptural texts and the issues under discussion in pPesaḥim 1:1 and 5:1. This, of course, would explain the lack of

53 Saul Lieberman, ירושלמי כפשוטו, p. 447, s.v. אף על פי שאין ראיה לדבר זכר לדבר.

54 Abraham Weiss, לחקר התלמוד, pp. 59–60.

55 Yaakov Elman, *Authority and Tradition*, pp. 80 and 84.

אף על פי שאין ראיה לדבר זכר לדבר in the original text of PT. If, however, the *baraita* parallels' sources are tannaitic *baraitot*, then the fact that they are cited as *memrot* may be due to their being vaguely known or remembered *baraita* traditions, or *baraitot* cited without stating that they are *baraitot*, or *baraitot* that the *amoraim* used in a way that differed from their original source. Any of these reasons might explain why the *amoraim* might take the credit or responsibility for these parallels.

אף על פי שאין ראיה לדבר זכר לדבר and *Asmakhta*

Our study of the midrashic phenomenon called אף על פי שאין ראיה לדבר זכר לדבר indicates that under most circumstances non-pentateuchal or pentateuchal narrative or poetic sources do not constitute "proof" or a substantive basis for a legal or even an aggadic view. Rather, such verses are used as proof-texts for law or lore. That being the case, we should view *midrashim* that use אף על פי שאין ראיה לדבר as distinct from tannaitic halakhic midrashic interpretations that appear without this formula preceding the *midrash*'s verse. That is, when a *midrash* did not include אף על פי שאין ראיה לדבר, then the *tannaim* considered the verse full proof for their *halakhah*.[56] Indeed, this idea resurfaces in the famous debate between Maimonides and Nachmanides about the nature of midrashic interpretations. Maimonides views almost all midrashic interpretations as "support *midrash*" for existing *halakhah* unless the Sages indicate otherwise.[57] Nachmanides holds that when *midrash* produces halakhic regulations, they have pentateuchal force.[58] In light of our findings, it appears that the *tannaim*'s sense of the status of *midrash* supports Nachmanides' view more than that of Maimonides. Yet both views, I believe, are strongly influenced by the phenomenon called אסמכתא (Aram., *asmakhta*, support), which many consider to be a form of mnemonic device.[59] Nachmanides claims that

56 A discussion in bYebamot 21a suggests that a law might be pentateuchal even though its details were determined by the Sages. Despite the passage's ultimate conclusion that the law in question, "incestuous relations of a second degree" (שניות לעריות), is a rabbinic enactment and the verse used to support it an אסמכתא ("support, but not source"), the initial description of the law as "רבנן דאורייתא ופירשו," "pentateuchal (law) but (its fine points) explained by the Rabbis," describes the tannaitic sense of their halakhic system perfectly. See also Abbaye's question addressed to R. Josef in bGittin 59b. It implies that Abbaye and R. Josef considered a midrashically derived or supported *halakhah* as "pentateuchal" even when tied to rabbinic ordinances enacted "for the sake of peace." This, of course, proves nothing about tannaitic attitudes towards *halakhot* derived by *midrash*, nor even about amoraic views in general, but it does indicate how at least two *amoraim* viewed such *halakhot* as pentateuchal in some sense.

57 ספר המצוות, שרש שני, ed. Frankel, pp. נא–נז.

58 הרמב"ן לספר המצוות להרמב"ם, ed. Frankel, pp. נב–נד, s.v. ועכשו אני חוזר וכו'.

59 For a full discussion of אסמכתא from a traditionalist perspective, see אנציקלופדיה תלמודית (Jerusalem: Enzyklopedia Talmudit, 1956–) v. 2. pp. קה–קח.

the existence of אסמכתא implies that anything not so categorized must be a full-fledged biblical proof. Maimonides, relying on the idea that אין המקרא יוצא מידי פשוטו, "Scripture always retains its plain meaning,"[60] holds that most *midrash* must be rabbinic support for various *halakhot*, because *midrash*, by definition, is not the text's plain meaning. While this is close to the idea of *asmakhta* as understood by other medieval authorities, Maimonides reserves *asmakhta* for situations in which there is not even a hint in the Bible for a particular *halakhah*. In those cases, according to Maimonides, the Sages often find a biblical text that can serve as a mnemonic device by which to remember the *halakhah*. According to him, such texts are *asmakhtot*.[61]

The Distinction between *Asmakhta* (Support) and זכר לדבר

While Maimonides considers an *asmakhta* a mnemonic allusion or support, it is not phenomenologically the same as זכר לדבר.[62] The rhetorical form "אף על פי שאין ראיה לדבר זכר לדבר" announces an honest conclusion about the status of an halakhic or aggadic view – namely, that it has no solid pentateuchal warrant. When we inspect the cases in which we find rhetorical introductions to *asmakhtot*, e.g., קרא אסמכתא בעלמא ("the verse is merely a support") or אסמכינהו רבנן אקרא ("the Sages connected it to a verse"), we discover that the function of אסמכתא is usually the resolution of some conflict between sources. For example, the Talmud might cite a midrashic source of an *halakhah*, and then cite another source which directly states that the *halakhah* is of rabbinic origin. At that point, someone, usually the anonymous voice of the Talmud (סתמא דגמרא), will resolve the conflict by stating, "קרא אסמכתא בעלמא," "the verse (used in the *midrash*) is a mere support (but not the source of the law)." The following selection from the Talmud will demonstrate how this rhetorical device operates:

תלמוד בבלי מסכת סוכה דף כח עמוד א–ב

...נשים ועבדים וקטנים פטורין מן הסוכה. קטן שאינו צריך לאמו – חייב בסוכה. מעשה וילדה כלתו של שמאי הזקן, ופיחת את המעזיבה וסיכך על גבי המטה בשביל קטן.

גמרא. מנא הני מילי? – דתנו רבנן: אזרח – זה אזרח +ויקרא כג+ האזרח – להוציא את הנשים. כל – לרבות את הקטנים....

אמר מר: כל – לרבות את הקטנים. והתנן: נשים ועבדים וקטנים פטורין מן הסוכה! – לא קשיא: כאן – בקטן שהגיע לחינוך, כאן – בקטן שלא הגיע לחינוך.

60 bShabbat 63a; bYebamot 11b and 24a.

61 *Mamonides' Introduction to his Commentary on the Mishnah*, ed. Kapah (Jerusalem: Sixth Printing, 1988), p. י and Mishnah Commentary, mShabbat 9:2.

62 Maimonides' Mishnah Commentary, Introduction, s.v. ועל כן כל דבר שאין לו רמז במקרא; ibid., mShabbat 9:2.

– קטן שהגיע לחינוך מדרבנן הוא! – מדרבנן, וקרא אסמכתא בעלמא הוא. . . .

Mishnah. Women, slaves, and minors are exempt from sukkah-dwelling. A minor who is independent of his mother is obliged to sukkah-dwelling. A case: The daughter-in-law of Shammai the Elder gave birth (to a son). He (Shammai) broke through the roof and covered it with boughs (for a sukkah) over (her) bed for the sake of the minor.

Gemara. Whence (do we know) these matters (i.e., the mishnaic laws). Our rabbis taught (in a *baraita*): "אזרח, a citizen"[63] – this means a full citizen (i.e., an adult Jewish male). "האזרח, the citizen"[64] – excludes women; "כל, every"[65] – includes minors. . . .

The Master said:[66] "כל, every" – includes minors. . . ." (But doesn't the Mishnah) teach: Women, slaves, and minors are exempt from sukkah-dwelling? There is no contradiction (between the halakhic *midrash* and the Mishnah). Here (in the midrashic *baraita* we are dealing) with a minor who has reached the age of training (for *mizvah* observance). There (in the *mishnah* we are dealing) with a minor who has not reached the age of training (for *mizvah* observance). (But isn't the law of) the minor who has reached the age of training (for *mizvah* observance) of rabbinic origin?![67] (True, its origin is) rabbinic, and the (cited) scriptural sources are merely *asmakhta* – a buttress for rabbinic legislation.

Let us review what occurred in the argument above. At a certain point after a contradiction between sources had been resolved, the resolution became problematic. That resolution claimed that the two sources in conflict, the Mishnah and a midrashic *baraita*, spoke of different kinds of minors: those ready to be educated to perform the commandments, and those who had not reached that age. But in the time of the anonymous spokesman in this passage, it was clear that the obligations imposed on minors being trained to take their eventual place in the Jewish community were rabbinic *halakhah*. Yet, there was a word, כל, in a legislative pentateuchal verse that a midrashist had interpreted as including minors, and that might mean that the obligation of minors to sukkah-dwelling was pentateuchal. How did that tally with

63 The generative verse for this *midrash* is Lev. 23:42: שבעת ימים תשבו בסכות כל האזרח בישראל ישבו בסוכות, "Seven days shall you dwell in huts; every citizen in Israel shall dwell in huts."

64 The *midrash* considers the addition of the definite article significant and, therefore, interprets it.

65 Since כל is inclusive, the midrashist uses it to include in the obligation of sukkah-dwelling parties who would have normally been exempted, i.e., minors.

66 This does not refer to any specific teacher. It is merely a formula for re-introducing a previously cited sources – in this case, a part of the midrashic *baraita*.

67 It is clear that the anonymous speaker holds, at least for argument's sake, that if a law is derived midrashically from the pentateuch's legal sections, it has pentateuchal standing.

what everyone in the anonymous redactor's time accepted about a minor's obligations? The answer provided was: the *midrash* was a mere support for the Rabbis' legislation, not its generative source.

To see how this bears no relationship to אף על פי שאין ראיה לדבר זכר לדבר we should consider whether the Talmud's anonymous interlocutor had to come to the conclusions he did. For example, there was no need in the first place to claim that the midrashic *baraita* and the *mishnah* were in contradiction: the *mishnah* itself said that minors who were independent of their mothers were obliged to sukkah-dwelling. The *baraita* might have been viewed as saying the same thing.[68]

Alternatively, the *mishnah* might have been conceived of as containing several different tannaitic views listed in the order of higher degrees of a minor's obligation: 1) All minors are exempt. 2) Independent minors are obliged. 3) Even dependent minors are obliged. If that is so, the *baraita* would reflect the most stringent tannaitic point of view: all minors must observe sukkah-dwelling. In short, it was not at all necessary for the Talmud's anonymous speaker to declare the *midrash* to be mere *asmakhta*. Indeed, it is quite likely that there was a significant tannaitic debate about the obligations of minors, with some *tannaim* holding that they were fully obliged to certain observances of the law.[69] By the time of the anonymous speaker in this passage, the view that minors were under no pentateuchal obligation to perform any of the *miẓvot* had become normative. How then was one to reconcile a tannaitic source that appeared to demand that minors observe the laws of sukkah-dwelling with the "normative" view? What proved to be the answer was the claim that that *midrash*'s results did not provide a pentateuchally-based legal claim on minors. Rather, the *midrash* provided a mere *asmakhta*-support for a piece of rabbinic legislation regarding Jewish male children.[70]

The difference between this and אף על פי שאין ראיה לדבר זכר לדבר should now be clear: what we have seen regarding *asmakhta* is that it is a *deus ex machina* to save the regnant halakhic viewpoint of later generations when

68 See חידושי הריטב״א – סוכה, ed. Lichtenstein (Jerusalem: 1982), pp. רס–רסא.

69 See, for example, mSukkah 2:8 and 3:15; mḤagigah 1:1 (defines קטן in a way that would require most male children under 13 to make the annual pilgrimages); mMegillah 2:4, cf. tMegillah (ed. Lieberman) 2:8. See also bᶜArakhin 2b–3a and the *baraitot* in support of the obligation of minors to certain *miẓvot*, and Yitzchak Gilat, "בן שלש-עשרה למצוות," מחקרי תלמוד א (Jerusalem: Magnes Press, 1990), pp. 39–53.

70 אסמכתא claims predicated on contradictory sources of a law can be found in bBerakhot 41b=Sukkah 6a, Pesaḥim 81b, ibid. 96b, Yoma 74a, ibid. 80, Moᶜed Qatan 3a, Yebamot 24a, ibid. 52b, ibid. 100b, Baba Meẓiᶜaᵓ 88b, Baba Batra 160b, Ḥullin 64b, ibid. 77a, Meᶜilah 15a. אסמכתא claims predicated on biblical prooftexts being used in cases where the Talmud claims to know that the law is a rabbinic enactment are found in bSukkah 28b, Moᶜed Qatan 3a, Ḥagigah 4a, Ḥullin 17b, Niddah 46b. אסמכתא claims based on miscellaneous considerations can be found in bYebamot 72a, Nedarim 49a, Sanhedrin 83a, ᶜAvodah Zarah 38a, Menaḥot 92b, and Niddah 25a.

that view runs into conflict with positions held by earlier authorities. אף על פי שאין ראיה לדבר זכר לדבר is the *tannaim*'s effort to distinguish between what they considered constitutionally mandated, i.e., pentateuchal, though derived by *midrash*, and what was not. Nevertheless, the existence of אף על פי שאין ראיה לדבר זכר לדבר, with its view that a *midrash* might provide a prooftext for a law rather than an actual proof for it, allows for the development of the notion of *asmakhta* despite their differences. Therefore, it is reasonable to view *asmakhta* as a talmudic device that develops out of the זכר לדבר phenomenon.

Summary

Our study has produced the following findings regarding the midrashic phenomenon introduced by the rhetorical formula אף על פי שאין ראיה לדבר זכר לדבר.

1. The prooftexts for midrashic interpretations of this sort are pentateuchal non-legal sources or non-pentateuchal biblical sources.

2. אף על פי שאין ראיה לדבר זכר לדבר *midrashim* are basically tannaitic creations. There is no solid evidence that the *amoraim* created *midrashim* of this kind.

3. The fact that some midrashic expositions are not considered genuine scriptural proof for a law implies that others are. Since the only midrashic interpretations marked as not being proof are those containing the formula אף על פי שאין ראיה לדבר זכר לדבר, all other midrashic expositions appear to be viewed by the *tannaim* as full scriptural support for the laws they produce. These laws would then have the status of what I call pentateuchal *halakhah*. During the Middle Ages, Nahmanides subscribed to this view.

4. The anonymous stratum of the Talmud often tries to explain why an אף על פי שאין ראיה לדבר זכר לדבר *midrash* does not constitute proof. This shows that those responsible for this stratum no longer knew the tannaitic criteria for a biblical verse to be considered solid proof for a law. Most likely this was the result of the *amoraim* having used pentateuchal non-legal texts and non-pentateuchal biblical verses as proofs for their *halakhot*. Given these facts, when the סתמא דגמרא is late or post-amoraic, it had no reason to exclude pentateuchal non-legal verses or non-pentateuchal verses from the category of "proof." Hence, when the plain meaning of verses used in an אף על פי שאין ראיה לדבר זכר לדבר *midrash* seemed to point directly to the *halakhah* or *aggadah* mentioned in an exposition, the late סתמא דגמרא found it necessary to explain why the verse was not solid proof for the proposition.

5. Some mishnaic passages contain interpretations based on non-pentateuchal sources in which the verses are cited using the standard introduction, שנאמר,

"as it is said." This phenomenon appears to run counter to our view that a rhetorical introduction like שנאמר introduces what the *tannaim* would have considered full scriptural proof. Under normal circumstances such proof should come only from a pentateuchal legal verse or pericope. However, the mishnaic cases appear to have been truncated as is indicated by the fact that the series of *mishnayyot* (mShabbat 8:7–9:4) begins and ends with the formula אף על פי שאין ראיה לדבר זכר לדבר. At least one example from this series (mMishnah Shabbat 9:3) has a BT *baraita* parallel that includes the אף על פי שאין ראיה לדבר formula.

6. A phenomenon called *asmakhta* has also been identified by some medieval commentators, notably Maimonides, as a mnemonic device. This is not actually the case in the Talmud. It is not equivalent to אף על פי שאין ראיה לדבר זכר לדבר *midrash*. The latter is an attempt to distinguish between what is pentateuchal legislation based on midrashic interpretation and what is not. *Asmakhta*, on the other hand, is a rhetorical device to solve textual difficulties, especially problems generated by contradictory views and sources. All claims that a midrashic interpretation is an *asmakhta* are no earlier than the fourth amoraic generation, and most are from the anonymous stratum of the Talmud, generally considered late.[71] Thus, the *asmakhta* phenomenon has its origins in the later amoraic period and its full flowering in the post-amoraic era.

In sum, the phenomenon introduced by the phrase אף על פי שאין ראיה לדבר זכר לדבר is a key to the tannaitic midrashists' understanding of the status of their interpretations and the apparent source of the development of the later phenomenon called *asmakhta*. It is also the earliest recognition and division of biblical literature into its distinct genres: law, narrative, and poetry, and for the *tannaim* an evaluation of the legal authority of those genres. It appears that for them only the legal sections of the Torah could produce what I call

71 There are four cases in which the phrase הילכתא נינהו ואסמכינהו רבנן אקראי, "it is a traditional law and the Sages attached it to verses," appears. In three of the four instances the party who is cited as saying this is Raba, a fourth-generation *amora*. In the printed edition of the Talmud, Sukkah 28a, Rabbah, a third-generation *amora*, is cited as having said this, but most mss. and incunabula have Raba. The Palestinian Talmud uses the terms סמכו למקרא and סמכו ... לתורה, the first in pShevi[c]it 1:1 (33a) and the second in pShevi[c]it 10:2 (39c). In the first case the term means "relied" and the implication is that the Torah served as proof for the law. In the second case, the case of *prosbul*, a device for avoiding cancellation of loans in the sabbatical year, the term means "they connected or based (the rabbinic ordinance enacted by Hillel) on the Torah." This is closer to the idea of אסמכתא, and interestingly enough the term is used by the anonymous stratum of the Palestinian Talmud. Nevertheless, its usage in that passage is different from ואסמכינהו רבנן אקראי. In the Palestinian Talmud the claim that *prosbul* was "connected to or based on the Torah" meant that the Torah itself no longer required any of the sabbatical year observances. Therefore, Hillel was free to enact the *prosbul*, which was, in fact, a stringency insofar as it required those who did not avail themselves of this enactment to cancel their debtors' obligations in the sabbatical year.

pentateuchal *halakhah*, rules that definitively determined the way a Jew should observe a *miẓvah* of the Torah. Any *halakhah* based on a pentateuchal narrative or non-pentateuchal scriptural source was nothing more or less than a piece of rabbinic legislation or a prooftext for pentateuchal *halakhah* that was not truly the source of the law.

We should not, however, be misled into thinking that the tannaitic Rabbis thought that the narrative and poetic sections of the Torah lacked the same revelational quality as its legal sections. Rather, regarding the literary character of the Torah, the *tannaim* concluded, as most readers would, that it was primarily a legal text. Nevertheless, according to the tannaitic teachers, its narrative and poetic sections created an argument for obedience to God and His law.[72] Therefore, since the narrative sections provided support for the claims of the Law, they were no less Torah revelation than the legal portions of the Pentateuch.

Conclusions

This section on אף על פי שאין ראיה לדבר includes two points that will have major significance for what follows in this study. The first is that for the Rabbis the canon of sacred works, especially of those sacred works that impact on the Rabbis' legal activities, had the potential to grow. The *tannaim* were willing

72 See *Mek. Baḥodesh*, 5, ed. Horovitz-Rabin, p. 291:

> מפני מה לא נאמרו עשרת הדברות בתחלת התורה, משלו משל למה הדבר דומה: לאחד שנכנס למדינה, אמר להם, אמלוך עליכם; אמרו לו, כלום עשית לנו טובה שתמלוך עלינו. מה עשה, בנה להם את החומה, הכניס להם את המים, עשה להם מלחמות. אמר להם: אמלוך עליכם; אמרו לו, הן הן. כך המקום הוציא ישראל ממצרים, קרע להם את הים, הוריד להם את המן, העלה להם את הבאר, הגיז להם את השלו, עשה להם מלחמת עמלק. אמר להם אמלוך עליכם, אמרו לו הן הן.

> "I am the Eternal, your God, (who took you out of Egypt)"– Why were the Ten Comandments not stated at the beginning of the Torah? They (the Sages) created a parable. To what is this matter comparable? To someone who entered a country. He said to them (i.e., the inhabitants), "I desire to rule over you." They said to him, "What benefit have you bestowed upon us that you should rule over us?" What did he do? He built a (protective) wall for them. He brought them water. He fought their battles. (Then) he said, "I desire to rule over you." They said to him, "Yes, yes!" So it is with the Omnipresent One. He took them (Israel) out of Egypt, split the sea for them, caused the manna to descend, raised the well for them, brought them the quail, and fought the war against Amalek. He said to them, "I desire to rule over you." They replied to him, "Yes, yes!"

The *Mekhilta*'s question "Why weren't the Ten Commandments stated at the beginning of the Torah?" implies that the Torah is essentially about its rules. Narratives about the Exodus, splitting the sea, supplying food to the Israelites in the desert, and fighting on their behalf could be viewed as irrelevant to the Torah's central purpose, which is communicating the Law to Israel. These narratives, however, provide an argument for the acceptance of God's legislation – namely, Israel should willingly obey God's Law because of all the benefits God has bestowed on them. Cf. *Mek. de-RSBY*, Exod 20:2, ed. Epstein-Melamed, p. 146, line 21.

to grant the authority of divinely revealed canon that allows for legislation only to the Pentateuch. The Prophets and Writings were holy for the *tannaim*, but they were not the sources of *mizvot* or *halakhot*. Hence, the level of revelation contained in them is different from and inferior to that of the Sinaitic revelation.

This was not the view of the *amoraim* and those who followed them. There is no question for them that Moses' prophetic stature was greater than that of any of the prophets who followed him and that the revelation to him was different in kind and quality from theirs. Nevertheless, it seems they held that the prophecies of Moses' successors were already present and included in the Sinaitic revelation. Therefore, for them it was legitimate to view post-Mosaic prophetic texts as sources for the derivation of *halakhot*.

The second major point that emerges from this part of our study is that some rabbinic legislation appears to be viewed by its creators as pentateuchal. The question that surfaces is, "Did the Rabbis of the tannaitic and early amoraic period think that their legislation was divinely revealed, or if they suggested that it was, did they mean it?" This question is obviously impossible to answer with certainty since we would have had to have lived among these men to know what they thought. Nevertheless, it appears to me that the *tannaim* as a group did not consider what they legislated to be the product of divine revelation. Rather, they considered their legislative midrashic activity as a pentateuchally legislated prerogative that allowed them as human agents to interpret the Torah in order to create a program for its observance.[73] What made their legislation "pentateuchal" was its scriptural source and the function it served in terms of providing the means for the observance of the Torah.[74]

73 See Deut 17:8–11. Regarding rabbinic interpretation as a form of divine revelation, see David Stern, *Midrash and Theory* (Evanston: Northwestern University Press, 1996), pp. 30–33 and Martin Jaffee, "How Much 'Orality' in Oral Torah? New Perspectives on the Composition of Early Rabbinic Tradition," *Shofar* (West Lafayette: Purdue University Press, 1992) 10:2:70. Jaffee has revised this view in his *Torah in the Mouth*, pp. 88–92.

74 Jaffee points to several midrashic passages that appear to equate or almost equate rabbinic legislation and interpretation as part of the revealed word of God. See above, n. 73, especially the reference to his *Torah in the Mouth*, pp. 88–92. He claims that this view is more characteristic of the Rabbis represented in the so-called halakhic *midrashim* than it is of the Rabbis represented in the Mishnah and Tosefta. This chapter's conclusions may explain this phenomenon, though in a different way than Jaffee did. That is, if the Rabbis who engaged in midrashic interpretation for the purposes of the derivation of *halakhah* considered the products of their interpretations "pentateuchal *halakhah*," when they say the "word of God" means the *halakhot*, or "that which God spoke" means the *halakhot*, they mean that that which God spoke as presently recorded in Scripture contains the *halakhot*. And, indeed, what else would we expect rabbinic interpreters of Scripture to say other than, "These *halakhot* need the midrashic process in order to make them explicit, but they already exist in the revealed scriptural 'word of God' as that word still addresses us."

2
Scriptural Discrepancies and their Resolution in Midrashic Interpretations

The problem of scriptural discrepancies exercised the rabbinic interpreters because for them the author of the Torah was God. This basic point of view finds its expression most pointedly in mSanhedrin 10:1, which lists those who have no share in the world-to-come. Among these is the one who says that "Torah is not from Heaven"– that is, it was not God-given.[1] *Sifre Deut.* also expresses the view that belief in "Torah from Heaven" is a litmus test for belonging to the circle of faithful Jews:

ספרי פרשת ראה פיסקא קב

אך את זה לא תאכלו (דברים יד, ז). א״ר עקיבא וכי משה קניגי ובליסטרי היה? מכאן תשובה לאומרים אין תורה מן השמים.

"But the following you may not eat" (Deut 14:7). R. Akiba said, "Was Moses a hunter or an archer (that he should have known the exact species and the specific number of them that were forbidden). This provides a response to those who say, "Torah is not from Heaven."

Similarly, *Sifre Deut.* 343 explicitly states that "Torah from Heaven" means that the Torah was God-given:

ספרי דברים פיסקא שמג

מימנו אש דת למו (דברים לג, ב). מגיד שדברי תורה משולים באש מה אש נתנה מן השמים כך דברי תורה נתנו מן השמים שנ׳ אתם ראיתם כי מן השמים דברתי עמכם.

"from his right hand (went) a fiery law for them" (Deut 33:2). This teaches that the words of the Torah are compared to fire. Just as fire was given from heaven, so the words of the Torah were given from heaven, as it says: "You have seen that I (God) have spoken with you from the heavens" (Exod 20:19).

The tannaitic authors of these statements could not actually take any other

1 ...ואלו שאין להם חלק לעולם הבא האומר שאין תחיית המתים בתורה ואין תורה מן השמים

position and remain within the circle of believing Jews who took the Torah's own words seriously. After all, verse after verse of the Pentateuch begins with "The Eternal spoke to Moses," and Lev 26:46 neatly sums up the Torah's sense of its own authorship, ואלה החקים והמשפטים והתורת אשר נתן ה׳ ,בינו ובין בני ישראל בהר סיני ביד משה "These are laws, rules, and instructions that the Eternal gave through Moses on Mount Sinai (as a covenant pact) between Himself and the Israelite people."

There are many implications to this idea of "Torah from Heaven." One of them is that God's Torah is perfect and cannot contradict itself, since that would be a sign of God's imperfection. Indeed, the biblical tradition points to this connection between the perfection of God's ways and the perfection of His statements. For example, we read in the parallel passages in 2 Samuel (22:31) and Psalms (18:31), ... האל תמים דרכו אמרת יהוה צרופה, "The way of God is perfect, the word of the Eternal is pure...."[2] The word "pure" is the English translation of צרופה, which actually means "refined by smelting." The implication is that as God's ways are perfect, so too God's word contains no alloy or impure mixture in it – that is, it too is perfect.[3] Yet, as we all know, the Bible contains many contradictions.

Rabbinic Judaism found itself caught between the perfection of God's Torah and those obvious contradictions. Nevertheless, because the rabbinic interpreters were certain that such contradictions were more apparent than real,[4] they developed an interpretive strategy that would obviate them. Thus, they developed the hermeneutic method called שני כתובים המכחישים זה את זה עד שיבוא הכתוב השלישי ויכריע ביניהם, generally translated as "two verses contradict one another until a third verse comes and reconciles them," thereby providing the strategy for reading contradiction out of the pentateuchal text.

2 See also Ps 12:7 and Prov 30:5.

3 G. Johannes Botterweck, Helmer Ringgen, and Heinz-Josef Fabry, eds., trans. Douglas W. Stott, *Theological Dictionary of the Old Testament* (Grand Rapids: William B. Eerdmans Publishing Company, 2003), 12:479:5:2.

4 Jay M. Harris, *How Do We Know This?* (Albany: SUNY Press, 1995), pp. 7–8, where Harris writes:

> The Book of Deuteronomy (24:16) states, 'Fathers shall not be put to death for sons, nor sons for fathers, a man shall be put to death for his own sin.' A modern reader... will have no difficulty in understanding the simple meaning (*peshat*) of this verse.... None of these readers is likely to be overly troubled by the verse's verbosity and redundancy. This the modern reader will attribute to stylistic preference.
>
> Those with some legal training, aware of statutory construction, may, however, be troubled by these features. They may... simply attribute verbosity to different legal standards or, perhaps, to sloppy construction.... But what if the option of sloppy construction were not available? What if one took for granted that the author was incapable of sloppy construction, indeed, incapable of less than perfect construction?... One would then be forced to find in each of the clauses a distinct statement that eliminates the redundancy.

What I will call "the two contradictory verses" hermeneutic is one of the most theologically informed of all the classical midrashic methods of interpretation. Because the *Baraita of R. Ishmael* includes it in its list of thirteen classical hermeneutics that appears in the Jewish prayerbook, this hermeneutical method is widely known.[5]

We will begin our study of this hermeneutic and its various forms with cases that conform completely to the hermeneutic activity as it is described above.

Two Cases of Harmonization in "Two Contradictory Verses" Expositions

1. The *Baraita* of Hillel's Seven Hermeneutical Methods

An example of "contradictory verses hermeneutics" appears among the examples provided in the *Baraita of Hillel's Seven Hermeneutics* to show how one performs the various hermeneutical actions described therein. In this case, the "two contradictory verses" *midrash* resolves a contradiction between verses by harmonizing the verses. The *midrash* based on the hermeneutic discusses the conditions under which Moses could enter the tent of meeting:

ספרא ברייתא דרבי ישמעאל פרשה א

(ח) כתוב אחד אומר ובבא משה אל אהל מועד לדבר אתו, וכתוב אחד אומר ולא יכול משה לבא אל אהל מועד הכריע כי שכן עליו הענן אמור מעתה כל זמן שהיה הענן שם לא היה משה נכנס לשם נסתלק הענן היה נכנס ומדבר עמו....

One verse says, "When Moses entered the tent of meeting to speak with Him" (Num 7:89), and another verse says, "and Moses was unable to enter the tent of meeting" (Exod 40:38).[6] The verse, "for the cloud dwelled

5 A perusal of commonly used prayer books' translations of this hermeneutical method's application shows they all hold its function to be harmonization. Dr. A. Th. Philips translates the description of the hermeneutic's interpretive action thus: "Similarly, when two passages are in contradiction to one another, the explanation can be determined only when a third text is found, capable of harmonizing the two." The Artscroll Siddur states somewhat clumsily, "... similarly, two passages that contradict one another – until a third passage comes to reconcile them." Rabbi Dr. Elie Munk, in his classic work *The World of Prayer*, provides the following clear translation, "Two statements seem to contradict one another. A third removes the difficulty." These translators agree that the hermeneutic's function is the resolution of a contradiction between scriptural verses. This perception is based on the example that appears in the *Baraita*, but as we shall see, the hermeneutic does not always reconcile or harmonize contradictions.

6 MS Assemani 66 includes the following:

אי איפשר לומ׳ ובבא משה שהרי כבר נאמ׳ ולא יכל משה, ואי איפשר לומ׳ ולא יכל משה שהרי כבר נאמ׳ ובבא משה, ...

> on it (and the glory of the Eternal filled the tabernacle)" (Exod 40:35) resolves the contradiction (הכריע). Say thus: whenever the cloud was there Moses would not enter; when the cloud left, he would enter and speak with Him. . . .

In this harmonization the two problematic verses are ultimately validated. The *midrash* accomplishes this goal by applying each verse to a different situation. The harmonizing verse, "for the cloud dwelled on it (and the glory of the Eternal filled the tabernacle)," allows this arrangement by providing a condition that would prevent Moses from entering the tent of meeting: the presence of the cloud of God's glory. When that condition was not present, Moses could enter the tent and speak with God.

2. *Sifre Numbers*, 58

Sifre Num., 58 (ed. Horovitz, pp. 55–6, lines 25–13) contains a short compilation of *midrashim* on the first verse in Leviticus.[7] It uses the typical *Mek. Sifre Num.* rhetorical formula to introduce the "two contradictory verses" interpretation that ends in a harmonization that applies the conflicting verses to different situations. The issue at hand is whether Moses heard God's voice from the tent of meeting or from above the ark cover:

ספרי במדבר פיסקא נח ד"ה (נח) ובבוא

נח) ובבוא משה אל אהל מועד לדבר אתו למה נאמר לפי שהוא אומר וידבר ה׳ אליו מאהל מועד לאמר (ויקרא א א) שומע אני מאהל מועד ממש תלמוד לומר

I.e., it is impossible to say ". . . when Moses came (into the tent of meeting)," because it has already said, ". . . and Moses was unable (to enter the tent of meeting)." And it is impossible to say, ". . . and Moses was unable (to enter the tent of meeting)," because it has already said, ". . . when Moses came (into the tent of meeting), . . ." This additional formula makes the contradiction even more blatant.

7 This is indicated by the appearance of a parallel to *Sif. Num.* 58 in *Sif. Nedabah* 2:1–2:

ספרי. ר׳ יהודה בן בתירה אומר הרי שלשה עשר מיעוטים מיעט אהרן מכל דברות שבתורה ואלו הן ובבוא משה אל אהל מועד לדבר אתו וישמע את הקול מדבר אליו, וידבר אליו ונועדתי לך שם ודברתי אתך (שמות כה כב) אשר אועד [לך] שמה (שם /שמות/ ל ו) לדבר אליך שם (שם /שמות/ כט מב) ביום צוותו (ויקרא ז לח) את אשר יצוה (שמות לד לד) את כל אשר אצוה אותך (שם /שמות/ כה כב) ואחת במצרים ואחת בסיני ואחת באהל מועד הרי שלשה עשר מיעוטים מיעט אהרן מכולם.

ספרא. (א) אליו, למעט את אהרן, אמר רבי יהודה בן בתירא י״ג דברות נאמרו בתורה למשה ולאהרן וכנגדן נאמרו י״ג מיעוטין ללמדך שלא לאהרן נאמר אלא למשה שיאמר לאהרן. (ב) ואלו הן ובבא משה אל אהל מועד לדבר אתו, וישמע את הקול מדבר אליו, וידבר אליו, ונועדתי לך, ודברתי אתך, אשר אועד לכם שמה לדבר אליך שם, ביום צוותו, את אשר צוה ה׳ אל משה, את כל אשר אצוה אותך אל בני ישראל, ויהי ביום דבר ה׳ אל משה בארץ מצרים, ואלה תולדות אהרן ומשה ביום דבר ה׳ אל משה בהר סיני, ויקרא אל משה וידבר אליו.

ונועדתי לך שם ודברתי אתך מעל הכפורת (שמות כה כב) אי אפשר לומר מאהל מועד שכבר נאמר מעל הכפורת ואי אפשר לומר מעל הכפורת שכבר נאמר מאהל מועד כיצד יתקיימו שני כתובים הללו זו מדה בתורה שני כתובים זה כנגד זה והרי הם סותרים זה על ידי זה יתקיימו במקומם עד שיבא כתוב אחר ויכריע ביניהם מה ת״ל ובבוא משה אל אהל מועד לדבר אתו מגיד הכתוב שהיה משה נכנס ועומד באהל מועד והקול יורד משמי שמים לבין שני הכרובים והוא שומע את הקול מדבר אליו מבפנים.

> "And when Moses went into the tent of meeting to speak with Him, (he would hear the Voice addressing him from above the cover that was on top of the ark of the covenant between the two cherubim. . . .)" (Num 7:89). Why was this verse necessary? Because it says, "and the Eternal spoke to him from the tent of meeting" (Lev 1:1). From this I might infer that God spoke from the tent of meeting itself. But the Torah says, "There I will meet you and I will speak to you from above the cover, (from between the cherubim that are on top of the ark of the covenant)" (Exod 25:22). It is impossible to say that (God spoke) from the tent of meeting because it says (He spoke) from above the ark cover; and it is impossible to say that (God spoke) from above the ark cover because it says (He spoke) from the tent of meeting. How can both these verses stand?
>
> This is a method of interpreting the Torah: Two verses are juxtaposed against one another and contradict one another. They stand in their place until a third verse comes and יכריע between them. Therefore the Torah says, "And when Moses went into the tent of meeting to speak with Him, (he would hear the Voice addressing him from above the cover that was on top of the ark of the covenant between the two cherubim. . . .)" (In this way,) the Torah tells us that Moses would enter and stand in the tent of meeting. The Voice would descend from the heaven of heavens to the area between the two cherubim, and he (Moses) heard the Voice speaking to him from within (the holy of holies).

The conclusion reached by this midrashic interpretation informs us that the meaning of יכריע in this context is to harmonize. The contradiction that this *midrash* resolves is between Lev 1:1, which says that Moses heard God's voice from the external area of the tent of meeting, and Exod 25:22, which states that Moses heard God's voice "from above the ark cover, from between the cherubim" that is, from the area of the inner sanctum. Num 7:89 ends the contradiction. It states, "When Moses went into the tent of meeting," thus explaining what Moses did and where he was when he heard God's voice. Thus Lev 1:1 is confirmed. Regarding God, the verse in Numbers states that God's voice emanated from above the ark cover, from where it could be heard by Moses in the area of the tent of meeting outside the inner sanctum. Thus Exod 25:22

is confirmed. The communication heard from the tent of meeting refers to Moses; the communication delivered from the ark cover refers to God, and there are, according to this *midrash*, no real contradictions at all.

In the two examples we have cited, יכריע means the resolution of a contradiction by applying the contradictory elements to different logical frameworks. Since a contradiction can only be sustained within a single logical framework, this form of resolution removes the contradiction. We should note that these expositions are unattributed and not subject to argument, which is sometimes a sign of the most classical and paradigmatic form of a hermeneutic.[8]

"Two Contradictory Verses" Interpretations Attributed to Named *Tannaim*

The "two contadictory verses" hermeneutic also appears in the halakhic *midrashim* with attributions. Indeed, the giants of the tannaitic midrashic period, R. Akiba and R. Ishmael, are said to use a form of it, although in their use it does not in fact completely harmonize the contradictory verses. Instead, according to this usage, two verses outweigh one verse, thereby putting the contradiction to rest. The following interpretation of R. Akiba, the only one of a halakhic nature that contains only a partial resolution of a contradiction, provides a good example of this hermeneutic action:

The Case of *Mekhilta*, *Pisḥa* 4

Mek. Pisḥa 4 attributes to R. Akiba an interpretation of Exod 12:5 in a discussion about what is the appropriate species of animal for the paschal offering:

> ר׳ עקיבא אומר כתוב אחד אומר וזבחת פסח ליי׳ אלהיך צאן ובקר וכתוב אחד אומר מן הכבשים ומן העזי׳ תקחו כיצד יתקיימו שני מקראות הללו אמרת זו מדה בתורה שני כתובים זה כנגד זה וסותרין זה על ידי זה מתקיימין במקומן עד שיבא כתוב שלישי ויכריע ביניהן תלמוד לומר משכו וקחו לכם צאן למשפחותיכם ושחטו הפסח. צאן לפסח ולא בקר לפסח.

> R. Akiba said: One verse says, "You shall sacrifice the passover to the Eternal, flocks and cattle" (Deut 16:2) and another verse says, "from the sheep or goats" (Exod 12:5). How can those verses both stand? You have said: this is a method of interpreting the Torah. Two verses are juxtaposed against one another and contradict one another. They remain in their place until a third verse comes and יכריע between them. Therefore the Torah says, "Draw forth and take for yourselves (of the) flock for your families and

8 Michael Chernick, מידת „גזירה שווה": צורותיה במדרשים ובתלמודים (Lod: Haberman Institute for Literary Research, 1994), p. 113.

slaughter the passover" (Exod 12:21). Of the flock (take) for the passover, but not of the cattle for the passover.

It is clear that the hermeneutical principle at work is the "two contradictory verses" midrashic method. I have left the Hebrew יכריע untranslated until we analyze what is recorded here as R. Akiba's interpretation. He notes that two verses contradict each other. One states that only young sheep and goats are acceptable for the paschal offering; another, in Deuteronomy, states that cattle would also be acceptable. A third verse, Exod 12:21, reiterates that only "flock" animals may be used for the passover offering. The *midrash* concludes that because two verses support the use of animals that come from "flocks," while only one verse supports the use of cattle, cattle cannot serve as paschal offerings. The contradictory verses have not been harmonized at all. Rather, one has been overturned by two working against it. The term יכריע thus means "outweighs," "overpowers," or "tips the scales in favor of," rather than "harmonizes." This hermeneutical device should therefore be described as "Two verses may contradict each other until a third comes and decides between them by two verses outweighing one."[9]

The meaning "outweigh" for the *hiph'il* of כ-ר-ע certainly fits well within its semantic range. Indeed, the majority of its use in Mishnah and Tosefta has that meaning.[10] What appears to lead the *midrash* attributed to R. Akiba in the direction of יכריע meaning "outweigh" is the fact that the third resolving verse in the *midrash* does not fully harmonize the contradiction between the initial Exodus and Deuteronomy verses about the animals fit for the paschal offering. Exod 12:21 does add information and indicates that the preponderance of scriptural evidence favors the use of "flock" animals for the paschal offering over cattle. These three verses are the only ones in all of the Bible that discuss the animals that may be used for the paschal sacrifice. Thus, faced with the lack of a third verse that fully resolves the scriptural contradiction, but possessing a third verse that does provide some information that indicates the tendency of Scripture regarding the animals fit for the paschal offering, the *midrash* attributed to R. Akiba redefines the meaning of the *hiph'il* of כ-ר-ע as "outweighs" or "tips the scales in favor of." Indeed, just as two contradictory verses possessing a fully harmonizing third verse may indicate an expression typical of Scripture that leads to the use of the "two contradictory verses" hermeneutic, so the presence of a verse that indicates Scripture's *tendenz* in a given case, even though it does not fully resolve a contradiction between

9 See *Mek. Pisḥa* 4, Horovitz-Rabin, p. 13, n. 20.

10 mᵓAvot 2:8; ibid. 6:6; Kelim 4:1; tPesaḥim 1:7; ibid. 3:7; ibid. 6:2; tḤagigah 1:1; tSheqalim 2:2; tSotah 5:12; tQiddushin 1:4; tSanhedrin 7:6; tZebaḥim 8:23; tMenaḥot 8:7; tZabim 4:8; *Mek. de-RSBY*, Exod 12:48; ibid. 21:1; *Sifra*, ᵓ*Emor* par. 1:13; *Sif. Deut.* 132; *Midrash Tannaim, Deut.* 16:18.

the verses, still may indicate that the "two contradictory verses" hermeneutic should be used.[11] This is especially so when the three verses are the only ones to discuss a particular issue. The next two examples of "two contradictory verses" *midrashim* will show this to be true.

Sifra, Aḥare Mot, par. 1:2

Sifra Aḥare Mot cites a *midrash* attributed to R. Akiba regarding the death of Aaron's sons, Nadab and Abihu. This *midrash* leaves no doubt that הכריע means the invalidation of one contradictory verse when two others agree.

ספרא אחרי מות פרשה א

(ב) בקרבתם לפני ה׳ וימותו, רבי יוסי הגלילי אומר על הקריבה מתו ולא מתו על ההקרבה, רבי עקיבה אומר כתוב אחד אומר בקרבתם לפני ה׳ וימותו, וכתוב אחד אומר ויקריבו לפני ה׳ אש זרה, הכריע בהקריבם אש זרה לפני ה׳ הוי על הקריבה מתו, ולא מתו על ההקרבה,[12] ר׳ אלעזר בן עזריה אומר כדיי קרבה לעצמה וכדיי קריבה לעצמה.

"(And the Eternal spoke to Moses after the death of the two sons of Aaron) when they came too close to the presence of the Eternal and died" (Lev 16:1) – R. Jose the Galilean said: They died for their approach (into God's presence), but they did not die for offering (alien fire). R. Akiba said: One verse says, "... when they came too close to the presence of the Eternal and died"; another verse says, "... and they brought alien fire into the Eternal's presence" (Lev 10:1). "(And Nadab and Abihu died) when they brought alien fire into the Eternal's presence" (Num 26:61) decides (whether Nadab and Abihu died for coming too close to God's presence or for offering alien fire). They died for offering (alien fire), but they did not die for approaching too close (to God's presence). R. Eleazar b. Azariah said, Their overly close approach was sufficient (to cause their deaths), and their offering was sufficient (to cause their deaths, i.e., both were causes of Nadab's and Abihu's deaths).

11 Azzan Yadin, *Scripture as Logos* (Philadelphia: University of Pennsylvania, 2004), p. 121. See also R. Joshua ha-Levi of Tlemcen, הליכות עולם (Tel Aviv: Shiloh, n.d.), p. כו א׳ (51) where a similar idea is used to explain *gezerah shavah*.

12 Both R. Abraham b. David of Posquierres and R. Hillel b. Elyakim have the following text for this exposition:

בקרבתם לפני ה׳ וימותו, רבי יוסי הגלילי אומר על הקריבה מתו ולא מתו על ההקרבה, רבי עקיבה אומר כתוב אחד אומר בקרבתם לפני ה׳ וימותו, וכתוב אחד אומר ויקריבו לפני ה׳ אש זרה, הכריע בהקריבם אש זרה לפני ה׳ הוי על ההקרבה מתו, ולא מתו על ההקריבה....

This version is also supported by the Gaon of Vilna in his glosses. It is this version that will appear in the English translation.

R. Akiba denies R. Jose the Galilean's position by using a "two contradictory verses" expositional approach. Because two verses support the idea that the cause of Nadab's and Abihu's death was their offering of alien fire, the single verse in Lev 16:1 that suggests otherwise is overridden.

Here, as in the previous case in *Mek. Pisḥa* 4, there are only three references in the entire Bible to the causes of the death of Nadab and Abihu, Aaron's sons. Two contradict each other and one indicates that the preponderance of evidence regarding the cause of their deaths favors their bringing of foreign fire. The third verse does not completely harmonize the contradiction that R. Akiba is cited as pointing out, but Scripture does not provide a verse that can do more. In the face of its inability to bring the contradiction between the two verses to a completely harmonized conclusion, the *midrash* attributed to R. Akiba redefines הכריע to mean "outweigh," and thereby determines that Aaron's sons died not because they approached the presence of God too closely but because they offered an unacceptable fire offering.

Mekhilta Baḥodesh, 9

A "two contradictory verses" *midrash* cited in the name of R. Ishmael in *Mek. Baḥodesh*, 9, also invalidates one of the three verses cited in the midrashic exposition.

מכילתא דרבי ישמעאל יתרו – מס' דבחדש יתרו פרשה ט ד"ה כי מן השמים

> כתוב אחד אומר, כי מן השמים, וכתוב אחד אומר (שמות יט כ) וירד ה' על הר סיני, כיצד יתקיימו שני מקראות הללו; הכריע השלישי (דברים ד לו) מן השמים השמיעך את קולו ליסרך, דברי רבי ישמעאל....
>
> One verse states, ("The Eternal said to Moses: Say thus to the children of Israel, 'You have seen that I have spoken to you) from the heavens'" (Exod 20:18). However, another verse says, "And the Eternal descended on Mount Sinai" (Exod 19:20). How can both verses be fulfilled? The third outweighs (one). "From the heavens He has made his voice audible to you in order to test you" (Deut 4:34), (these are) the words of R. Ishmael. . . .

Here again information about God's locus during the Sinaitic revelation is limited to three scriptural verses. Two say that the revelation emerged from heaven, and one says that God descended onto the peak of Mount Sinai. Further, the three verses do not combine to form a full harmonization of the contradiction between them.[13] Consequently, the *midrash* uses the verses at hand

13 Some might argue that the "two contradictory verses" interpretation attributed to R. Ishmael is not a case of two verses "outweighing" one verse. Those who would argue in this way might claim that the use of the *hiph'il* of the Hebrew root ש-מ-ע in Deut 4:36 implies that God caused His voice to be heard on earth, though it emanated from the heavens. According to this view, the

to determine the *tendenz* of the Torah regarding this matter. Since the majority say that God spoke from heaven, then that is the resolution of the contradiction. R. Akiba resolves the issue differently, as the continuation of the *Mekhilta* passage indicates:

רבי עקיבא אומר [כתוב אחד אומר, כי מן השמים, וכתוב אחד אומר, וירד ה׳ על

---

first clause of Deut 4:36 would support Exod 20:18, which says God spoke from the heavens. The causative *hiph'il* in that clause, suggesting that God caused His voice to be heard on earth, would explain what Exod 19:20 meant when it said that God descended onto Mount Sinai.

My preference for viewing the *derashah* attributed to R. Ishmael as being the "outweighing" form of the "two contradictory verses" hermeneutic is based on two considerations:

1. The use of the *hiph'il* of ש-מ-ע is unnecessary if the midrashist is trying to resolve the contradiction of the revelation proceeding from heaven or from Mount Sinai. If the midrashist had wanted to do that in a convincing manner, all he needed to do was cite the final clause of Deut 4:36: ועל הארץ הראך את אשו גדולה ודבריו שמעת מתוך האש "and on the earth He caused you to see His great fire, and from the midst of the fire you heard His words." This would have resolved the contradiction between Exod 20:18 (the revelation came from heaven) and Exod 19:20 (the revelation came from the top of Mount Sinai) in the following manner: The first clause in Deut 4:36, which states that God caused His voice to be heard from heaven, supports Exod 20:18, which makes essentially the same claim. However, the vehicle God used for His communication on earth was the great fire on Mount Sinai described in Exod 19:18, which was the symbol of God's descent onto the mountain, mentioned in Exod 19:20. This is supported by the final clause of Deut 4:36. There is, however, no support in manuscript traditions of the *Mekhilta* itself to support a reading for the Deut 4 citation that includes its final clause, though Buber's פסיקתא זוטרתא adds ועל הא׳ הראך וגו׳ and the glosses to *Mekhilta* called איפת צדק (mid–18th century) in the Vilna edition suggest that the Deuteronomy citation in the Ishmael *midrash* should be completed with the final clause of Deut 4:36. פסיקתא זוטרתא, however, is a medieval work completed in the early 12th century. Its author, Tobiah b. Eliezer, neither cites his sources nor quotes them verbatim (H. L. Strack and Guenther Stemberger, *Introduction to the Talmud and Midrash* [Minneapolis: Fortress Press, 1992, second edition 1996], p. 356). It is therefore not a reliable source for the reconstruction of the *Mekhilta*'s text, which is also obviously the case regarding איפת צדק. Both פסיקתא זוטרתא and איפת צדק may have been trying to reconstruct our Ishmael "two contradictory verses" *derashah* to match the majority "two contradictory verses" interpretations, which harmonize contradictions between verses. See *Scripture as Logos*, pp. 117–19, for Yadin's critique of David Henschke's attempt to reconstruct this "two contradictory verses" *midrash* along the lines of פסיקתא זוטרתא and איפת צדק.

2. The formulation דברי ר׳ ישמעאל, ר׳ עקיבא אומר is typically a dispute formulation. When this formulation is used in pericopes where R. Ishmael and R. Akiba appear, it always indicates a difference of opinion whether the issue is halakhic or aggadic. See Pisḥa 14, ed. Horovitz, p. 49, lines 1–2; Nezikin 10, p. 285, lines 9–10, see n. 10 and critical apparatus to line 10; Baḥodesh 4, p. 219, lines 1–2; Baḥodesh 7, p. 231, lines 1–2; Baḥodesh 9, p. 235, lines 8–9; Nezikin 14, p. 296, lines 17–19; Nezikin 18, p. 313, lines 1–3 (R. Akiba's position should be understood as restricting the law to widows and orphans). Kaspa 19, ibid., p. 317: see critical apparatus to line 12 because of the oddity of the formulation. Consequently, there is no reason to consider the interpretation in Baḥodesh 9 anything other than a dispute about both midrashic method and the place from which God spoke at the Sinaitic revelation.

הר סיני אל ראש ההר],[14] מלמד שהרכין הקב״ה שמים העליונים על ראש ההר ודבר עמהן מן השמים, [שנאמר, מן השמים וגו׳];[15] וכה״א+תהלים יח י+ ויט שמים וירד וערפל תחת רגליו.

> R. Akiba says: [One verse says, "From the heavens (I spoke to you)" (Exod 20:18) and another says, "And the Eternal descended on Mount Sinai" (Exod 19:20).][16] This teaches that the Holy Blessed One tipped the highest heavens toward the mountain top and spoke from the heavens.... And thus it says, "He tipped heaven and descended, and there was thick cloud beneath His feet" (Ps 18:10).

This resolution of the contradiction is more elegant than the one attributed to R. Ishmael, but it also reads more into the Torah's text than is actually there. The fact that the *midrash* attributed to R. Akiba avoids the "two contradictory verses" approach is somewhat contrary to the approach attributed to R. Akiba in two other sources. Nevertheless, it is possible that where a contradiction can be totally resolved, a midrashic interpreter like R. Akiba might prefer that solution over any other.

"Two Contradictory Verses" in the *Midrashim* of Named *Tannaim* Conclusions

The use of the attributed "two contradictory verses" hermeneutic has three things in common wherever it is used: 1) The scriptural rubric that the midrashist interprets contains three verses that are the only ones that discuss that rubric – e.g., animals fit for the paschal sacrifice. 2) Two of the verses that discuss the rubric contradict one another and the third does not completely resolve the contradiction. It only sides with one verse, which indicates a scriptural *tendenz* in one direction rather than another. 3) This causes the midrashic interpreter to redefine הכריע or יכריע as "outweigh" or "tip the scale in favor of," and this partial resolution is considered resolution enough.

The association of the "outweighing" form of the "two contradictory verses" hermeneutic with R. Akiba and R. Ishmael may be completely accurate. The attribution of it to them may also point to the second half of the second generation of the *tannaim* as the period in which this development in the "two contradictory verses" hermeneutic took place. The attribution of the "outweighing"

14 Horovitz's edition contains bracketed material at this point. As his critical apparatus indicates, this material does not appear in most manuscripts.

15 The bracketed material is found only in מדרש חכמים (Aptowitzer).

16 The bracketed material appears only in a single manuscript, MS Oxford of the *Mekhilta*.

form of the "two contradictory verses" hermeneutic to R. Akiba and R. Ishmael also provides this hermeneutic method, which does not fully solve the theological problem of scriptural contradictions, with the authority of these giants of the tradition.

Two Contradictory Verses Without a Third Resolving Verse

שני כתובים המכחישים זה את זה became the model for the removal of contradictions between verses in the Pentateuch and elsewhere in the Bible even where no third verse could be found to help resolve the two verses' contradiction. As we have noted, it seems reasonable that the "two contradictory verses" hermeneutic came into existence primarily as a response to the theological problem of God's words contradicting themselves. The existence of a verse that would end the contradiction meant that God himself intervened to remove the problem in accordance with the idea that "God shall not violate His covenant, nor change what He has uttered. . . ." (Ps 89:35).[17]

But what shall one do when there is no third verse to undo a contradiction? The answer for many rabbinic exegetes lay in the formula that appears in most "two contradictory verses" interpretations in the tannaitic *midrashim*: זו מדה שבתורה: שני כתובים זה כנגד זה והרי הם סותרים זה על ידי זה וכו'. For them, "This is a rule of interpretation (found) in the Torah" meant that the Torah itself provided the model for requiring the resolution of contradictions that crop up in the Pentateuch, and by extension throughout the *TaNaKh*. Hence, when there is no third harmonizing or resolving verse, the Rabbis, basing themselves on the Torah's paradigm, resolve the contradiction by midrashic interpretation or logic. This is clearly the view of R. Abraham b. David of Posquierres (henceforth, *RAbaD*) in his commentary on *Sifra*, which seems substantially right regarding the impetus for rabbinic resolutions of biblical contradictions. *RAbaD* writes:

> ומזו ההכרעה שהכריע הכתוב השלישי ותקן שני כתובים המכחישין זה את זה למדו רז"ל למקומות אחרים שמכחישים זה את זה ולא בא הכתוב השלישי להכריע... והגירסא הנכונה כפי דעתי כך היא: ושני כתובים המכחישים זה את זה עד שיבא הכתוב השלישי וגו'. וכך פירושו: זו מדה נוהגת בתורה. שיש כתובים המכחישים זה את זה, כלומר שהם נראין כמכחישים זה את זה, עד שיבא הכתוב השלישי ומתרץ אותם. הילכך מכאן יש לנו ללמוד ולתרץ כל שני כתובים שהן קשין זה על זה, ולא שנדחה אחד מהם ולא שנחזיק את התורה בשבוש.

17 In rabbinic *midrash*, Ps 89:35 is used to describe the consistency of God's dictates even though the reference in Psalms is to promises God made to David. See Rashi, Gen 22:12, for an example of this use.

> From this resolution (found in the example section of the *Baraita of R. Ishmael*) in which the third verse resolved and properly ordered the two conflicting verses, our Sages, of blessed memory, learned (what to do) in other cases where two verses conflict and there is no third verse to resolve (the contradiction).... And this is the explanation (of how the "two contradictory verses" hermeneutic operates). This is an interpretational activity used in the Torah, because there are contradictory verses – that is, they appear to be contradictory, until a third verse resolves them (and shows them to be free of contradiction). Therefore, we should learn from this to resolve two contradictory verses rather than reject one and presume the Torah to be in error.[18]

Because the great number of contradictory statements in the Pentateuch and elsewhere in the *TaNaKh* do not have a third verse that reconciles the contradiction in some way, the largest number of interpretations resolving contradictions do so without reference to any verse at all. In those cases, the Rabbis resolve contradictions by creating "divided applications." What is most striking about these interpretations is that they are not referred to as שני כתובים המכחישים זה את זה or הכרעה. This terminology is apparently reserved for situations in which a third verse plays some role, which bears out my general thesis that the tannaitic midrashists were extremely careful in the use of their midrashic terminology and naming of hermeneutical methods. Those hermeneutics that followed specific rules as a condition for their application – for example, גזירה שוה – were given specific names; those that carried out similar actions but did not follow the rules required to qualify as a classical hermeneutic were given no designation at all.[19] This seems to be true of the "two contradictory verses" hermeneutic as well. None of the formulas using the *hiph'il* of כ-ר-ע that introduced the application of the "two contradictory verses" hermeneutic are used in what I will now refer to as "resolution of a contradiction" *midrashim*.[20]

18 *RAbaD* seems not to recognize that some of the examples in the tannaitic *midrashim* in fact discard a verse, which, at least, raises the question of why we have a misleading or useless verse in the Torah. Since *RAbaD*'s comments refer solely to the first example of שני כתובים in the *Baraita of R. Ishmael*, which totally harmonizes conflicting verses, it is not surprising that he overlooked the problems caused by the phenomenon of שני כתובים that "resolved" conflicts by denying the validity of a verse when it was outweighed by two others. *RAbaD* would be especially tempted to overlook those phenomena if he viewed the example in the *Baraita of R. Ishmael* as the most accurate portrayal of the "two contradictory verses" hermeneutic.

19 See Michael Chernick, לחקר מידת גזירה שווה, chap. 5, in which I distinguish between true גזירות שוות (*gezerah shavah* interpretations) and what I call השוואות מילים (comparisons of the same or similar biblical words).

20 Because Azzan Yadin did not distinguish between authentic "two contradictory verses" and the

Some Examples of "Resolution of Contradictions" in the Tannaitic *Midrashim*

A good example of a "resolution of a contradiction" *midrash* brought about by rabbinic reasoning is found in *Sifre Deut.*, 124. The issue is the contradictory commands regarding firstborn animals that are *kasher*. Lev 27:26 says they cannot be dedicated as sacrifices; Deut 15:19 ordains that they should be dedicated as sacrifices. R. Ishmael reconciles the conflict thus:

ספרי דברים פיסקא קכד ד"ה תקדיש לה'

תקדיש לה' אלהיך, רבי ישמעאל אומר כתוב אחד אומר תקדיש וכתוב אחד אומר +ויקרא כז כו+ לא יקדיש [אי איפשר לומר תקדיש שכבר נאמר אל יקדיש ואי איפשר לומר אל יקדיש שכבר נאמר תקדיש אמור מעתה מקדישו אתה הקדש עילוי ואין אתה מקדישו] הקדש מזבח.

"(All firstlings....) you shall dedicate to the Eternal, your God" (Deut 15:19). R. Ishmael said: One verse says, "Dedicate" and another verse says, "One shall not dedicate" (Lev 27:26). [It is impossible to say, "Dedicate," because it says, "One shall not dedicate;" and it is impossible to say, "One shall not dedicate," because it says, "Dedicate." Say (i.e., reason) from this that one may dedicate its additional value, but one may not dedicate it] for sacrifice. (*Sifre Deut.*, 124)[21]

R. Ishmael's resolution of the contradiction between Leviticus and Deuteronomy regarding the disposition of a firstborn is essentially a "divided application." According to him, the command to dedicate the firstborn, "תקדיש," applies to the firstborn's "additional monetary worth."[22] Leviticus's prohibition

"resolution of a contradiction" midrashic method, he regards them as synonymous. This led to a somewhat forced analysis of two examples of "the two contradictory" hermeneutic. See *Scripture as Logos*, pp. 109–10ff.

21 My formulation of the *Sif. Deut.* passage is based on Friedmann-Ish-Shalom's textual revision based on *Pesikta Zutrata* ad loc., and Finkelstein's proposal in his edition of *Sif. Deut.*, p. 183, note to line 1.

22 Firstlings, which are technically priestly property, may still be given by the firstborn's owner to a priest of his own choice. The right of choice could be sold along with the firstborn to another person, as long as the firstborn was given to a priest. In the scenario presented for the estimation of "additional value," an Israelite wishes to purchase a firstborn to give to his priestly grandson, the son of his daughter and her priestly husband. The amount he must pay for this right is called עילוי, "additional value," i.e., value beyond the basic cost of the firstling. A firstling's owner may dedicate the firstborn's estimated additional value to a priest or to the Temple in the form of *ḥerem*. Alternatively, the firstling's owner may donate it for the Temple's upkeep (בדק הבית, *bedeq habayit*). No matter how the additional value of a firstborn is disbursed, the firstling's owner will still have to give the firstling to a priest since the Torah grants the priest proprietary rights over firstlings.

on dedicating firstborns, "לא יקדיש אותו," applies to dedicating a firstborn for some sacrificial purpose rather than giving it to a priest.

The term הכרעה does not appear here because the resolution of the contradiction does not result from a third verse. The entire *midrash* is not designated as a case of שני כתובים המכחישים זה את זה (a case amenable to "two contradictory verses" interpretation) despite the fact that two verses do contradict one another. Clearly, the lack of a third conciliating verse fails to conform to the requirement of the "two contradictory verses" hermeneutic: עד שיבוא הכתוב השלישי ויכריע ביניהם "until a third verse appears and decides between (or balances, or harmonizes) them." This places the *midrash* outside the realm of the classical form of the "two contradictory verses" hermeneutic and, therefore, the typical formulas associated with that hermeneutic are not present.

Another example appears in *Midrash Tannaim*. This one is particularly interesting because it involves three verses, all of which are in conflict. The conflict is created by the different formulations of the requirement which the Rabbis called "counting the *ᶜomer*" (ספירת העומר). In Lev 23:15 it says that one should count from the day after the Sabbath. In 23:16 it says the count should continue "until you shall have counted fifty days." In Deut 16:9 the formula is "seven weeks shall you count. . . ." These various formulas provide the potential for mutual contradiction. Leviticus's count of a full seven Sabbaths starting with Sunday as the day after the Sabbath and ending on the seventh Sabbath could result in a 52 day count. Because Deuteronomy provides no absolute starting point for the seven week count, theoretically one could start counting on any day of the week after the Sabbath, which, according to the Rabbis, is the day after the first day of Passover. This might lead to a count of more than fifty days from the day after the first day of Passover. For example, if Passover fell on Wednesday and the count of weeks started only on Sunday, one would have counted 53 days from the second day of Passover by the seventh week. Finally, if one takes the notion of a seven-week count literally, then the proper count of the *ᶜomer* is always forty-nine days. How can all these discrepancies be reconciled? *Midrash Tannaim* cites R. Ishmael's and R. Akiba's answers. I will cite only Akiba's response:

מדרש תנאים לדברים פרק טז פסוק ט

> ר' עקיבה אומר כתוב אחד אומר שבעה שבועות וכת' אחד אומר וספרתם לכם כיצד יתקיימו שני כתובים הללו וכשהוא אומר תס' חמ' יום ימים מסרתי לך לא מסרתי לך שבתות הא כיצד חל להיות מן הימים את מונה מן הימים חל להיות מן השבתות את מונה מן השבתות:

> R. Akiba said: One verse says, "Seven weeks (shall you count for yourself)" (Deut 16:9), and another verse says, "You shall count for yourselves (seven complete Sabbaths) (Lev 23:15). How can both of these verses be sustained? And when it says, "You shall count up to fifty days" (the problem

is exacerbated because it implies that God said) I have given to you days (to count), but I have not given you Sabbaths (to count). How can (all this) be? If it (i.e., Passover) falls on a weekday, you count days. If it falls on the Sabbath, you count Sabbaths. (The end result is the count will always be 49 days, i.e., seven weeks.)

As in the previous *midrash* of R. Ishmael, the "resolution of the contradiction" is achieved by assigning the various verses' requirements to different situations, thereby obviating discrepancies. R. Akiba does not call his solution הכרעה, probably because he is not willing to use the term הכרעה in reference to a resolution based on logic; only a reconciliation based on a third verse could truly qualify as a hermeneutical הכרעה. The problematic verses also do not produce a situation in which a "two contradictory verses" *midrash* is possible: more than two verses stand in contradiction, and no other verse is available to undo the verses' conflicting requirements. Hence, there is no mention of the "two contradictory verses" hermeneutic or its formula. R. Akiba's *midrash* is a "resolution of contradictions" *midrash*, but not an example of שני כתובים המכחישים זה את זה.[23]

"Two Contradictory Verses" Further Developments

Elsewhere I have noted that as time went on, there was a tendency to conflate *midrashim* and midrashic methods that were once clearly separate and distinguishable. In the case of כלל ופרט וכלל and ריבוי ומיעוט, by then end of the amoraic period or, perhaps in the post-amoraic period, these two *middot* took on characteristics of one another. ריבוי ומיעוט וריבוי took on the formal order of כלל ופרט וכלל and כלל ופרט וכלל of the later period accepted as כללים terms, like verbs, that were considered exclusively ריבויים in the halakhic *midrashim*.[24] A similar phenomenon occurred in instances in which there was a "two contradictory verses" *midrash* and an alternative interpretation to it. At a later point in the development of the hermeneutic and examples of its use, the two *midrashim* conflated into one.

23 The following sources in the tannaitic *midrashim* are examples of "resolution of contradiction" *midrashim*: *Mek. Pisḥa* 8=*Pisḥa* 17=*Sifra*, *ᵓEmor* 10=*Sifre Deut.* 134=*Midrash Tannaim, Deut.* 16:8; *Pisḥa* 14; *Baḥodesh* 8; *Kaspa* 20; *Shabbata* 1; *Mek. de-RSBY*, *Exod* 23:10; *Sifre Num.* 42; ibid., 62; *Sifre Zuta, Num.* 6:26; ibid., *Num.* 7:89; *Sifre Deut.* 40; ibid., 70; ibid., 134; *Midrash Tannaim, Deut.* 15:4.

24 לחקר המידות „כלל ופרט וכלל" ו„ריבוי ומיעוט" במדרשים ובתלמודים, pp. 57–62, 113–26; 128. In regard to similar developments in the גזירה שוה hermeneutic, see לחקר מידת „גזירה שווה" במדרשים ובתלמודים, (Lod: Haberman Institute, 1994), chap. 7.

The Phenomenon of the *Baraita of R. Ishmael*'s Example of the Contradictory Verses Hermeneutic

The so-called *Baraita of R. Ishmael* that serves as an introduction to *Sifra* contains two parts: a list of the 13 hermeneutical principles of R. Ishmael and a section containing examples of the application of those principles. The formulation of the example for the "contadictory verses hermeneutic" is closely parallel to the exposition in *Mek. Baḥodesh* 9. However, it deviates from the *Mekhilta*'s *midrash* in a significant way – namely, it conflates the views of R. Ishmael and R. Akiba in *Mekhilta*. By doing so it accomplishes what no other "two contradictory verses" interpretation has, the total harmonization of every scriptural element cited in the *midrash*:

ספרא ברייתא דרבי ישמעאל פרשה א

> (ז) שני כתובים המכחישים זה את זה עד שיבא השלישי ויכריע ביניהם, כיצד כתוב אחד אומר וירד ה׳ על הר סיני אל ראש ההר וכתוב אחר אומר מן השמים השמיעך את קולו ליסרך, הכריע השלישי כי מן השמים דברתי עמכם מלמד שהרכין הקדוש ברוך הוא שמי שמים העליונים על הר סיני ודבר עמהם, וכן אמר דוד בספר תלים /תהלים/ ויט שמים וירד וערפל תחת רגליו.

> Two verses that contradict each other until a third arrives and יכריע between them. How (does this operate). One verse says, "And the Eternal descended on Mount Sinai, to the mountain top" (Exod 19:20), and another verse says, "From the heavens He made His voice heard to you, to try you" (Deut 4:36). The third verse הכריע: "For from the heavens I spoke with you" (Exod 20:18) – this teaches that the Holy Blessed One bent the uppermost heavens onto Sinai and spoke with them. And thus said David in Psalms, "He tipped the heavens and descended, and thick cloud was beneath His feet" (Ps 18:10).[25]

In my translation of the *Baraita*'s example of the "contradictory verses hermeneutic," I have refrained from translating יכריע and הכריע, which in the interpretations of R. Akiba and R. Ishmael meant "outweighed," "tipped the scales in favor of" one verse over another, or simply "decided between" two verses. Here, however, the meaning of these terms has shifted slightly once more, and

25 The formulation of this *midrash* in *Sifra* MS Vatican Assemani 66, ed. Finkelstein, is even closer to *Mek. Baḥodesh* 9:

> שני כתובים מכחישים זה את זה עד שיבא כתוב שלישי ויכריע ביניהן, כת׳ אחד או׳ וירד ייי על הר, סיני אל רא׳ ההר, וכת׳ אחר או׳ אתם ראיתם כי מן השמים דברתי עמ׳ , הכריע מן השמים השמיעך את קולו ליסרך, מלמד שהרכין ה׳ק׳ב׳ה׳ שמי שמים העליונים על ראש ההר ודבר עמהן מן השמים (שנ׳) [וכן הוא אומ׳] ויט שמים וירד וערפל תחת רגליו.

now עד שיבוא הכתוב השלישי ויכריע ביניהם means "until a third verse arrives and harmonizes (all the contradictions)." This new meaning for יכריע emerges from the *Baraita* example's melding of R. Ishmael's and Akiba's expositions in *Mek. Baḥodesh.* In its conflation of their essentially different *midrashim* and concepts, the *Baraita* example has reduced R. Ishmael's words to a purely linguistic formula whose entire function is to serve R. Akiba's view through harmonization.

This phenomenon, as I noted above, is not totally new. There is evidence that the examples that appear in the *Baraita of R. Ishmael* are later additions onto the original material.[26] Hence, it would not be surprising that later amoraic or even post-amoraic forms of the hermeneutic would appear there. Beyond this, a full harmonization would, over time, be preferable to the more radical activity of completely overriding a biblical verse or even reconciling contradictions by applying the contradictory verses to different situations. This, as noted, is the single example of this form of "two contradictory verses" interpretation, which is actually an *ersatz* version of the hermeneutic and its interpretive use. The reality is that the example is nothing but R. Akiba's exposition in *Mek. Baḥodesh* 9 made to look as if it is a "two contradictory verses" *midrash.*

A Talmudic Case of שני כתובים pSotah 1:7 (17a)

There are no cases of "two contradictory verses" hermeneutical interpretations in the Babylonian Talmud, at least not formulated as such. The only mention of שני כתובים, "two verses," is in a hermeneutic called שני כתובים הבאים כאחד, "two verses teaching the same principle."[27] Thousands of what I have called "resolutions of contradictions" *midrashim* do appear in the halakhic *midrashim*, PT, and BT. The Palestinian Talmud, though, does contain a "two contradictory verses" interpretation. PT identifies a contradiction between Num 5:21, 22, and 27 in the biblical section about the ordeal of the suspected wife. Num 5:21 describes the woman's hard-to-visualize thigh falling and her stomach distending as a result of drinking the ordeal's bitter waters. 5:22 reverses the order: the woman's stomach swells first and then her thigh falls. In 5:27 the order of the ordeal's results agree with Num 5:21. In this case, PT's formu-

26 *Sifra*, ed. Finkelstein, p. 9, n. 33 and Michael Chernick, לחקר המידות, p. 33 and p. 168, n. 3. There I propose that some of the material in the examples section of the *baraita* is, in fact, amoraic. See also Moshe Zucker, "לבעית פתרון ל״ב מדות ו׳משנת ר׳ אליעזר׳," *PAAJR* 23: א–לט (December 1954). Zucker suggests that the examples for the 32 hermeneutics are of geonic provenance. Clearly the examples represent a commentary on the original *baraita*, and there is nothing about them that demands that we view them as integral to the *Baraita of R. Ishmael.*

27 See chap. 4.

lation implies that the two verses outweigh the third:

תלמוד ירושלמי מסכת סוטה פרק א דף יז עמוד א/ה"ז

כתוב אחד אומר לצבות בטן ולנפיל ירך וכתוב אחר אומר וצבתה בטנה ונפלה ירכה וכתוב אחר אומר בתת יי׳ את ירכך נופלת ואת בטנך צבה מקרא אחד מכריע שני מקראות אמר רבי מנא כאן למעשה וכאן לתנאין אמר רבי אבין ואפילו תימר כאן וכאן למעשה כאן וכאן לתנאין לצבות בטן ולנפיל ירך לבועל וצבתה בטנה ונפלה יריכה לאשה הדעת מכרעת ירך התחילה בעבירה תחילה ואחר כך הבטן לפיכך תלקה הירך תחילה ואחר כך הבטן....

One verse says, "... to cause the womb to sag and the thigh to fall;" and another verse says, "... and her womb shall sag and her thigh fall"; yet another verse says, "When God shall make her thigh fallen and her womb distended." One verse outweighs two.[28] R. Mana said: (The two verses) refer to the factual situation;[29] the single verse refers to the conditions (stated by the priest overseeing the ordeal when he administers the *sotah*'s oath to the woman).[30] R. Abin said: You might even say that all the verses

28 In the context of the passage in PT, the "two contradictory verses" *midrash* stands in conflict with mSotah 1:7 and thus presents the Talmud with an issue to resolve. mSotah 1:7 states:

משנה מסכת סוטה פרק א משנה ז

במדה שאדם מודד בה מודדין לו היא קשטה את עצמה לעבירה המקום ניולה היא גלתה את עצמה לעבירה המקום גלה עליה בירך התחילה בעבירה תחלה ואחר כך הבטן לפיכך תלקה הירך תחלה ואחר כך הבטן ושאר כל הגוף לא פלט:

By the measure a person measures, so it is meted out to him/her: she (the suspected wife) bedecked herself for sinful purposes, so God made her unkempt; she advertised herself for sinful purposes, so God advertises her as a sinner; her thigh began the sin followed by the womb, therefore she is punished first in the thigh and then in the womb, and the rest of her body does not escape.

According to the *mishnah*, the suspected wife's punishment begins with the falling of her thigh. According to the *midrash* cited in PT, her punishment starts with her womb, if we accept that two verses outweigh one. Cf. *Sifre Num.* 18, ed. Horovitz, p. 22, lines 12–14, which may hold a similar view regarding the order of the adulterous wife's punishments as our *midrash*. See also *Malbim*, *Num.* 5:27, #עג. *Sifre Zuta* clearly follows the Mishnah's tradition. See *Sifre Zuta*, *Num.* 5:21, ed. Horovitz, p. 236, lines 5–7.

29 The bitter waters used in the ordeal "investigate" the woman in the natural order of their movement through her body. Anatomically, the womb would receive them first and the thigh afterward. Cf. bSotah 9b, starting with הירך התחילה. It is possible that BT (Abbaye) was aware of the general content of part of the PT *sugya* but not of its exact formulation. It therefore reformulated it in its own way. Alternatively, BT recognized the contradiction between verses independently and resolved the contradiction in much the same way as PT.

30 That is, the priest's adjuration of the suspected adulteress should begin with mention of her thigh and then of her womb. See Num 5:19–21.

> refer either to the facts or the conditions (in the priest's administration of the *sotah*'s oath).[31] (Rather, the better interpretation of the Numbers verses mentioned above is:) "to cause the thigh to fall and the belly to sag"– refers to the adulterous man; "and her belly shall sag and her thigh fall"– refers to the adulterous woman.[32] (Then,) reason decides the matter: the thigh began the sin and then the belly (womb), therefore she is punished first in the thigh and then in the belly and all the rest of her body did not escape. . . .

A contemporary philological reading of this PT passage would probably consider the "two contradictory verses" *midrash* an independent tannaitic source. Though it follows tannaitic rules and usages, its formulas are unlike any found in "two contradictory verses" *midrashim* in the classical tannaitic halakhic *midrash* collections. Nevertheless, given the possibility of PT's reformulation of its traditions, there is no reason to deny it a tannaitic provenance. This is especially true in view of the *midrash*'s independent stance that contradicts the Mishnah. In this respect this "two contradictory verses" *midrash* appears to be an alternative tannaitic tradition which, typically, the *amoraim* harmonize with the Mishnah's view.[33]

Because of the difficulty of the latter part of this passage, I feel that an explanation of it is due. Though this explanation is conjectural since the connections between the passage's units are not always clear, it attempts to show how R. Mana and R. Abin may have tried to resolve the contradiction between the "two contradictory verses" *midrash* and the Mishnah. In order to make this explanation more comprehensible, I will present it in step-by-step form:

Step 1. R. Mana tries to resolve the contradiction between the verses in the "two contradictory verses" *midrash* by "harmonizing" or "balancing" the verses rather than allowing the *midrash* to stand as a case of two verses outweighing one. This was accomplished by applying Num 5:21 (=the bitter waters af-

31 That is, the order of the afflictions that descend on the woman really is not significant. Sometimes the waters have one effect, sometimes another. Similarly, the priest's adjuration of the suspected adulteress can begin either with a mention of her womb or her thigh. (*Penei Mosheh*, s.v. אמר ר' אבין). *Penei Mosheh* correctly recognizes this as an argument against R. Mana's interpretation. R. Abin seems to resolve the contradiction between Num 5:21 and Num 5:22 and 27 by viewing them as complimentary rather than contradictory.

32 Cf. *Sifre Num.* 15, ed. Horovitz, p. 20, lines 2–3 and *Sifre Zuta, Num.* 5:22, ed. Horovitz, p. 236, lines 15–16.

33 R. Mana and R. Abin are fifth-generation Palestinian *amoraim*. By the fifth generation no *amora* would have considered any source superior to the Mishnah. *Amoraim* would have declared any source in opposition to the Mishnah "non-normative" and, therefore, overruled, or they would have brought the source into congruence with the Mishnah by reinterpreting it. The latter route was taken by R. Mana and R. Abin.

fect the thigh first) to the priest's adjuration of the woman and Num 5:22 and 27 (=the bitter waters affect the womb first) to the actual events of the woman's punishment by the bitter waters. This resolution of the contradiction between the Numbers verses also resolves the contradiction between the *midrash* and the Mishnah's tradition to a degree. Num 5:21, describing the priest's official formula of adjuration reflects the Mishnah's official theological position that the limb that began the sin suffers first.

Step 2. R. Abin argues against R. Mana's resolution. He holds that all the verses may be applied either to the actual event of the suspected adulteress's punishment or to the formula for the priest's adjuration. The result would be that the actual event of the adulteress's punishment might start either with her womb or her thigh. Regarding the priest's adjuration, this interpretation would allow him to adjure the suspected adulteress in any order he chose – that is, either by her womb or her thigh first. According to this, the Numbers verses complement rather than contradict one another. This resolution of the contradiction between Num 5:22 and 27 and Num 21 resolves the contradiction in the "two contradictory verses" *midrash*, but does not resolve the contradiction between the *midrash* and the Mishnah. Since the actual event of the adulteress's punishment may begin with her womb, this fails to jibe with the Mishnah's view that punishment starts with the thigh.

Step 3. Therefore, R. Abin seems to conclude that the tradition of the "two contradictory verses" *midrash* cannot be brought into congruence with the Mishnah's view. Therefore, he cites another midrashic tradition.[34] This applies Num 5:22 to the adulterer and Num 27 to the adulteress.[35] This leaves Num 5:21, which refers to the bitter waters afflicting the woman's thigh first. However, R. Abin does not cite this verse but rather cites the (probably reconstructed) formulation of the *midrash* that says הדעת מכרעת. This means that reason rather than midrashic interpretation decides in favor of the Mishnah's

34 See *Synopse zum Talmud Yerushalmi*, ed. Shaefer and Becker (Tuebingen: Mohr-Siebeck, 1998), p. 3:85, pSotah 1:7/6–7. There the section including the "two contradictory verses" *midrash*, R. Mana's resolution, and what I believe to be the beginning of R. Abin's resolution constitutes unit 1:7/6. The *derashah* about the bitter waters affecting both the adulterer and the adulteress is part of a new unit 1:7/7. Unit 1:7/7 may have been separated from unit 1:7/6 because there is an addition to the *derashah* by R. Abba b. R. Pappi, a fourth-generation *amora*. What precedes this material comes from fifth-generation *amoraim*.

35 See *Sifre Num.* 16, ed. Horovitz, p. 20, lines 1–7 and compare this to pSotah 1:7 from "לנפיל בטן" – זה הבועל to מדת הטובה על אחת כמה וכמה. This comparison indicates that the Palestinian *amoraim* had a general knowledge of the *Sifre Num.*'s *derashah* or one like it and reconstructed it in their own way. R. Abba b. R. Pappi's added completion suggests this even more strongly. See David Weiss-Halivni, מקורות ומסורות – נשים (Tel Aviv: Dvir, 1968) p. תרמה and idem., מועד (Jerusalem: Jewish Theological Seminary), p. פא. See also Michael Chernick, "כלל ופרט וכלל" ו"ריבוי ומיעוט", לחקר המידות (Lod: Habermann Institute for Literary Research, 1984), pp. 125 and 127.

tradition.[36] The *midrash* that R. Abin cites may have taken this route because if it reflects the content of *Sifre Num.*, then that tradition also contradicts the Mishnah because it holds that the bitter waters punish the womb first.[37] This does not produce a support for the Mishnah's view. Hence, only logic is left to generate the Mishnah's tradition that the adulteress's thigh suffers punishment first.[38]

The late amoraic resolutions of the contradiction between a *midrash* and the Mishnah is one of the clearest testimonies to the victory of Mishnah as the rabbinic constitutional document *par excellence*. I have discussed this issue elsewhere,[39] and it seems to me that as rabbinic Judaism developed, it changed its fundamental constitutional document. At the outset, proto-rabbinic Judaism shared the Torah as constitution with all other varieties of Judaism. As rabbinic Judaism more clearly defined itself as distinct from other forms of Judaism – for example, Qumranic Judaism or Jewish Christianity – it created a specifically rabbinic form of expression: *mishnah*. This form gained its ultimate expression in "The Mishnah," which then became the official constitution of rabbinic Jewry.[40] *Midrash*, with all its potential for creating legal norms

36 *Penei Mosheh*, s.v., הדעת מכרעת. Though I do not agree with *Penei Mosheh*'s explanation of R. Abin because it is too forced, this explanation of הדעת מכרעת is what at first glance most would accept as its meaning.

37 See n. 28 above.

38 It is possible, though rather forced, that הדעת מכרעת may mean that, having used Num 5:22 and 27 to include both the adulterer and the adulteress in the punishment of the bitter waters, it stands to reason that we should use Num 5:21 to support the Mishnah. See Zeev Wolf Rabinovitz, שערי תורת ארץ ישראל (Jerusalem: I. Rabinovitz, 1940), p. 364. See, however, how הדעת מכרעת is used in pYebamot 10:3 (10d)||pKetubot 2:3 (26b). Further, neither *ed. princ.* Venice nor MS Leiden nor MS Vatican preserve the reading suggested by Rabinovitz.

39 Michael Chernick, לחקר מידת גזירה שווה (*Hermeneutical Studies: Gezerah Shavah*), p. 229.

40 See for Tanḥuma (Buber), פ׳ וירא, סי׳ ו, p. 88 and n. מו there:

> אמר ר׳ יהודה הלוי ב״ר שלמה: בקש משה שתהא אף המשנה בכתב. וצפה הקב״ה על שעתידין אומות העולם לתרגם את התורה ולקרות אותה יוונית, והן אומרין: אף אנו ישראל. א״ל הקב״ה: אכתוב לך רובי תורתי ואם כן כזר נחשבו (מבוסס על הושע ח, יב). וכל כך למה? אלא שהמשנה מסטורין שלו של הקב״ה, ואין הקב״ה מגלה מסטורין שלו אלא לצדיקים....

See also bGittin 60a for R. Joḥanan's view that the covenant is most essentially related to Israel's acceptance of the Oral Law. For R. Johanan, that would most likely mean at least some of the *halakhot* in the Mishnah. If we accept *Midrash ha-Gadol*'s attribution of the statement to R. Nathan, the equivalence between Oral Law and Mishnah would be even greater.

For a contemporary treatment of Mishnah as "mystery" (מסטורין), see Marc Bregman, "Mishnah and LXX as Mystery: An Example of Jewish Christian Polemic in the Byzantine Period," *Continuity and Renewal in Byzantine-Christian Palestine*, ed. Lee Levine (Jerusalem: Dinur and Jewish Theological Seminary of America, 2004), pp. 333–42. The Hebrew version, "משנה כמסטרין" appears in מחקרי תלמוד, ed. Yaakov Sussman and David Rosenthal (Jerusalem: Magnes Press, 2005) p. 101–9.

in conflict with mishnaic law through new interpretations of the Torah, stood to undermine the mishnaic constitution. Is it any wonder, then, that the chief spokesmen for rabbinic Judaism "defanged" the midrashic enterprise by subordinating it to the mishnaic constitution?[41]

Conclusions

Our study of the "two contradictory verses" hermeneutic has shown us that this hermeneutic existed in a number of forms. One form harmonized contradictions by suggesting the possibility of what I have called a "divided application." In this situation, verse A would apply to situation X, and verse B to situation Y. Now that the midrashist could propose what we might describe as an "apples and oranges" situation, he could resolve the contradiction. The classical examples of this form of the "two contradictory verses" hermeneutic in the tannaitic halakhic *midrashim* are in the "example section" of the *Baraita of Hillel's Seven Hermeneutics* and *Sif. Num.*, 58. Resolutions of contradiction by "divided application" became a favored means for dealing with scriptural inconsistencies even when no third verse was available. Though these are not referred to as "two contradictory verses" interpretations, they are certainly extensions of the method. This seems to be a second stage in the development of this hermeneutic, which does not mean that the interpretations based on this method are not as old as the ones generated by the "two contradictory verses" hermeneutic itself. There is only one odd case of total harmonization of verses without recourse to "divided application." That appears in the late, possibly geonic, example of the "two contradictory verses" hermeneutic in the *Baraita of R. Ishmael.*

Another form of the "two contradictory verses" method simply declares one conflicting verse invalid, thereby ending the contradiction. Notably, this occurs only once regarding a legal matter. In that case, the most radical reading of the "two contradictory verses" *midrash* would claim that a commandment,

41 This process does not start before the late amoraic period and beyond. By "the late amoraic period" I mean from the fourth amoraic generation. Jacob Neusner has suggested that Mishnah and *midrash* were at loggerheads ideologically even during the tannaitic period. See, for example, his statement in *Sifra: An Analytical Translation*, Introduction, pp. 30–31 and n. 11 there; 38ff. Jay Harris and Azzan Yadin provide a useful corrective to Neusner's view that Mishnah and the halakhic *midrashim* stand in a polemical relationship with one another. Both authors argue that *midrash*'s most basic agenda is not informed by its relationship to Mishnah or Tosefta but by its interest in the interpretation of Scripture. See Jay Harris, *How Do We Know This?*, pp. 10–11 and nn. 36–39 ad loc.; Azzan Yadin, *Scripture as Logos*, pp. 1–3. I find Harris's and Yadin's arguments persuasive. See Harris's remark: "Neusner's position strikes me as attending only to the formal and rhetorical presentation of the midrashic passages, but not their content. Form and rhetoric are important, but no more so than content."

or at least a permission, to use cattle as a Passover offering was invalidated by two verses requiring the use of flock animals.

Not surprisingly, the other examples of this type of "two contradictory verses" *midrash* apply to aggadic matters. Differing over the details of a biblical narrative, even to the point of denying the validity of a verse's description of events, is less theologically challenging than declaring a legal verse invalid. The fact that the tradition preserves only three of this kind of "two contradictory verses" *midrashim*, or four if we include an example in PT, is testimony to its problematic nature.

Whatever the history of this hermeneutic may be, and it is not one which can be easily delineated or documented, it is clear that the theologically untenable notion of contradiction in the Torah was the force that caused the development of the various forms of the "two contradictory verses" hermeneutic. Thus, we see that rabbinic thought, which apparently could not accept the possibility that God contradicted himself in the Torah, led to the creation of a reading strategy that would resolve those contradictions. This strategy crystallized into a hermeneutical method – in this case, the "two contradictory verses" hermeneutic in all its various forms.[42] Ultimately, when the Mishnah emerged as the pre-eminent tannaitic work, a reading strategy regarding anti-mishnaic midrashic interpretations had to be developed. Many tannaitic *midrashim* themselves underwent a process of harmonization when they contradicted a mishnaic tradition. In such cases, as PT's example shows, logic or alternative (amoraic) midrashic approaches might trump even the best (tannaitic) "two contradictory verses" or other forms of midrashic interpretations if they did not readily conform to the Mishnah's views. This, as we shall see, indicates a change in rabbinic thought about the status of Mishnah and other tannaitic works as divinely revealed documents. This change will ultimately affect how the later Rabbis will read these documents and how hermeneutics will develop or change in order to accommodate those Rabbis' readings.

"There is No Contradiction" (לא קשיא) A Post-tannaitic Form of Contradiction Resolution

It is interesting to see how the need to resolve contradictions continued beyond the period of the *tannaim*. The standard formulation of the resolution is לא קשיא, "there is no contradiction." There are about 900 cases of this, all of them in BT. Most of these are anonymous, but many are cited using the

42 Azzan Yadin suggests that the fact that there were third verses that could resolve contradictions between two verses in the Torah signaled that this was a characteristic form of literary expression in the Torah and that interpreters should use it. That is, rather than the *middot* being inductive, they were deductive. This is, of course, possible. See above, n. 11.

name of an amoraic Sage. When a named early *amora* – that is, an *amora* who lived and taught before the fourth Babylonian amoraic generation – uses this formula, there are two different approaches that he might take, depending upon whether the contradiction is between or within scriptural passages or between or within rabbinic sources. If the contradiction is connected with Scripture, לא קשיא functions exactly like the "two conflicting verses" hermeneutic that assigns each aspect of the contradiction to a different situation. If, however, the source of the contradiction is a tannaitic source, the early *amoraim* resolve the contradiction by claiming that different *tannaim* are the authors of the different opinions. In a sense, the contradiction is not really resolved. It is merely identified as a debate.

In the case of the late amoraic and anonymous לא קשיא, these resolutions usually attempt to remove the contradiction entirely. The *amora* or *stam* accomplishes this by assigning one element of the contradiction to one situation and the other to a different one. This method was already current during the tannaitic period for the resolution of contradiction between two scriptural verses in cases where there was no available third harmonizing verse. The late amoraic and anonymous לא קשיא functions in this fashion whether the contradiction results from conflicts between or within scriptural or rabbinic sources.

The following are examples of different rabbinic periods' approaches to contradictions that appear in Scripture and in tannaitic and amoraic sources.

The Early Amoraic Approach to Contradiction Resolution in Scriptural Sources

bBerakhot 35a–b. In discussing the idea that one should not benefit from the world's goodness without reciting a blessing prior to enjoying it, R. Levi supports this notion by resolving a contradiction between two Psalms verses:

> רבי לוי רמי: כתיב „לה׳ הארץ ומלואה" (תהילים כד, א), וכתיב „השמים שמים לה׳ והארץ נתן לבני אדם" (שם קטו, טז). לא קשיא.[43] כאן לפני ברכה; כאן לאחר ברכה.

> R. Levi contrasted (two verses). It is written, "The earth and its fullness is the Eternal's" (Ps 24:1), and it is written, "The heavens, the heavens are the Eternal's, but the earth He has given to humanity" (ibid. 116:16). This is not a contradiction. Here (in the first verse the situation) is before the recitation of a benediction. There (in the second verse the situation is) after the recitation of a benediction.

43 לא קשיא: כ״י א״פ OPP. ADD. fol 23: הא כיצד. לפי גירסא זו הרי הוא יותר ברור שהפירוקא מיסודו של ר׳ לוי.

This resolution of the contradiction between these two verses is no different from what we find in tannaitic "two contradictory verses" *midrashim*. In this respect, this method of contradiction resolution continues from the period of the *tannaim* through the amoraic period and into the period of the anonymous redactors. The amoraic use of לא קשיא in relation to rabbinic sources is, however, different from that of the *stam*.

The Early Amoraic Approach to Contradictions in Rabbinic Sources

bBerakhot 9a. In bBerakhot 9a, the *sugya* discusses a conflict between the Mishnah and a *baraita*. In mBerakhot 1:1 there is a short list including two activities that according to the Torah may be performed all night until the dawn. These are the burning of the fats and limbs left over from the sacrifices and eating sacrificial food whose consumption must take place in one day. By rabbinic enactment, one may perform these actions only until midnight. The Talmud questions why the Mishnah did not include other night observances like the consumption of the Passover offering and cites a *baraita* whose contents contradict the mishnaic list:

> הקטר חלבים: ואילו אכילת פסחים לא קתני. ורמינהו: קריאת שמע ערבית והלל בלילי פסחים ואכילת פסחים – מצותן עד שיעלה עמוד השחר. אמר ר׳ יוסף: לא קשיא. הא רבי אלעזר בן עזריה, הא רבי עקיבא. דתניא: ... ר׳ אלעזר בן עזריה אומר ... .אמר ליה[44] ר׳ עקיבא....

> (Mishnah:) The burning of fats (and limbs and the consumption of sacrifices that may be eaten for only one day may take place until dawn). But (this *mishnah*) does not teach the consumption of the Passover offering?! And it is contradicted (by the following). The recitation of the *Shema*[c] and of the *Hallel* on Passover nights, and the consumption of the Passover offerings – their *mizvah* is until the dawn.
>
> R. Yosef said: This is not a contradiction. This (the Mishnah reflects the view of) R. Elazar b. Azariah; that (the *baraita* reflects the view of) R. Akiba.[45]

44 אמר ליה: רוב כי״י יש בהם או „אמר לו״ (פירנצה, א״פ OPP. ADD. fol. 23) או „א״ל״ (כי״מ, פריז). הגירסא „אמר ליה״ מופיעה לראשונה בדפוס שונצינו 1484.

45 R. Elazar b. Azariah is reported to have held that the consumption of the Passover offering was permitted by Torah law only until midnight. Hence, the Mishnah, which supposedly reflects his view, does not include the consumption of the Passover offering since it lists actions permitted until dawn. R. Akiba, who purportedly held that the Torah permitted the consumption of the Passover offering until dawn, has the *baraita* that permits its consumption until dawn assigned to him.

R. Yosef, a third-generation Babylonian *amora*, does not resolve the dissonances between the Mishnah and *baraita* by applying each to a different case. Rather, he assigns each source to a different tradent. This does not truly resolve the contradiction. Instead, it states that the sources are at variance because they have different authors with different views.[46]

bBerakhot 16a. The above example is not the only case in bBerakhot where a named *amora* resolves a contradiction by assigning two contradictory positions to tannaitic Sages rather than opting for assigning each part of the contradiction to a different situation. bBerakhot 16a provides us with another example. At issue there is how workers should conduct themselves in relation to certain religious obligations that take up work time that they legally owe to their employer. The *sugya* states:

> תנו רבנן: הפועלים שהיו עושין מלאכה אצל בעל הבית קורין קריאת שמע ומברכין לפניה ולאחריה, ואוכלין פיתן ומברכין לפניה ולאחריה, ומתפללין תפלה של שמונה עשרה, אבל אין יורדין לפני התיבה ואין נושאין כפיהם. והתניא: מעין שמונה עשרה? אמר רב ששת: הא רבן גמליאל, הא רבי יהושע....
>
> Our Rabbis taught (in a *baraita*): Workers who were doing work for a householder recite the *Shema*ᶜ and recite the blessings before and after it. They eat their bread and recite the benedictions before and after it. They recite the ᶜ*Amidah* of eighteen (benedictions), but they do not pray as a group and (the priests) do not raise their hands (in the priestly blessing of the congregation). But is it not taught: (They recite the ᶜ*Amidah* of) the essence of the eighteen (benedictions)?[47]
>
> There is no contradiction (between these sources). This one (the first *baraita* is in accordance with) Rabban Gamliel; that one (the second *baraita* accords with the view of) R. Joshua.

As in the previous example of the amoraic use of לא קשיא, the resolution does not come from applying the two different *baraitot* to two different situations. Rather, R. Sheshet says that the difference between the views in these *baraitot* is the result of their reflecting the debate between Rabban Gamaliel and R. Joshua (mBerakhot 4:3). Again, such a resolution does not actually undo the contradiction between these *baraitot*. Nor can it; because in the case of a debate one cannot speak of a contradiction between views. Rather, each view is internally coherent unto itself, but different from the other. This approach

46 Compare pBerakhot 1:1 (3a).

47 I.e., they recite a truncated version of the Eighteen Benedictions, rather than the Eighteen Benedictions themselves.

differs from the late amoraic and anonymous לא קשיא method, which, as we will see, tries to eliminate conflict completely.[48]

Late Amoraic Applications of לא קשיא to Contradictions in Rabbinic Sources

bMegillah 8b–9a. In bMegillah we find a contradiction between a *mishnah* (mMegillah 1:8) and a *baraita*. The *mishnah* states:

> אין בין ספרים לתפילין ומזוזות אלא שהספרים נכתבין בכל לשון, ותפילין ומזוזות אינן נכתבות אלא אשורית....

> There is no difference between scriptural scrolls (lit., Books, Heb., ספרים) and *tefillin* and *mezuzot* except that sacred scrolls may be written in any language, and *tefillin* and *mezuzot* must be written only in Assyrian script (i.e., the square Hebrew script).

The *gemara* then cites the following *baraita* as a contradiction:

> מקרא שכתבו תרגום, ותרגום שכתבו מקרא ובכתב עברי, אינו מטמא את הידים עד שיכתבנו בכתב אשורית על הספר בדיו.

> (A scroll of) Scripture that one wrote in Aramaic (lit., [the language of] *targum*), or (a section of Scripture that is in Aramaic, for example, יגר שהדותא in Gen 31:47) that one wrote in (the language of) Scripture or (in the ancient) Hebrew (script), does not defile hands until one writes it in Assyrian script on parchment with ink.[49]

The conflict between these two sources is fairly obvious. The Mishnah allows the writing of Scripture in any language, while the *baraita* seems to indicate that Scripture written in any language other than Hebrew does not qualify as sacred text. Rava, the fourth-generation Babylonian *amora,* enters the dis-

48 See Kalmin, *Sages, Stories*, pp. 48–49, 52, and 55 and n. 22 there. Kalmin notices this phenomenon in relation to the teachings of Rav and Samuel. He documents the fact that this process begins during the fifth generation of Babylonian *amoraim*. The *amoraim* I have cited so far are third-generation Babylonians.

49 Writings that had full scriptural status defiled one's hands if one touched them (mYadayim 3:8). This may have been a rabbinic enactment in order to protect the writing on the scrolls, though bShabbat 14a attributes a different explanation to R. Mesharshia. The Talmud reports that he said that sanctified food was at one time stored with sanctified scrolls. It was discovered that rodents were damaging these holy texts. In order to prevent this form of storage of sacred food, the Sages declared that sacred Writings would render one's hands impure. If one then touched the sacred food, it would become unfit for use.

cussion with a resolution: אמר רבא: לא קשיא. כאן בגופן שלנו, כאן בגופן שלהן, "Rava said: There is no contradiction (between these sources). This (the Mishnah) refers to our writing (Assyrian script). That (the *baraita*) refers to their writing (that is, the script used in the foreign language)."[50]

The continuation of this *sugya* is interesting in terms of Abbaye's use of לא קשיא. Abbaye, also a major fourth-generation Babylonian *amora,* responds to Rava's resolution with a challenge: If your solution is correct, the *baraita* should not have restricted its cases to Scripture being written in Aramaic, or an Aramaic section of Scripture being written in Hebrew. Rather, it should even have included Scripture written in Hebrew using non-Hebrew characters or an Aramaic section of Scripture written in Aramaic using non-Hebrew characters since the *baraita* requires the writing to be in "square Hebrew letters on parchment with ink." Abbaye appears to respond to his own challenge by saying that the way out of the contradiction is not by assigning the *mishnah* to one situation (the transliteration of Scripture in Hebrew script) and the *baraita* to another (the foreign language translation of Scripture in the foreign language's characters). Rather, say that the *mishnah* reflects the views of the majority of the Sages, and the *baraita* reflects the opinion of R. Simeon b. Gamaliel. Abbaye's use of לא קשיא returns to the early amoraic usage of that form of "contradiction resolution" namely, claiming that the two sources reflect the views of disputants.

bMegillah 24a–b. A second example of the use of this type of לא קשיא to resolve contradictions between rabbinic sources appears in Abbaye's name in bMegillah 24a. At issue is how to resolve the following contradiction: the Mishnah in Megillah rules that one is not permitted to skip from one pericope to another when one reads the Torah. In Yoma 7:1, however, it rules that on Yom Kippur the high priest should first read Lev 16:1–34, which describes the special rites of the day. Then he should skip to Num 29:7–11, which describes the additional offerings of the day. The resolution attributed to Abbaye in most of the manuscripts settles the contradiction in this way:[51] The mishnaic

50 I.e., the Mishnah allows the writing of Scriptures in any language as long as the scribe uses the square Hebrew script. The *baraita* declares Scriptures written in a foreign language or obsolete Hebrew script invalid for use, but only if they are written in the foreign language's script. According to Rava, if they are written in transliteration in square Hebrew script on parchment with ink, they are acceptable.

51 All the manuscript text witnesses except Munich 95 mention Abbaye only once in the *sugya*. They report his dictum as being: לא קשיא כאן בעניין אחד כאן בשני עניינים. This appears with small variations in spelling, but not in content. This reading appears in Goettingen 3, Lond. BL Harl. 5508 (400), NY-Columbia X 893T 141, Oxford Opp. Add. fol. 23, and Vatican 134. MS Munich appears to be the source for the printed editions, Pisaro 1516 and later Vilna.

"skipping prohibition" in Megillah applies when skipping from a pericope that discusses one issue to another that discusses a different matter. The mishnaic "skipping permission" in Yoma applies when skipping takes place between pericopes that are subject related. What is noteworthy here is that the Talmud attributes to Abbaye the same use of לא קשיא as it did to Rava. In short, the impression one gets from BT is that a change in the use of לא קשיא for the resolution of contradictions between rabbinic sources begins only in the fourth Babylonian amoraic generation.

The *Stam* and the Application of לא קשיא to Contradictions in Scriptural Passages

bBerakhot 7a. The *stam* resolves a contradiction between two scriptural positions regarding children being punished for their forebear's iniquities. One scriptural view is that children suffer for their progenitor's misdeeds; another view insists that each person suffers only the consequences of his or her own sins. The *stam* resolves the discrepancy in the following manner:

> ...והא כתיב: „פקד עון אבות על בנים" (שמות לד, ז) וכתיב „ובנים לא יומתו על אבות" (דברים כד, טז) ורמינן קראי אהדדי. ומשנינן: לא קשיא. הא כשאוחזין מעשה אבותיהם בידיהם; הא כשאין אוחזין מעשה אבותיהם בידיהם.

> ... it is written, "He visits the sin of the fathers on the children" (Exod 34:7) and it is (also) written, "and children shall not be put to death for (their) fathers' (sins)" (Deut 24:16). And we contrast the verses with each other (and find a contradiction). And we undo the contradiction (thus). It is no contradiction. This (the first verse obtains) when they (the children) maintain the practices of their fathers. That (the second verse obtains) when they do not maintain the practices of their fathers.

In this case, there is no difference between how the *stam* handles the contradiction that emerges from these two verses and how the *tannaim* would handle it. This methodology has a long history, and as we have seen, the early *amoraim* also use it.

The *Stam* and the Application of לא קשיא to Contradictions in Rabbinic Sources

bBerakhot 14b.

> ...[ה]תניא: החופר כוך למת בקבר פטור מקראית שמע ומן התפלה ומן התפילין ומכל מצוות האמורות בתורה. הגיע זמן קריאת שמע, עולה ונוטל ידיו ומניח

תפילין וקורא קריאת שמע ומתפלל.[52] הא גופא קשיא! רישא אמר פטור, וסיפא חייב. הא לא קשיא: סיפא בתרי, ורישא בחד.

> ... Is it not taught: One who digs a sepulchre in a grave for a corpse is exempt from reciting the *Shema*ᶜ, from the Prayer, and from *tefillin* and from all the (positive commandments) mentioned in the Torah. If the time of reading the *Shema*ᶜ arrives, he should climb out, wash his hands, put on *tefillin*, recite the *Shema*ᶜ, and pray.[53]
>
> This is self-contradictory! The first section (of this *baraita*) says (the grave digger) is exempt, and the second section (says) he is obliged. This is not a contradiction: the second section deals with two (grave diggers) and the first with one.

Whether this resolution is convincing or not, its methodology is clear. This is how the *tannaim* would resolve a contradiction within a single verse or a contradiction that emerged from several verses. In sum, this Babylonian *baraita* has been treated as if it were Scripture. We should note, however, that there may not be a true contradiction within this source. The first section indicates that while digging the sepulchre, the digger is in fact exempt. The second section advises him, however, to renounce this exemption and recite the *Shema*ᶜ and the *ᶜAmidah* and don *tefillin*.

It is more likely, however, that the conflict between the first and second parts of this Babylonian *baraita* is the result of the amalgamation of a Babylonian and Palestinian tradition. The Babylonians may have held that digging a grave constituted a *miẓvah* while the Palestinian Sages did not. If the Babylonians considered grave digging a *miẓvah*, then in accordance with a toseftan principle known to and accepted by both *Talmudim*,[54] they would have exempted grave diggers from *Shema*ᶜ, the *ᶜAmidah*, and *tefillin*. It seems that the Palestinian Sages considered burial itself a *miẓvah*, but preparation of a burial site was perhaps too unrelated to the actual act of burial to qualify as an activity that would grant exemption from the performance of *miẓvot*.

bBerakhot 23b. In bBerakhot 23b we find two sources between which BT finds a contradiction. The sources have to do with placing *tefillin* in a turban cloth.

52 עיין ירוש׳ ברכות פ״ב, ה״ג ומועד קטן פ״ג, ה״ה. שם איתא רק הסיפא דברייתא וממילא אין קושיא מרישא לסיפא. הברייתא שבירושלמי מופיעה בשינויים ניכרים.

53 See pBerakhot 2:3 (4c) and pMoᶜed Qatan 3:5 (83a). There a *baraita* similar to the Babylonian *baraita* is cited, but only the second section thereof. This, of course, eliminates the contradiction between the first and second section of the *baraita*. The Palestinian version of the *baraita* contains noticeable variations from the Babylonian text.

54 tBerakhot, ed. Lieberman, 1:3; pBerakhot 1:3 (3c). bBerakhot 11a and 16a, bSukkah 25a.

The *sugya* states:

> תני חדא: צורר אדם תפיליו עם מעותיו באפרקסות. ותניא אידך: לא יצור. לא קשיא. הא דאזמניה. הא דלא אזמניה.

> One *baraita* teaches: A man may wrap his *tefillin* with his coins in his turban cloth. But another (*baraita*) teaches: He may not wrap (them). This is not a contradiction. This (*baraita* speaks of) when he dedicated it, and that (*baraita* speaks of) when he did not dedicate it.

Here, too, the anonymous voice of the Talmud resolves a conflict between the two *baraita* traditions it knows. As in the previous case, it does so by assigning the elements of the conflict to different situations, thereby eliminating the basis of the contradiction. In this case, the *baraita* that rules that one may not wrap *tefillin* and coins in one cloth applies when the cloth has been designated specifically for holding *tefillin*. The *baraita* that permits wrapping *tefillin* and non-sacred items like coins together in a cloth speaks, according to the *stam*, of a cloth that one has not designated specifically for holding *tefillin*.[55]

The differences between the לא קשיא methodologies of the early *amoraim*, the later *amoraim*, and the *stam* suggests that the three groups had differing views of the sources. The early *amoraim* seem to accept that rabbinic sources can be in conflict because they represent the views of different people. These views are not the product of revelation, but of legitimate human debate. For the *stam*, however, disputes appear to be unacceptable. Is this because they conflict with the notion that the Torah and its practical observance spelled out in the rabbinic *halakhot* are the products of God's revelation? Or to put it as the Talmud does, "Can there be doubt in Heaven?" (bBerakhot 3b; Gittin 6b). This question is one that we will keep before us and one that we will try to answer once we have seen more of the hermeneutical behaviors of the *tannaim*, *amoraim*, and the *stam*.

55 Other similar examples in bBerakhot of the *stam*'s use of לא קשיא appear in bBerakhot 7b; 8a; 16a; 22b; 23b; 24a; 24b; 29a; 34b; 36b; 40a; 45b; 50b; 51a; 53a; 55a; 56b; 58b; 59a; 59b. See Appendix B for more examples of the use of לא קשיא among the early and late *amoraim* and the *stam*.

3

The Transfer of Pentateuchal Rules from One Rubric to Another

This chapter contains an extensive study of a hermeneutic that, unlike those I have analyzed until now, appears in every stratum of rabbinic literature. The first part of my analysis will address the action or midrashic method and outcome of this hermeneutic and how these change from period to period in rabbinic literature. The chapter concludes with an intellectual history of the theologies of revelation and canonization that informed the reading methods and hermeneutic practices of the Rabbis from their tannaitic beginnings to the end of the talmudic era.

In the exegetical *midrashim* and the *Talmudim* we find a hermeneutical method that I will call אם אינו ענין. This name is taken from the longer formula that introduces midrashic interpretations using this interpretational rule, namely, אם אינו ענין ל...תניהו ענין ל...., "if (the biblical rule under discussion) is inapplicable to subject A, apply it to subject B." This formula indicates that in all cases of אם אינו ענין, a verse clearly deals with one issue, while its *midrash* shifts the verse's legal content to another. Our examination of the earliest stratum of this interpretational method will concentrate upon the hermeneutic's action within a midrashic interpretation and upon the choice of the alternative subject to which a verse's rules are applied. The latter issue is a matter of interest because it raises the question, "What relationship, if any, exists between the verse's original subject and the new subject that the אם אינו ענין *midrash* proposes?"

אם אינו ענין *Midrash* as a Form of *Ribbui*

A study of the cases of אם אינו ענין interpretations in the classical tannaitic exegetical *midrashim* shows that they are, generally speaking, a form of ריבוי (*ribbui*) *midrash*.[1] That is, they are interpretations that rely on superfluity, repetition, or highly inclusive language to produce their halakhic conclusions.

1 Early authorities recognized that אם אינו עניין interpretations were a form of *ribbui*. They spoke of these interpretations as resting on a יתור (*yittur*), i.e., an extraneous or superfluous element. See R. Samson of Chinon, ספר הכריתות (Warsaw: 1885), p. 34, letter כ; R. Malachi b. Jacob Hakohen, יד מלאכי (reprinted, no publisher, Brooklyn, 1974), letter ב.

The *ribbui* midrashic method rests on the theological proposition that the Torah's text, as an expression of God's revelation, would not include uselessly repetitive or superfluous elements. Once the rabbinic interpreters of Scripture accepted that position, they deemed any case of repetition or superfluity as merely apparent. From their point of view, each repetition or superfluity was a new piece of the revelation of God's Law. Regarding an inclusive formula in the Torah, the rabbinic interpreters sought to answer the question, "What does this formula incorporate?" This quest for definition produced *ribbui midrashim* that delineated, at least for the midrashist, the *halakhot* that the inclusive word or phrase encompassed.

What separates אם אינו ענין interpretations from typical *ribbui* expositions is that אם אינו ענין interpretations based on superfluity and inclusive words and phrases use verses or elements from different pericopes. In contrast, the classical *ribbui* operates within a single pericope and usually within a single verse. The following example from *Sifre Num.* 118,[2] should help clarify how the אם אינו ענין hermeneutic operates:

ספרי במדבר פיסקא קיח ד"ה אך פדה

אך פדה תפדה, שומע אני אף שאר בהמה טמאה במשמע ת"ל ופטר חמור תפדה בשה (שמות יג יג) פטר חמור אתה פודה ואי אתה פודה בכור כל שאר בהמה טמאה או פטר חמור תפדה בשה ושאר כל בהמה טמאה בכסות וכלים ת"ל עוד במקום אחר (שמות לד כ) ופטר חמור תפדה בשה בשה אתה פודה ואי אתה פודה בכסות וכלים א"כ מה ת"ל אך פדה תפדה אם אינו ענין שפודים בהמה טמאה תניהו ענין שמקדישים בהמה טמאה לבדק הבית וחוזרין ופודין אותה מהקדש בדק הבית.

"[B]ut you shall "certainly redeem (the firstborn of humans, and the firstborn of unclean animals shall you redeem)" (Num 18:15) – from this I might understand that all unclean animals were implied; (therefore) the Torah says, "The firstborn of an ass you shall redeem with a lamb" (Exod 13:13) – the firstborn of an ass you redeem, but not the firstborn of other unclean animals. But perhaps (from this I might deduce that) the firstborn of an ass one redeems with a lamb, but the firstborn of other unclean animals (one redeems) with clothing and vessels. (Therefore,) the Torah repeats elsewhere, "the firstborn of an ass you shall redeem with a lamb" (Exod 34:20).[3] (This being the case,) why does the Torah say, "[B]ut you shall certainly redeem (the firstborn of humans and the firstborn of

2 This *Sifre Num.* source has a parallel in *Mek. Pisḥa* 18, ed. Horovitz-Rabin, p.71, lines 8–14. The *Sifre Num.* passage is clearer.

3 This repetition serves to reiterate the specificity of the law of redemption: the only ritually unclean animal the Torah requires one to redeem is an ass, and the medium of redemption is a lamb.

> unclean animals shall you redeem)"?[4] If it is not (necessary for) the issue of the redemption of an unclean animal, apply it to the issue of the dedication of an unclean animal for the upkeep of the Temple. (In which case, the law requires that) one return and redeem the unclean animal from its dedicated status.[5]

An outline of this midrashic argument will clarify the issues in it. 1) Num 18:15 implies that all firstlings of impure animals are subject to redemption. 2) Exod 13:13 counters this by applying the rule of redemption to the firstlings of asses alone. The medium of redemption is a lamb. 3) The *midrash* suggests that perhaps the firstlings of asses are redeemed with a lamb, while other impure animals may be redeemed with clothing or vessels, i.e., other objects of worth. 4) This position is refuted by the repetition of the rule regarding redemption of an ass's firstling by use of a lamb (Exod 34:20). This leaves the question of why the Torah even raises the matter of redemption of impure animals in general if it is totally superfluous. 5) The *midrash* answers that the superfluity should be used to establish the rule that one must redeem the impure animals one dedicated for the purpose of the Temple's physical upkeep.

What we should note regarding this *midrash*'s form is that the superfluity of the Numbers verse results from its interaction with the Exodus verses. This is what I mean when I speak of אם אינו ענין *midrash* as a form of *ribbui*-interpretation in which the *ribbui* element draws from two or more biblical pericopes instead of one.

Another example from *Sifra* will show this to be a common characteristic of אם אינו ענין midrashic interpretations. In this example, the issue is whether there is any source for the idea that one who sacrifices a thank-offering must have in mind the proper rules for eating these sacrifices when he slaughters them:

ספרא צו פרשה ז

(ב) ביום קרבנו יאכל אין לי אלא אכילתם ליום אחד ומנין אף תחילת זביחתן לא תהא אלא על מנת לאכול ליום אחד. (ג) תלמוד לומר וכי תזבחו זבח תודה לה׳ לרצונכם תזבחו ביום ההוא יאכל, שאין תלמוד לומר אלא אם אינו ענין לאכילה תניהו ענין לזביחה שאף תחלת זביחתה לא תהא אלא על מנת להיאכל ליום אחד.

4 The verse appears to be totally superfluous since all issues related to the redemption of unclean animals seem to have been covered by the two Exodus verses. Therefore, what is left for Num 18:15 to teach?

5 One may dedicate an unclean animal to the Temple treasury for the upkeep of the Temple. When it comes time for using it for that purpose, however, it must be redeemed for its money value and not used as is.

> "On the day of its sacrifice shall it be eaten" (Lev 7:16)[6] – (from this) I know only the rule regarding the consumption (of thank-offerings, namely, they may be eaten) for one day. Whence (do I know) that even from the beginning of their being slaughtered that (the slaughter must be) for the sake of eating them for only one day? The Torah says: "When you slaughter a sacrifice of thanks to the Eternal, according to your free will shall you slaughter it, on that day shall it be eaten" (Lev 19:6). The Torah did not have to state this (having stated it previously in Lev 7:16). But if it (Lev 19:16) is not necessary for the matter of consumption, use it for the issue of slaughter; namely, even from the beginning of the thank-offering's slaughter, it must (slaughtered) be for the sake of consuming it in one day.

As we can see, the verse in Leviticus 7 discusses the slaughter and eating rules for the thank-offering. Nevertheless, Leviticus 19 repeats these matters. Because of this superfluous repetition, *Sifra*'s midrashist reapplies the rules of sacrificial consumption to the intentions that must accompany the thank-offering's slaughter. Though superfluous elements regularly constitute "excessive" elements (i.e., *ribbuyim*) that the midrashist may use to generate or support halakhic legislation, the midrashic process here makes no reference to the root *r-b-h* that normally accompanies *ribbui-midrash* interpretations. Rather, we find אם אינו ענין ל... תניהו ענין ל- ..., "If the verse is not applicable to issue A, then apply it to issue B." The reason appears to be that the "*ribbui*" emanates from two distinct Leviticus pericopes rather than from within a single one.[7]

Logical Extraneity as the Source of אם אינו ענין Interpretations

In several cases the basis for an אם אינו ענין interpretation is superfluity based on logic rather than on purely textual considerations.[8] A passage in *Mek. de-RSBY*

6 The context is the *shelamim* and thank offering pericope in Lev 7:11–37.

7 This phenomenon repeats itself in the following sources in the tannaitic halakhic *midrashim* pericopes: *Mek. de-Rashbi*, Exod 12:18; *Sifra Nedabah* par. 12:7 = *ʾEmor* 12:9; ibid. *Ẓav* 12:3; ibid. 13:2; ibid. *Shemini* 4:3; ibid. *Qedoshim* 1:1; ibid. *Qedoshim* 9:7; ibid. *Qedoshim* 10:2; ibid. *ʾEmor* 9:1; ibid. Behar 5:5; Sif. Num. 118. This accounts for well over half the cases of אם אינו ענין interpretations in the tannaitic *midrashim*. The approximate number of such interpretations, counting repetitions, is 15 or 16.

8 This was recognized by the author of the article on אם אינו עניין in the *Enzyklopedia Talmudit*, 3:25, s.v. אם אינו עניין, who wrote:

> מדת אם אינו ענין נדרשת כשאי אפשר לפרש שכוונת הפסוק לגופו. לאי אפשרות זו היא באחד משני אופנים: א) כשאין צורך להשמיענו את הדבר, שכן כבר ידוע הוא לנו אם ממקרא זה עצמו, או ממקרא אחר, או מאחת מהמדות שהתורה נדרשת בהן; ב) כשהדבר כמו שהוא נסתר, אם מהמקרא עצמו, או ממקום אחר, או מסברא.

provides a good example of this phenomenon. The pentateuchal context of *Mek. de-RSBY*'s discussion is the death of a non-Israelite slave caused by his Israelite master. The midrashic interpretation discusses the culpability for the slave's death when two people have partial ownership of the slave.

מכילתא דרבי שמעון בר יוחאי פרק כא פסוק כ

ומת תחת ידו מה אני צריך והלא אפלו מת לעשר שעות הרי זה חייב מה ת״ל ומת תחת ידו אלא אם אינו ענין למיתה תניהו ענין לשעבוד מכאן אתה אומר האומר לחברו עבד זה מכור לך לאחר שלשים יום ר׳ אליעזר אומר זה וזה אינו בדין יום או יומים הראשון מפני שאינו תחתיו והשני מפני שאינו עבדו <ר׳ יוסי אומר שניהם ישנן בדין יום או יומים זה מפני שהוא תחתיו וזה מפני שהוא כספו>

"And he (the non-Israelite slave) dies under his hand" (Exod 21:20)[9]– why do I require this (statement). Is it not the case that even if (the slave) dies within ten hours (the master) is culpable? Why then does the Torah say, "and he dies under his hand?" Rather, if (the verse) is not meaningful regarding the matter of (the slave's) death, apply it to the matter of (what constitutes the legal definition of the terms of a slave's) servitude. From here you learn[10] (the rule regarding) one who says to his fellow, "This slave is sold to you after thirty days." (In such a case) R. Eliezer says, "Neither party is subject to the rule of 'a day or two days';[11] the first party because the slave is no longer fully "under his hand";[12] the second party because (the slave) is not (yet completely) his slave.[13] R. Jose said, "Both of them are subject to the rule of 'a day or two days'; this party (i.e., the

---

> The hermeneutic אם אינו ענין is used in interpretation when it is impossible to explain the verse's intention in consonance with the verse itself. The impossibility arises in two ways: 1) when there is no need to inform us of the matter (in the verse) because it is already known from the verse itself, from another verse, or from a midrashic interpretation; 2) when the matter as it stands presently is contradicted by Scripture itself, or by some other source, or by logic.

Because the *Enzyklopedia*'s statement is a useful opening for our work (though it makes no distinctions between tannaitic, amoraic, and post-amoraic אם אינו ענין phenomena) I have followed its basic division of אם אינו ענין interpretations based on textual superfluity or logical impossibility.

9 *Mek. de-RSBY*'s understands the phrase "under his hand" to mean "immediately"– i.e., while the slave is under the master's hand receiving a fatal beating. Its alternative meaning, "in the master's possession," is used later in this midrashic interpretation.

10 Lit., from here you may say. . . .

11 I.e., the rule that if the slave lives for a day or two, the master who beat him or her is not culpable for his or her death. That is, both "masters" are completely free from culpability.

12 See n. 9. The first owner no longer has full dominion over the slave since s/he has been promised for sale.

13 I.e., he has neither dominion over nor possession of the slave.

master) because he (i.e., the slave) is still in his possession (since the sale has not yet been finalized), and that one (i.e., the buyer) because he (i.e., the slave) is his property (by virtue of the sale being fully agreed upon).

Regarding this midrashic interpretation's form, it is clear that the "excessive" *ribbui*-like element is the product of superfluity produced by logic. If the Torah holds culpable the master who beats his servant so savagely that he dies within twenty-four hours, there is no doubt that it regards the master who kills his slave on the spot guilty of murder. Hence, the Torah's statement, "and he (i.e., the slave) dies under his hand (i.e., on the spot)" is superfluous by virtue of *a fortiori* reasoning (קל וחומר). This variety of superfluity is common in midrashic interpretations based on גזירה שווה that appear in *Mekhilta* and *Sifre Numbers*. In those interpretations, similar words are compared in order to link two legal rubrics found in the Torah. Since this could lead to midrashic anarchy, the words used in these comparisons must be superfluous מופנה (*mufneh*), according to *Mekhilta* and *Sifre Numbers*. Frequently, the necessary superfluity is the product of a successful *a fortiori* argument.[14] The phenomenon here is essentially the same. Since, however, this element was not exactly a *ribbui* or *mufneh*, it was introduced by a different rhetorical formula – namely, אם אינו ענין ל... תניהו ענין ל....

אם אינו ענין in a Single Pericope

There are cases of אם אינו ענין *midrash* that derive from a single pentateuchal pericope. In fact, the previous example is such a case. The most likely reason for this is that there is no other pericope in the Torah that deals with bludgeoning a slave to death. The exegetical *midrashim* contain two other similar cases, and in both cases the reason for the phenomenon appears to be that the pericopes involved are the only ones that discuss their particular subjects. One case is in *Sifra, Behar* 5:5. Its result is that one who redeems property that has been sold by his relative follows the same redemption procedures applicable to his relative. That point is not clearly stated in the pentateuchal text, but *Sifra* derives it as follows:

ספרא בהר פרשה ג ד"ה פרק ה

(ה) ואם לא מצאה ידו, מה ת"ל (מנין אתה אומר)[15]אם אינו ענין לבעל השדה

14 Michael Chernick, מידת "גזירה שווה": צורותיה במדרשים ובתלמודים (Lod: 1994), pp. 39–40. I would now add that I believe that the name of the first hermeneutic in the Baraita of R. Ishmael is מקל וחומר ומגזירה שווה, "(interpretation using) *a fortiori* and word comparison."

15 לפי הפירוש המיוחס לר"ש משאנ"ץ והפירוש לספרא של ראב"ד משמע שצריך למחוק המוסגר. וכן הגיה הגר"א.

תניהו ענין לגואל שיגאל כסדר הזה ת"ל אם לא מצאה ידו, לא ילוה, די השיב לו, ואינו גואל חציים.

"If he cannot find sufficient (funds to redeem his property)" (Lev 25:28) – why does the Torah state this (i.e., isn't it obvious that if one has insufficient funds he cannot redeem his sold real estate)? (The Torah states this to teach:) if this matter is now inapplicable to the original owner of the field, apply it to the (field's) redeemer. (This implies) that he (i.e., the relative) should redeem it according to the (same) procedures (applicable to the original owner). Therefore the Torah says, "If he cannot find sufficient funds"– he shall not borrow; "enough to recover it" (ibid.,) – nor shall he redeem half of it.[16]

The form of this אם אינו ענין *midrash* is somewhat different from others we have seen. It is not immediately obvious what is extraneous in the verse or verses that would generate the *midrash*. However, inspection of this pentateuchal pericope will show that it began thus:

ויקרא פרק כה

(כה) כי ימוך אחיך ומכר מאחזתו ובא גאלו הקרב אליו וגאל את ממכר אחיו: (כו) ואיש כי לא יהיה לו גאל והשיגה ידו ומצא כדי גאלתו: (כז) וחשב את שני ממכרו והשיב את העדף לאיש אשר מכר לו ושב לאחזתו: (כח) ואם לא מצאה ידו די השיב לו והיה ממכרו ביד הקנה אתו עד שנת היובל....

If your brother becomes poor and sells part of his real estate, his nearest kinsman must come and redeem his brother's sale. And if a man has no one (who can act as a) redeemer, but he (himself) succeeds and finds enough for redemption purposes, then he shall compute the years since the sale, refund the difference to the man to whom he sold, and return to his property. If he lacks sufficient means to recover it, what he sold shall remain with the purchaser until the jubilee year. . . . (Lev 25:25–28)

The phrase והשיגה ידו ומצא כדי גאלתו ... ושב לאחוזתו, "but he (himself) succeeds and finds enough for redemption purposes . . . and he returns to his property" (Lev 25:26–27), already implies that "If he lacks sufficient means to recover it, what he sold shall remain with the purchaser until the jubilee year. . . ." (Lev 25:28) without the text actually having to state it. The fact that the text does clearly state this rule creates a superfluous element on which to base the אם אינו ענין interpretation.[17] Note, it is logic that is drawn on here

16 According to *Sifra*, these rules apply to the original owner who sold his land. See *Sifra*, *Behar* 5:2. Now, according to this midrashic interpretation, they apply to the land's redeemer as well.

17 See the *Sifra* Commentaries of R. Samson of Sens and R. Abraham b. David of Posquieres, ad loc.

to create a *ribbui*- or *mufneh*-like element, and the result is essentially the same as in the previous *midrash* in *Mek. de-RSBY*. Thus, when אם אינו ענין emerges from a single pentateuchal pericope, it is generally logic rather than the repetition of the same regulation in several pericopes that the midrashist calls upon to generate textual superfluity. The *midrash* then undoes the logical superfluity of the pericope's rule by applying it to another closely related subject. In this case in *Sifra*, the rules of redemption by the original seller of the property are transferred to the redeemer, a relative who will act to keep the property in the family.

An example of אם אינו ענין derived completely from a single pericope also appears in *Sifre Zuta* on Num 19:2. It shares similar methodological characteristics with the previous examples. There the *midrash* addresses the required physical traits of the red heifer whose ashes are used to create a medium for restoring ritual purity. The *midrash* concludes that the heifer must be perfectly red, i.e., not blemished by having any other color hair:

ספרי זוטא פיסקא יט

ויקחו פרה, יכול מולבנת או מושחרת ת״ל אדומה או אדומה יכול בזמן שרובה מאדים ת״ל תמימה אם לומר שהיא תמימה מן המומין והלא כבר נאמר אשר אין בה מום אלא מה אני מקיים תמימה אם אינו ענין למומין תנהו ענין לאדומות:

"They shall take a heifer" (Num 19:2) – I might think a white or black one, but the Torah says, "red." I might think (the heifer would be acceptable) if it was mostly red. The Torah teaches, "perfect."[18] If you wish to say that the heifer must be "perfect," meaning free of blemishes, hasn't it already been stated, "(a heifer) that has no blemish in it" (Num 19:2). So how shall I fulfill "perfect" (without redundancy). If "perfect" is unnecessary when applied to blemishes, apply it to the matter of (the heifer's) redness.

This אם אינו ענין *midrash* uses logical linguistic analysis to produce a superfluity that will lead to the application of the term תמימה, "perfect," to redness rather than to other physical traits. It is like the אם אינו ענין *midrash* we have seen in Lev 25:25–28. By virtue of its placement in the verse, the adjective תמימה, "perfect," could refer to the heifer's redness or to the heifer itself. Hence, the verse might be parsed, "They shall take for you a heifer that is perfectly red," or "They shall take for you a red heifer that is perfect." Because the verse contains the phrase "(a heifer) that has no blemish in it," primacy is given to the former reading in order to remove the potential redundancy.

Again this form of אם אינו ענין *midrash* emerges from a pericope that does

18 The verse reads ...ויקחו אליך פרה אדומה תמימה אשר אין בה מום..., "... they shall take for you (Moses) a perfect red heifer that has no blemish in it. . . ."

not appear again in the Torah. Numbers 19 is the single source for the laws of the red heifer. Since it contains a redundancy, it is a candidate for אם אינו ענין interpretation. Nevertheless, the *midrash* here is more exegetical than other logic-oriented אם אינו ענין interpretations. It determines that the referent of the ambiguous adjective, תמימה, "perfect," is the heifer's hair color.

The Distinction Between *Ribbui* and אם אינו ענין in a Single Pericope

Despite all the similarities between logically derived מופנה, the extraneous word or phrase that allows for a word comparison *midrash* (גזירה שווה) and אם אינו ענין, it is easy to understand why they are distinguished from one another. אם אינו ענין, unlike מופנה, does not lead into a גזירה שווה. What, however, is the difference between אם אינו ענין that emerges from a single pericope and *ribbui*? It appears that two factors generate an אם אינו ענין *midrash* rather than a *ribbui*: 1) אם אינו ענין in a single pericope is the product of superfluity uncovered by logic or linguistic analysis; *ribbui* results from more obvious literary superfluity.[19] 2) אם אינו ענין is generally based on full phrases or verses; *ribbuyim* are based on single words or even particles.[20] Thus, when logic creates a superfluity that generates a *midrash*, it will be an אם אינו ענין interpretation. If, however, the superfluity is obvious and based on a single word or particle, it will generate a *ribbui* interpretation.

The Logic of אם אינו ענין Applications

The second question that אם אינו ענין interpretations raise is related to the section of the interpretation that contains the rhetorical introduction, "תניהו ענין ל....," "apply (superfluous matter A) to subject B." What, if any, logic guides the choice of the application of the rules stated regarding scriptural rubric A to a new scriptural rubric, B?

It appears that these factors determine what "subject B" will be: 1) It appears

19 The biblical constructions איש איש or אמֹר יאמר are examples of what some rabbinic interpreters would have considered obvious superfluity based on repetition. While such repetitions imply emphasis in the Torah, they suggest a lack of literary economy to some schools of rabbinic interpreters.

20 *Sifra*'s midrashic interpretation of Lev 1:2 illustrates this well. The verse states: דבר אל בני ישראל ואמרת אלהם אדם כי יקריב מכם קרבן לה׳....., "Speak to the Israelites and say to them: a person from among you who brings a sacrifice to the Eternal. . . ." The *midrash* states: "אדם" – לרבות את הגרים; "מכם" – להוציא את המומרים...., "a person"– to include (Heb., לרבות, *le-rabbot* – indicating a *ribbui*) proselytes; "from among you"– to exclude apostates. . . . The single word "אדם," "any person," generated the *ribbui* because of its inclusiveness.

in one of the two or multiple pericopes that serve as the basis for the אם אינו ענין interpretation. 2) Or both subjects A and B appear in the single pericope that generates the אם אינו ענין interpretation. 3) Or "subject B" is closely related to "subject A" in some way.

Subject B Appears in One of the Generative Verses of the אם אינו ענין Interpretation

Sifra Ẓav, 12:9. In *Sifra Ẓav*, 12:9 we find an example of factor 1 at work. This midrashic interpretation is based on two verses. The first is Lev 7:16, whose context is, among other things, the *shelamim* sacrifice (JPS *TaNaKh*, 1985 translates this as "offering of wellbeing"). That verse states, ואם נדר או נדבה קרבנו ביום הקריבו את זבחו יאכל וממחרת והנותר ממנו יאכל, "If his offering is a vow or pledge, on the day he brings it and the morrow it may be eaten, and that which is left over of it may be eaten." Lev 19:5–6 supplies the second verse, וכי תזבחו זבח שלמים לה׳ לרצנכם תזבחהו, ביום זבחכם יאכל וממחרת והנותר עד יום השלישי באש ישרף "When you slaughter an offering of wellbeing to the Eternal, you shall slaughter it so that it shall be accepted on your behalf; on the day you slaughter it and the morrow it shall be eaten, and that which is left over on the third day shall be burned in fire." While the first verse speaks primarily of eating the *shelamim*, the second one speaks of both slaughtering and eating it. It is this connection between slaughtering and eating in the latter verse that creates the result of this *Sifra midrash*: "If there is superfluity caused by repetition of the rules governing eating the *shelamim*, apply that extraneous element to the issue of having to slaughter the *shelamim* with the intention of eating it for two days."[21]

Subjects A and B Appear in the Same Pericope

Mekhilta de-RSBY, Exod 12:18. The following אם אינו ענין interpretation in *Mek. de-RSBY* to Exod 12:18 provides a good illustration of one of these methods of transferal from scriptural subject A to scriptural subject B. It notes that Exod 12:18 explicitly requires the eating of *maẓẓah* (subject A) on Nisan 14, the eve of Passover. When Deut 16:3 undermines this by requiring the consumption of *maẓẓah* only on the night of Nisan 15, the אם אינו ענין interpretation applies the obligation (subject A) to subject B, the destruction of *ḥameẓ* (i.e., leavened products). The resultant rule is that *ḥameẓ* must be destroyed on Nisan 14, Passover eve:

21 A variation of this *midrash* appears in *Sifra*, *Ẓav*, 12:3=*ʾEmor* 9:1 where the thank-offering is discussed. The thank-offering is very similar to the *shelamim*, but its meat and bread offerings may only be eaten for one full day. Other אם אינו ענין interpretations in which the new application relates to an issue mentioned in the same pericope appear in *Sifra*, *Ẓav*, par. 1:15; *Sifra*, *Be-*

מכילתא דרבי שמעון בר יוחאי פרק יב פסוק (יח)

יכול את חייב מצה בארבעה עשר ת״ל עליו (דב׳ טז ג) עליו אתה חייב מצה ואין אתה חייב מצה בארבעה עשר אם כן למה נאמר בארבעה עשר אם אינו ענין לאכילת מצה תניהו ענין לביעור חמץ.

I might have thought that one is required (to eat) *mazzah* on the 14th (day of Nisan),[22] but the Torah says: "(seven days) on it [i.e., on Passover alone, which begins on Nisan 15] shall you eat *mazzah*, the bread of poverty)" (Deut 16:3). If so, why does it say "on the fourteenth"? (Rather), if this rule is not applicable to the issue of eating *mazzah*, apply it to the issue of the destruction of leavened products.[23]

Given the results of this אם אינו ענין *midrash*, one might regard the shifting of the explicitly stated obligation of eating *mazzah* on Nisan 14 to the matter of the destruction of *ḥamez* as the height of arbitrariness. Yet, it is clear that the obligation to eat *mazzah* begins only with the actual onset of Passover. It is not only the Deuteronomy passage that says so; this is also the clear statement of Num 28:17, ובחמשה עשר יום לחדש הזה חג; שבעת ימים מצות יאכל, "And on the fifteenth day of the month (there shall be a) seven day celebration; *mazzot* shall be eaten." So it is not strange to ask: What is the meaning of a requirement to eat *mazzah* on the fourteenth? Since the documentary hypothesis was not a theologically possible consideration for the Rabbis, some resolution of the contradictions had to be found. In fact, it is somewhat odd that we do not find a "two contradictory verses" *midrash* here.[24] Be that as it may, however, the אם אינו ענין interpretation solves the texts' contradictions thus:

Earlier in the Exodus pericope it states, שבעת ימים מצות תאכלו אך ביום הראשון תשביתו שאר מבתיכם..., "Seven days you shall eat *mazzah*; but on the first day you shall destroy leaven from your houses. . . ." (Exod 12:15). Since the topic of *ḥamez* destruction appears in the pericope, it apparently becomes a natural choice for an alternative to the contradictory rule that one must eat *mazzah* on the fourteenth of Nisan. This application is further supported

---

har, 5:5; *Sifre Zuta* on Num 19:2.

22 This is because the verse in Exod 12:18 states, "בראשן בארבעה עשר יום לחדש בערב תאכלו מצת...." "On the first day, on the fourteenth of the month in the evening, you shall eat *mazzot*. . . ."

23 This is the second interpretation in *Mek. de-Rashbi* in which logical analysis uncovers an extraneity. There is a third אם אינו ענין in *Mek. de-Rashbi*. It, too, appears to be a case of logical generation of an extraneity leading to the אם אינו ענין, Apparently the redactor(s) of *Mek. de-Rashbi* accepted only this form of אם אינו ענין *midrash*.

24 See chap. 1. It is possible that the "two contradictory verses" hermeneutic does not appear here because there is no third verse to harmonize or outweigh the conflicting verses. Further, the resolution of this contradiction is not amenable to the typical assignment of one aspect of the contradiction to one legal rubric and the other to another.

by the use of the term ביום הראשון, "on the first day," in Exod 12:15 and the appearance of בראשון, "on the first," in Exod 12:18. In the latter verse, "the first" is equivalent to the fourteenth. Thus it takes only several small steps to arrange the following argument: 1) since "the first day" and the fourteenth of Nisan are one and the same, and 2) since Exod 12:15 identifies the first day as the day for *ḥameẓ* destruction, 3) then "if it (the fourteenth of Nisan) is irrelevant to the requirement of *maẓẓah* consumption due to information found in Deut., let us apply it to the obligation of *ḥameẓ* destruction. This interpretive result is especially useful because the date implied in the phrase ביום הראשון in Exod 12:15's discussion of *ḥameẓ* destruction is undefined. The *midrash* now defines it as the fourteenth, which, it appears, is the major point of this interpretation.[25]

Subject B is Closely Related to Subject A

Sifre Numbers, 118. These examples, however, do not explain other cases of the application of the rules of subect A to subject B in all the tannaitic אם אינו ענין interpretations. In the *Sifre Numbers* exposition on the redemption of unclean animals we found the following אם אינו ענין *midrash*:

ספרי במדבר פיסקא קיח ד"ה אך פדה

אך פדה תפדה, שומע אני אף שאר בהמה טמאה במשמע ת"ל ופטר חמור תפדה בשה (שמות יג יג) פטר חמור אתה פודה ואי אתה פודה בכור כל שאר בהמה טמאה או פטר חמור תפדה בשה ושאר כל בהמה טמאה בכסות וכלים ת"ל עוד במקום אחר ופטר חמור תפדה בשה בשה אתה פודה ואי אתה פודה בכסות וכלים[26] א"כ מה ת"ל אך פדה תפדה אם אינו ענין שפודים בהמה טמאה תניהו ענין שמקדישים בהמה טמאה לבדק הבית וחוזרים ופודים אותה מהקדש בדק הבית.

"But you shall certainly redeem (the firstborn of humans and impure animals)" (Num 18:15) – (from this) I might understand that all impure animals are included, but the Torah says, "the firstborn of an ass you shall redeem with a sheep" (Exod 13:13) – the firstborn of an ass you redeem, but not the firstborn of other impure animals. Or perhaps the firstborn

25 This *midrash* is one of several trying to prove that *ḥameẓ* destruction must occur on the day prior to Passover. See the various interpretive attempts in this direction in *Mek. Pisḥa* 5, ed. Horovitz-Rabin, pp. 27–28 and *Mek. de-RSBY*, ed. Epstein-Melamed, p. 17. In fact, this is one of the more successful attempts.

26 The Mekhilta's version reads: פטר חמור אתה פודה, ואי אתה פודה בכור שאר בהמה טמאה, "the firstborn of an ass you redeem, but you do not redeem the firstborn of other impure animals." This formulation is superior to the one in *Sifre Num*. See *Sifre Num*., ed. Horovitz, p. 139, note to line 1. Horovitz cites the Mekhilta formula incorrectly. It should read as I have presented it above.

> of an ass you redeem with a sheep and the firstborn of other impure animals with clothing and vessels? (Therefore,) the Torah says in another place, "the firstborn of an ass you shall redeem with a sheep" (Exod 34:20) – (to teach) that one redeems (only) with a sheep but not with clothing or vessels. If so, why does the Torah say, "But you shall certainly redeem (the firstborn of humans and impure animals)"? (To teach that) if it is not necessary for the issue of redemption of (the firstborn of) impure animals, apply it to the rule that people who dedicate an impure animal for the upkeep of the Temple must return and redeem it from the upkeep fund of the Temple (and the redemption fee becomes part of the upkeep fund).[27]

It is clear that there is no mention in the biblical citations in this אם אינו ענין of anything related to the fund for the upkeep of the Temple. However, there is a pentateuchal pericope that speaks of the redemption of impure animals without any reference to the firstborn of asses, just as Num 18:15 does. It is the pericope about הקדשות, dedicatory vows, in Leviticus 27. There, in verse 27 we find: ואם בבהמה הטמאה ופדה בערכך ויסף חמשתו עליו, ואם לא יגאל, ונמכר בערכך, "And if (what one dedicates is from) among the impure animals, one shall redeem it for its assessed value with a fifth added; and if it is not redeemed, it should be sold for its assessed worth." This verse follows immediately upon a reference to the redemption of ritually clean firstborn animals and may, according to the verse's plain meaning, refer to firstborn ritually unclean animals. If so, these verses parallel the order of rules in Numbers, thereby creating a perfect intertextual allusion for the midrashist's אם אינו ענין. Nevertheless, the rabbinic interpreter understands Lev 27:27 to refer to unclean animals dedicated to the Sanctuary, probably because the term בערכך, "at its assessed worth," appears in this verse as it does in most of the other verses in this pericope dealing with dedicatory vows. According to this interpretation, since this dedicated ritually unclean animal is useless for sacramental purposes, it is redeemed or sold for the benefit of the Temple or Sanctuary. The אם אינו ענין *midrash* indicates that despite the impression that redemption and sale are equivalent options according to the Torah, there is, in fact, a preference for the original owner to redeem his offering, thereby increasing the Sanctuary's profits by the added fifth. Thus, if none of the pericopes used in the creation of an אם אינו ענין interpretation provides a subject B to which subject A's rules may be transferred, then the midrashist may choose a literarily and legally related subject for this purpose.

27 Since redemption means paying not only the determined worth of the animal but an additional fifth, the Temple upkeep fund profits beyond the mere worth of the dedicated impure animal.

Mekhilta de-RSBY, Exod 20. Another case of this phenomenon appears in *Mek. de-RSBY.* In its discussion of the Torah's warning and sanction against violating the Sabbath labor prohibition,[28] *Mek. de-RSBY* states the following:

מכילתא דרבי שמעון בר יוחאי פרק כ

י) ויום השביעי שבת אין לי אלא מצות עשה מצות לא תעשה מנין ת״ל לא תעשה כל מלאכה. אין לי אלא מצות עשה ומצות לא תעשה מיתה מנין ת״ל כל העושה מלאכה ביום השבת מות יומת (שמ׳ לא טו). עונש שמענו אזהרה לא שמענו ת״ל ושמרו בני ישראל את השבת (ש״ם ט״ז) אין לי אלא עונש ואזהרה למלאכת יום עונש ואזהרה למלאכת לילה מנין ת״ל מערב עד ערב (ויק׳ כג לב) אם אינו ענין ללילי יום הכפורים תניהו ענין ללילי שבתות.

> "And the seventh day is the Sabbath" (Exod 20:10) – I only have (here) the positive commandment, whence (do I know) the prohibition? The Torah says, "You shall do no work." (Ibid.) I now have the positive commandment and prohibition, whence (do I know that Sabbath violation is punished by) death? The Torah says, "Anyone who does labor on the Sabbath day shall surely be put to death" (Exod 31:15). We have (now) heard the punishment, but not the forewarning. (Therefore,) the Torah says, "The children of Israel must keep the Sabbath" (Exod 31:16). I now have the forewarning and punishment for work (done on the Sabbath) day, whence (do I know the) forewarning and punishment for work done (during the Sabbath) night? The Torah says (regarding Yom Kippur), "from evening until evening shall you observe your Sabbath (i.e., Yom Kippur)" (Lev 23:32). If this verse serves no purpose regarding the night of Yom Kippur, apply it to the night of the Sabbath.

This אם אינו ענין *midrash* is quite difficult, but its meaning appears to be as follows: Because there is no other pericope that deals specifically with the night of Yom Kippur, Lev 23:32 is the single frame of reference for the prohibitions applicable to that time. The full text of Lev 23:32 is שבת שבתון הוא לכם ועניתם את נפשתיכם בתשעה לחדש בערב, מערב עד ערב תשבתו שבתכם, "It is a Sabbath of complete rest for you; you shall practice self-denial; on the ninth day in the evening, from evening to evening, you shall observe your Sabbath." The phrase "in the evening, from evening to evening" provides the opportunity to claim superfluity: Why not simply say, "On the ninth day of the (seventh) month from

28 In the rabbinic view of the Torah's laws, every rule that carries a sanction like death or excision must have a verse that provides a forewarning. The verse containing the warning does not mention any punishments for infractions. The punishment verse does. *Mek. de-Rashbi* is seeking a verse about Sabbath violation that does not include any reference to punishment and another verse that includes mention of punishment for Sabbath violations.

evening until evening shall you observe your Sabbath," leaving "in the evening (בערב)" aside? Under normal circumstances we might view בערב as a simple *ribbui* that should add some halakhic information about the observance of Yom Kippur evening, but there apparently is nothing more to add. The verse merely reiterates all the Yom Kippur prohibitions and requirements. The *midrash* of the phrase בתשעה לחדש, "on the ninth of the month," provides the idea of תוספת יום הכיפורים, the extension of the sanctity of Yom Kippur, to some amount of normally profane time. בערב means straightforwardly that the observance of Yom Kippur starts with the evening and, as the Torah clearly states, proceeds until the next evening. There is apparently no further issue related to Yom Kippur night that could be derived from the extraneous phrase בערב or מערב עד ערב. Consequently, the *midrash* concludes that the text provides more than a simple *ribbui* and interprets the verse in accordance with the principles of אם אינו ענין. It then applies the Yom Kippur eve verse to the weekly Sabbath since that is the only other holy day referred to as שבת שבתון, "a Sabbath of Sabbaths."[29]

On the basis of the examples we have cited, we may conclude that the following are the characteristics of an אם אינו ענין application that extends beyond the boundaries of its generative pericopes: 1) the superfluous elements that are part of what we have been calling "subject A" share linguistic or formulary similarities with "subject B," the reapplication rubric; and 2) the superfluous elements that are part of subject A do not provide any further halakhic information about subject A, i.e., they cannot function as *ribuyyim*. These pentateuchal linguistic *sigla* and constricted application potentials join to create a "literary logic" and sometimes shared legal characteristics for אם אינו ענין applications that shift the rules of one biblical context to closely related alternatives.[30]

An Anomalous Case
Midrashic "Eisegesis" as a Source of the
אם אינו ענין Interpretation

In one rather odd instance of אם אינו ענין in *Sifre Num.* 78, midrashic "eisegesis" of a verse rather than the verse itself produces the logical inconsistency that

29 See Exod 31:15; Exod 35:2; and Lev 23:3. The term is used twice in reference to Yom Kippur, once in Lev 16:31 and again in our verse, Lev 23:32. It is also used in reference to the seventh year of fallow and debt cancellation. Since the last is not a twenty-four hour observance, it is not a candidate for an אם אינו ענין application.

30 Another example of this kind of אם אינו ענין application appears in *Sifra Nedabah*, par. 12:8 and *Ẓav*, 13:2=*Sifra Qedoshim* 1:4. The interpretation in *Sifra Nedabah* applies the rules regarding wheat-flour offerings to barley-flour offerings with the result that neither can be brought from the new harvest. The Torah speaks of only two kinds of grain for meal offerings (מנחות), wheat and bar-

generates an אם אינו ענין interpretation. In another deviation from the norm, the interpretation produces more than one transferral suggestion. None of these suggestions appear to have a scriptural basis, thus giving the impression of being completely arbitrary choices. Deeper analysis of these suggestions will show this not to be the case, just as it has not been the case in any of the other אם אינו ענין interpretations we have analyzed. Finally, in further deviations from the formal characteristics we have seen in אם אינו ענין expositions, *Sifre Num.* expounds a verse in Ezekiel, thereby going beyond the Pentateuch, which, until now, has been the only source for these interpretations. The pentateuchal verse it uses is derived from a narrative rather than legal section of the Torah. Indeed, it is possible that the use of pentateuchal narrative in this אם אינו ענין *midrash* generates all its oddities. That is, once the interpreter "violated" what had been a basic rule of אם אינו ענין interpretation, he could permit himself further licenses.

The midrashist finds the basis for his אם אינו ענין interpretation in a contradiction between a verse in Ezekiel and the pentateuchal verse as understood midrashically. Thus, formally, a logical problem generates this אם אינו ענין. On the one hand, the *midrash* of Num 10:29 implies that there are no land allotments in the Land of Israel that are apportioned to non-Israelites, even excluding the גר, the Bible's equivalent of a "naturalized citizen." On the other hand, the verse in Ezekiel apportions to such a citizen a נחלה, a term that usually means a land allotment, within Israelite tribal areas:

> אל המקום אשר אמר ה׳ אותו אתן לכם – ואין לגרים בו חלק ומה אני מקיים והיה השבט אשר גר הגר אתו שם תתנו נחלתו (יחזקאל מז כג) אלא אם אינו ענין לירושה תניהו ענין לכפרה שאם היה בשבט יהודה מתכפר לו בשבט יהודה בשבט בנימין מתכפר לו בשבט בנימין ד״א אם אינו ענין לירושה תניהו ענין לקבורה ניתן לגרים קבורה בארץ ישראל.

". . . to the place that God has said, 'I shall give it to you.' . . ." (Num 10:29) – (this implies that) proselytes have no portion in it. (If so,) how shall I uphold (the verse which states:) "You shall give the stranger his allotment within the tribe where he resides. . . ." (Ezek 47:23). If it (the Ezekiel verse) is not applicable to the issue of inheritance (given the Numbers verse's midrashic implications), apply it to the issue of atonement. If he (the proselyte) lives within the tribe of Judah, he receives atonement with the tribe of Judah; if he lives with the tribe of Benjamin, he receives atonement with the tribe of Benjamin.

---

ley. See, for example, Exod 29:2, Exod 34:22. and Num 5:15. Hence, these are the only frames of reference to which the Torah's rule regarding grain offerings may apply. Superfluity regarding a rule operative in the area of wheat offerings is therefore likely to lead to the rule being transferred to barley offerings.

> Another interpretation: If it (the Ezekiel verse) is not applicable to the issue of inheritance (given the Numbers verse's midrashic implications), apply it to the issue of burial, namely, that burial rights in the Land of Israel are granted to proselytes.

It is clear that the verse in Ezekiel implies that גרים have land ownership rights in the tribal areas where they reside. The Torah, without midrashic embellishment, conceivably concurs. Therefore, the denial of real estate ownership within the Israelite tribal allotments to a גר depends completely on a midrashic, eisegetical reading of Num 10:29. Thus it is only a meaning read into the pentateuchal verse that causes the verse in Ezekiel to function as a contradiction.

Of course, assuming there had been a real contradiction between the Numbers source and the Ezekiel verse, one might have argued that the law had changed over time or that Ezekiel viewed the law of the in-dweller differently from the Pentateuch. That view would have been impossible for the rabbinic midrashist. Here again, a rabbinic theology of Scripture informs his position – namely, the Pentateuch is the first and last revelation and no prophet can reveal any new law.[31] All laws in subsequent prophecies must therefore conform to the Torah of Moses, and Ezekiel is no exception. Consequently, the rabbinic midrashist, who viewed his interpretation of Num 10:29 as a proper one, found the verse in Ezekiel at odds with it.[32] Therefore, if Ezekiel's ruling could not be understood in terms of land ownership without contradicting "the Torah," it had to be understood in terms of some other right or entitlement allotted to converts.[33]

One midrashic interpreter chose to apply the verse in Ezekiel to the right of the convert to receive atonement through the expiatory offering brought for an entire tribe's unwitting transgression.[34] Another midrashic interpreter offered an alternative application of the Ezekiel verse: the tribe in whose midst the convert lives must provide him or her with a burial plot in the Land of Israel.

What appears clear from both interpretations is that there is a strong emphasis on ethnicity in determining Jewish identity and its entitlements. Indeed, ethnicity trumps theology and practice. Converts, according to this view, are naturalized citizens with many rights, but not with rights equal to those of the native born. The verse in Ezekiel certainly confounded this view because on its face it equalizes the naturalized citizen or convert and the tribe member. As noted, the Pentateuch and Ezekiel could by themselves bear this

31 See *Sifra* Beḥuqotai, par. 8, 13:7: „אלה המצות" – אין נביא רשאי לחדש דבר מעתה.

32 Ezekiel's alteration of pentateuchal rules and procedures presented the rabbinic world with difficulties that it admitted and promptly interpreted away. See bShabbat 13b.

33 This case of *midrash* is another support for our view that the rabbinic interpreters of Scripture considered their interpretations to have pentateuchal status since they "inhered" in Scripture.

34 See Lev 4:13–22 and the rabbinic understanding of it in mHorayyot 1:5.

interpretation, but the world view expressed in *Sifre Num.* and elsewhere in rabbinic literature could not. Therefore, the rabbinic midrashists represented in this midrashic exposition apportioned those rights to the convert they believed the Ezekiel verse indicated.

The first suggested transferral applied Ezekiel to purely spiritual matters: converts receive atonement along with the tribe in which they live for any unwitting communal transgression caused by following an erroneous decision of the Sanhedrin. In essence, converts are sufficiently members of the Jewish community to be obliged to the *mizṿah* system and subject to the jurisdiction of the Sanhedrin. Consequently, they would not be obliged to bring personal sin offerings at their own expense, which is the case when individuals transgress by following the ruling of an erring Sanhedrin. According to this first interpretation, land ownership by a convert is simply a non-issue.

According to the second midrashic interpretation, the גר's right to a parcel of land in the Land of Israel is a matter for discussion. The question the midrashist appears to address is, "How hard and fast is the rule that only born Israelites inherit land in the Land of Israel?" His interpretation seems to hold that converts who die among the tribes are granted the privileges of כבוד המת, honoring the dead, which are applicable to all members of the community. Therefore, the requirement to bury them applies to the community, and burial implies a burial place.[35]

On the surface, there is every reason to view these choices as arbitrary. However, the Ezekiel verse's central term, נחלתו, "his portion, allotment," does, in fact, have two usages in the *TaNaKh*: a land allotment, which accounts for the overwhelming majority of its use in the Bible, and a literary connection to forgiveness of sin. The midrashist responsible for the alternate interpretation (דבר אחר) section of our *Sifre Num.* passage accepted the "land allotment" definition and read the verse in Ezekiel thus: "You shall give the convert the land allotment specifically due him within the tribe where he resides." Since that allotment cannot be construed as an inheritable estate under the terms of the *midrash*, "logic" suggests it would be land set aside for some other purpose, in this case burial.

Another use of a form of the Hebrew radical נ-ח-ל appears in Exod 34:9. As part of Moses' plea for forgiveness for the Israelites after the episode of the golden calf, he begs God, וסלחת לעוננו ולחטאתנו ונחלתנו, "and pardon our iniquity and our sin, and take us for Your own."[36] Mandelkern notes in his con-

35 See Deut 21:23 and its rabbinic interpretation that if the honor of speedy burial is given to the criminal, it is certainly given to every member in good standing of the community.

36 Translation according to the Jewish Publication Society's *TANAKH, A New Translation of the Holy Scriptures* (Philadelphia, New York and Jerusalem: 1985).

cordance that the original might have been ומחלתנו, "and forgive us," and that seems to be quite appropriate given the context; but Mandelkern is also aware that the root מ-ח-ל never appears in the *TaNaKh*.[37] Yet, it is possible that ונחלתנו had that meaning or, more likely, that the midrashic interpreter decided to assign that meaning to it. If this hypothesis is correct, then the interpreter read the Ezekiel verse thus: "You shall give the convert his forgiveness within the tribe where he dwells." Thus, the choices for the אם אינו ענין *midrash*'s new applications of the Ezekiel verse are considerably less arbitrary than they appear.

The Tannaitic אם אינו ענין Interpretation Summary

Our survey of the tannaitic אם אינו ענין interpretation has shown the following:

1. The initial section of אם אינו ענין *midrashim* is essentially a form of *ribbui*, i.e., an extraneous or superfluous element. It is unlike the standard form of *ribbui* because it is generally based on a verse or full phrase rather than on a single word or particle. There are times when the superfluity is obvious; at other times it is the product of a logical deduction.

2. Under most circumstances, an אם אינו ענין *midrash* depends on two verses in two separate pericopes. This is another reason that the superfluous elements in these interpretations do not qualify as *ribbuyim*. This is not only important for defining the nature of the superfluous element in אם אינו ענין *midrashim*, but also for a more articulated definition of the nature of *ribbuyim*. The latter are part of a dialectic within a single *parashah* (biblical pericope), but not between pericopes.

3. Single pericopes do occasionally generate an אם אינו ענין *midrash*. In those cases the extraneous element in the interpretation is usually a product of logical deduction rather than another verse within the pericope. This phenomenon usually occurs when the pericope is the only one that discusses a particular law. For example, legal matters like murdering a slave, the rites of the red heifer, and the law of real estate redemption after sale appear only once in the Torah. In all these cases we have a single pericope אם אינו ענין *midrash* in which superfluity is the product of logic rather than of the repetition of a law.

4. There is one case in which the midrashic interpretation of a pentateuchal verse, rather than the verse itself, creates the logical impossibility that generates the אם אינו ענין. This passage is exceptional in so many ways that I am

37 Solomon Mandelkern, ספר היכל הקדש (ed. princ., Leipzig, 1846; Israel, no date), p. 734, columns 3–4.

tempted to hypothesize that it is a post-tannaitic addition into *Sifre Num.*, but there is no support for this view in the manuscript traditions of this *midrash*.

5. Perhaps the more significant matter in our study of אם אינו ענין is the workings of the section that begins תנ(י)הו ענין ל-, "If the verse is superfluous or inapplicable to subject A, apply its rule to subject B." Is the new application a matter of the interpreter's whim? Is he trying to give established rabbinic norms a grounding in the Written Law as best he can? Or is his choice determined by firm rules of interpretation? Our sense is that the midrashic interpreter's new application of the extraneous element in an אם אינו ענין interpretation is certainly guided, if not totally determined, by firm interpretational regulations.

6. The "firm rules" that guide the "new application" aspect of an אם אינו ענין interpretation are the following: a) An אם אינו ענין interpretation may apply the rule applicable to its superfluous subject A to alternative subject B when subject B appears in one of the generative pericopes of the אם אינו ענין; b) when subjects A and B appear in a single pericope; c) when an intimate linguistic-formulary or legal connection exists between subject A and subject B.

7. The source of every tannaitic אם אינו ענין is the tannaitic Rabbis' sensitivity to redundancy and illogic in the Torah. Therefore, when they came upon these formulary phenomena, they recognized a religious obligation to solve these forms of textual difficulties.[38] Their response was to undo redundancy by applying the rules applicable to rubric A to rubric B. The same was true when illogic appeared. If the illogic could be resolved by transferring the rules applicable to one rubric of the Torah to another, then they did so in order for a sensible meaning of the Torah to stand firm. Hence, there is a relationship between rabbinic expectations about the appropriate formulation of what they considered canonical works, in this case the Pentateuch, and the hermeneutical reading strategies they used to fulfill those expectations.

We now turn to the analysis of the אם אינו ענין hermeneutic in the Palestinian and Babylonian Talmuds. We first discuss developments in the form of the hermeneutic and what appear to be problematic formal patterns in אם אינו ענין interpretations. Though this fairly lengthy detour temporarily shifts our fo-

38 See Deut 17:8–11. See also *Sifre Deut.* 336:

„כי לא דבר רק הוא מכם" – אין לך דבר ריקם בתורה שאם תדרשנו שאין בו מתן שכר בעולם הזה והקרן קיימת לו לעולם הבא....

"For it (the Torah) is no empty matter for you"— there is no (apparently) empty word in the Torah. If one will only interpret it (i.e., such a word), it will provide one with a reward in this world and a standing account for one in the world-to-come....

See also *Midrash Tannaim, Deut.* 32:47, though this source may not be tannaitic.

cus away from rabbinic views of what constituted the sacred canon and the reading strategies the Rabbis employed to interpret that canon, it is a necessary excursus that leads back to the main point of our work. Eventually, this more formal and historical-critical analysis of examples of אם אינו ענין will reveal the stages of the development of the later talmudic Rabbis' view that their predecessors' traditions were a form of divinely revealed Torah.

אם אינו ענין in the Palestinian Talmud

There are approximately 18 examples of אם אינו ענין in the Palestinian Talmud. None of the them are truly parallel to interpretations in the classical halakhic *midrashim* or *Mek. de-RSBY*, *Sifre Zuta*, or *Midrash Tannaim*. As we would expect, some of them follow the patterns we have uncovered in the tannaitic אם אינו ענין midrashic interpretations, but other examples indicate the development of an אם אינו ענין that uses the form of reasoning used in the midrashic אם אינו ענין on non-biblical sources. Between these two poles there are new forms of the midrashic אם אינו ענין found in the Palestinian Talmud. We will begin with אם אינו ענין interpretations generated by redundancies in two pericopes and logical problems, but we will concentrate initially on examples from PT and BT that differ in some way or ways from their tannaitic antecedents. Eventually, we will try to determine when these "deviations" occurred with the intention of creating a chronology of developments in rabbinic thinking about Scripture and their impact on the אם אינו ענין hermeneutic.

אם אינו ענין Based on Two Pentateuchal Pericopes

pḤallah 2:2. In a discussion about agricultural laws applicable only in the Land of Israel, the Mishnah discusses the case of produce growing in soil from outside Israel on a ship anchored at the shores of the Land. An anonymous view in mḤallah 2:2 obligates such produce to all the agricultural laws applicable to the Land of Israel without qualification. R. Judah holds that the obligations only exist when the ship actually touches the Land's shores. The Rabbis of Caesarea citing R. Ḥanina claim that the dispute depends on what form of *midrash* one applies to Deut 11:14. The midrashic interpretation that supports the unqualified application of the agricultural laws of the Land to foreign soil on a ship is an אם אינו ענין *midrash*:

תלמוד ירושלמי מסכת חלה פרק ב דף נח עמוד ב/מ"א

רבנין דקיסרין בשם רבי חנינה במחלוקת[39] כל מקום אשר תדרך כף רגליכם בו לכם יהיה אין בכלל אלא מה[40] שבפרט וכרבי יודה מתיבין לרבי יודה אם בספרי

39 במחלוקת: בכ"י ל: כמחלוקת.

40 „אלא מה": נוסף ע"י הסופר בכ"י ל.

ארץ ישראל והכתיב מהמדבר והלבנון הזה ועד הנהר הגדול נהר פרת כל ארץ החתי׳ ועד הים הגדול מבוא השמש יהיה גבולכם אלא[41] אם אינו ענין לספרי ארץ ישראל תניהו ענין לספרי חוץ לארץ....[42]

> The Rabbis of Caesarea citing R. Ḥanina (said): (The mishnaic dispute about produce growing in soil on a ship that came from outside Israel) depends on a difference of opinion (about how to interpret the verse,) "Every place where your sole shall tread shall be yours; (from the wilderness to Lebanon, from the river – the river Perat – to the Great Sea shall be your border)" (Deut 11:24). There is nothing (implied) in the general clause that is not (specified) in the particular clause. And this accords with R. Judah's view.[43] They (i.e., the authors of the Mishnah's anonymous view) would respond to R. Judah: If the verse (in Deuteronomy) was discussing the borders of Israel, has it not been written: "From the wilderness to Lebanon and until the great river, the river Perat, all the land of the Hittites until the Great Sea where the sun sets shall be your border" (Josh 1:4)?[44] Rather, if the verse is extraneous in relation to the borders of Israel, apply it to the borders of lands beyond Israel.[45]

In terms of the attribution chain leading to R. Ḥanina, the אם אינו ענין *midrash* in this passage appears to be clearly amoraic. What distinguishes it from some of its tannaitic counterparts is that the verses that serve as the basis for the interpretation are not all pentateuchal. With one extreme exception in *Sifre Num.* 78, the rule for tannaitic אם אינו ענין interpretations is that only the Pentateuch

41 נמחק (אבל) ונוסף במקומו [אלא] ע״י הסופר.

42 The order of verses in the אם אינו ענין is attested to in all the major mss. and early imprints. This factor will be important in later discussions of this type of אם אינו ענין in PT.

43 I.e., the general clause, "Every place where your sole shall tread" is fully defined by "from the wilderness to Lebanon, etc." Thus, only that which is in the biblical borders of Israel is subject to the Land's agricultural laws. This accords with R. Judah's view in the Mishnah that only when the ship with its foreign soil touches Israel's shores does the produce that grows from that soil become subject to the Land's agricultural laws.

44 The full context of Joshua includes the statement, "Every place your sole shall tread I have given you as I have spoken to Moses. From the desert and the Lebanon unto the great river, the river Perat, etc." (Josh 1:3–4). Apparently the Rabbis of Caesarea held that this exact repetition in another biblical pericope produced a redundancy. Redundancy, as we have noted, opens the way for interpretation that extends existent legal perameters.

45 I.e., there is the possibility of making foreign territory into the territory of the Land of Israel by bringing the foreign territory under Israelite/Jewish control. If a ship filled with foreign soil was brought to Israel where Jewish control of it could be asserted, any produce growing from that soil would be subject to the agricultural laws of the Land whether it was within the borders of the Land or not. This explanation is based on the commentary of R. Jacob David of Slutzk (פירוש הרידב״ז), who applied it to the debate between R. Eliezer and R. Akiba in pḤallah 2:1.

serves as a source for אם אינו ענין interpretations.[46] Consequently, if tannaitic midrashists had considered constructing such an interpretation, they would have looked for a redundancy between the descriptions of the borders of the Land of Israel that are found in Numbers and Deuteronomy respectively.

Another difference exists between this אם אינו ענין interpretation and its tannaitic forebears. It appears from PT's wording that the verse in Joshua renders the Deuteronomy verse redundant rather than the reverse. If anything, we would have imagined that a posterior repetition of a formula would form the redundant or superfluous element.[47] Indeed, the seeming illogic of the order of elements in the PT interpretation is glaring in light of the tannaitic *midrash* of Deut 11:24 in *Sifre Deut.* 51:

ספרי דברים פיסקא נא

> כל המקום אשר תדרוך כף רגלכם בו (דברים יא כד), אם ללמד על תחומי ארץ ישראל הרי כבר נאמר מן המדבר והלבנון מה תלמוד לומר כל המקום אשר תדרוך אמר להם כל מקום שתכבשו חוץ ממקומות האלו הרי הוא שלכם....

> "Any place your sole shall tread (shall be yours)" (Deut 11:24) – if this was meant to teach us about the borders of the Land of Israel, has it not already been stated, "From the desert and the Lebanon . . . (shall be your border)" (ibid.).[48] Then why say, "Any place your sole shall tread (shall be yours)?" He (Moses) said to them, "Any place you conquer besides the places (that I have specified) shall be yours (as well). . . . "

This *midrash* is a perfect case of *ribbui*, which is why there is no mention of אם אינו ענין in it. The midrashist infers that if the borders of the Land of Israel have already been listed, the extensive כל in Deut 11:14 expands potential

46 See chap. 2 for a discussion of this phenomenon in the case of the hermeneutic action called אף על פי שאין ראיה לדבר and what the phenomenon implies. There, too, there are significant differences between the midrashic methods of the *tannaim* and *amoraim*. The *tannaim* use only pentateuchal legal passages for "true" derivation or support of *halakhot*. The *amoraim* feel free to use any part of the *TaNaKH* in their halakhic *midrash*. As stated in the previous chapter, this is due to different views of the standing of the Pentateuch in relation to other sections of the Scriptures. For the *tannaim* only the Pentateuch functioned as the relevant revelation for legislative interpretation. For the *amoraim*, God either revealed the whole body of the Hebrew Scriptures at Sinai or the Prophets and Writings had to be consonant with the Sinaitic revelation.

47 This is not the case with אם אינו ענין *midrashim* based on either logic or textual contradictions because verse order does not matter in those cases. Logical objections and contradictions will exist no matter what the verse order is.

48 Both מלבי"ם and מאיר עין hold the second half of Deut 11: 24 to be the source of *Sifre Deuteronomy*'s *midrash*. מאיר עין states that this is the verse he has in his manuscript text of *Sifre Deuteronomy*; Malbim has it as an alternate version. His original version uses the verse from Joshua. Finkelstein has simply מן המדבר והלבנון with no other versions in his critical apparatus. That would point to our Deuteronomy citation since the verse in Joshua begins "מהמדבר וכו'."

Israelite territory to places beyond those borders.

Therefore, it appears to me that in their attempt to reconstruct a vaguely recollected source whose content was similar to that of *Sifre Deut.* or some similar *midrash*, the *amoraim* created a new אם אינו ענין interpretation. This probably occurred because they felt constrained not to acknowledge the word כל, "all," as a *ribbui* since it did not function as one in the first *midrash* in the PT passage. There the word כל generated a כלל, a general clause, which was overridden by its פרט, the specific clause listing the biblical borders of Israel.[49] According to PT's description of R. Judah's opponents' view, if כל could not serve as a *ribbui* to extend the legal parameters of Land-oriented *miẓvot*, a redundant biblical verse might. Since the passage in Joshua repeated Deut 11:24 almost verbatim, it became the prime candidate for the required redundant element.

The fact that these *amoraim* applied אם אינו ענין to a case of redundancy between what they considered two pericopes indicates that they were still aware of the formulary rules that permitted the application of אם אינו ענין hermeneutics to pentateuchal verses. What they did not seem to agree with any longer was the specific manner in which the *tannaim* established redundancy in two pericopes. We should view the PT phenomenon of "reverse order redundancy" as a significant development in the form of the אם אינו ענין hermeneutic. This form of superfluity also generates אם אינו ענין interpretations in pSanhedrin 9:1 (26d), pPesaḥim 2:2 (28d), pRosh ha-Shanah 1:1 (56c), and pShebuᶜot 1:2 (32d).

Why did some of the *amoraim* and the anonymous interlocutors of PT (סתמא דירושלמי) use "reverse order redundancy" in a departure from the methodology of their predecessors? The answer lies in the nature of the verses creating the redundancy. In all cases in PT where a posterior verse renders an anterior verse redundant, the second verse provides more details than the first. In this case, the verse in Joshua provides a more detailed description of the borders of the Land of Israel than does Deuteronomy.

The development of the "reverse order redundancy" format relies to a great extent on a formal trait of the Pentateuch. There are many examples of pericopes that present a rather general statement of the Torah's law followed by more detailed accounts in a later pericope. For example, Exod 20:24–26 offers a general statement about an altar and the laws of sacrifice. Regarding the latter, Leviticus 1–17 contain detailed descriptions of the sacrificial system, and Exod 30–40 presents more detailed information about the altars. Similarly, Exod 23:10–11 introduce the reader to the idea of a seventh year fallow, but it is Lev 25 and Deut 15 that detail the rules of the fallow and the obligation to remit debts during the seventh year.

49 There were different midrashic schools that viewed inclusive or extensive terms like כל in different ways. One school viewed such terms as *ribbuyim*. The other viewed them as *kelalim*, inclusive generalizations open to further definition if the Torah provided specifics. PT originally viewed כל as an inclusive generalization, not a *ribbui*.

We could multiply examples of this sort at least enough times to claim that this literary format typifies much of the legislative material in the Pentateuch. Therefore, it appears that the *tannaim* held that repetition alone was sufficient to create superfluity, while the midrashists in PT who used "reverse order redundancy" looked more carefully at the content of the verses and recognized a pattern: the Torah places more detailed enumeration of its laws after a more generalized opening statement of a rule. For the PT midrashists the issue was, "What do we need the introductory verse for? It is already included in and surpassed by the later verse." Thus, the latter, more detailed verse renders an earlier, less specific statement of a law superfluous. אם אינו ענין is the rabbinic means for removing the theologically unacceptable "flaw" of literary superfluity from the perfect revelation of the One who gave Israel the Torah.

In terms of the transferral or reapplication section of this אם אינו ענין, there is no persuasive logic supporting the new application of the verse in the Book of Joshua to the borders of foreign lands. That is because, as we have noted above, the amoraic *midrash* replaces a tannaitic *ribbui-midrash* with an אם אינו ענין interpretation. A *ribbui* provides the interpreter with a license to interpret beyond the text more or less as he sees fit. In tannaitic circles, as we have seen, אם אינו ענין did not function this way. Rather, it had a literary or formal logic that determined its halakhic outcome. The amoraic replacement of *ribbui* with אם אינו ענין left the latter without the kind of logic it had when the *tannaim* applied it.

pBaba Meẓiᶜaᵓ 3:1. A similar form of אם אינו ענין interpretation appears in pBaba Meẓiᶜaᵓ 3:1 (9a). There the *midrash* supports the mishnaic law that grants an unpaid bailee the multiple repayments the Torah requires of certain thieves.[50] This occurs when the bailee pays for any losses during his guardianship that the bailor sustained. According to pentateuchal law as interpreted by the Rabbis, the bailee could have freed himself of all liability by taking an oath.[51] The PT *sugya* uses אם אינו ענין to prove the point:

תלמוד ירושלמי מסכת בבא מציעא פרק ג דף ט עמוד א

ה״א/ המפקיד אצל חברו כו׳ מנן תיתי ליה אם המצא תמצא בידו הגניבה וכי אין אנו יודעין שאם ימצא הגנב ישלם שנים ומה תלמוד לומר שנים ישלם[52] אם אינו ענין לו תניהו ענין לשלפניו...[53]

50 The Torah requires a thief caught in possession of what he stole to repay twice the value of the theft. If he stole animals and sold or slaughtered them, he pays four or five times their worth depending on whether he stole a sheep or an ox. See Exod 21:37 and 22:3, 6 and 8.

51 See Exod 22:6–7 and compare it to Exod 22:10.

52 שנים ישלם: כ״ה בכי״ל. בכ״י אסקוריאל: חיים שנים ישלם.

53 The arrangement of verses in this interpretation is attested to by the major PT mss.

> One who deposits (an object) with his fellow, etc: Whence do we derive this?[54] (From) "If the theft is found in his hand (... he shall pay double)" (Exod 22:3). But don't we know that "if the thief is found he shall pay double" (from Exod 22:6)?[55] So why does the Torah say, "He shall pay double" (Exod 22:3). If it is superfluous in regard to itself, apply it to the matter which is ahead of it....[56]

A comparison of this *midrash* with the version in *Mek. de-RSBY*, Exod 22:6 again points out the compositional problems with the PT interpretation:

> מכילתא דרבי שמעון בר יוחאי פרק כב
>
> אם ימצא הגנב מה אני צריך והלא כ[בר] נאמר אם המצא תמצא בידו הגנבה (שמ׳ כב ג) מה ת״ל אם ימצא הגנב מגיד שאם שלם לבעל הפקדון ואחר כך נמצא גנב משלם תשלומי כפל וד׳ וה׳ לשני....[57]
>
> "If the thief is found (he shall pay double)" (Exod 22:6) – why do I need (this verse). Has it not already been stated, "If the theft is found in his hand (... he shall pay double)" (Exod 22:3). So why does it say "If the thief is found (he shall pay double)" (Exod 22:6)? (In order to inform us) that if he (the bailee) paid the bailor, and later the thief was found, he (the thief) pays the double payment or four or fivefold payment to the second one (i.e., the bailee)....

In this *midrash*, Exod 22:6 is viewed as redundant because it repeats the rule stated earlier in Exod 22:3 using almost the same formula (שנים ישלם, "double he shall pay" and ישלם שנים, "he shall pay double," respectively). This redundancy creates an opportunity to have the first verse, which appears in a sub-paragraph of the pentateuchal law of animal and human damagers, provide the standard rule: a thief pays the party from whom he stole. The superfluous repetition of the same rule in another sub-paragraph of this larger pericope on bailees provides an interpretational opportunity to grant the thief's repayment to the voluntary bailee.

In the Palestinian *midrash*, this orderly progression of redundancy is re-

54 I.e.,when an unpaid bailee pays the bailor rather than swearing an oath, what is the biblical source that informs us that he receives the thief's payment when the thief is found.

55 MS Escorial explicitly cites Exod 22:3, "If the animal is found alive in his possession he must repay double."

56 I.e., a pericope further along; in this case, Exod 22:6–8, which, according to rabbinic interpretations, discusses the obligations of unpaid bailees in the case of loss of the bailor's property.

57 See the version in *Mek. de-RSBY*, p.200, critical apparatus line 6: מ: או תשלומי ארבעה וחמשה לשומר.

versed, producing a convoluted midrashic logic. According to PT, Exod 22:3 is rendered extraneous by Exod 22:6. The superfluity at Exod 22:3 is then applied back to 22:6. But, as we have seen, it is actually Exod 22:3 that sets the standard of payment, and Exod 22:6 that unnecessarily repeats the known rules creating a superfluity that can be applied *in situ.*

Further, in the PT *midrash*, Exod 22:3 and 6 are not viewed within subparagraphs that are part of a larger pericope, but as verses within two separate pericopes. Again, the presumably amoraic midrashists of PT have apparently reconstructed a vaguely remembered tradition of a tannaitic *midrash* originally based on a *ribbui* using אם אינו ענין. They also use "reverse order redundancy" because Exod 22:6, which seems to be addressing a similar issue as Exod 22:3, is more inclusive. Exod 22:3 requires double payment for theft of animals alone. Exod 22:6ff. ultimately requires payment for the theft of all forms of chattels. Thus, the posterior verse in Exod 22 includes everything that the anterior one has and surpasses it in scope.

As in the prior example of a PT אם אינו ענין, the transferral of the rules of Subject A (Exod 22:3) to Subject B (Exod 22:6) is not particularly persuasive. The outcome is supposed to be that if the bailee pays rather than swears, should the one who stole the bailment be found, the bailee will receive the double payment owed by the thief. Yet, the Torah never actually discusses the issue of the bailee paying. It only knows of the bailee and the bailor coming before God or judges, the latter being the meaning the Rabbis assign to the term אלהים (Heb., *elohim*, usually meaning God). The litigants do this in order to determine, perhaps by oath, whether the bailee made improper use of the bailment or stole it himself.

Despite Scripture's plain sense, it is not surprising that the tannaitic *ribbui-midrash* provides a "scriptural basis" for the *halakhah* that a bailee who recompenses the bailor for the loss of the the bailment becomes entitled to the thief's double payment. After all, it is the nature of *ribbui-midrashim* to engage in "loose constructionist" interpretations of Scripture. Tannaitic אם אינו ענין *midrashim*, however, treat Scripture more conservatively, thereby indicating the amoraic provenance of the *derashah.*

אם אינו ענין Generated by Logic in a Single Pentateuchal Pericope

PT also contains an example of an אם אינו ענין *midrash* generated by a single pericope – namely, Exod 12:1–20, especially verses 14–20. The *midrash* provides a biblical basis for the destruction of leaven on the 14th of Nisan, the day prior to Passover:

תלמוד ירושלמי, פסחים פ"א, ה"א (כז א)

כתיב ושמרתם את המצות כי בעצם היום הזה הוצאתי את צבאותיכם מארץ מצרים. בראשון בארבעה עשר יום לחדש בערב תאכלו מצות וגומר. מה אנן קיימין אם לאכילת מצה כבר כתיב שבעת ימים מצות תאכלו. ואם לומר שמתחיל בארבעה עשר והכתיב עד יום האחד ועשרים לחודש. אלא אם אינו ענין לאכילת מצה תניהו ענין לביעור חמץ.

It is written: "You shall watch over the *mazzot* for on this very day I took your hosts forth from the Land of Egypt; in the first (month), on the fourteenth day of the month, you shall eat *mazzot* in the evening, etc." (Exod 12:17–18). With what are we dealing? If with (the requirement of) eating *mazzah*, it is already written, "Seven days shall you eat *mazzot*. . . ." (Exod 12:15);[58] and if (the verse means) to say that we begin (eating *mazzah*) on the fourteenth, is it not written,". . . until the twenty-first day of the month" (Exod 12:18)?[59] Rather, if it (Exod 12:18) is superfluous in regard to eating *mazzah*, apply it to the matter of the destruction of leaven (which according to this new application should take place on the 14th of Nisan). . . . (pPesaḥim 1:1 [27a])

On the surface this PT *midrash* gives the impression of being parallel to the tannaitic *midrash* in *Mek. de-RSBY*, Exod 12:18.[60] Yet it differs from all the tannaitic אם אינו ענין *midrashim* we have seen in one significant way: It renders Exod 12:18 superfluous twice within a single interpretation.

The first time, the *midrash* points out the superfluous repetition of the command to eat *mazzah,* stated in Exod 12:15 and then again in Exod 12:18. The second time, the *midrash* demonstrates how the 14th of Nisan mentioned in Exod 12:18 could not be a beginning point for the required consumption of *mazzah*. The verse's final clause states that *mazzah* should be eaten until the twenty-first of Nisan. If the 14th was the beginning of this period, *mazzah* consumption would be required for eight days. This, of course, would conflict with the seven day requirement of *mazzah* consumption previously stated in verse 15. This leaves Exod 12:18 without any acceptable meaning, which is itself a form of superfluity.

All this suggests that the *amoraim* knew of the existence of a tannaitic אם אינו ענין interpretation about the destruction of *hamez*. Whether changes in formulation of the *baraita* were due to oral transmission, scribal errors, or other

58 Thus, the verse in Exod 12:18 is extraneous.

59 If eating *mazzah* started on the fourteenth of Nisan and ended on the twenty-first, eight days of *mazzah* consumption would have taken place. Obviously, this would conflict with the commandment in Exod 12:15.

60 See above, pp. 111.

factors, the *amoraim* no longer possessed it in its exact original form.[61] Therefore, they reconstructed the *midrash* as best they could and according to their rules for the construction of אם אינו ענין *derashot.* As in other cases of this sort, this may be why what seems to be a derivation from a *baraita* is not introduced as such.[62]

As regards the new application section of the *midrash*, it follows a completely tannaitic pattern. The close if not interlocked connections in the pericope between eating *maẓẓah* and the destruction of leavened products (Exod 12:15; 12:18–19) create the framework for a literary logic that easily allows for the application of the superfluous rules about the consumption of *maẓẓah* to rules governing the disposal of leaven.

אם אינו ענין Based Solely on Logic

A single case of אם אינו ענין based on a discrepancy in logic appears in PT. It is part of a response of R. Bun to another אם אינו ענין interpretation. That first אם אינו ענין tries to prove that those who ritually defile the Sanctuary bring an *ʾasham*-offering whose value is commensurate with their economic status only when they know of their impure state, forget it, and remember it again. The same rule applies to those who eat sacred food in a state of ritual contamination. The first אם אינו ענין bases this idea on two consecutive verses, Lev 5:2–3. R. Bun suggests an alternative approach:

...אית דבעי נישמעינה מן הכא והוא ידע ואשם והלא כבר נאמר והוא טמא ואשם אלא אם אינו ענין לידיעה בתחילה תניהו ענין לידיעה בסוף רבי בון בעי אם לא נודע לו בסוף היך מביא קרבן אלא אם אינו ענין לידיעה בסוף תניהו לידיעה בתחילה....

... Some seek to derive it (the principle of "realization (of transgression) at the outset, realization (of transgression) at the end, and forgetting in between") from here: "and he knew and he was guilty" (Lev 5:3). But was it not already stated that "he was impure and guilty" (Lev 5:2). Rather, if

61 See Steven Fraade, "Literary Composition and Oral Perfromance in Early Midrashim," *Oral Tradition* (1999) 14:33–51. For a discussion of the impact of a combination of literacy and orality on Toseftan *baraitot*, see Yaakov Elman, *Authority and Tradition*, pp. 71–75; 79–80. Though the discussion there is about the Tosefta, it arguably has implications for midrashic *baraitot* as well. See also David Weiss Halivni, מקורות ומסורות – נשים (Tel Aviv: Dvir, 1968), pp. 8–9.

62 It is quite possible that PT considered this source a *baraita*. PT often does not identify *baraitot* as such. See Michael Higger, אוצר הברייתות (New York: De-be Rabbanan, 1939), 2:227; Chanoch Albeck, מחקרים בברייתא ותוספתא, p. 4=מבוא לתלמודים, p. 21; H. L. Strack and Günter Stemberger, *Introduction to the Talmud and Midrash*, p. 177; E. Z. Melamed, מדרשי הלכה של התנאים בתלמוד הירושלמי (Jerusalem: Magnes Press, 2000), p. לג.

(Lev 5:3) does not refer to knowledge (of cultic impurity) at the outset, apply it to knowledge (of cultic impurity) at the end.

R. Bun raised a question: If (the transgressor) had no knowledge (of his or her transgression) at the end,[63] why would (he or she) bring (an expiatory) sacrifice? Rather, if the issue of "realization (of transgression) at the end" is superfluous (from the point of view of logic), apply it (i.e., Lev 5:3) to "realization (of transgression) at the outset."

R. Bun, a third- to fourth-generation Palestinian *amora*, objects to the first אם אינו ענין because he sees nothing in Lev 5:2 that directly states the need for "knowledge at the outset." Rather, R. Bun believes the אם אינו ענין rests on a superfluity generated by logic. Why, he says, would a person bring an expiatory offering if he did not know of his sin? Therefore, "knowledge at the end"– that is, recognition of transgression temporally proximate to when one brings his or her *ʾasham*, is gainsaid. Hence, there is no need for Lev 5:3 to say, "and he knew... and he was guilty" in reference to "knowledge at the end." That being the case, a reasonable alternative application of Lev 5:3 is to "knowledge at the outset," when one first transgressed. This form of אם אינו ענין also conforms to the tannaitic model in which a logical problem with a verse substitutes for superfluous repetition, and its reapplication section also follows the tannaitic pattern of transferral of an idea from one rubric to a closely related one. In this case, the single rubric is "realization of transgression." Logical problems usually generate אם אינו ענין interpretations when the discussion of a particular legal rubric appears in a single scriptural pericope, which is the only one to discuss that rubric. Here, too, this is the case because only this pericope discusses bringing an *ʾasham* whose value fluctuates according to the economic status of the one who transgresses by entering the Sanctuary or eating sanctified foods in a state of cultic impurity.

אם אינו ענין that Supports a Rabbinic Law

PT contains a new development in אם אינו ענין that applies its superfluous element to a rabbinic enactment rather than to a biblical law. The example of this development is in the *gemara* of pShebiᶜit 1:1 (33a). There a *midrash* supports the *halakhah* of adding some time onto the sabbatical year fallow period at its beginning and at its end. According to mShebiᶜit 2:1, the practical result of this rule was that fields with trees in them could be plowed only until Shabuᶜot and fields without trees only until Passover. Nevertheless, R. Kruspai cites R. Johanan who said that R. Gamaliel abolished these prohibitions. His ability to do so indicates these regulations were of rabbinic origin, which is

63 I.e., at the point in time when the transgressor decided to bring his or her expiatory sacrifice.

the implication of the entire discussion in the Palestinian *gemara* on 33a.[64] The following is the אם אינו ענין *midrash* that supports adding on to the period of the sabbatical year fallow:

תלמוד ירושלמי מסכת שביעית פרק א דף לג עמוד א/מ"א

כתי' ששת ימי' תעש' מעשיך וביו' השביעי תשבות[65] וכתיב בחריש ובקציר תשבות מה אנן קיימין אם לענין שבת בראשית והלא כבר נאמר ששת ימים תעבד ועשית כל מלאכתך ואם לענין שבתות שנים והלא כבר נאמר שש שנים תזרע שדך ושש שנים תזמר כרמך אלא אם אינו ענין לשבת בראשית ולא לענין שבתות שנים תניהו ענין באיסור שני פרקים....[66]

It is written: "Six days shall you do your (work) activities and on the seventh day you shall rest" (Exod 23:12), and it is written: "You shall rest from plowing and harvesting" (Exod 34:21). What are we dealing with? If (you say) with the matter of the weekly Sabbath, has it not already said, "Six days shall you work and do all your (work) activities (and on the seventh day you shall rest)" (Exod 20:8–9). And if (you say regarding the verse in Exodus 34) that it is a reference to the sabbatical year, has it not already said, "Six years shall you sow your field and six years shall you dress your vineyard (and bring in its produce; but in the seventh year there shall be a Sabbath for the land)" (Lev 25:3–4). Rather, (if the redundancies produce no new information) regarding the weekly Sabbath or the sabbatical years, apply them to the prohibition of (working treeless fields and orchards) in the two seasons (i.e., Passover and Shabu^cot respectively)....

This אם אינו ענין *midrash* differs from any of the tannaitic אם אינו ענין *midrashim* we have seen previously. Unlike them, it discusses two rubrics, the weekly Sabbath and the sabbatical year, rather than one. In the case of each rubric, two pericopes generate redundancies.

The opening argument of the exposition raises the possibility that there is

64 See Maimonides' פירוש המשניות (ed. Kapah), mShebi[c]it 1:1, which affirms this understanding of the PT *gemara*. See also Maimonides' decision in *Mishneh Torah*, Laws of the Sabbatical Year and Jubilee, 3:1.

65 *Pene Mosheh* insists that the intended verse is Exod 34:21. None of the manuscripts or incunabula support him with the exception of MS London. See n. 59.

66 The manuscripts and early printed editions of PT are substantially in agreement regarding the formulation of this אם אינו ענין *midrash*. MS London, however, reads thus: ...אלא מה אני מקיים: אם אינו ענין לשבת בראשית ולא לענין שבתות שנים, תנהו ענין לתוספת שביעית. ואתו רבנן ותקינו שני פרקים הראשונים. The impression that this version makes is that the *midrash* generates a biblical requirement to add onto the sabbatical year. The Rabbis fulfilled the Torah's requirement by mandating the "prohibition of the two periods." See *Pene Mosheh* ad loc., who seems to understand the pShebi[c]it passage in the same way. Given *Pene Mosheh*'s emendations and understanding of the passage, one wonders whether he had access to a text similar to MS London.

a relationship between the Sabbath prohibition on work in general and the specific prohibitions on plowing and harvesting mentioned in Exod 34:21. Perhaps these specified activities define completely what is prohibited on the Sabbath.[67] Exodus 20:8–9 disabuses us of that notion by forbidding all forms of work, thereby rendering the verse prohibiting plowing and harvesting superfluous in regard to the weekly Sabbath. That being the case, perhaps we should apply the prohibition on plowing and harvesting to the issue of the sabbatical year. The *midrash* cuts off that avenue of interpretation by pointing out that Leviticus 25 has already dictated a Sabbath for the land, presumably one like the weekly Sabbath, which requires total cessation of all agricultural work. Bounded on one side by superfluity related to the weekly Sabbath and on the other by superfluity related to the sabbatical year, the verse prohibiting plowing and harvesting (34:21) appears to be totally unnecessary. PT's *gemara* uses an אם אינו ענין interpretation in its attempt to avoid leaving 34:21 devoid of meaning. Its midrashic conclusion is that the verse applies "to the 'prohibition of the two seasons.'"

This midrashic interpretation is quite ingenious. Since 34:21 is superfluous regarding two matters, the Sabbath and specific work prohibitions, it produces halakhic prohibitions on plowing for two different periods of time affecting two different kinds of fields. Furthermore, the prohibited time periods for plowing, Passover and Shabuᶜot, are outside the two temporal periods actually mentioned in the Torah – namely, the weekly Sabbath and the sabbatical year.

Regarding the reapplication section of this אם אינו ענין, we find that in this case typical tannaitic logic will not succeed. The "prohibition of the two seasons" is not a closely related pentateuchal rubric to the Sabbath or the sabbatical year because it is not a pentateuchal concept at all. This also precludes finding this prohibition within one of the pericopes that serves as the basis of the אם אינו ענין. In sum, then, the PT אם אינו ענין interpretation is novel in its use of two different rubrics, each with its own superfluous elements and its function as a support for a rabbinic enactment. Unfortunately, no other examples of this sort of אם אינו ענין appear in PT.

Tannaitic Midrashic Supports for Rabbinic Enactments

While this אם אינו ענין appears somewhat strange at first glance, it is not the earliest attempt to ground rabbinic enactments in the Torah. Tannaitic literature already records instances of this phenomenon. For example, *Sifre Deut.* provides a midrashic warrant for Hillel's enactment circumventing the

67 See Maimonides' פירוש המשניות, mShebiᶜit 1:1.

prohibition on collection of debts that had not been retrieved prior to the sabbatical year:

ספרי דברים פיסקא קיג

את אחיך תשמט ידך, ולא המוסר שטרותיו לבית דין מיכן אמרו התקין הלל פרוסבול מפני תיקון העולם שראה את העם שנמנעו מלהלוות זה את זה ועברו על מה שכתוב בתורה עמד והתקין פרוסבול וזהו גופו של פרוסבול מוסרני אני לכם פלוני ופלוני הדיינים שבמקום פלוני כל חוב שיש לי שאגבנו כל זמן שארצה והדיינים חותמים למטה או העדים.[68]

("That which is due you which is presently) with your brother you shall remit" (Deut 15:3) – excluding the one who turns his notes of indebtedness over to the court.[69] From here they (i.e., the Sages) said: Hillel enacted the *prosbul*[70] for the benefit of good communal order. For he saw that the populace refused to lend to one another (as the seventh year approached), and thus they violated that which was written in the Torah.[71] He (therefore) arose and enacted the *prosbul*. And this is the essence of the *prosbul*: (the one wishing to take advantage of it says,) "I am turning over to you, Sir A and Sir B, the judges in place C, every debt that is owed me in order that I may collect them whenever I wish. And the judges or the witnesses sign on the bottom (of the *prosbul* record).

Similarly, the Sages are credited with creating an enactment regarding the special ceremonial recitation required of those presenting their first fruits. Their enactment required that the special recitation that those who brought first fruits were obliged to pronounce should be read to both the literate and illiterate. Thereby both classes of individuals would be able perform

68 The formulation in *Midrash Tannaim*, Deut 15:3 is even clearer than that in Sifre Deut. There Hillel himself is depicted as using a midrashic interpretation of Deut 15:3 to underpin his enactment:

ואשר יהיה לך את אחיך תשמט ידך לא המוסר שטרותיו לבית דין מיכן התקין הלל פרוזבול וכך דרש הלל ואשר יהיה לך את אחיך לא המוסר שטרותיו לבית דין:

"That which is due you (which is presently) with your brother you shall remit"– but not the one who turns over his bills of indebtedness to the court. From this Hillel enacted the *prosbul*. And thus Hillel interpreted midrashically: "That which is due you (which is presently) with your brother you shall remit"– excluding the one who turns over his bills of indebtedness to the court.

69 Thereby making this private loan between himself and "his brother" into a public loan between "his brother" and the court. The loan is no longer due to the lender, and he is, therefore, under no obligation to remit.

70 A Greek loan word meaning "before the court." This essentially describes the activity of going before the court to turn one's notes of indebtedness over to it.

71 See Deut 15:9, which warns against refusing to lend as the sabbatical year approached.

this recitation equally well. Consequently, the illiterate would be spared the embarrassment that had kept them from fulfilling their obligation to bring their first fruit offerings to the Temple. The *midrash* in *Sifre Deut.* 301 tells us that the Sages who legislated this arrangement "relied on Scripture" in doing so:

ספרי דברים פיסקא שא

(ה) וענית ואמרת, נאמר כאן עניה ונאמר להלן עניה מה עניה האמורה להלן בלשון הקדש אף עניה האמורה כאן בלשון הקדש מיכן אמרו בראשונה כל מי שהוא יודע לקרות קורא ושאינו יודע לקרות מקרים אותו נמנעו מלהביא התקינו שיהו מקרים את היודע ואת מי שאינו יודע סמכו על המקרא וענית אין עניה אלא מפי אחרים.[72]

"And you shall respond and say" (Deut 26:5) – It states here "response" and it states there "response."[73] Just as "response" there implies (response)

72 Another midrashic interpretation of this sort appears in *Sifra*, *Behar* 4:5:

וכי תאמרו עתידים אתם לומר מה נאכל בשנה השביעית הן לא נזרע ולא נאסף את תבואתינו, אם אין אנו זורעים מה אנו אוספים, אמר רבי עקיבא מיכן סמכו חכמים על הספיחים שיהו אסורים בשביעית וחכמים אומרים אין ספיחים אסורים מדברי תורה אלא מדברי סופרים.

"And if you say" (Lev 25: 20) – in the future you will say, "What shall we eat in the seventh year? Behold, we have not sown nor gathered our produce. . . ."– if we do not sow, what do we reap? R. Akiba said: From here the Sages relied (on Scripture) in order to prohibit (produce generated by) spontaneous growth during the sabbatical year. And the Sages say: Spontaneous sabbatical growth is not prohibited according to Torah law but only according to rabbinic enactment.

The formulation of R. Akiba's statement is strange in light of the Sages' response. R. Akiba, as his view is formulated here, stated that the Sages declared spontaneous sabbatical growth prohibited on the basis of a midrashic inference drawn from Lev 25:20, but his colleagues retort that the prohibition of spontaneous sabbatical growth is not Torah law but rabbinic enactment. According to this, R. Akiba holds that the Sages' reliance on the verse and its *midrash* produces a pentateuchal rule.

This formulation also appears in the Yalqut's citation of *Sifra*. However, in the *Sifra* commentaries of R. Abraham b. David of Posquierres and Rabbenu Hillel, the citation contains several formulary differences. Of importance to us is the word חכמים, "Sages," which does not appear in their versions of R. Akiba's dictum. This is of small help since סמכו, "they relied," does appear, begging the question of who "they" are if not the Sages. The formulation of the *midrash* according to bPesaḥim 51b is "מכאן לספיחים שהן אסורין," "from here (we derive) that spontaneous sabbatical growth is prohibited." This formulation makes no reference to the problematic elements, "Sages" and "relied," that we have seen in other versions. Furthermore, R. Samson of Sens's version of *Sifra* as cited in his Mishnah commentary, mShebiᶜit 9:1, mirrors bPesaḥim's formula.

In sum, while it appears that R. Akiba considered spontaneous sabbatical growth prohibited according to Torah law (see also pMaᶜaserot 5:4 [51d]), the role or function of the Sages in determining that the prohibition is pentateuchal or rabbinic is not completely clear.

73 See Deut 21:7 and *Sifre Deut.*, 210.

> in the holy tongue (i.e., Hebrew), so "response" here implies in the holy tongue. From here they have said: At the outset all who knew how to read (the ceremonial formula that was part of offering the first-fruits) would read (on their own). Those who did not know how to read, others helped them recite (the formula). They (i.e., the illiterates) ceased to bring (their first fruits because they were distinguishable from the literate by being helped to recite the ritual formula and were embarrassed).[74] They (i.e., the Sages) passed an enactment that they should help both the literate and illiterate to read the formula. (In legislating thus) they relied on Scripture: "and you shall respond"– response only (occurs) in relation to (that which comes) from the mouths of others.[75]

These two examples of tannaitic halakhic midrashic support for rabbinic enactments represent part of a somewhat larger pool of examples such as *Sifra*, *Zabim* 4:6 and *Sifra*, *Behar* 1:3 and 4:5. Since tannaitic sources already provide support for rabbinic *taqqanot* and *gezerot*, it is no surprise that we can find amoraic sources that do the same.

It is interesting to note that several of the rabbinic enactments that receive midrashic support using the rhetorical form מיכן (מכאן) סמכו are supposedly from the pre-Destruction period.[76] The two cases we analyzed fall into this

74 *Midrash Tannaim*, *Deut.* 26:5, states directly that the embarrassment of the illiterate was the reason for the enactment:

> מיכן אמ׳ בראשונה כל מי שהוא יודע לקרות [קורא] ושאינו יודע מקרין אותו נמצאו נמנעין מלהביא בכורים כדי שלא יכלמו התקינו שיהו מקרין את היודע כמי שאינו יודע וסמכו על המקרא הזה וענית אין ענייה אלא מפי אחרים.

> From this (verse, Deut 26:5) they said: At the outset all those who knew how to read, read; those who did not know how to read, others helped them read. When it was discovered that they (i.e., the illiterate) ceased to bring their first-fruits so as not to be embarrassed, they (i.e., the Sages) enacted that others should help both those who knew how (to read) and those who did not know (how to read). They relied on this scriptural verse (Deut 26:5 in order to make this enactment), "And you shall respond/answer)"– response only (occurs) in relation to (that which comes) from the mouths of others.

75 That is, one responds to the one helping him to read by repeating what he says.

76 Rescinding the "prohibition of the two periods" is attributed to Rabban Gamaliel. PT claims that when the Sages put it into force, למקרא סמכו, they relied on or connected their decision to Scripture, and they did the same when they rescinded it. According to our claim, the Rabban Gamaliel and the Sages who retracted the prohibition is Rabban Gamaliel I. There are two other contenders, however: R. Gamaliel of Yavneh (II) and R. Gamaliel, son of R. Judah ha-Nasi. The *variae lectiones* in MS Vatican, London, and Yalqut Shim'oni have the formula רבן גמליאל הנשיא, Rabban Gamaliel the Prince (head of the Sanhedrin). See also Saul Lieberman, תוספתא כפשוטה – שביעית, p. 483, n. 15, in which he indicates several other sources that include this reading. This suggests that Rabban Gamaliel I is meant. On the other hand, see Saul Lieberman, תוספתא כפשוטה – שביעית,

category. Similarly, the *Sifra Zabim* source cites R. El'azar b. 'Arakh, who claims that Lev 15:11 served as a support for the *gezerah* about "cleanness of the hands," which BT and PT attribute to Hillel and Shammai. A Babylonian *baraita* directs us to Exod 22:16 as the source upon which the Sages relied when they enacted the requirement of the *ketubah*, an enactment that another BT *baraita* attributes to Simeon b. Shetaḥ.[77] Perhaps the use of מיכן (מכאן) סמכו in these instances is an attempt to valorize the early (Pharisaic?) masters. Claiming that they would legislate only with the Torah's license would indicate their modesty. That they could find such license showed their interpretive ingenuity.

There are, however, several purportedly pre-Destruction rabbinic enactments that have either no pentateuchal verse to support them or no scriptural support at all.[78] There are also rabbinic enactments that are not assigned to the pre-Destruction period that have the rhetorical formula מיכן (מכאן) סמכו attached to them.[79] These cases suggest that the use of the מיכן (מכאן) סמכו formula may have had a more rhetorically oriented function. Namely, the formula indicates rabbinic legislation that has support from a pentateuchal verse with legal content but is nevertheless not "pentateuchal" *halakhah*. This makes מיכן (מכאן) סמכו a close relative to אף על פי שאין ראיה לדבר when the latter supports halakhic legislation.

אם אינו ענין Interpretations Based on Rabbinic Texts

pRosh ha-Shanah 1:10=pMegillah 3:7. Another interesting phenomenon in PT is the application of the אם אינו ענין hermeneutic to rabbinic texts rather than

---

p. 482–3, line 5. R. Samuel Sirilio in his Mishnah commentary to mShebiᶜit 1:1, s.v. למה נאמר, holds that R. Gamaliel is R. Judah ha-Nasi's son. While there is considerable support for the eldest Rabban Gamaliel (I) as the one who rescinded the "prohibition of the two periods," the matter remains uncertain.

77 See bKetubot 10a and Shabbat 14b. Both these Babylonian *baraitot* have no corroboration from other sources that they are actually tannaitic. In fact, the closest parallel to the *baraita* that ascribes the enactment of the *ketubah* to R. Simeon b. Shetaḥ is in pShabbat 1:4 (3d)=pPesaḥim 1:6 (27d) and pKetubot 8:11 (32c) in the names of the following *amoraim*: R. Zeʿira b. R. Abuna in the name of R. Jeremiah, or R. Zeʿira (Zeʿura), R. Abina (Abuna) citing R. Jeremiah, and R. Jonah (in Pesaḥim: R. Juda). For some of the explanations of why Palestinian *memrot* appear in BT as *baraitot*, see Introduction, p. 21 and n. 29 there. On the basis of these sources, it seems that BT created its own "history" of the *ketubah*.

78 See, for example, mSotah 9:9–10. There no scriptural source supports the action of Johanan the High Priest. A source in Hosea supports the action of R. Johanan b. Zakkai regarding the ordeal of the suspected wife, but no source supports the abolition of the rite of the beheaded heifer. See also the previous note. In the sources mentioned there, there are references to enactments that declared the "land of the gentiles," glassware, and metalware impure. The extant formative rabbinic literature provides no scriptural supports for any of this rabbinic legislation.

79 See *Sifra, Behar* 1:3 and 4:5, bBeẓah 15b.

biblical ones.[80] One of the best examples appears in pRosh ha-Shanah 1:10 (57d) = pMegillah 3:7 (73c). The question the passage addresses is whether the harvesting of the *ᶜomer* overrides the Sabbath if it is performed during the day.[81]

רשב״ל בעי קצירת העומר מהו שתדחה את השבת ביום התיב ר׳ אביי והא תנינן מצותו לקצור בלילה נקצר ביום כשר ודוחה השבת. ולא קיבלה. א״ר אחא חזר רשב״ל מן הדא כיון שחשיכה אמר להן בא השמש אומר הין בא השמש אומר הין מה אנן קיימין אם ללילה כבר הוא אומר אלא אם אינו ענין ללילה תניהו ענין ליום....

R. Simeon b. Laqish asked, "Does the harvesting of the *ᶜomer* override the Sabbath (when it is performed) during the day?" R. Abbaye responded, "Is it not taught (mMenaḥot 10:9), 'The normal requirement is to harvest (the *ᶜomer*) at night; if (however) it is harvested in the day, it is fit, and it overrides the Sabbath.'" He (R. Simeon b. Laqish) did not accept (this response).[82] R. Aḥa said, "R. Simeon b. Laqish retracted (his rejection of R. Abbaye's response) based on this (mMenaḥot 10:3):[83] 'once it became dark

80 This phenomenon was already recognized by R. Isaiah di Trani, פסקי הרי״ד (Jerusalem: Makhon ha-Talmud ha-Yisraeli, 1964), pp. רכ״ט-ר״ל. For specific examples, see I. H. Weiss, דור דור ודורשיו (Jerusalem: Dor, 1910, reprinted most recently in Jerusalem and Tel Aviv: Ziv, 1963), 3:10 and recently Yaakov Elbaum, "Prospective *Derash* and Retrospective *Peshat*," in *Modern Scholarship in the Study of Torah*, pp. 229–32.

81 The requirement to harvest an *ᶜomer*'s measure of barley is found in Lev 23:10–11. According to rabbinic interpretation of Lev 23:9–14, the waving of this wheat permits the consumption of grain that has grown before the second day of Passover. The rabbinic interpretation of this passage also requires, under normal circumstances, the harvesting of the *ᶜomer* at night. If the cutting of the *ᶜomer* falls on the Sabbath, it overrides the prohibition of harvesting on the Sabbath.

82 Various suggestions as to why R. Simeon b. Laqish did not feel this *mishnah* was conclusive have been given. *Pene Mosheh* suggests that R. Simeon b. Laqish might have parsed the *mishnah* in such a way that what he understood to be the first mishnaic clause discussed the issues of *prima facie* performance and "after the fact" acceptability of the cutting of the *ᶜomer*. The next clause discussed overriding the Sabbath, and it applied only to the proper performance of the ceremony. In that case the *mishnah* would be translated thus: מצותו לקצור בלילה, נקצר ביום כשר. ודוחה השבת. "The normal requirement is to harvest it at night, but if it is harvested during the day it is fit. And it overrides the Sabbath (when performed properly)." This is also the view of R. Jacob David of Slutzk in his תוספות הרי״ד and one interpretation in *Qorban ha-ᶜEdah* also accepts this position.

83 The fact that PT reports that R. Aḥa (Palestinian *amora*, primarily fourth generation) commented on the discussion between R. Simeon b. Laqish and R. Abbaye gives some support to the accuracy of the attributions and the content of the argument. See the criteria that Jacob Neusner lists for the verification of attributed statements, criterion 3, in *The Pharisees, Rabbinic Perspectives* (New York: KTAV, 1985), pp. 233–35. Nevertheless, Neusner disallows the use of these criteria in relation to attributions and concepts that appear in the *Talmudim*. See David Kraemer's succinct recapitulation of Neusner's views in his "On the Reliability of Attributions," p. 176. The rest of that article seeks to demonstrate that, in a general sense, talmudic attributions are, indeed, reliable. See, especially, pp. 182–89. For a more detailed treatment of this issue, see David Krae-

> he (the one harvesting the ᶜomer) says, "Has the sun set? The assemblage responds, "Yes." (He repeats), "Has the sun set?" The assemblage responds, "Yes." (. . . On the Sabbath he says to them, "Is it the Sabbath?" They reply, "Yes." He repeats, "Is it the Sabbath?" They reply, "Yes.") With what are we dealing? If with the night,[84] it has already been stated (in mMenaḥot 10:3). Therefore, if it (mMenaḥot 10:9) is superfluous (regarding the nighttime harvesting of the ᶜomer which overrides the Sabbath), apply it to the matter of (harvesting the ᶜomer) during the day. . . .[85]

In this case of אם אינו ענין interpretation there is no reference to a biblical passage at all. The texts that generate the interpretation are two mishnaic pericopes within a single chapter of tractate Menaḥot. The logic of the interpretation seems to be as follows: The issues of harvesting the ᶜomer at night and and on the Sabbath are directly addressed in mMenaḥot 10:3. R. Simeon b. Laqish's initial interpretation of mMenaḥot 10:9 also seems to understand the *mishnah*'s final clause as referring to nighttime harvesting of the ᶜomer, which the *mishnah* declares to be permitted on the Sabbath. This makes mMenaḥot 10:9 into a superfluous repetition of the rules already stated in mMenaḥot 10:3.[86] Therefore, an אם אינו ענין interpretation based on these two mishnaic pericopes transfers the application of the redundancy to the issue of a daytime harvesting of the ᶜomer, which is a subject also mentioned in mMenaḥot 10:9. This application changes mMenaḥot 10:9 from a redundant *mishnah* into one that adds to the information we already know. We now discover two things about the ᶜomer harvested during the day: 1) it is, after the fact, fit for the ceremonial waving on the second day of Passover, and 2) it overrides the Sabbath despite its failure to conform to the rule that the ᶜomer should be harvested at night. Implicitly, this approach suggests a belief that the Mishnah, like the Torah, does not contain any gratuitous redundancies. Does this im-

---

mer, *The Mind of the Talmud* (Oxford: Oxford University Press, 1990). For our purposes, assigning the discussion of R. Simeon b. Laqish and R. Abbaye to the second amoraic generation, even if not exactly to these *amoraim*, is sufficient and will contribute significantly to our discussion of the application of אם אינו ענין to rabbinic sources in PT. See also David Goodblatt, "Towards the Rehabilitation of Talmudic History," *The History of Judaism – The Next Ten Years*, Brown Judaica Series 21, ed. Baruch M. Bokser (Chico: Scholars Press, 1980), pp. 37–38.

84 In mMenaḥot 10:3 it says clearly "once it became dark." Further, the *mishnah* discusses both weekdays and the Sabbath. Hence, the case of overriding the Sabbath on the night of the ᶜomer harvesting is completely covered by this *mishnah*.

85 I.e., that the daytime harvesting of the ᶜomer should also override the Sabbath.

86 Note that R. Simeon b. Laqish's אם אינו ענין follows the tannaitic form for redundancy: the second citation is the redundant one since it gratuitously repeats the information contained in the first citation. We will argue further in this chapter that the earliest *amoraim* continued to use the tannaitic form of אם אינו ענין.

ply that the Mishnah has acquired scriptural status? This is an issue to which we will return.

pSotah 3:6. A second example of this phenomenon appears in pSotah 3:6 (19a–b). There, according to R. Simeon, a penitent priest's meal-offering (מנחת חוטא) is subject to the removal of a token handful of flour (קמיצה) to be offered on the altar. R. Simeon also holds that the remainder of the offering should be burned on the altar separately from the token handful in accordance with the Torah's decree that priestly meal-offerings should be offered *in toto* (Lev 6:16). The Palestinian *gemara* then seeks information regarding the remainder's status. Is it still holy and similar to the token handful, or has the removal of the handful desanctified it? The *gemara* cites R. Elazar b. Simeon, R. Simeon's son, in what appears to be a slightly different formulation of R. Simeon's viewpoint. It is here that the אם אינו ענין interpretation enters to draw a distinction between R. Simeon's view and his son's position.

> ...אילין שיריים משם מה הן באין משם קומץ משם שיריים. אין תימר משום קומץ אינו נותנן בלילה ואינו נותנן לאחר מיתה. ואינו מחשב להן ואין תימר משום שיריים נותנן בלילה ונותנן לאחר מיתה. מהו שיחשב להם. נישמעינה מן הדא רבי אלעזר ברבי שמעון[87] אומר הקומץ קרב לעצמו והשיריים מתפזרין על גבי הדשן. רבי יוחנן בעי מה אנן קיימין אם בדשן שלמעלן כבר אמר׳ ר׳ שמעון אלא אם אינו ענין לדשן של מעלן תניהו ענין לדשן של מטן. הדא אמרה נותנן בלילה ונותנן לאחר מיתה ומחשב להן....

> ... those remainders (of the meal-offering), what is their status: (that of) the token handful or (the desanctified) remainders? If you say (their status is equivalent to) the handful, then one may not place them on the altar at night or after the death (of the one who dedicated the offering). Also, one may not have any disqualifying intention regarding them.[88] If, however, you say that their status is (that of desanctified) remainders (of the meal-offering), one may place them on the altar at night, or after the death (of the donor). But what is the rule regarding improper intention?[89]

87 רבי אלעזר ברבי שמעון: בכי״ל ר׳ שמעון ברבי אלעזר, ובהמשך הסוגיא, ר׳ אלעזר ברבי שמעון. וכ״ה בתוספתא (צוקרמנדל) מנחות פ״ח, ה״ד .

88 It was prohibited to offer sacrifices at night, and once a sacrifice was ownerless, it lost its status. Improper intention had to do with offering the sacrifice with the intention of eating it in a place where such consumption was unacceptable according to the Torah or at a time beyond the limits set by the Torah.

89 *Pene Mosheh* explains the issue thus: This matter is in question because the rules governing improper intention apply to offerings that become permitted either for human use or for sacrifice. The remnants of a penitent priest's sin offering may not be fit for either. They may not be eaten because a priest's meal-offering must be totally offered; hence, they may still have some sort of

> Let us resolve this matter by means of this (citation). R. Elazar b. Simeon says, "The token handful (of the penitent priest's meal-offering) is brought by itself, and the remnants (of it) are scattered on the ashes."[90] R. Johanan asked, "What are we dealing with (in R. Elazar b. Simeon's statement). If with the "upper" ashes (that are on the altar itself), R. Simeon already has said (this).[91] Rather, if (R. Elazar b. Simeon's statement) is extraneous regarding the "upper" ashes, apply (his words) to the "lower" ashes.[92] That means that one can place them (i.e., the meal-offering's remnants on the altar) at night or after (the donor's) death, and one may have improper intention (regarding them without penalty). . . .

Here, as in the previous example, no biblical verses play a role in the formation of the אם אינו ענין interpretation. The source is a *baraita* in tMenaḥot which we might have interpreted as a son explaining his father's views with greater precision. That is, we might have understood R. Elazar b. Simeon's statement about the remnants of a penitent priest's meal-offering being scattered on the ashes as a more detailed explanation of R. Simeon's statement, "They were brought separately." After all, there was a place on the altar where the ashes were piled.[93] But R. Johanan's analysis implies that R. Simeon's statement already referred to the ashes piled on the altar and, therefore, R. Elazar b. Simeon's statement had to mean something else in order not to be redundant. In this case, it meant depositing the burnt remnants of the penitent priest's meal offering on the ash heap at the altar's base or elsewhere in the Temple precincts or beyond them. אם אינו ענין serves as R. Johanan's means of showing how R. Elazar b. Simeon's opinion must differ from his father's view.

---

sacred status. But if one claims the remnants are desacralized, then they are not fit for sacrificial purposes. Since they may not be fit for human use or sacrifice, are they or are they not subject to the rules of improper intention? *Pene Mosheh* draws his view from R. Jose b. R. Bun's comment on the conclusions drawn from the *sugya*'s אם אינו ענין.

The *Qorban ha-ᶜEdah* simplifies the question: Is the act of placing the remnants of a penitent priest's meal-offering on the altar a sacrificial act since the Torah requires the total consumption of a priest's meal-offering on the altar, or is is merely an act of disposal? Saul Lieberman claims the whole section refers back to mSotah 3:7. See תוספתא כפשוטה – סוטה, p. 632–33, lines 38–39, especially p. 633.

90 Both R. Simeon's and R. Elazar b. Simeon's statements appear together in tMenaḥot 8:3–4: ... רבי שמעון אומר: מנחת חוטא של כהנים נקמצות. הקומץ קרב לעצמו ושירים קריבין לעצמן. ר׳ אלעזר בר׳ שמעון אומר: הקומץ קרב בעצמו והשירים מתפזרין על גבי הדשן. As Lieberman notes in תוספתא כפשוטה – סוטה, p. 632, n. 31, this is one unit despite Tosefta Zuckermandel's separation of R. Simeon's statement from his son's.

91 PT understands the phrase קריבין לעצמן ("offered by themselves") to mean offered on the altar. This is the standard meaning of קרב.

92 I.e., on the ash heap at the altar's base where desacrilized remnants of the sacrifices were placed.

93 See *Pene Mosheh* ad loc., s.v. אם בדשן שלמעלן.

Again we find that PT reports that a second-generation *amora*, R. Johanan, applied אם אינו ענין to a tannaitic source. As noted in the Introduction to this work, the subject of attributions is a matter of significant controversy, which would place the attribution of this אם אינו ענין to R. Johanan in doubt. In this case, however, there is external testimony in BT that supports that R. Johanan discusses the issue attributed to him.[94] This testimony appears in bMenaḥot 72b (Mishnah) and 73b–74a (*gemara*), which parallels the *sugya* in PT in many ways. The following citations of the PT and BT *sugyot* show the relationship between the two sources:

pSotah 3:6

1. ... תמן תנינן: ר׳ שמעון אומר: מנחת חוטא של כהן נקמצת והקומץ קרב לעצמו והשיריים קריבין לעצמן. ושניהן מקרא אחד דורשין: „והיתה לכהן כמנחה.״

2. רבנין אמרין כמנחת נדבתו. מה מנחתו קריבה בכלול,[95] אף זו קריבה בכלול. ר׳ שמעון אומר: הרי עשירית האיפה של כהן כעשירית האיפה של ישראל. מה עשירית האיפה של ישראל נקמצת, אף זו נקמצת. אי מה זו נאכלת, אף זו נאכלת? ת״ל: וכל מנחת כהן כליל תהיה לא תאכל.

3. אילין שיריים משם מה הן באין משם קומץ משם שיריים. אין תימר משום קומץ אינו נותנן בלילה ואינו נותנן לאחר מיתה ואינו מחשב להן. ואין תימר משום שיריים נותנן בלילה ונותנן לאחר מיתה. מהו שיחשב להם? נישמעינה מן הדא: רבי אלעזר ברבי שמעון אומר הקומץ קרב לעצמו והשיריים מתפזרין על גבי הדשן. רבי יוחנן בעי מה אנן קיימין אם בדשן שלמעלן כבר אמר׳ ר׳ שמעון אלא אם אינו ענין לדשן של מעלן תניהו ענין לדשן של מטן. הדא אמרה נותנן בלילה ונותנן לאחר מיתה ומחשב להן....

4. רבי בא בר ממל בעי: הך ר׳ אלעזר בי ר׳ שמעון בשיטת חכמים או בשיטת אביו? אין בשיטת אביו יקרב למעלן, אין בשיטת חכמים, לא יקמוץ. בשיטת אביו הוא. ר׳ שמעון אומר: הרי עשירית האיפה של כהן כעשירית האיפה של ישראל. מה עשירית האיפה של ישראל נקמצת, אף זו נקמצת. אי מה זו נאכלת, אף זו נאכלת? ת״ל: וכל מנחת כהן כליל תהיה לא תאכל. ותהא כליל. ולא[96] תאכל הקשתי׳, לא הקשתי׳ לכליל תקטר....

94 Externality means that "one source is demonstrably independent of the source in question." See Kraemer, "On the Reliability of Attributions." Even Jacob Neusner, whose skepticism about attributions is well known, admits that PT and BT "assuredly stand autonomous from one another." See Jacob Neusner, *The Bavli and Its Sources: The Case of Tractate Sukkah* (Atlanta: Scholars Press, 1987), p. 50. David Kraemer makes use of this externality to verify attributions. See Kraemer, "On the Reliability of Attributions," pp. 179–81. Our sources are analogous to the pBerakhot and bShabbat sources that Kraemer analyzed.

95 בכלול: בכי״ל: „בבלול״ בשני המקומות. נראה כט״ס, ותוקן בדפוס וונציה.

96 ולא: נמחק הוי״ו ע״י הסופר של כי״ל, והוסיף מגיה א׳ למ״ד. מזה התהוותה גירסא הנקראת כך: ללא תאכל הקשתי׳, לא הקשתי׳ לכליל תקטר.

bMenaḥot

1. מתני׳... ר״ש אומר מנחת חוטא של כהנים נקמצת והקומץ קרב לעצמו, ושיריים קריבין לעצמן.

2. גמרא: מנה״מ? דת״ר: ״והיתה לכהן כמנחה״ – שתהא עבודתה כשרה בו. אתה אומר שתהא עבודתה כשרה בו או אינו אלא להתיר מנחת חוטא של כהנים? ומה אני מקיים ״וכל מנחת כהן כליל תהיה לא תאכל״? מנחת נדבתו, אבל חובתו תהא נאכלת. תלמוד לומר: ״והיתה לכהן כמנחה״ – מקיש חובתו לנדבתו. מה נדבתו אינה נאכלת, אף חובתו אינה נאכלת. אמר ר׳ שמעון: וכי נאמר ״והיתה לכהן כמנחתו״? והלא נאמר אלא ״כמנחה״! אלא להקיש מנחת חוטא של כהנים כמנחת חוטא של ישראל. מה מנחת חוטא של ישראל נקמצת אף מנחת חוטא של כהנים נקמצת. אי מה מנחת חוטא של ישראל נקמצת ושיריה נאכלין, אף מנחת חוטא של כהנים נקמצת ושיריה נאכלין? ת״ל: ״לכהן למנחה״ – לכהן למנחה ולא לאשים למנחה. הא כיצד? קומץ קרב בעצמו, ושיריים קריבין לעצמן....

3. תניא אידך: מנחת חוטא של כהנים נקמצת והקומץ קרב לעצמו, ושיריים קריבין לעצמן. רבי אלעזר ברבי שמעון אומר הקומץ קרב לעצמו והשיריים מתפזרין על גבי הדשן. א״ר חייא בר אבא: הוי בה רבי יוחנן: בית הדשן דהיכא? אי דלמעלה, היינו אבוה! אי דלמטה, יש לך דבר שקרב למטה?

א״ל ר׳ אבא: דילמא לאיבוד? אחיכו עליה. וכי יש דבר שקרב לאיבוד?

4. תני אבוה דר׳ אבין: ״וכל מנחת כהן כליל תהיה לא תאכל״ – לאכילה הקשתיה לא לדבר אחר....[97]

I have arranged the sections of these two *sugyot* numerically to indicate where there is similarity between them. The mishnaic starting point (1) of both citations is the same. PT only summarizes the debate between R. Simeon and the Sages about how a penitent priest's meal offering is to be handled (2). R. Simeon says that one who offers a penitent priest's meal offering takes a token handful from it and places the remnants on the ash heap of the altar. The Sages require that one who offers the meal offering should treat it like a priest's free-will offering – namely, he should offer it completely on the main altar without separating a token handful. BT 2, however, cites a complete *baraita* that includes this dispute and full midrashic justification for it.[98]

Section 3 in PT contains a well developed discussion about the status of the remnants of a penitent priest's meal offering. It includes R. Johanan's question regarding which ash heap R. Elazar b. Simeon intended in his ruling. This ends with the אם אינו ענין that determines that R. Elazar b. Simeon opined that the

97 אין בכה״י ש״נ חשובים להבנת בסוגיא, וכולם גורסים ״א״ר חייא בר אבא: הוי בה רבי יוחנן: בית הדשן דהיכא? אי דלמעלה, היינו אבוה! אי דלמטה, יש לך דבר שקרב למטה?״ בש״נ קטנים מכ״י לכ״י.

98 The BT *baraita* is parallel to *Sifra*, *Ḥobah*, 19:11.

remnants of meal offering should be scattered on the ash heap at the bottom of the Temple's main altar. This implies that the remnants are not sacred and can be treated accordingly. BT 3 does not even raise the issue of the status of the remnants of a penitent priest's meal offering. Rather, it contains only an investigation of the implications of R. Elazar b. Simeon's opinion in tMenaḥot 8:4. This investigation includes PT's citation of R. Johanan's query, but it does not resolve it using אם אינו עניין. Rather, BT cites an unsuccessful attempt by R. Abba to answer R. Johanan's question. This does not appear in PT at all.

Section 4 in PT starts with R. Abba b. Memel's question about whether R. Elazar b. R. Simeon's position is more closely related to the Sages' opinion or to his father's view. The discussion concludes that his position is more closely related to that of his father. PT then cites a midrashic *baraita* attributed to R. Simeon. The Palestinian *sugya* then comments on this *baraita* and concludes that a penitent priest's offering is analogized to the prohibition on eating a priestly offering, but it is not analogized to the obligation to burn the offering completely. As the commentators on PT understand this sequence of citation and comment, the *baraita* is supposed to show that both R. Simeon and R. Elazar b. R. Simeon agree that the meal offering of a penitent priest is not to be offered *in toto*. They only disagree about where the disposal of the remnants of the meal offering should take place.

BT 4 cites what purports to be a midrashic *baraita* in the name of the father of R. Abin. The citation contains the verse of the midrashic *baraita* that PT cites in its section 4, but BT concludes the *midrash* with what appears in PT 4 as the anonymous comment on the midrashic *baraita* of R. Simeon. The *midrash* of the father of R. Abin seems to be a short summary, perhaps for mnemonic purposes, of the longer *midrash* of R. Simeon cited in BT 2. The issue of whether R. Elazar b. R. Simeon agrees more with the Sages or with R. Simeon does not appear in BT 4.

I have undertaken this detailed description of the relationship between the PT and BT sources in order to demonstrate that the attribution of the אם אינו עניין interpretation of tMenaḥot – or at least its general context – to R. Johanan is sound. That R. Johanan's אם אינו עניין interpretation does not appear in BT may be due to the derivation of PT's and BT's traditions from related but different Palestinian sources. One source may have possessed R. Johanan's own answer to his question in the form of his אם אינו עניין interpretation. The other may have had R. Abba's response to R. Johanan's query instead of the אם אינו עניין. The former source entered PT; the latter source became part of BT's *sugya*. Nevertheless, both sources identify R. Johanan as the author of a similar comment about R. Elazar b. Simeon's opinion.[99]

99 See for this hypothesis J. N. Epstein, מבואות לספרות האמוראים (Jerusalem and Tel Aviv: Magnes Press and Dvir, 1962), pp. 292 and 321–22. Other possibilities exist, and I list them here in what

אם אינו ענין Interpretations of Rabbinic Sources Summary

The two examples of the application of אם אינו ענין to a *mishnah* and to an opinion in a toseftan *baraita* emerge from the second generation of Palestinian *amoraim*, more specifically from R. Johanan and his student, R. Simeon b. Laqish. The two interpretations also share formal characteristics. In each case, the אם אינו ענין interpretation results from a redundant repetition of a law. This redundancy occurs within a single chapter of Mishnah or Tosefta, and the second repetition of the law is the source of the redundancy. The fact that the redundancy occurs within a single chapter of Mishnah or Tosefta differentiate these אם אינו ענין *derashot* from tannaitic ones. In tannaitic *midrash* of the Pentateuch, this would more likely lead to a *ribbui* rather than an אם אינו ענין *derashah*. However, the fact that the second repetition of a rule generates the redundancy distinguishes this form of אם אינו ענין interpretation from all the other PT cases of אם אינו ענין. These two אם אינו ענין interpretations are also unlike any of the other PT examples insofar as they interpret rabbinic sources while all the others interpret scriptural verses. Since the first, late third- to fourth-, and fifth-Palestinian amoraic generations produce all the other attributed examples of אם אינו ענין in PT, and the anonymous ones differ in form from the ones we have just analyzed, it appears that the type of אם אינו ענין that interprets rabbinic sources is a specifically second-generation Palestinian amoraic phenomenon.

On the basis of the application of אם אינו ענין to mishnaic and toseftan texts, should we conclude that tannaitic sources attained a quasi-scriptural status in

---

I believe to be a descending order of likelihood. 1) At an early stage of development, R. Johanan may have asked his question about R. Elazar b. R. Simeon's opinion and found himself unable to answer it. R. Abba tried to answer it but failed. At a later date, R. Johanan answered his own question using אם אינו ענין. BT preserves the earlier stage of development; PT preserves the later one. 2) Oral transmission may have led to both lacunae and additions in the original Palestinian source in its final Babylonian form. This may explain the lack of R. Johanan's אם אינו ענין interpretation in BT's formulation and its replacement with R. Abba's response to R. Johanan's question. See Zechariah Frankel, מבוא הירושלמי, pp. מג–מד. 3) The Babylonians may have consciously rejected R. Johanan's אם אינו ענין interpretation because it was applied to a "*mishnah* form" source. I raise this possibility, though I believe it is unlikely, because a search of the Bar Ilan database of all the BT cases of אם אינו ענין showed that they interpreted only scriptural verses or tannaitic or amoraic midrashic sources, i.e., sources containing scriptural verses. The same holds true for all PT אם אינו ענין interpretations other than the two attributed to R. Johanan and R. Simeon b. Laqish. See David Rosenthal, "מסורות ארץ-ישראליות ודרכן לבבל" ("The Transformation of Eretz Israel Traditions in Babylonia"), *Cathedra* 92 (Jerusalem: Yad Izhak Ben-Zvi Press, 1999), p. 8, especially Rosenthal's citation of his father, E. S. Rosenthal, and p. 11 and notes ad loc.

the early amoraic period? It is tempting to do so,[100] but I think we must answer, "No." R. Johanan's and R. Simeon b. Laqish's liberal attitude to revising and "correcting" the Mishnah suggests it has great but not inviolate authority.[101] R. Johanan and R. Simeon b. Laqish are not alone in these activities and this view of the Mishnah and *baraitot*. PT and BT report that other Palestinian and Babylonian *amoraim* share a similar approach to the Mishnah and tannaitic *baraitot*.[102]

The question this conclusion raises is, "Why did R. Johanan and R. Simeon b. Laqish apply אם אינו ענין to a toseftan *baraita* and to a *mishnah* if they did not consider those sources to have scriptural or quasi-scriptural canonical status?" Analysis of the formulation of the sources to which R. Johanan and R. Simeon b. Laqish applied אם אינו ענין will, I believe, provide an answer to this question.

100 For example, Jacob Neusner in his later writings assigns to the Rabbis the belief that Mishnah and other formative rabbinic works are in the category of divinely-revealed Oral Law, a view he did not subscribe to in his summation of his work on the Mishnah, *Judaism: The Case of Mishnah*. See also פסקי הרי״ד, ברכות-שבת (Jerusalem: 1964), pp. 229–30, where R. Isaac di Trani claims the *amoraim* approached the Mishnah as the *tannaim* approached the Torah. I believe the quasi-scriptural status of Mishnah and other tannaitic sources is a late phenomenon primarily found in the anonymous layer of the Talmud (סתמא דגמרא), though some earlier *amoraim* may have subscribed to this view either in actuality or for propagandistic purposes. See M. Chernick, לחקר המידות „כלל ופרט וכלל" ו„ריבוי ומיעוט" במדרשים ובתלמודים, p. 78, n.72. Beyond these statements is the fact that R. Johanan is responsible for many of the principles of halakhic decision (כללי הפסק) used to decide disputes in the Mishnah. This may suggest that he was trying to establish the Mishnah as a constitutional document. In order to invest it with that level of authority, he may have treated the Mishnah as he would have treated the Scriptures.

101 For PT's tendency to revise and "correct" tannaitic sources, see Zechariah Frankel, מבוא הירושלמי (Breslau: 1880, reprinted Jerusalem: 1977), pp. יט-כא and Louis Ginzberg, *A Commentary on the Palestinian Talmud* (New York: Jewish Theological Seminary, 1971), Hebrew Introduction, p. נה. In regard to R. Johanan and R. Simeon b. Laqish, J. N. Epstein, מבוא לנוסח המשנה (Jerusalem and Tel Aviv: Magnes Press and Dvir, 1948; reprinted, 1964), pp. 262–68; 270–78; 290 (#2). Despite the tendency to revise and "correct," PT attributes the statement, "אני, אין לי אלא משנה" to R. Yoḥanan. See pBerakhot 7:1 (11a), Terumot 2:1 41c=Shabbat 3:1 (5d), and Shabbat 3:7 (6c). PT attributes the statement, "משנה תמימה (שלימה) שנה לנו רבי" to R. Simeon b. Laqish. See pKilaim 1:6 (27a). Shabbat 14:1 (14b)||Pesaḥim 7:11 (35a)||Sanhedrin 8:2 (26a). Baba Qama 5:8 (5a). This statement implies the superiority of the Mishnah over other sources of authority. See also R. Johanan's view about *halakhah le-Mosheh mi-Sinai* and the Mishnah in pPeah 2:4 (17a)=pHagigah 1:8 (76d). It is reasonable to hypothesize that his view in pPeah and pHagigah would apply even more to a *baraita*.

102 J. N. Epstein, מבוא לנוסח המשנה, pp. 349–50 (These pages summarize pp. 166–234; see the prior pages he refers to for Epstein's more detailed documentation of the views of Rav, Samuel, and R. Yannai. For later Palestinian generations, see pp. 395–404. Whether these attributions are to be trusted or not, it is clear that the *Talmudim* do not ascribe to most of the *amoraim* the notion that *mishnayyot* and *baraitot* have canonical parity with Scripture. See also bShabbat 106a=Baba

The Formulation of tMenaḥot 8:3–4 and R. Yoḥanan's אם אינו ענין

tMenaḥot 8:3–4, R. Johanan's source, states:

> רבי שמעון אומר מנחת חוטא של כהנים נקמצות הקומץ קרב לעצמו ושירים קריבין לעצמן ר' אלעזר בר' שמעון אומר הקומץ קרב בעצמו והשירים מתפזרין על גבי הדשן:
>
> R. Simeon says, "A handful of the meal offering of a penitent priest is taken and is sacrificed by itself and the remnants (of the meal offering after the removal of the handful) are sacrificed by themselves. R. Elazar b. R. Simeon says, "The handful is sacrificed by itself and the remnants are scattered on the ash pile.

The use of the term "sacrificed" in R. Simeon's statement implies that the token handful of the meal offering and what remains of the offering after the handful has been removed are both placed on the altar.[103] That each is sacrificed "by itself" seems to mean that each part of the meal offering is placed in a different area on the altar. Since it is clear that the token handful is a true sacrifice, it stands to reason that it goes on the altar itself. This would imply that the meal offering's remnants go onto the altar's ash heap.

R. Elazar b. R. Simeon says that the remnants of the penitent priest's meal offering are "scattered" on the ash heap. "Scattering" and "sacrificing" are not the same act, yet the term דשן or ash heap is used.[104] The use of "scattered" as opposed to "sacrificed" suggests the possibility that R. Elazar b. R. Simeon held that the remnants of the penitent priest's meal offering were not sacred and therefore should be scattered on an ash heap that was not on the altar; and in fact there were two ash heaps for the disposal of unfit sacrifices and non-sacred remnants of sacrifices. One ash heap was outside the Temple precincts and the other was in the Temple's courtyard.[105]

Yet, how could one be sure that this was the implication of R. Elazar b. R. Sime-

---

Qama 34b; bBeẓah 12b; Yebamot 43a; Ketubot 81b; ibid. 82a; Baba Qama 39b (סתם); ibid. 40b; Ḥullin 82a; Bekhorot 56a; and Niddah 13b.

103 See Saul Lieberman, תוספתא כפשוטה, באור ארוך לתוספתא – סוטה (New York: Jewish Theological Seminary of America, 1973), p. 632, lines 37–38.

104 Tosafot Yom Tov makes note of this point in his critique of Bartenuro's comment. See Tosafot Yom Tov, mSotah 3:6, s.v. ושבעלה. For the context of Tosafot Yom Tov's remarks, see R. Obadiah Bartenuro's Mishnah Commentary, mSotah 3:6, s.v. וכל הנשואות לכהן.

105 Rashi in bMenaḥot 74a holds that the meaning of דשן in tMenaḥot 8:3–4 is the ash heap outside the Temple (s.v. אלא אבית הדשן דלמטה). Tosafot holds that the *baraita* refers to the ash heap on the Temple's premises.

on's opinion? On one hand, perhaps he was just explaining R. Simeon's view in clearer terms. On the other, one had to consider the differences in linguistic formulation between R. Simeon's and R. Eliezer b. R. Simeon's views and the fact that the *baraita* casts their positions in the dispute form, "Rabbi A says. . . . Rabbi B says. . . ." Thus, the preponderance of evidence suggests that R. Elazar b. R. Simeon did not hold the same view as R. Simeon. R. Johanan sought to eliminate all doubt about this.

Therefore, R. Johanan applied אם אינו ענין in order to make the distinction between R. Simeon's position and R. Elazar b. R. Simeon's position absolutely clear. This is not the same as the tannaitic application of אם אינו ענין to the Pentateuch. In the tannaitic אם אינו ענין, the midrashists are trying to solve the problem of redundancy and superfluity in what they hold to be a divinely revealed text. They accomplish this by finding a new, not particularly obvious, application for a verse.[106] R. Johanan's application of אם אינו ענין to tMenaḥot 8:3–4 confirms what the general formulation of the *baraita* and the specific wording attributed to R. Elazar b. R. Simeon already implies. Thus, the meaning of R. Johanan's statement is something like, "If R. Elazar b. Simeon is discussing the ash heap on the altar, then he and R. Simeon say the same thing. (If so, why is there a difference in the formulation of their statements and why are their opinions formulated as a debate?) Therefore, if R. Elazar b. R. Simeon's view does not seem to address the same issue that R. Simeon discusses (אם אינו ענין לדשן של למעלן, "if the discussion is not about 'sacrifice' of the remnants on the altar's ash heap"), assume his view is about scattering the remnants of the penitent priest's meal offering on the ash heap that is not on the altar." This is in the category of clarifying commentary rather than *midrash*.

The Formulation of mMenaḥot 10:9 and R. Simeon b. Laqish's אם אינו ענין

R. Simeon b. Laqish's use of אם אינו ענין is similar to that of R. Johanan. As the *sugya* reports, R. Simeon b. Laqish raised the question of whether the ceremony of cutting the *ᶜomer* overrode the Sabbath if performed during the day. The attempt by R. Abbaye to solve this problem in favor of the daytime ritual overriding the Sabbath using mMenaḥot 10:9 did not meet with R. Simeon b. Laqish's approval. R. Aḥa, however, reported that R. Simeon b. Laqish reversed himself. What brought about this change of heart seems to be the recognition that one *mishnah* in mMenaḥot 10 adds something to another *mishnah* in the same chapter. R. Abbaye tried answering R. Simeon b. Laqish's query by referring to the last clause in mMenaḥot 10:9:

106 Yaakov Elman, "Prospective *Derash* and Retrospective *Peshat*," pp. 229–30.

...מצות העומר לבא מן הקמה, לא מצא יביא מן העמרים. מצותו לבא מן הלח, לא מצא יביא מן היבש. מצותו לקצור בלילה, נקצר ביום כשר, ודוחה את השבת.

> The proper performance of the (rite of the) *ᶜomer* is (for it) to come from standing grain. If one did not find (standing grain), one may bring it from bundled grain. Its proper performance is (for it) to come from fresh grain. If one did not find (fresh grain), one may bring it from dry grain. Its proper performance is to harvest (it) at night. If (however) it was harvested during the day, it is fit, and it overrides the Sabbath.

The phrase, "If it was harvested during the day, it is fit, and it overrides the Sabbath," would seem to be incontrovertible proof that daytime harvesting of the *ᶜomer* sets aside the Sabbath. Yet, one could parse the *mishnah* thus: "Its proper performance is to harvest (the *ᶜomer*) at night. If (however) it was harvested during the day, it is fit. And it (the properly performed *ᶜomer* ceremony) overrides the Sabbath." The reason that one might do this is because of the literary balance that exists in the two clauses leading up to the final clause of this *mishnah*. That is, the *mishnah* first states the proper way to perform the rite of the *ᶜomer* ("the *ᶜomer* is cut at night"). It then follows this with a ruling about what is acceptable after the fact ("and if it is cut during the day, it is fit"), and there is where the *mishnah* should have ended if it intended to create a balanced unit.[107] However, it continues with an additional clause, "and it overrides the Sabbath," which disturbs its formal balance. This clause creates a crux in need of clarification. On one hand, the final clause may allow Sabbath violation only for the fully acceptable form of harvesting the *ᶜomer* during the night.[108] On the other hand, it may refer to the rule that immediately precedes it: "If (however) it was harvested during the day, it is fit." In order for R. Simeon b. Laqish to determine whether daytime harvesting of the *ᶜomer* sets aside the Sabbath, he must resolve this crux.

According to R. Aḥa, R. Simeon b. Laqish realized that mMenaḥot 10:3, which discussed the procedure for the nighttime harvesting of the *ᶜomer* on the Sabbath, provided a means to interpret mMenaḥot 10:9. mMenaḥot 10:3 contains a full discussion of the ceremony of harvesting the *ᶜomer* on the night of

107 Interestingly, BT, ed. princ. Venice רפ"ט, preserves the following reading of a Babylonian *baraita* that serves as a midrashic support for mMenahot 1:9: ...מנין שאם נקצר ביום כשר ת׳ל תקריב ודוחה את השב׳ ת׳ל תקריב. Note how the issue of the fitness of harvesting the *ᶜomer* by day is separated from the issue of the *ᶜomer* ceremony abrogating the Sabbath in this version. No other MS or early imprint of this *midrash* has this reading. All of them have מנין שאם נקצר ביום כשר ודוחה את השבת ת"ל... with insignificant variations in spelling caused by abbreviations. There is no claim here that this reading is the correct one. Rather, it merely indicates how it is possible to separate the penultimate clause of the *mishnah* from its final one.

108 See mMenaḥot 10:3.

the 16th of Nisan. This discussion includes the rules governing the nighttime ceremony when it takes place on the Sabbath. In such a case, mMenaḥot 10:3 holds that setting aside the Sabbath is acceptable. Consequently, mMenaḥot 10:3 provides all the information we need about the abrogation of the Sabbath in the case of the proper performance of the the *ᶜomer* ceremony. Therefore, according to R. Simeon b. Laqish, we should apply the clause, "and it overrides the Sabbath," to a situation where we need information. That situation is the case of harvesting of the *ᶜomer* during the day. Thus, mMenaḥot 10:9 covers two points: 1) the status of an incorrectly performed *ᶜomer* ceremony as fit; and 2) the determination that because it is fit, it abrogates the Sabbath.

Again, we should pay attention to the fact that mMenaḥot 10:9 had the potential to be understood just as R. Simeon b. Laqish is said to have finally understood it. R. Abbaye had understood it that way *ab initio*, and generally speaking if one clause immediately follows another, we would expect the last clause to refer to the one immediately preceding it. What R. Simeon b. Laqish sought was conclusive proof that mMenaḥot 10:9 should be read thus and in no other way. His use of אם אינו ענין decided the matter for him.

Here, as in the case of R. Johanan's application of אם אינו ענין to a toseftan *baraita*, we are not dealing with *midrash* in its classical style. Simeon b. Laqish does not produce an *halakhah* that goes beyond the "plain meaning" of the text. Rather, his אם אינו ענין determines what for him is the plain meaning of the Mishnah. In that respect, his use of אם אינו ענין is more in the realm of clarifying commentary on Mishnah than "*midrash*" of it.[109]

To summarize: there is a qualitative difference between the uses of אם אינו ענין attributed to R. Johanan and his student, R. Simeon b. Laqish, and the application of אם אינו ענין to scriptural sources by *tannaim* and *amoraim*. In the case of application of אם אינו ענין to rabbinic sources, R. Johanan uses אם אינו ענין to determine the meaning of a distinctive but somewhat confusing linguistic formulation in a *baraita*, and R. Simeon b. Laqish determines what constitutes the referent of a mishnaic clause. In the case of the halakhic *midrashim*, tannaitic and amoraic midrashists use אם אינו ענין to "uncover" *halakhot* that are not immediately obvious when one reads the scriptural text.

אם אינו ענין in the Palestinian Talmud Summary of Findings

1. As we have noted, the אם אינו ענין interpretations in the Palestinian Talmud differ in significant ways from the examples in the tannaitic *midrashim*. In

109 There is a similar application of אם אינו ענין in tannaitic midrashic literature. That is the resolution of the crux created by the term תמימה in *Sifre Zuta* 19. See above, pp. 108.

the interpretations that approximate tannaitic interpretations, the אם אינו ענין gives the impression of being reconstructions of tannaitic *ribbui* interpretations. In the case of a PT אם אינו ענין based on two pericopes, one of the pericopes is not a pentateuchal source. This is not characteristic of אם אינו ענין interpretations in tannaitic sources, though *Sifre Num.* 78 contains an אם אינו ענין *midrash* that made use of a verse from Ezekiel. It is hard to determine whether the *Sifre Num. midrash* is a tannaitic model for the PT interpretation, or whether it is a post-tannaitic interpolation into *Sifre Num.*[110] Whatever the case, there is a continuation of a pattern in אם אינו ענין interpretations that we saw in the "prooftext *midrash*" interpretations (אף על פי שאין ראיה לדבר, זכר לדבר). The *amoraim*, in contrast to their tannaitic predecessors, dispensed with the "prooftext *midrash*" interpretations because they apparently deemed non-legal sections of the Pentateuch, biblical narratives, and biblical poetry acceptable sources of support for or derivation of *halakhah*. Similarly, the *amoraim* drew from the entire corpus of the Hebrew Scriptures in their אם אינו ענין expositions, unlike the *tannaim*, who restricted the use of Scripture in their אם אינו ענין *midrashim* to the Pentateuch. As we stated in our study of "prooftext *midrash*" interpretations, this suggests a shift in rabbinic views of the nature of scriptural revelation. For the *tannaim*, only the laws in the Torah revealed to Moses could produce law. For the *amoraim*, all subsequent revelation of Scriptures could also serve this purpose because it either was essentially Sinaitic or had to conform to what was revealed to Moses.[111]

In the single PT example in which only one pentateuchal pericope generates the אם אינו ענין, the *midrash* differs from its tannaitic antecedents by turning what the *tannaim* would have considered a *ribbui* into an אם אינו ענין interpretation. It also differs from the tannaitic אם אינו ענין format by including two cases of superfluity. There are no tannaitic אם אינו ענין *midrashim* that have more than one superfluous element. Since the exposition has two reapplications of pentateuchal rubrics, the double superfluity may be a required element to achieve this result.

2. The Palestinian Talmud's אם אינו ענין frequently constructs superfluity differently from the tannaitic *midrashim*. In several instances where the PT אם אינו ענין *midrash* approximates the tannaitic *midrash* in some way, the repeated mention of a subject renders the first pentateuchal verse superfluous rather than the second, repeated verse. This counters the seemingly more logical tan-

110 I have not found any version of *Sifre Num.* that does not include this *midrash*. If it did not appear in some version of *Sifre Num.*, it would be easier to claim later interpolation. As it stands, one can argue for a tannaitic or post-tannaitic provenance for this *midrash* only on the basis of form; but lacking more proof, arguments in either direction are circular.

111 See *Sifra*, *Beḥuqotai* 13:6.

naitic formulation which regards the repetition of a matter as the superfluous element. In all cases of "reverse order redundancy," however, the second verse amplifies the first one in some way and thereby subsumes the first verse. This subsumption renders the first verse unnecessary: if we had only the second verse, we would have all the information about a rubric that we might need. The transferral of subject A to subject B of the Palestinian talmudic אם אינו ענין interpretation, like that of its tannaitic predecessors, removes the superfluity uncovered by the main section of the exposition.

3. PT contains one אם אינו ענין interpretation that supports rabbinic legislation. The Pentateuch itself contains no hint that one is forbidden to work various kinds of fields within the "two seasons," from Passover until the beginning of the sabbatical year in one case, and from Shabu^{c}ot until the sabbatical year in another. Yet, PT finds midrashic support for this rabbinic regulation, ultimately rescinded by R. Gamaliel, by use of אם אינו ענין hermeneutics. The PT interpretation does not appear in tannaitic midrashic sources, nor is there any mention of the "prohibition of the two periods" in that literature. Nevertheless, the phenomenon of finding midrashic support for rabbinic enactments is not new; only the use of אם אינו ענין for that purpose is.

4. Finally, PT contains cases of אם אינו ענין that have no connection to biblical verses at all. Rather, this hermeneutic is applied to mishnaic and *baraita* texts. אם אינו ענין in these cases is truly exegetical, helping us to parse a Mishnah passage accurately in one case and to choose the correct meaning of an otherwise ambiguous *baraita* in another. No examples of this sort of אם אינו ענין surfaced in tannaitic literature.

5. Although אם אינו ענין was applied to Scripture in order to support a rabbinic enactment and was used in the interpretation of Mishnah and *baraita* passages, it is not likely that these phenomena indicate that tannaitic sources achieved scriptural status during the period of the Palestinian Talmud's development. PT's *amoraim* and *stam* still use *midrash* in much the same way as the *tannaim* did, though in general they use logical argument more often than midrashic interpretation.[112] Furthermore, PT maintains a rather strict distinction between scriptural and rabbinic law and between *midrash* that generates one or the other.[113] Nevertheless, these phenomena may represent the first opening towards regarding the rabbinic corpora as a form of revealed Torah.

112 E. Z. Melamed, פרקי מבוא לספרות התלמוד (Jerusalem: 1973), pp. 312 and 314.

113 PT's Sages and anonymous voice (*stam*) use terms such as דבר תורה and מחוור/ת to designate what they consider matters of pentateuchal law. דברי סופרים and דבריהם indicates rabbinic law. Some examples of the term מחוור in reference to *midrashim* that PT believes produce pentateuchal law either according to all the Sages or according to some are found in p^{c}Erubin 10:1

אם אינו ענין in the Babylonian Talmud

The Babylonian Talmud contains about 60 examples of אם אינו ענין interpretations. Only four of these are parallel to interpretations in the tannaitic halakhic *midrashim*: 1) *Sifra Nedabah* 12:7–8=bMenaḥot 84b;[114] 2) *Sifra Ẓav* 13:2=*Sifra Qedoshim* 1:4=bZevaḥim 28a–b;[115] 3) *Sifra Qedoshim*, par 10, 9:6–7=bSanhe-

---

(26a). Pesaḥim 2:1 (28c). Shabbat 9:4 (12a)=Yoma 8:3 (45a)=Taᶜanit 1:6 (64c). Some examples of דבר תורה without *midrash* can be found in pPe'ah 1:1 (15a). Kila'im 3:1 (28c). Shebiᶜit 2:5 (34a). Some PT examples of דבר תורה with *midrash* can be found in pBerakhot 7:1 (11a). Shebiᶜit 6:1 (36b). Sukkah 4:1 (54b). Gittin 5:1 (46c)=Baba Meẓiᶜaᵓ 9:2 (12b). Some PT examples of rabbinic law supported by halakhic *midrash* on pentateuchal verses can be found in pBerakhot 3:1 (5d). Berakhot 3:5 (6d). Berakhot 4:1 (7a) see also pBerakhot 3:3 (6b). Berakhot 6:1 (9d). Berakhot 7:1 (11a). Examples of דבריהם and דברי סופרים in contrast to דבר תורה appear in p'Orlah 1:1 (60d). Yebamot 7:3 (8a–b). Qiddushin 1:1 (58c). and Taᶜanit 2:12 (66a).

114 ספרא ויקרא – דבורא דנדבה פרשה יב

(ז) קרבן ראשית שיהא ראשית לכל המנחות וכך הוא אומר והקרבתם מנחה חדשה לה׳ שתהא חדשה לכל המנחות אין לי אלא מנחת חיטין מנחת שעורין מנין וכשהוא אומר וביום הבכורים בהקריבכם מנחה חדשה לה׳ בשבועותיכם אם אינו ענין למנחת חטין תנהו ענין למנחת שעורין. (ח) ומנין שיקדימו לבכורים תלמוד לומר בכורי קציר חטים אין לי אלא של חטין של שעורים מנין ת״ל אשר תזרע, אין לי אלא שיזרע עלה מאליו מנין ת״ל אשר בשדה, אין לי אלא שבשדה שבגג ושבחצר ושבחרבה מנין ת״ל בכורי כל אשר בארצם, ומנין שיקדימו לנסכין ולפירות האילן ת״ל בכורי מעשיך ואומר באספך את מעשיך מן השדה.

תלמוד בבלי מסכת מנחות דף פד עמוד ב

איתיביה רבי אחא בר אבא לרבה: +ויקרא ב׳+ קרבן ראשית – שתהא ראשית לכל המנחות, וכן הוא אומר: +במדבר כ״ח+ בהקריבכם מנחה חדשה לה׳ בשבועותיכם, אין לי אלא חדשה של חטים, חדשה של שעורים מנין? תלמוד לומר: חדשה חדשה, אם אינו ענין לחדשה של חיטין, תנהו ענין לחדשה של שעורים; ומנין שתהא קודמת לביכורים? תלמוד לומר: +שמות ל״ד+ וחג שבעות תעשה לך בכורי קציר חטים; ואין לי אלא בכורי קציר חטים, קציר שעורים מנין? ת״ל: +שמות כ״ג+ וחג הקציר בכורי מעשיך אשר תזרע בשדה; ואין לי אלא שתזרע, עלו מאליהן מנין? תלמוד לומר: בשדה; ואין לי אלא בשדה, מנין לרבות שבגג ושבחורבה ושבעציץ ושבספינה? ת״ל: +במדבר י״ח+ בכורי כל אשר בארצם; מנין שתהא קודמת לנסכים ופירות האילן? נאמר כאן בכורי מעשיך ונאמר להלן +שמות כ״ג+ באספך את מעשיך מן השדה, מה להלן נסכים ופירות אילן, אף כאן נסכים ופירות אילן....

115 ספרא צו פרק יג

(ב) הין אם פסלה מחשבה בזמן שהזמן נוהגת בבמה תפסול מחשבה במחיצה שאין מחשבה נוהגת בבמה, תלמוד לומר בפרשת קדושי׳ אם האכל יאכל ביום השלישי פיגול הוא לא ירצה שאין תלמוד לומר אלא אם אינו ענין לחוץ זמנו תניהו ענין לחוץ למקומו....

ספרא קדושים פרק א

(ד) אם האכל יאכל ביום השלישי, פיגול הוא לא ירצה שאין תלמוד לומר אלא אם אינו ענין לחוץ לזמנו תניהו ענין חוץ למקומו.

תלמוד בבלי מסכת זבחים דף כח עמוד א–ב

אמר אביי: כי אתא רב יצחק בר אבדימי [אמר, רב] סמיך אדתני תנא, כשהוא אומר שלישי

drin 66b;[116] and 4) ibid. 10:1–2=bSanhedrin 54b.[117] BT also contains other אם אינו ענין interpretations attributed to *tannaim*. We will examine these first.

בפרשת קדושים תהיו, שאין ת"ל, שהרי כבר נאמר: +ויקרא ז+ ואם האכל יאכל מבשר זבח השלמים ביום השלישי אם אינו ענין לחוץ לזמנו תנהו לענין חוץ למקומו....

116 ספרא קדושים פרק ט

(ו) כי איש איש אשר יקלל את אביו ואת אמו, בשם, אתה אומר בשם או אינו אלא בכנוי תלמוד לומר בנקבו שם יומת שאין תלמוד לומר שם ומה ת"ל שם אלא להביא את המקלל אביו ואמו שלא יהא חייב עד שיקללם בשם (המפורש) דברי רבי אחי בר ר' יאשיה, רבי חנניא בר אידי אומר הואיל ואמרה תורה השבע ואל תשבע קלל ואל תקלל מה השבע בשם אף אל תשבע בשם. (ז) מות יומת בסקילה אתה אומר בסקילה, או באחת מכל המיתות שבתורה, תלמוד לומר דמיו בו ולהלן נאמר דמיהם בם מה דמיהם בם שנאמר להלן בסקילה אף דמיו בו שנאמר כאן בסקילה, עונש שמענו אזהרה לא שמענו תלמוד לומר אלהים לא תקלל, ואם נשיא הוא אביו הרי הוא בכלל ונשיא בעמך לא תאור, אינו לא דיין ולא נשיא אלא בור הרי את בבנין אב מבינין שניהם, לא ראי דיין כראי נשיא ולא ראי נשיא כראי דיין הצד השוה שבהם שהן בעמך ואתה מוזהר על קללתן, אף אביך שבעמך אתה מוזהר על קללתו, אי מה הצד השוה שבהן שהם גדולים ומעמך וגדולתן גרמה להן ואתה מוזהר על קללתו, אף אביך שהוא גדול ומעמך וגדולתו גרמה לו ואתה מוזהר על קללתו תלמוד לומר לא תקלל חרש דבר הכתוב באמללין של אדם, מה לחרש שכן חרישותו גרמה לו נשיא ודיין יוכיחו מה לנשיא ודיין שכן גדולתן גרמה להן חרש יוכיח הרי את דן בבנין אב מבינין שלשתן לא ראי דיין כראי נשיא ולא ראי נשיא כראי דיין ולא ראי זה וזה כראי חרש ולא ראי חרש כראי שניהם הצד השוה שבהם שבשלשתן שהם בעמך ואתה מוזהר על קללתן אף אביך שהוא בעמך את מוזהר על קללתו מה להצד השוה שבהן שכן משונין א"כ נכתוב קרא אלהים וחרש או נשיא וחרש אלהים ל"ל אם אינו ענין לגופו תנהו ענין לאביו.

תלמוד בבלי מסכת סנהדרין דף סו עמוד א

תניא, רבי מנחם ברבי יוסי אומר: +ויקרא כ"ד+ בנקבו שם יומת, מה תלמוד לומר שם – לימד על מקלל אביו ואמו שאינו חייב עד שיקללם בשם. תנו רבנן: איש, מה תלמוד לומר+ויקרא כ'+ איש איש – לרבות בת, טומטום, ואנדרוגינוס. אשר יקלל את אביו ואת אמו – אין לי אלא אביו ואמו, אביו שלא אמו, אמו שלא אביו מניין? תלמוד לומר אביו ואמו קלל דמיו בו אביו קילל, אמו קילל, דברי רבי יאשיה. רבי יונתן אומר: משמע שניהן כאחד ומשמע אחד בפני עצמו, עד שיפרוט לך הכתוב יחדו. מות יומת – בסקילה. אתה אומר בסקילה, או אינו אלא באחת מכל מיתות האמורות בתורה? נאמר כאן דמיו בו ונאמר להלן +ויקרא כ'+ דמיהם בם, מה להלן בסקילה – אף כאן בסקילה. עונש שמענו, אזהרה מניין? תלמוד לומר +שמות כ"ב+ אלהים לא תקלל וגו'. אם היה אביו דיין – הרי הוא בכלל אלהים לא תקלל, ואם היה אביו נשיא הרי הוא בכלל +שמות כ"ב+ ונשיא בעמך לא ולא ראי דיין כראי נשיא. לא ראי דיין כראי נשיא – שהרי דיין אתה מצווה על הוראתו, כראי תאר, אינו לא דיין ולא נשיא מניין? אמרת: הרי אתה דן בנין אב משניהן: לא ראי נשיא כראי דיין, נשיא – שאי אתה מצווה על הוראתו. ולא ראי נשיא כראי דיין – שהנשיא אתה מצווה על המראתו, כראי דיין – שאי אתה מצווה על המראתו. הצד השוה שבהם – שהן בעמך, ואתה מוזהר על קללתן – אף אני אביא אביך שבעמך ואתה מוזהר על קללתו. מה להצד השוה שבהן – שכן גדולתן גרמה להן! תלמוד לומר +ויקרא י"ט+ לא תקלל חרש – באומללים שבעמך הכתוב מדבר. מה לחרש – שכן חרישתו גרמה לו! נשיא ודיין יוכיחו. מה לנשיא ודיין – שכן גדולתן גרמה להן, חרש יוכיח. וחזר הדין, לא ראי זה כראי זה, ולא ראי זה כראי זה, הצד השוה שבהן: שהן בעמך ואתה מוזהר על קללתן – אף אני אביא אביך, שבעמך, ואתה מוזהר על קללתו. מה לצד השוה שבהן – שכן משונין. אלא אם כן נכתוב קרא או אלהים וחרש, או נשיא וחרש, אלהים למה לי? אם אינו ענין לגופו – תנהו ענין לאביו.

117 ספרא קדושים פרק י

bYoma 26b. In a discussion of the Mishnah's statement that the daily sacrifice was offered by up to a dozen priests, there is a statement that the second daily offering in the afternoon was accompanied by eleven priests. Nine carried the various pieces of the sacrifice, and two others carried two pieces of wood. The *gemara* seeks a source for the requirement that two priests carry two pieces of wood, and finds it in this *midrash*:

> תניא, רבי שמעון בר יוחאי אומר: מניין לתמיד של בין הערבים שטעון שני גזירי עצים בשני כהנים – שנאמר +ויקרא א+ וערכו עצים, אם אינו ענין לתמיד של שחר, דכתיב[118]+ויקרא ו+ ובער עליה הכהן עצים בבקר בבקר וערך עליה – תניהו ענין לתמיד של בין הערבים.
>
> It was taught (in a *baraita*). R. Simeon b. Yoḥai says: Whence (do we know) that the afternoon daily sacrifice requires two pieces of wood (carried) by two priests? As it is said, "... and they shall arrange wood (on the fire that is on the altar)" (Lev 1:7). If this verse is inapplicable to the morning daily offering, as it is written, "... and the priest shall burn on it (i.e., the altar) pieces of wood (עצים) each morning...." (Lev 6:5), apply it to the afternoon daily offering.

This אם אינו ענין *midrash* is problematic primarily because it follows a pattern of rendering a verse superfluous that we have seen in PT – namely, the verse that is in an earlier chapter of the Pentateuch is rendered extraneous by a later

---

> (א) ואיש להוציא את הקטן אשר יתן שכבתו בבהמה בין גדולה בין קטנה מות יומת בסקילה. אתה אומר בסקילה או באחד מכל המיתות שבתורה תלמוד לומר ואת הבהמה תהרוגו נאמר כאן הריגה ונאמר להלן הריגה מה הריגה האמורה להלן סקילה אף כאן סקילה. (ב) למדנו עונש לשוכב נשכב מנין תלמוד לומר כל שוכב עם בהמה מות יומת אם אינו ענין לשוכב תנהו לנשכב למדנו עונש בין לשוכב בין לנשכב אזהרה מנין תלמוד לומר ובכל בהמה לא תתן שכבתך לטמאה בה למדנו אזהרה לשוכב אזהרה לנשכב מנין תלמוד לומר לא יהיה קדש מבני ישראל ואומר וגם קדש היה בארץ דברי ר' ישמעאל....
>
> תלמוד בבלי מסכת סנהדרין דף נד עמוד ב
>
> תנו רבנן: +ויקרא כ'+ איש – פרט לקטן, אשר יתן שכבתו בבהמה – בין גדולה בין קטנה, מות יומת – בסקילה. אתה אומר בסקילה, או אינו אלא באחת מכל מיתות האמורות בתורה? נאמר כאן תהרגו ונאמר להלן +דברים י"ג+ כי הרג תהרגנו, מה להלן בסקילה – אף כאן בסקילה. למדנו עונש לשוכב, עונש לנשכב מנלן? תלמוד לומר +שמות כ"ב+ כל שוכב עם בהמה מות יומת, אם אינו ענין לשוכב – תניהו ענין לנשכב. למדנו עונש בין לשוכב בין לנשכב, אזהרה מניין? – תלמוד לומר +ויקרא י"ח+ ובכל בהמה לא תתן שכבתך לטמאה בה. למדנו אזהרה לשוכב, לנשכב מניין? תלמוד לומר +דברים כ"ג+ לא יהיה קדש מבני ישראל ואומר +מלכים א' י"ד+ וגם קדש היה בארץ וגו', דברי רבי ישמעאל....

118 דכתיב: בצורה זו או בצורת „דכתב" איתא בכל כתבי היד ובדפוס ספרדי ובדפוס ונציה, "as it is written": This appears in Aramaic in all the mss. and in an early Spanish imprint and in ed. princ. Venice.

verse. In this case, Lev 1:7 is rendered superfluous by Lev 6:5. In tannaitic אם אינו ענין *midrash*, as we have seen above, the verse that appears later in the Pentateuch usually becomes the extraneous element applied to some new context. Is this אם אינו ענין interpretation an exception to the rule, another form of tannaitic אם אינו ענין that we have not seen until now, or something else?

The answer is that this אם אינו ענין is not tannaitic at all. One immediate clue is the appearance of the Aramaic דכתיב, "as it is written," in the middle of the *midrash*. This formula does not appear in tannaitic *midrashim*, which are in rabbinic Hebrew. Further, the formulation of the Yoma passage in the relatively early commentary of R. Ḥananel (990–1055 C.E.) does not include any reference to the אם אינו ענין, though it includes a reference to a *midrash* that makes the same point.[119] It appears that the *midrash* R. Ḥananel alludes to is *Sifra, Nedabah* 5:11:

> וערכו עצים על[120] האש, עצים על גבי האש לא האש על גבי עצים, אמר רבי שמעון מנין לרבות שני גזרי עצים למערכה על תמיד של בין הערבים תלמוד לומר וערכו עצים על האש.
>
> "And they (the priests) shall lay out the wood" (Lev 1:7) – wood (should be placed) on the fire, not fire on the wood. R. Simeon says: Whence (do we know) that two pieces of wood should be added to the altar pile with the afternoon daily offering? The Torah says, "And they shall lay out wood (עצים, plural) on the fire."

According to this reading, the *midrash* arrives at its conclusions without recourse to אם אינו ענין. But how? The answer lies in a response to a question raised regarding this *midrash* by many medieval commentators – namely, how does a verse in the pericope about voluntary burnt offerings teach anything about obligatory burnt offerings? The *Sifra* commentary attributed to

119 מנא לן שתמיד של בין הערבים טעון שני גזירי עצים? שנאמר: „וערכו עצים על האש." ודרשינן ליה בתמיד של בין הערבים, ומשמע „וערכו" שנים....

Whence do we know that the afternoon daily offering requires two pieces of wood? As it says, "and they shall lay out wood on the fire." And we interpret this midrashically in reference to the afternoon daily offering. And "they shall lay out" implies two (priests because it is in the plural form)....

120 *Sifra Assemani* 66: עם. This also indicates that BT's *baraita* is a Babylonian *baraita* because it includes the rule regarding the two priests who according to it must carry the pieces of wood. As we note later, this is most likely a reformulation of the *baraita* in order for it to support and match mYoma 2:8. See J. N. Epstein, מבואות לספרות התנאים, pp. 680–81. See in regard to the present case of אם אינו ענין and others that we will analyze, Shamma Friedman's citation of and comments on RAbaD's *Sifra* commentary in "הברייתות בתלמוד הבבלי ויחסן למקבילותיהן בתוספתא," p. 199.

R. Samson of Sens responds:

> אף על גב דהאי קרא בעולת נדבה כתיב, יליף מינה שפיר לתמיד. וכן לנתחים ילפינן מכאן לתמיד.
>
> Though this verse is written about a freely donated burnt offering, *Sifra* properly derives from it (rules appropriate to) the obligatory daily offering. And similarly we derive from here (Lev 1:7) that the daily offering must be cut into pieces.

We may extend R. Samson's point thus: the information in Lev 1:1–9 can be applied wherever the rules of burnt offerings need clarification. It is not necessary to make the point about two pieces of wood regarding the morning daily sacrifice. There it explicitly refers to the priest burning pieces of wood (Lev 6:5). Furthermore, the use of "priest" in the singular in Lev 6:5 would, if taken literally, imply that in the morning only one priest need carry the wood. The only burnt offering whose arrangements are not clear is the daily afternoon offering. Therefore, the *Sifra midrash* provides a necessary clarification – namely, the rule regarding the addition of two pieces of wood. Once it supplies that information, all the other aspects of its prooftext, Lev 1:7, apply to the afternoon daily offering as well. Consequently, because the verse declares that "they (pl., וערכו) shall lay out the pieces of wood," we derive that a minimum of two priests must add the wood at the afternoon daily offering. This is exactly how R. Ḥananel concludes his comments on the *baraita* in Yoma: וערכו משמע שנים, "And 'they shall arrange' implies two."[121] Though *Sifra* itself does not discuss the issue of the two priests, bYoma does. This is probably because its *baraita* is formulated in light of mYoma 2:8, which speaks of two priests carrying two pieces of wood to be added to the altar pile as part of the afternoon daily offering.

As we have seen, the first part of the talmudic *baraita* prior to the אם אינו ענין *midrash* basically parallels the *Sifra baraita*, and we should view that material as an independent source. The אם אינו ענין *midrash* is an appended commentary to explain how Lev 1:7 applies to the afternoon daily offerings. After all, Lev 1:7 makes no obvious reference to any of the daily offerings, let alone the afternoon one. In response to this problem, an amoraic or post-amoraic midrashic commentator suggests that this difficulty can be overcome if we use אם אינו ענין hermeneutics. Thus, he claims to make explicit what he believed was implicit in the *Sifra midrash*. Thus, it is not surprising that this commentary takes the form of a post-tannaitic אם אינו ענין *midrash*.

121 So, too, RAbaD on *Sifra*: "'they'" implies (minimally) two (priests). 'pieces of wood' implies (minimally) two pieces.

Baba Meẓiᶜaᵓ 60b–61a. Baba Meẓiᶜaᵓ 60b–61a presents a midrashic *baraita* that defines prohibited interest. Two terms are used for interest in the Torah, and the *midrash* wishes to clarify whether they both apply to borrowed food and money or whether one form of interest applies only to money and the other only to food. It concludes that despite differences in biblical terminology applied to interest – namely, נשך (*neshekh*, advance interest) and מרבית (*marbit*, accrued interest), they are legally the same and apply equally to money and foodstuffs:

תלמוד בבלי מסכת בבא מציעא דף ס עמוד ב–סא עמוד א

> תנו רבנן: +ויקרא כ״ה+ את כספך לא תתן לו בנשך ובמרבית לא תתן אכלך – אין לי אלא נשך בכסף ורבית באוכל, נשך באוכל מנין, תלמוד +דברים כ״ג+ נשך אכל.[122] רבית בכסף מנין, תלמוד לומר נשך כסף אם אינו ענין לנשך כסף – שהרי כבר נאמר[123] +דברים כ״ג+ לא תשיך לאחיך, תנהו ענין לרבית כסף....[124]

122 נשך אכל: אסקוריאל 3-ל: לא תשיך לאחיך נשך כסף נשך אוכל. המבורג 165: לא תשיך לאחיך נשך כסף נשך אכל . MSS Escorial 3-ל and Hamburg 165: "You shall not lend to your brother on interest, interest of money or interest of food."

123 שהרי כבר נאמר: המבורג 165: דהא כתי'. כי"מ: דהא כתיב. פירנצה: דהכת'. MSS Hamburg, Munich, and Florence: (in Aramaic) "for it is written. . . ."

124 MS Hamburg 165 preserves a significantly different version of this *baraita*. It reads as follows:

> תנו רבנן: +ויקרא כ״ה+ את כספך לא תתן לו בנשך ובמרבית לא תתן אכלך – אין לי אלא נשך בכסף ותרבי' אכל במלוה. נשך באוכל ורבית בכסף במלוה, ונשך ורבית בין באוכל בין בכסף בלוה מניין? ת״ל: לא תשיך לאחיך נשך כסף נשך אכל. רבית בלווה בין בכסף בין באוכל מניין? ת״ל, נשך כסף נשך אכל. אם אינו ענין לא בכסף ולא באוכל דהא כתי' לא תשיך דמשמע בין בכסף בין באוכל תנהו ענין לרבית בין בכסף בין באוכל....

> Our Rabbis taught (in a *baraita*). "You shall not give your money to him (i.e., a borrower) on advance interest, nor shall you give him your foodstuffs on accrued interest (מרבית)"– (from this) I only know (the rule governing) one who lends on advance interest involving money and on accrued interest involving foods. Whence (do I learn the rule governing) one who lends on advance interest involving foods and on accrued interest involving money and (the rule governing) one who borrows whether on advance or accrued interest involving either food or money? The Torah says, "You shall not lend to/borrow from your brother with interest of money or interest of food." Whence do I learn (the rule governing) one who borrows whether money or food on accrued interest? The Torah says, "interest of money, interest of food"– if this has no application to advanced interest of money or food, for it is written, "You shall not lend to/borrow from . . . ," which implies both money and food, apply it to accrued interest of both money and food. . . .

The text is corrupt since it repeats the question about the borrower's culpability when he borrows money or food on advance or accumulated interest. Its opening, however, is interesting and different from all other manuscript and early imprint versions of this *baraita* insofar as it raises the issue of the culpability of the borrower and lender on interest along with the various permutations of the prohibited kinds of interest that are possible. Other versions of this *baraita* first determine what sorts of interest are prohibited and then turn their inquiry to which parties are culpable for involving themselves in dealings involving one type of prohibited interest or another.

> Our Rabbis taught: "You shall not give your money to him (i.e., a borrower) on advance interest (נשך), nor shall you give him your foodstuffs on accrued interest (מרבית)" (Lev 25:37) – (from this) I only know that advance interest (applies) to money and accrued interest to foods; whence (do I learn that) advance interest applies to foods? The Torah says, "advance interest of food" (Deut 23:20). Whence (do I know) accrued interest of money? Since it (the phrase "advance interest of money" in Deut 23:20) is extraneous (in regard to monetary advance interest) because it has previously been stated (at the outset of the verse), "You shall not cause your brother to charge advance interest"[125] (Deut 23:29), apply it to the matter of accrued interest on money. . . .

In this *midrash* we also encounter problems related to form. The use of Deut 23:20 and 23:29 as a basis for an אם אינו ענין interpretation flies in the face of the common tannaitic form that bases אם אינו ענין on two different pericopes unless no other pericope deals with a particular subject. The prohibition on charging interest appears in several pentateuchal passages, some of which appear in the *midrash* itself (for example, Exod 22:24; Lev 25:36–37; Deut 23:19–20). Notably, there is another formulation of this *baraita* preserved in the commentaries of R. Ḥananel, Alfasi, *Sefer ha-Terumot*[126] and in the Yemeni *midrash* collection *Midrash ha-Gadol*:

> ... [ת]נו רבנן: „את כספך לא תתן לו בנשך ובמרבית" (ויקרא כב, לז) – אין לי אלא נשך בכסף ורבית באוכל, נשך באוכל מנין? ת"ל „נשך אוכל" (דברים כג, כ). רבית בכסף מנין? ת"ל „נשך כסף" (דברים כג, כ) – אם אינו ענין לנשך כסף שהרי נאמר „את כספך לא תתן לו בנשך" (שם), תנהו ענין לרבית כסף.

> Our Rabbis taught: "You shall not give your money to him (i.e., a borrower) on advance interest (נשך), nor shall you give him your foodstuffs on accrued interest (מרבית)" (Lev 25:37) – (from this) I only know that advance interest (applies) to money and accrued interest to foods; whence (do I learn that) advance interest applies to foods? The Torah says, "advance interest of food" (Deut 23:20). Whence (do I know the prohibi-

125 I have translated according to the rabbinic understanding of this verse – namely, that it refers to the borrower and his obligation not to borrow on interest. This will be important in our discussion of this *baraita*. I do not describe this interpretation as midrashic because תשיך is, in fact, in the causitive form. Thus, the verse might mean, "Do not cause your brother to charge advance interest." See Ibn Ezra's commentary on the verse as well as A. S. Hartom's in *TaNaKH* (Tel Aviv, Yavneh Publishing, Ltd., 1996). Nevertheless, RaSHbaM in his commentary and the Aramaic, Syriac, and Greek translations hold that the verse refers to the lender.

126 אוצר מפרשי התלמוד – בבא מציעא, ed. Makhon Yerushalaim (Jerusalem: 1989), 3:32, n. 2.

> tion of) accrued interest (applies to) money? The Torah says, "advance interest of money" (Deut 23:20). Since (this phrase) is superfluous (regarding the) issue (of monetary advance interest) because it already was stated, "you shall not give your money to him on advance interest (נשך) . . ." (Lev 25:37), apply it to monetary accrued interest. . . .

The *baraita* in this form conforms completely to the typical two pericope tannaitic אם אינו ענין. This version seems to solve our problem, but we still must ask, "How did the Talmud's version develop?"

According to the rabbinic interpretation of Deut 23:20, it is the only verse in the Torah that refers to an interest prohibition in regard to the borrower. It is also the only verse that by itself and through a superfluity generates an אם אינו ענין *midrash*, proving that the prohibition on advance and accrued interest applies equally to both money and foodstuffs. Since all the other verses dealing with interest do not achieve this and since they all refer to lenders, this is a good example of a tannaitic "single pericope" אם אינו ענין. This form of אם אינו ענין seems to be the basis for the printed edition of the Talmud's version of our *baraita* in Baba Meẓiᶜaᵓ and the version prevalent in Ashkenaz.

The version of the *baraita* preserved in North African, Yemeni, and Sephardic sources represents an alternative form of tannaitic אם אינו ענין. It is the more typical "two pericope" form of this hermeneutic. Using information about interest from the two most definitive pentateuchal sources on the subject, it finds a superfluous element and produces an אם אינו ענין interpretation that proves that the prohibition on advance and accrued interest applies to food and money. To do this, it compared a verse referring to a lender and one referring to a borrower. Since, however, the *baraita*'s inquiry was not about the parties involved in violating the interest prohibition but about the definition of the prohibition itself, the midrashist considered the shift from lender to borrower irrelevant. The author of the talmudic *baraita*, however, did not agree that the shift from lender to borrower was an insignificant matter. Therefore, he used verses from a single pericope dealing with the borrower alone.

In sum, both of these *baraita* versions contain אם אינו ענין interpretations that conform to tannaitic standards. One version seems to have circulated in Ashkenaz and the other in Sepharad, North Africa, and the Middle East. The two differ over whether an אם אינו ענין *midrash* must draw on verses from within the context of its new application section or whether it can draw from other contexts. The Talmud's *baraita* demands that the context of the verses of an אם אינו ענין be the same as the context of the new application section of the *midrash*; the version preserved by R. Ḥananel, Alfasi, *Sefer ha-Terumot*, and *Midrash ha-Gadol* rejects this limitation.

Sanhedrin 83b=Zebaḥim 17a. A midrashic *baraita* containing an אם אינו ענין interpretation appears in bSanhedrin and bZebaḥim. It deals with the status of a person who has gone through all the procedures to remove ritual impurity but must wait until the sun sets in order to become completely pure. This individual is known as a טבול יום (*tebul yom*, i.e., someone who has undergone ritual immersion during the day). In rabbinic law such a person is, on one hand, ritually impure enough to be barred from participating in Temple rites and to render the priestly gift called תרומה (*terumah*, heave offering) contaminated. On the other hand, the *tebul yom* was sufficiently pure not to create more than three removes of impurity. Thus, if a *tebul yom* touched sacrificial flesh, it became impure to a third degree. Under normal circumstances, if that flesh came into contact with other sacrificial meat, it contaminated it to a fourth degree of impurity, at which point the possibility of further contamination ended. In the case of the *tebul yom*, however, the possibility of contamination ended at the third level of impurity. Other leniencies also extended to the *tebul yom*, whose status was somewhat pure and somewhat impure.

The Talmud presents the midrashic *baraita* we will now analyze as the pentateuchal basis for the law that a *tebul yom* who performs a sacrificial service profanes it. In Zebaḥim this is the whole matter; in Sanhedrin the discussion extends to the subject of the death penalty for the act of profanation. The *baraita* states:

> [ו]טבול יום ששימש. מנלן? דתניא, רבי סימאי אומר: רמז לטבול יום שאם עבד[127] חילל מניין – תלמוד לומר +ויקרא כ"א+ קדשים יהיו לאלהיהם ולא יחללו, אם אינו ענין לטמא ששימש,[128] דנפקא לן מוינזרו[129] – תניהו ענין לטבול יום ששימש.[130]

> Whence (do we know) that a *tebul yom* who performs the sacrificial rites (profanes the sacrifice). As is it is taught (in a *baraita*). R. Simai says: Whence (do we find a) hint regarding the *tebul yom* who performs sacrificial rites that he profanes (the sacrifice). The Torah says, "They shall be holy to their God and not profane" (Lev 21:6).[131] If this is superfluous regarding the matter of someone ritually impure who performs the sacrificial service – (a rule) derived from "and they shall separate themselves"

127 עבד: כ"י מ: עבר (כנראה ט"ס).

128 לטמא ששימש: כ"י יד הר' הרצוג: לטמא.

129 מוינזרו: כ"י פירנצה 9–7 11: מוינזרו מקדשי בני ישר'. זבחים כ"י וטיקן 118: דנפקא לי מנייהו מוינזרו. זבחים כ"י וטיקן 121: דנפיק מוינזרו.

130 לטבול יום ששימש: כ"י יד הר' הרצוג: לטבול יום. וכ"ה בזבחים כי"י וטיקן 118, 121, וקולומביה 141x893.

131 The full verse says: "They shall be holy to their God and not profane the name of their God, for they offer the sacrifice of their God, and shall be holy."

(Lev 22:1)[132]– apply it to the matter of the *tebul yom* who performs the sacrificial service.

In spite of the attribution of this *midrash* to R. Simai, it does not conform to the typical form of tannaitic אם אינו ענין because the later pentateuchal verse mentioned in the *midrash* renders the earlier one redundant. This format is, as we have noted several times now, typical of post-tannaitic אם אינו ענין interpretations.[133] This problem is, however, very minor because the reference to the later pentateuchal verse, Lev 23:1–2, appears in what is obviously an Aramaic gloss.[134] Given the fact that the gloss is based on a third-generation amoraic midrashic interpretation by R. Joseph,[135] it cannot be the source for R. Simai's tannaitic אם אינו ענין.

We should also consider that R. Simai was seeking a רמז (*remez*), a hint to his notion, not proof.[136] There are no other cases of רמז in the halakhic *midrashim* or Talmuds that contain an אם אינו ענין component.[137] There are, however, elusive Babylonian talmudic רמז interpretations that have commentary added to them in an attempt to clarify them.[138] The commentary is sometimes attributed to a known authority, usually an *amora*, and at other times it is presented anonymously. Our אם אינו ענין is a case of this type of

132 (ב) דבר אל אהרן ואל בניו וינזרו מקדשי בני ישראל ולא יחללו את שם קדשי אשר הם מקדשים לי אני ידוד: (ג) אמר אלהם לדרתיכם כל איש אשר יקרב מכל זרעכם אל הקדשים אשר יקדישו בני ישראל לידוד וטמאתו עליו ונכרתה הנפש ההוא מלפני אני ידוד:

Speak to Aaron and his sons that they may be scrupulous about the sacred offerings of the Israelites that they sanctify to Me, so that they shall not desecrate My holy name. Say to them, "(A rule) for all your generations: any man of your seed in a state of ritual impurity who approaches the sanctified offerings that the Israelites sanctify to the Eternal shall be extirpated from before Me. I am the Eternal.

133 See above, pp. 123 and 126–27 for examples.

134 See R. Barukh Halevi Epstein's formulation of the אם אינו ענין in his *Torah Temimah*, Lev 21:6 and n. מא.

135 The *midrash* about "one who is impure who performs the sacrificial service" earlier in bSanhedrin 83b is attributed to R. Joseph. His application of Lev 22:1ff. to the act of performing the sacrificial service is neither the plain meaning of those verses nor the tannaitic understanding of them. The *tannaim* interpreted Leviticus 22 as pertaining to eating sanctified foods. See *Sifra*, ʾ*Emor*, par. 4:5.

136 A רמז is based on a verse that in its context does not actually deal with the midrashic interpreter's point. The midrashist recognizes and honestly reveals this. The existence of רמז, like that of זכר לדבר, suggests that other verses used in midrashic contexts were regarded as true pentateuchal proofs for the midrashist's legislation.

137 See *Sifre Num.* 116; *Midrash Tannaim*, Deut 21:23: ibid., Deut 24:13: bShabbat 103b=Taʿanit 2b; Yoma 74b; ibid., 78a; Yebamot 21a; Yebamot 54b; Nedarim 39b; Qiddushin 80b=Sanhedrin 21a=ʿAvodah Zarah 36b; Sanhedrin 10a=Makkot 2b; ibid., 46b; and Ḥullin 42a.

138 See bYebamot 21a; Sanhedrin 10a; Ḥullin 42a.

post-tannaitic commentary on R. Simai's elusive *midrash*. Consequently, it makes perfect sense for our אם אינו ענין interpretation to follow post-tannaitic norms of formulation.

R. Simai's prooftext for profanation of the sacrifices by a *tebul yom* who offers them needs clarification. Where is there any "hint" regarding a *tebul yom*? A comparison of his "hint" *midrash* with other tannaitic "hint" *midrashim* will solve the problem.

R. Simai's Hint in View of other Tannaitic "Hint" *Midrashim* An Excursus

Sifre Num. 116 presents a *midrash* that serves as a "hint" for the rule that the Levites must sing during the presentation of the obligatory sacrifices. It derives this, it appears, from the last clause of Num 18:3, ושמרו משמרתך ומשמרת כל האהל אך אל כלי הקדש ואל המזבח לא יקרבו ולא ימתו ,גם הם גם אתם "And they (the Levites) shall perform their duty to you (Aaron) and to the entire Tent, but they shall not come in contact with the furnishings of the Shrine or the altar lest they die, both they and you." גם הם גם אתם, a repetitive phrase that literally means "also they and also you," serves as the scriptural basis for the *midrash* though this part of the verse itself does not appear in *Sifre Number*'s presentation. Nevertheless, it is the only element that makes a connection between the Levites' and the priests' duties in the sanctuary.[139] It is clear from the verse that the Levites may not perform the sacrificial service. What then is their role in that service? The *midrash* concludes that it is the Levites' song.

What are the formal characteristics of this "hint" *midrash*? It contains a repetitive phrase; its plain meaning relates to the dismantling and re-erection of the sanctuary; and the issue it hints at is not actually mentioned in the biblical

139 Cf. *Sifre Num*. 116 and b^cArakhin 11a–b. The latter directly refers to the last clause of Num 18:3. The issue under discussion in ^cArakhin is the same as in *Sifre Num*. 116: the source for the requirement of song at the sacrificial service.

ספרי במדבר פיסקא קטז

ר׳ נתן אומר מיכן רמז לשיר מן התורה אלא שנתפרש ע״י עזרא. ר׳ חנניה בן אחי ר׳ יהושע אומר אין צריך שהרי כבר נאמר משה ידבר והאלהים יעננו בקול (שמות יט יט) מיכן רמז לשיר מן התורה:

תלמוד בבלי מסכת ערכין דף יא עמוד א–ב

חנניא בן אחי רבי יהושע אמר, מהכא +שמות י״ט+ משה ידבר והאלהים יעננו בקול....רבי יונתן אמר, מהכא: +במדבר י״ח+ ולא ימותו גם הם גם אתם, מה אתם בעבודת מזבח, אף הם בעבודת מזבח.

R. Jonathan's and R. Nathan's names interchange frequently in the literature given the similarity of their Hebrew spelling.

verse that serves as the *midrash*'s source. This characterizes yet another "hint" *midrash* in *Midrash Tannaim*.

In *Midrash Tannaim*, Deut 21:23, we find the following "hint" *midrash* based on the verse לא תלין נבלתו על העץ כי קבור תקברנו ביום ההוא כי קללת אלהים תלוי ולא תטמא את אדמתך אשר ידוד אלהיך נתן לך נחלה ("Do not allow his corpse to remain (hanging) on the gibbet, rather you shall surely bury him; for a hung criminal is a reproach to God. You shall not defile the land that the Eternal, your God, has given you as an inheritance.") The *midrash* is based on the repetitive clause כי קבור תקברנו, "rather you shall surely bury (lit., 'bury, you shall bury') him."

> ר׳ [שמעון בן] יהודה אומר משום ר׳ שמעון בן יוחאי מנ׳ למלין את מתו שהוא עובר בלא תעשה ת״ל כי קבור שאין ת״ל תקברנו אם כן מה ת״ל תקברנו מיכן רמז למלין את מתו שהוא עובר עליו בלא תעשה:
>
> R. (Simeon b.) Judah said in the name of R. Simeon b. Yoḥai: Whence (do we know that) one who detains the burial of his dead violates a negative commandment? The Torah says, "rather certainly bury (כי קבור)." This obviates the need for the Torah to say, "you shall bury him" (תקברנו). Why then does the Torah state "you shall bury him" (תקברנו)? From this (repetition) there is a hint to the violation of a negative commandment by one who detains the burial of his dead.

This "hint" *midrash*, like the previous one, contains 1) a repetitive phrase (כי קבור תקברנו), 2) a verse whose actual context is the public display of an executed criminal's body rather than the speedy burial of an upright individual, and 3) no actual reference to a negative commandment related to these upright individuals.[140] These characteristics all apply to R. Simai's "hint" *midrash*.

In R. Simai's *midrash*, the generative verse includes a repetition. At the verse's beginning we find the phrase, קדשים יהיו, "they shall be holy." This holiness refers to the prohibitions found in Lev 21:1–5 against priests defiling themselves or mutilating their bodies. What then could the repetition of the holiness requirement in the last clause of the verse indicate to R. Simai? The answer seems to be a state of holiness that goes beyond the limits of actual defilement and extends even to borderline impurity, i.e., the impurity of a *tebul yom*. This *midrash* fits the general pattern of "hint" *midrashim* we have established. It contains a repetition; its verse actually refers to the profanation of God's name rather than to the profanation of the sacrifices; and the subject of the "hint," the *tebul yom* who performs sacrificial rites, is not actually mentioned in the verse.

140 The prohibition לא תלין נבלתו על העץ, "do not maintain his corpse on the gibbet," refers only to executed criminals.

Sanhedrin 54b. Sanhedrin 54b presents us with another serious challenge to the claims we have made about the order of the verses in the tannaitic אם אינו ענין. A *baraita* cited there is parallel to *Sifra, Qedoshim* 10 (11). 1–2. The *baraitot* discuss various aspects of the prohibition on bestiality:

ספרא קדושים פ"י (יא), הל' א–ב

(א) ואיש להוציא את הקטן אשר יתן שכבתו בבהמה בין גדולה בין קטנה מות יומת בסקילה. אתה אומר בסקילה או באחד מכל המיתות שבתורה תלמוד לומר ואת הבהמה תהרוגו נאמר כאן הריגה ונאמר להלן הריגה מה הריגה האמורה להלן סקילה אף כאן סקילה. (ב) למדנו עונש לשוכב נשכב מנין תלמוד לומר כל שוכב עם בהמה מות יומת אם אינו ענין לשוכב תנהו לנשכב למדנו עונש בין לשוכב בין לנשכב אזהרה מנין תלמוד לומר ובכל בהמה לא תתן שכבתך לטמאה בה למדנו אזהרה לשוכב אזהרה לנשכב מנין תלמוד לומר לא יהיה קדש מבני ישראל ואומר וגם קדש היה בארץ דברי ר' ישמעאל ר"ע אומר אינו צריך הרי הוא אומר לא תתן שכבתך לא תתן שכיבתך.

תלמוד בבלי מסכת סנהדרין דף נד עמוד ב

תנו רבנן: +ויקרא כ' + איש – פרט לקטן, אשר יתן שכבתו בבהמה – בין גדולה בין קטנה, מות יומת – בסקילה. אתה אומר בסקילה, או אינו אלא באחת מכל מיתות האמורות בתורה? נאמר כאן תהרגו ונאמר להלן +דברים י"ג+ כי הרג תהרגנו, מה להלן בסקילה – אף כאן בסקילה. למדנו עונש לשוכב, עונש לנשכב מנלן? תלמוד לומר +שמות כ"ב+ כל שכב עם בהמה מות יומת, אם אינו ענין לשוכב – תניהו ענין לנשכב. למדנו עונש בין לשוכב בין לנשכב, אזהרה מניין? – תלמוד לומר +ויקרא י"ח+ ובכל בהמה לא תתן שכבתך לטמאה בה. למדנו אזהרה לשוכב, לנשכב מניין? תלמוד לומר +דברים כ"ג+ לא יהיה קדש מבני ישראל ואומר +מלכים א' י"ד+ וגם קדש היה בארץ וגו', דברי רבי ישמעאל. רבי עקיבא אומר: אינו צריך, הרי הוא אומר לא תתן שכבתך – לא תתן שכיבתך.

"A man"[141]– to the exclusion of a minor. "Who has carnal relations with (lit., gives his semen into) a beast"– whether (the beast) is young or mature. "He shall surely die"– by stoning. You say by stoning, or perhaps it is by one of the other capital punishments mentioned in the Torah? It states here "(and the beast) you shall kill." It says here "you shall kill" and it says further on "you shall certainly kill him" (Deut 13:10). Just as there (in Deuteronomy, the penalty is) stoning, so here too the penalty is stoning.

We have learned the punishment for the one who actively lies (with a beast), whence (do we derive) punishment for the passive participant in bestiality? The Torah says, "Anyone who lies with a beast shall surely

141 The *midrash* is based on Lev 20:15. In this case, a single translation will suffice insofar as the two sources are virtually the same.

> die" (Exod 22:18) – if this is not applicable to the active participant in bestiality (due to redundancy in light of Leviticus 20), apply it to the passive participant.
>
> We have learned the punishment for the active and passive participants in bestiality, whence (do we know) the warning (against such behavior)?[142] The Torah says, "You shall not have carnal relations with any beast to defile yourself thereby. . . ." (Lev 18:23).
>
> We have learned the warning for the active participant; whence (do we derive) a warning for the passive participant? The Torah says, "There shall be no male prostitutes among the children of Israel" (Deut 23:18), and it says, "Also there were male prostitutes in the land. . . ." (1 Kgs 14:24), (these are the) words of R. Ishmael. R. Akiba said, "(All) this is unnecessary. It says, "Do not give שכבתך (i.e., your semen)"– i.e., do not give שכיבתך ("your lying," i.e., either actively or passively).

This *baraita*'s formulation of its אם אינו ענין has the second verse in the interpretation, Lev 20:15, rendering the earlier verse, Exod 22:18, redundant. Redundancy in all other tannaitic "two pericope" אם אינו ענין interpretations has been the result of a second verse repeating the ideas already established in an earlier verse. In fact, that could have been the situation here. Exodus 22 potentially prohibits all forms of bestiality by its use of the inclusive כל שוכב עם בהמה, "all who lie with an animal." In view of this, Leviticus 20 could have been considered redundant, but neither the *baraita* in *Sifra* nor in the Talmud suggests this arrangement. Is this case a true exception to the general tannaitic formulary rule for אם אינו ענין or not? If it is, how do we explain this single deviation from all the other cases of tannaitic אם אינו ענין?

In this case a great deal hinges on the formulation of the *baraita* as it appears in the oldest *Sifra* manuscript we possess, Assemani 66.[143] There we find the following:

ספרא אסמני 66

„ואיש" להוציא את הקטן „אשר יתן שכבתו בבהמה מות יומת" בסקילה. אתה אר׳ בסקילה או אינו אילא באחת המיתות שבתורה תל׳ לו׳ ואת הבהמה תהרגו נא׳ כן הריגה ונא׳ להלן הריגה מה הריגה שנ׳ להלן סקילה אף הריגה שנאמרה כן סקילה. עונש שמענו אזהרה לא שמענו תל׳ לו׳ „ובכל בהמה לא תתן שכבתך

142 The rabbinic tradition holds that every punishable crime has a verse that serves as a warning. The warning verse contains only the prohibition without mention of the punishment for the crime.

143 Regarding the age of MS Assemani 66, see Louis Finkelstein, Introduction (Heb.) to the manuscript. Scholars prior to Finkelstein dated it between the eighth and tenth centuries C.E. Finkelstein dates it between the tenth and twelfth centuries. Nevertheless, it is certainly one of the oldest among the manuscripts of formative rabbinic literature.

> לטמאה בה.״ אין לי אילא שוכב נישכב מנ׳ תל׳ לו׳ „כל שוכב עים בהמה״ קרא הכתוב הנישכב שוכב עונש שמענו אזהרה לא שמענו תל׳ לו׳ „ולא יהיה קדש מבני ישראל״ ואומר „גם קדש היה בארץ עשו ככל תועבות הגוים אשר הוריש יי מפני בני ישראל....[144]

> "A man"– to the exclusion of a minor. "Who has carnal relations with a beast shall surely die"– by stoning. You say by stoning, or is it perhaps by any other capital penalty mentioned in the Torah? The Torah says, "and the beast shall you kill." The verse here (Lev 20:15) speaks of killing, and it speaks further on (in Deut 13:10) of killing. Just as the killing referred to there is by stoning, so the killing mentioned here is by stoning. We have heard the punishment (for bestiality), but we have not heard the warning. (Therefore,) the Torah says, "You shall not have carnal relations with any beast to defile (yourself) thereby" (Lev 18:23). I only have (information about) the active participant in bestiality; whence (do I derive) the passive participant? The Torah says, "All who lie with a beast (shall surely die)" (Exod 22:18). Scripture calls the passive participant "one who lies."[145] We have heard the (passive participant's) punishment, but we have not heard (his) warning. (Therefore) the Torah says, "There shall be no male prostitute among the children of Israel" (Deut 23:18) and it says, "Also there were male prostitutes in the land who did according to all the abominations of the peoples that the Eternal drove out from before the children of Israel. . . ." (1 Kgs 14:24).

Though this *baraita* contains all the information we find in the printed *Sifra*'s and Talmud's *baraita*, its method is completely different. For our purposes

144 This *baraita* is parallel to *Mek.*, *Nezikin* 17:

> כל שוכב עם בהמה מות יומת. למה נאמר, לפי שהוא אומר +ויקרא כ טו+ ואיש אשר יתן שכבתו בבהמה, בסקילה. אתה אומר בסקילה, או אינו אלא באחת מכל מיתות האמורות בתורה, תלמוד לומר +ויקרא כ טו+ ואת הבהמה תהרוגו, נאמר כאן הריגה ונאמר להלן הריגה, מה להלן בסקילה, אף כאן בסקילה. עונש שמענו, אזהרה מנין, תלמוד לומר +שם /ויקרא/ יח כג+ ובכל בהמה לא תתן שכבתך; אין לי אלא עונש ואזהרה לשוכב, עונש לנשכב, מנין תלמוד לומר כל שוכב עם בהמה מות יומת, קרא הכתוב לנשכב כשוכב, מה זה בסקילה אף זה בסקילה. עונש שמענו, אזהרה לא שמענו, תלמוד לומר +דברים כג יח+ לא תהיה קדשה מבנות ישראל ולא יהיה קדש מבני ישראל, ואומר +מ״א=מלכים א׳= יד כד+וגם קדש היה בארץ עשו מכל תועבות הגוים אשר הוריש יי.

The formulation of this *baraita* indicates that it is taken from a *midrash* on Leviticus, probably the one represented in *Sifra Assemani* 66, and used in reference to the same subject in Exodus.

145 That is, once Scripture uses the inclusive כל ("all") and the preposition עם ("with"), every form of lying with a beast is included. Thus, "one who lies with a beast" can refer to either the active or passive participant in bestiality. Either way he or she is having carnal intercourse with the animal. One might reach this conclusion without resorting to אם אינו ענין. See R. Meir Leibush Malbim, התורה והמצוה, Lev 20:15, n. קי״ד (114).

the most striking difference is the lack of the אם אינו ענין component in the *midrash*. This raises the possibility that the oldest and, perhaps, most original version of *Sifra* that included *baraitot* interpreting the Torah's sexual prohibitions did not make any reference to an אם אינו ענין *midrash*. We cannot, however, be sure of this because of a comment by Abbaye, one of the most prominent fourth-generation *amoraim*.

In a continuation of the discussion of the punishment for bestiality, Abbaye tries to determine how many sin offerings one would have to bring if he had mistakenly violated the bestiality prohibition, as follows:

> אביי אמר: אפילו לדברי רבי ישמעאל נמי אינו חייב אלא אחת, דכי כתיב לא יהיה קדש בגברי כתיב. – אלא לרבי ישמעאל אזהרה לנשכב מנא ליה? – נפקא ליה +שמות כ״ב+ מכל שכב עם בהמה מות יומת, אם אינו ענין לשוכב – תניהו ענין לנשכב. ואפקיה רחמנא לנשכב בלשון שוכב, מה שוכב – ענש והזהיר, אף נשכב – ענש והזהיר.
>
> Abbaye said: Even according to R. Ishmael, (the passive partner in bestiality) is only obligated for one (sin offering if he commits this sin without knowing one is liable for it). Because when (the Torah) writes, "There shall be no male (temple) prostitute," it refers to (relations between) human beings (and not to bestiality; hence the passive partner in bestiality does not violate this prohibition and is not required to bring a sin offering for it). And whence does he (i.e., R. Ishmael) derive a warning against being a passive partner in bestiality? From "all who lie with a beast shall surely be put to death" (Exod 22:18) – if this verse is superfluous in regard to an active partner (see Lev 20:15), apply it to a passive partner. Scripture derives the passive partner using the language of active partnership. Just as (Scripture) punishes and warns the active partner, so it punishes and warns the passive partner. (And since both are derived from the use of language applicable to the active partner in bestiality, it is as if active and passive partnership are all one matter. Hence, one who violates the bestiality prohibition in error, whether actively or passively, commits one sin and brings one sin offering.)

Abbaye's comment virtually recapitulates our *Sifra baraitot* in its own way and in Aramaic. This indicates that Abbaye did not know the original form of the tannaitic *midrash* on bestiality, for if he did, he would most likely have cited it.[146] Nevertheless, his comment shows he had knowledge of the *baraita*'s

146 PT also shows that the *Sifra baraita*'s form was unknown, but some of its contents were vaguely remembered. See pSanhedrin 7:7 (25a). I suggest that there was a progressive uncovering of the original form of the *baraita*. See pSanhedrin 7(14):9 (24d–25a). *Pene Mosheh* tries to bring the PT material into line with BT – a phenomenon noted in our discussion – but PT's text does not

contents. But which *baraita* did Abbaye know? Perhaps he knew aspects of two different *baraitot* that proved the same point using different methods. I would suggest, however, that he probably knew only the content of a *baraita* similar to the one in *Sifra Assemani* 66=*Mek. Nezikin* 17. However, in order to clarify how the active verb שוכב in Exod 22:18 could be construed as a reference to the passive participant in bestiality (הנשכב), he added an explanatory gloss in the form of an אם אינו ענין *midrash*.[147] Removal of the אם אינו ענין *midrash* from the printed *Sifra*'s and Talmud's *baraita* would not affect their midrashic interpretation of the bestiality prohibition. It would just make the interpretation of R. Ishmael in the *Sifra* and talmudic *baraita* virtually equivalent to *Sifra Assemani* 66. When later talmudic Sages or redactors recovered the original tannaitic *baraita*, they included Abbaye's explanatory *midrash* as part of it in order to explain the relationship between Exodus 22 and Leviticus 20.[148] If this is so, then the אם אינו ענין is amoraic and not surprisingly follows the formulary rules of the *amoraim*.

Regarding the *baraita* text in the printed editions of *Sifra*, it is possible scribes replaced the original *Sifra baraita* with the talmudic one because the latter is easier to understand and also includes R. Akiba's view. Furthermore, it was and still is a common practice for traditional rabbinical scholars to "correct" non-Babylonian talmudic works using the Babylonian Talmud. Consequently, they may have "corrected" our *Sifra baraita* according to this method, and eventually this "correction" became the dominant version.[149] Notably, the oldest *Sifra* commentaries show that their authors had texts that were the same as the *baraita* in Assemani 66, which apparently was the original *Sifra baraita*.[150]

---

support his comments. The discussion in PT is reminiscent of Abbaye's and R. Abbahu's discussions in BT. It is likely that BT's discussion was influenced by Palestinian sources.

147 Rabbenu Hillel's *Sifra* commentary shows how this process might have worked. The text R. Hillel (tenth century) comments on is exactly equivalent to *Sifra Assemani* 66. He explains that text, using the אם אינו ענין *midrash* found in the Talmud and in Abbaye's discussion of the bestiality prohibition. R. Hillel then informs us that this is the version found in the Talmud, i.e., as opposed to what is in *Sifra*.

148 The phenomenon of amoraic commentary being added into original *baraita* material has been noted by many, but especially by Ch. Albeck, מחקרים בברייתא ובתוספתא (Jerusalem: 1969), pp. 23–31; Judith Hauptman, *Development of the Talmudic Sugya: Relationship Between Tannaitic and Amoraic Sources* (Lanham, New York and London: 1988), p. 217.

149 Traditional commentators on PT have generally tried to bring the Palestinian material into line with BT. See above, n. 146 for an example. Bringing *Sifra* formulations into line with the language of BT parallels is basic to R. Elijah of Vilna's glosses to *Sifra* called הגהות הגר"א. See Louis Finkelstein, "הערות ותיקוני-נוסח בתורת כהנים," *Louis Ginzberg Jubilee Volume on the Occasion of his Seventieth Birthday*, eds., Saul Lieberman, Alexander Marx, Shalom Spiegel, and Solomon Zeitlin (New York: Jewish Theological Seminary, 1945), pp. שה–שח.

150 We have already mentioned Rabbenu Hillel. See also the *Sifra* commentary attributed to R. Samson of Sens. The comment is virtually the same as Rabbenu Hillel's, though it is formulated dif-

Summary
The Tannaitic אם אינו ענין in BT

The tannaitic *midrashim* containing אם אינו ענין interpretations that appear in BT fall into two categories: 1) exact or nearly exact parallels of original tannaitic *baraitot*; and 2) material presented in BT as tannaitic *baraitot* containing אם אינו ענין *midrash* that deviates from the characteristic tannaitic forms of אם אינו ענין. In most of the latter cases the אם אינו ענין component is an obvious addition or gloss to the original contents of the *baraita*. Often variants in manuscripts or in the texts witnessed to by early commentators corroborate this. We may therefore conclude that any *baraita* containing an אם אינו ענין *midrash* with non-tannaitic features indicates either 1) an amoraic or post-amoraic explanatory addition into the original *baraita* in the form of an אם אינו ענין interpretation; or 2) an incorrect understanding or reconstruction of a tannaitic אם אינו ענין's form generated by an amoraic or post-amoraic glossator's misidentification of the *midrash*'s pentateuchal sources. None of the examples indicate any new formal developments in the tannaitic אם אינו ענין.

It has also become evident that the *amoraim* and those who followed them did not always have a clear knowledge of the pentateuchal sources of tannaitic אם אינו ענין interpretations. As we study BT's amoraic and post-amoraic אם אינו ענין, we will try to determine when this break in the continuum of tradition took place. As my other works on rabbinic hermeneutics show,[151] changes in forms and formal discontinuities between the tannaitic, amoraic, and post-amoraic periods are the norm. Here, I will try to delineate when this took place in regard to אם אינו ענין and why.

Amoraic אם אינו ענין *Midrashim*

In many cases it was not possible to date the אם אינו ענין *midrashim* in PT because they appeared anonymously. Often this was because PT אם אינו ענין interpretations were reconstructions of *midrashim* originally based on other hermeneutical methods, especially *ribbui*, or amoraic attempts to recreate the thought processes of tannaitic teachers. In our study of אם אינו ענין in the Babylonian Talmud we will analyze in chronological order only those אם אינו ענין *midrashim* that are identifiably amoraic. We begin with an אם אינו ענין exposition attributed to R. Joshua b. Levi, a first-generation Palestinian *amora*.

Pesaḥim 23b. bPesaḥim 23a–24b presents a long variation on a theme based on אם אינו ענין interpretations. Four generations participate in the passage's

---

ferently. Its author also uses bSanhedrin 54b to explain the less clear, but more original version of his *Sifra* text, which was the same as *Sifra Assemani* 66.

151 See Michael Chernick, לחקר המידות „כלל ופרט וכלל" ו„ריבוי ומיעוט" and לחקר מידת „גזירה שווה".

creation: R. Joshua b. Levi (first generation, Palestine), R. Samuel b. Nahmani (third generation, Palestine), Abbaye (fourth generation, Babylonia), and Abbaye's student, R. Papa (fifth generation, Babylonia). However, because each אם אינו ענין takes what is presented as R. Joshua b. Levi's אם אינו ענין *midrash* as its basic model,[152] we discover little about the formal development of אם אינו ענין over the generations. Therefore, I will concentrate on his interpretation alone.

The issue that forms the basis of the talmudic discussion in Pesaḥim 23b is whether a prohibited food is forbidden only in regard to eating or whether the prohibition extends to beneficial use as well.

> יתיב ההוא מרבנן קמיה דרבי שמואל בר נחמני, ויתיב וקאמר משמיה דרבי יהושע בן לוי:[153] מנין לכל איסורין שבתורה דכי היכי דאסורין באכילה הכי נמי אסורין בהנאה, ומאי ניהו – חמץ בפסח ושור הנסקל מנין.... דכתיב +ויקרא ו+ כל חטאת אשר יובא מדמה וגו׳. שאין תלמוד לומר באש תשרף ומה תלמוד לומר באש תשרף? אם אינו ענין לגופו, דכתיב[154] +ויקרא י+ והנה שרף – תנהו ענין לכל איסורין שבתורה. ואם אינו ענין לאכילה – תנהו ענין לאיסור הנאה.[155] אי מה כאן בשריפה – אף כל איסורין שבתורה בשריפה! אמר קרא +ויקרא ו+ בקדש באש תשרף, בקדש – בשריפה, ואין כל איסורין שבתורה בשריפה.
>
> A certain student sat in R. Samuel b. Naḥmani's presence. He (R. Samuel b. Naḥmani) sat and cited R. Joshua b. Levi (thus). Whence (do we know that) all prohibited (foods mentioned) in the Torah that are forbidden for consumption are also forbidden for beneficial use? And what are these things? Leavened items on Passover and (the flesh of) an ox that has been stoned (for killing a human being) [excursus]. . . . Whence (do we know this). As it is written: "Any *ḥattat*-offering whose blood has been brought (into the Tent of Meeting to make atonement in the Sanctuary shall not be eaten; it shall be burned in fire)" (Lev 6:23). It was superfluous for the Torah to state "it shall be burned in fire."[156] Why, therefore, does the Torah

152 All mss. attribute this citation to R. Joshua b. Levi. See below. PT, as we will see, attributes it to R. Johanan. R. Ḥananel, an early commentator on BT, attributes it only to an unnamed party. Even if the *midrash* is not accurately attributed, its provenance would appear to be within the first to third generation of *amoraim*, all of whom are considered to be within the circle of R. Johanan either as teacher or students. At the very least, both PT and BT attest that there was a question of prohibited benefit that was decided midrashically in the same way in both *Talmudim*.

153 כ״ה בכל כי״י.

154 דכתיב: בשאר כל כי״י איתא בצורה זו או בצורה דומה לה כגון „דהא כתיב״ או „דנפקא ליה״ חוץ מכ״י מ. שם איתא: וכל חטאת אשר יובא מדמה אל אהל מועד לכפר בקדש לא תאכל באש תשרף שאין ת״ל באש תשרף ומת״ל באש תשרף אינו ענין לגופו תנהו ענין לכל איסורין שבתורה.

155 אם אינו ענין לאכילה – תנהו ענין לאיסור הנאה: בכי״י א״פ, ביה״מ לרבנים EMC 1623 ,271, כי״מ 6: ליתא. ועי׳ דקד״ס, פסחים כד ע״א, הערה ש .

156 I.e., the Torah could simply have stated "it shall be burned." The phrase "in fire" is gratuitous.

> state "it shall be burned in fire?" If the phrase is not relevant for the issue under discussion – as it is written (דכתיב): "and behold, it was burned" (Lev 10:16)[157]– apply it to all the prohibited (foods mentioned) in the Torah. And if it is not applicable to the issue of eating,[158] apply it to the issue of benefit. (Say then) just as here (in Lev 6:23 there is a requirement to dispose of the prohibited food) by burning, so too all prohibited foods (must be disposed of) by burning! The Torah says, "(to make atonement) in the Sanctuary... shall be burned in fire"– (that which comes into the) Sanctuary (is subject to the requirement of) burning; but all (the other) prohibited foods are not (subject to the requirement of) burning.

R. Joshua b. Levi's *midrash* appears to be an amoraic אם אינו ענין because the later pentateuchal verse, Lev 10:16, renders the earlier verse, Lev 6:23, superfluous. This would seem to allow us to conclude that the amoraic אם אינו ענין existed from the first generation of the Palestinian *amoraim*. There are, however, many indications that R. Joshua b. Levi's midrashic interpretation is not actually an אם אינו ענין *midrash* at all.

The first issue we must consider is that R. Joshua b. Levi's *midrash* may be a Babylonian rendition of a Palestinian source. There is much to support this possibility. The citation of R. Joshua's midrashic interpretation contains a relatively high use of of Aramaic. This is quite atypical in the presentation of early amoraic dicta, which tend to be formulated in Hebrew. Further, there is a rather lengthy Aramaic and anonymous excursus separating the opening question of R. Joshua's *midrash* from its prooftext. The resumptive repetition of מנין, "Whence (do we know this)?" indicates an interruption that entered into the original text at a later date.[159] This would indicate late, possibly post-amoraic, reconstruction of or commentary on the original midrashic text.[160] Above all, the Babylonian *sugya* in bPesaḥim 23b–24a parallels much of the

157 This cryptic reference is to Lev 10:16–20. On the day of the dedication of the Tabernacle, two sons of Aaron died. At a certain point in the dedicatory rites, Moses inquires about the goat that Aaron had slaughtered as a *ḥattat*-offering. Discovering that it had been burned, Moses becomes angry and states that since its blood had not been brought into the Sanctuary to effect atonement, the *ḥattat* was properly offered and should have been eaten. He blames Aaron for failing to carry out his obligations, thereby withholding atonement from Israel. Aaron explains his actions and Moses recognizes that Aaron's behavior was correct.

158 Logically, that which has been completely destroyed by burning cannot be eaten. Since the prohibition against eating counters the logic of the verse, it is devoid of sensible meaning, and is therefore superfluous. The אם אינו ענין removes the superfluity.

159 Shamma Friedman, "על דרך חקר הסוגיא," *Texts and Studies: Analecta Judaica*, ed. H. Z. Dimitrov-sky (New York: Jewish Theological Seminary, 1977), 1:303.

160 R. Ḥananel's presentation of the Babylonian *sugya* in his commentary also does not include any reference to R. Joshua b. Levi. Indeed, his formulation of the material reduces the use of Aramaic in the *midrash*'s opening and indicates clearly that the excursus is an addition by introducing it

material we find in pPesaḥim 2:1 (28c), and one section of the Palestinian *sugya* is of particular note:

> רבנן דקיסרין רבי אבהו בשם רבי יוחנן כל מקום שנאמר לא תאכל לא תאכלו אין את תופש איסור הנייה כאיסור אכילה לא תאכל לא יאכל את תופש איסור הנייה כאיסור אכילה בניין אב שבכולן וכל חטאת אשר יובא מדמה אל אוהל מועד לכפר בקודש לא תאכל באש תשרף.
>
> The Rabbis of Caesarea (cited) R. Abbahu (who reported this tradition) in the name of R. Johanan: Wherever it says "you shall not eat" (sing., לֹא תֹאכַל) or "you shall not eat" (pl., לֹא תֹאכְלוּ), you cannot claim there is a prohibition on beneficial use as there is on eating. (But) wherever it says "it shall not be eaten" (passive fem., לֹא תֵאָכֵל) or "it shall not be eaten (passive masc., לֹא יֵאָכֵל), you can claim there is a prohibition on beneficial use as there is a prohibition on eating. The paradigmatic verse (that one may use to interpret) all the other verses is, "Any *ḥattat*-offering whose blood has been brought (into the Tent of Meeting to make atonement in the Sanctuary shall not be eaten [לֹא תֵאָכֵל]; it shall be burned in fire)" (Lev 6:23).

According to this midrashic interpretation, the connection between the prohibition on eating and the requirement to burn the flesh of the invalid *ḥattat*-offering, thereby preventing any further use of its remains, creates a paradigm for interpreting every other prohibition on eating stated in the passive form. Thus, according to R. Johanan, the designated author of this *midrash*, a pentateuchal verse using just the passive form of the verb א-כ-ל (*a-k-l*) generates a prohibition on consumption of a forbidden food and all forms of beneficial use of it as well.

Though there is no mention of R. Joshua b. Levi in this citation,[161] this Pal-

with ואמרינן, "and we say." R. Ḥananel uses this introductory formula to indicate anonymous glosses. R. Ḥananel's presentation of the beginning of the *sugya* is as follows:

> יתיב ההוא מרבנן וקאמר: מנין לחמץ ושור הנסקל שאסורין בהנאה? ואמרינן ותיפוק ליה מלא תאכל....
>
> A student sat and said, "Whence (do we know that) leavened products (on Passover) and the ox executed by stoning are prohibited for beneficial use?" And we say (in Aramaic), derive it from "you shall not eat" etc.

More interestingly, when R. Ḥananel resumes the *midrash* after the anonymous excursus, he introduces its response and prooftext section with the formula ופרשינן, "and we explain," which he uses to introduce anonymous responses to questions. Does he wish to imply that the student asked a question to which the *stam* responded? While that is possible, I believe R. Ḥananel is proposing that the response and proof sections of the *midrash* in their BT formulation are a hybrid mix of original amoraic and later anonymous material that cannot be given full amoraic status.

161 See previous footnote and n. 152 above.

estinian *midrash* based on Lev 6:23 contains all the halakhic information that the BT's *midrash* presents without using the אם אינו ענין hermeneutic. On these grounds, I believe that the *midrash* attributed to R. Joshua b. Levi included only this:

> מנין לכל איסורין שבתורה דכי היכי דאסורין באכילה הכי נמי אסורין בהנאה? דכתיב +ויקרא ו+ כל חטאת אשר יובא מדמה וגו׳.
>
> Whence (do we know that) all the prohibitions in the Torah that are prohibitions on eating are also prohibitions on beneficial use? As it is written, "Any *ḥattat*-offering whose blood has been brought (into the Tent of Meeting to make atonement in the Sanctuary shall not be eaten; it shall be burned in fire)" (Lev 6:23).

In this form, the *midrash* is not an אם אינו ענין interpretation at all. Rather, it is a simple בנין אב, the use of a well-defined verse as a paradigm for interpreting other less-defined verses with similar formulary characteristics. The אם אינו ענין *midrash* in BT is, in my view, a purely Babylonian commentary on the original Palestinian interpretation, the workings of which the Babylonian recipients did not fully understand. This is not surprising because there is no mention of the paradigmatic nature of the verse in BT's version of this *midrash*. Had there been, the Babylonians would have recognized the *midrash* as a בנין אב, and no further comment would have been necessary. I believe Abbaye is the author of this commentary and of the אם אינו ענין it contains.[162] The

162 On bPesaḥim 24a there is the citation of a *midrash* of Exod 29:34 attributed to R. Jonathan. This *midrash* also seems to be a בנין אב, i.e., a *midrash* based on a paradigmatic verse, similar to the interpretation cited in R. Joshua b. Levi's name. It too supports a prohibition on eating forbidden foods and the extension of that prohibition to beneficial use of the forbidden foodstuff. Like the *midrash* in R. Joshua b. Levi's name, it receives what I consider to be a commentary based on אם אינו ענין. Abbaye rejects what BT reports as R. Jonathan's verse as the source of the prohibitions, and defends what appears as R. Joshua b. Levi's *midrash*.

BT's report of Abbaye's defense of R. Joshua b. Levi's *midrash* demands considerable re-reading of Lev 6:23, while Exod 29:34, R. Jonathan's verse, seems to work perfectly without emendation. If we read Abbaye independently of the excursus attached to R. Jonathan's *midrash*, his objection to R. Jonathan's interpretation might be that it is based on a verse that describes a one-time event, the dedication of the desert Sanctuary. Abbaye therefore prefers R. Joshua's *midrash*, which is drawn from a verse describing a regular sacrifice and its rules. The following is Abbaye's comment:

> אמר אביי: לעולם מקרא קמא, ואיפוך. דליכתוב באש תשרף ולא בעי לא תאכל, מה תלמוד לומר לא תאכל? אם אינו ענין לגופו, דנפקא ליה מדרבי אלעזר – תנהו ענין לכל איסורין שבתורה. (ואם אינו ענין לאכילה) [עיין תוס׳ ד״ה ואם אינו ענין לאכילה] – תנהו ענין לאיסור הנאה.
>
> Abbaye said: (The best proof is) from the first citation (Lev 6:23), but one must reverse (elements of the verse). Let the verse write (first) "it shall be burned in fire" and (then the phrase) "it shall not be eaten" would be unnecessary. Why then does the Torah state, "it

stam then applied his commentary to other verses and their interpretations that appear in bPesaḥim 23b–24a.

Thus, I believe that what is cited as R. Joshua b. Levi's *midrash* does not provide us with any information about the date of the development of the amoraic אם אינו ענין. Rather, the commentary on his *midrash*, which contains an אם אינו ענין interpretation, tells us only what form the אם אינו ענין interpretation took in some amoraic generation, perhaps Abbaye's. Assuming my reconstruction of this midrashic material is correct, we still do not know whether the amoraic אם אינו ענין emerged earlier than Abbaye's time. Therefore, we continue our investigation of what appears to be an אם אינו ענין *midrash* of Hezekiah, a first-generation Palestinian *amora*.

A First-Generation Amoraic אם אינו ענין

Menaḥot 72b. An אם אינו ענין *midrash* attributed to Ḥezekiah, a first-generation Palestinian *amora*, provides a scriptural base for the rule in mMenaḥot 6:1, which grants the priests the desanctified remainders of barley flour offerings like the *ᶜomer* (עמר) and the offering of the suspected wife.

> מנלן? אמר חזקיה,[163] דאמר קרא: +ויקרא/ז׳/י׳+ וכל מנחה בלולה בשמן וחרבה לכל בני אהרן תהיה, אם אינו ענין לבלולה של חיטין – תנהו ענין לבלולה של שעורין, ואם אינו ענין לחרבה של חיטין – תנהו ענין לחרבה של שעורים.
>
> Whence (do we know that the remnants of barley offerings go to the priests). Ḥezekiah said:[164] Scripture says, "Every meal offering whether mixed with oil or dry shall belong to the sons of Aaron" (Lev 7:10). If it (the verse) is inapplicable to a mingled offering of wheat (flour), apply it to a mingled offering of barley (flour). and if it (the verse) is inapplicable to a dry offering of wheat (flour), apply it to a dry offering of barley (flour).

The logic of this אם אינו ענין is: 1) The Torah generally required flour offerings to be of fine flour, which, by definition, meant wheat flour (Lev 2:1). 2) The remainders of the mingled flour offerings belonged to the priests (Lev 2:3 and 2:10), and the remainders of dry wheat flour offerings also went to the priests

---

shall not be eaten"? If it is not necessary for itself (i.e., for a prohibition on eating), which we derive from (an interpretation of) R. Elazar, apply it to all the prohibitions (on consumption) in the Torah (in order to generate a) prohibition on beneficial use.

See Tosafot s.v. אם אינו ענין לאכילה.

163 חזקיה: כ״ה בכל כתבי היד.

164 Ḥezekiah appears in all the extant mss. and in the first Venice printing of BT.

(Lev 5:11 and 5:13). Hence, the Torah's statement, "Every meal offering whether mixed with oil or dry shall belong to the sons of Aaron," is redundant. Ḥezekiah's *midrash* undoes the redundancy by applying it to the as yet undefined realm of rules regarding barley offerings. The result is that as the Mishnah rules, the remainders of barley offerings, like those of wheat offerings, go to the priests.

In terms of its basic form, Ḥezekiah's אם אינו ענין is no different from the tannaitic אם אינו ענין.[165] Regarding the application of Lev 7:10 to barley offerings, this is also consistent with tannaitic usage in which new applications were found within a single rubric. Here the general rubric is flour offerings. There are only two varieties of such offerings, wheat and barley. Hence, if the Torah has made known all the rules governing flour offerings of wheat, a redundant verse teaches rules about the alternative variety of flour offerings – barley offerings – whose rules are undefined.

We may conclude that the first amoraic generation, to the rather limited extent it is represented in BT, appears to have known the tannaitic rules and forms for אם אינו ענין. Ḥezekiah, assuming he is not citing a tannaitic *midrash*, followed his predecessors' methods and forms when he constructed his own אם אינו ענין interpretation. It is not surprising that he maintained the traditional form of אם אינו ענין since it simply existed and was available. It is new development that is the more interesting phenomenon and the one that demands an explanation.

A Second-Generation Amoraic אם אינו ענין

Yebamot 95a. A *baraita* citing R. Judah's view about a dispute between the Shammaites and Hillelites appears as an opening into an אם אינו ענין interpretation by R. Ami (3, Palestine) citing Resh Laqish (2, Palestine). R. Judah held that Bet Hillel and Bet Shammai never disagreed over the law regarding a man who had relations with his mother-in-law. This forbidden sexual act definitely prohibited his wife from continuing marital relations with him. R. Ami cited Resh Laqish's explanation of R. Judah's position:

> אמר רבי אמי אמר ריש לקיש:[166] מאי טעמא דרבי יהודה? דכתיב: +ויקרא כ׳+ באש ישרפו אותו ואתהן, וכי כל הבית כולו בשרפה? אם אינו ענין לשרפה, תנהו ענין לאיסורא.

165 See *Sifra*, *Nedabah*, par. 12:7, which may have served as a paradigm for Ḥezekiah. The *midrash* also appears in pSotah 3:1 (18c) as a *baraita* that R. Zeira taught to R. Isaac of 'Attush. To the extent that תנא דבי חזקיה in BT and תני (ר׳) חזקיה in PT accurately portray Ḥezekiah as a collector and "reciter" of midrashic *baraitot*, the *midrash* attributed to him here may in fact be of tannaitic origin. In that case, what we are encountering here may be the phenomenon of a *baraita* cited as an amoraic teaching, a phenomenon we have discussed above. See Introduction, pp. 21–22.

166 אמר רבי אמי אמר ריש לקיש: בכ״י א״פ Opp. 248 (367): א״ר זריקא א״ר אביי מ״ט (דר״ל) דר׳ יהודה.

> R. Ammi cited Resh Laqish:[167] What is R. Judah's rationale (for saying that the Houses agreed that a wife was prohibited to her husband if he had relations with her mother). As it is written: "In fire shall they be burned, he and them" (Lev 20:14). And is it really possible that the entire household[168] is (subject to) burning?[169] Hence, if (the verse) is not applicable to burning (because that is logically inconceivable if justice is to be done), apply it to the matter of prohibition (of a wife to her husband if he had relations with her mother).[170]

This אם אינו ענין uses logic to create superfluity. That is, Lev 20:14 is rendered logically untenable if justice means anything. Hence, Resh Laqish suggests that we apply it to a prohibition on conjugal relations between the wife and her husband rather than maintaining that the innocent wife receive capital punishment along with her guilty mother and spouse.

Why does Resh Laqish think that Lev 20:14, a verse that discusses punishment, should be understood as applying to prohibition? I would suggest he was guided by the fact that the only other discussion of the sexual offense of

---

כי"מ: א"ר זריקא א"ר אמי אמר ריש לקי'. כי"מ 141: א"ר זריקא א"ר אמי אמר ר' שמעון בן לקיש. דפוס פיזרו: א"ר אמי אמ' ריש לקיש.

167 All major mss. have either "R. Ammi cited Resh Laqish" or "R. Zeriqa cited R. Ammi, who cited Resh Laqish (or R. Simeon b. Laqish)." MS Oxford Opp. 248 (367) has "R. Zeriqa cited R. Abbaye, 'What is the rationale (of Resh Laqish) of R. Judah. . . .'"

168 I.e., husband, wife, and mother-in-law.

169 I.e., why should the wife be executed by burning? What sin has she committed?

170 This *midrash* has a parallel in pYebamot 10:6 (11a). There "the comrades" (חבריא) cited R. Johanan as its author:

> חבריא בשם ר' יוחנן: מאי טעמא דרבי יודה? באש ישרפו אותו ואתהן. מה אנן קיימין? אם לענין שריפה, אין נשרפת אלא אחת. אלא אם אינו ענין לשריפה, תניהו ענין לאיסור.

> The comrades citing R. Johanan (said): What is R. Judah's rationale (for saying that the Houses agreed that a wife was prohibited to her husband if he had relations with her mother). "In fire shall they be burned, he and them" (Lev 20:14). With what are we dealing? If with the matter of burning, (then) only one of them is burned. Rather, if there is no application to the matter of burning (as related to the wife), apply the verse to the issue of prohibition (of the wife to her husband if he had relations with his mother-in-law).

Though there are differences in attribution, including one to R. Abbaye (second generation, Palestinian *amora*), the content of this *midrash* is essentially the same in BT and PT, and both sources, with exception of one ms., attribute it to the two of the best known second-generation Palestinian *amoraim*. Additionally, the Talmuds link R. Johanan and Resh Laqish (R. Simeon b. Laqish) as teacher and student. On the basis of this conception of the relationship of these two Sages, it is not hard to imagine how attribution from one to another of them might take place. No matter who the original author of this midrashic tradition is, those who cite it view it as emerging from the second Palestinian amoraic generation. See Kraemer, "On the Reliability of Attributions" pp. 179–81; Kalmin, *Sages, Stories*, p. 14.

a man having sexual relations with a woman and her daughter appears in Lev 18:17. There the Torah only declares this behavior prohibited, but it does not mention any sanctions. Consequently, Resh Laqish suggests that while the wife did not deserve the death penalty, nevertheless Lev 20:14 requires some action in relation to her husband and her. After all, the verse prohibiting the relationship of a man with a daughter and her mother spoke of punishment for "him and them" (fem. pl., אתהן). Lev 18:17 provides the choice of a prohibition on sexual contact between the wife and her husband.

There is nothing in Resh Laqish's *midrash* that is not fully consonant with the tannaitic form of אם אינו ענין. Therefore, we must conclude that whatever changes took place in this hermeneutic and midrashic form occurred later than the second amoraic generation. We will turn now to a group of אם אינו ענין interpretations by R. Elazar (third generation, Palestine), the majority of which are similar in form and method to the tannaitic אם אינו ענין.

Third-Generation R. Elazar, Tannaitic Forms

Shebu^c ot 16b. mShebu^cot 2:3 discusses the case of a person who becomes ritually contaminated while in the Temple court. R. Elazar's *midrash* provides a scriptural basis for punishing the contaminated person with extirpation (כרת) for willful violation of this prohibition or obliging him or her to bring a sin-offering if the violation was unwitting:

טומאה בעזרה מנלן? א"ר אלעזר, כתוב אחד אומר: +במדבר י"ט+ את משכן ה' טמא, וכתוב אחד אומר: +במדבר י"ט+ כי את מקדש ה' טמא, (אם אינו ענין לטומאה שבחוץ, תנהו ענין לטומאה שבפנים.)[171]

171 This line of Talmud was deleted by R. Solomon Luria (seventeenth century). See, however, *Diqduqe Soferim*, Shebu^cot 16b, n. פ. All the major manuscripts and incunabula witness the presence of this אם אינו ענין *midrash*. pShebu^cot 2:3 (34a), however, contains this *midrash* without the אם אינו ענין element:

ניטמא בעזרה כו' רבי חזקיה רבי אמי בשם רבי לעזר כתוב אחד אומר את משכן יי' טמא וכתוב אחר אומר את מקדש יי' טמא הא כיצד ליתן חלק בין למיטמא בפנים למיטמא בחוץ מיטמא בפנים עד שיכניס ראשו ורובו מיטמא בחוץ עד שישהא כדי השתחויה....

R. Ḥezekiah cited R. Ammi who cited R. Lazar (= Elazar). One verse says, "... he contaminated the dwelling place of the Eternal," and another says, "... for he contaminated the sanctuary of the Eternal." What is the implication (of these two repetitive verses)? (They) provide a distinction between one who becomes ritually impure within (the Temple precincts) and one who becomes ritually impure outside (the Temple precincts). One who becomes ritually impure within (the Temple precincts is not culpable) until he has caused his head and most of his body to enter (the Temple). One who becomes ritually impure outside (the Temple precincts is not culpable) until he stays (in the Temple precincts for the) amount of time it takes to prostrate oneself.

> Whence (do we know that) ritual contamination (which one incurs) in the Temple court (requires expiation). R. Elazar said: One verse says, "... he contaminated the dwelling place of the Eternal" (Num 19:13), and another says, "... for he contaminated the sanctuary of the Eternal" (19:20). If (the latter verse) has no application to contamination (incurred) outside (the Temple), apply it to contamination (incurred) within (the Temple).

This *midrash* follows the formal and methodological principles typical of tannaitic אם אינו עניין interpretations. While Num 5:1–4 discusses the requirement to remove those who are ritually contaminated "from the camp"—understood by the Rabbis as the area of the desert sanctuary or, after the Temple was built, the Temple precincts – it does not discuss sanctions for the contamination of sacred space. Only Numbers 19 discusses that matter. Hence, R. Elazar deems it the single scriptural pericope that generates our אם אינו עניין. In the *midrash*, Num 19:20 unnecessarily repeats the contents of Num 19:13; thus the later pentateuchal verse in the *midrash* creates the requisite superfluity for an אם אינו עניין *derashah* in the style of the *tannaim*.

The logic of the reapplication of the redundant verse to some new area of the law is that the kind of impurity Numbers 19 discusses, namely, corpse-impurity, is usually encountered outside the sanctuary precincts and brought from there into the sanctuary's environs. This is the case because the sanctuary itself is carefully guarded against all forms of contamination.[172] Repetition of a discussion of the contamination of the sanctuary by corpse-impurity is redundant, thereby forcing a re-interpretation of the verse to remove the redundancy. Therefore the verse is applied to the rules covering the less frequent case of contamination that occurs within the sanctuary space itself. All this

---

The traditional commentators on PT revise the conclusion of this passage so that the one who is contaminated outside the Temple is culpable for entering the Temple in that state once he puts his head and most of his body into the sacred precincts. The one who is contaminated within the Temple becomes culpable for being in the Temple in an impure state when he or she has been there for the time it takes to prostrate oneself. The critical edition of MS Leiden published by the Academy for the Hebrew Language also notes that the formulation above is problematic.

On the basis of PT's formulation of R. Elazar's midrash it is possible that BT tradents received only the verses and the most basic elements of the halakhic conclusion that R. Elazar reached using some midrashic method. If so, BT seems to have reconstructed this *derashah* as best it could. Similar phenomena are noted by David Weiss Halivni, מקורות ומסורות – שבת (Jerusalem: Jewish Theological Seminary, 1982) p. רסו; מקורות ומסורות – עירובין–פסחים (Jerusalem: Jewish Theological Seminary, 1982), p. כט, n. 11; מקורות ומסורות – מועד (Jerusalem: Jewish Theological Seminary, 1975), p. תב and nn. 8*–10*. If so, the אם אינו עניין midrash attributed to R. Elazar may not in fact be his. Rather, it may be a redactor's reconstruction of what he thought was R. Elazar's midrashic basis for his halakhic view. The fact that the redactor's reconstruction replicated the tannaitic form of אם אינו עניין would then be serendipitous.

172 See Num 5:1–4.

conforms to typical tannaitic methodology and formulation of אם אינו ענין *midrashim*.

One more of R. Elazar's אם אינו ענין interpretations also follows the formulas and methods that the *tannaim* used – namely, the one in bZebaḥim 36a.[173] Yet, there are three other אם אינו ענין interpretations attributed to R. Elazar that, at least according to their present formulation in BT, follow what we have called the amoraic form.

Sanhedrin 61a = ᶜAvodah Zarah 51a = Zebaḥim 106a. In Sanhedrin, ᶜAvodah Zarah, and Zebaḥim the Talmud cites another אם אינו ענין *midrash* by R. Elazar. The *midrash* discusses whether idolatrous intention connected to an atypical act of idol worship creates culpability. Not surprisingly, the *midrash* concludes that it does:

> אמר רבי אליעזר:[174] מניין לזובח בהמה למרקוליס שהוא חייב – שנאמר +ויקרא י, ז+ ולא יזבחו עוד את זבחיהם לשעירם,[175] אם אינו ענין לכדרכה, דכתיב[176] איכה יעבדו,[177] תניהו ענין לשלא כדרכה....
>
> R. Elazar said: Whence (do we know that) one who slaughters an animal to Mercury is culpable (for idolatry). As it says (שנאמר), ". . . they shall no longer slaughter their offerings to the goat-demons. . . ." (Lev 17:7). If this verse is not applicable to the normal way (of serving Mercury), as it is

173 תלמוד בבלי מסכת זבחים דף לו עמוד א

> אמר רבי אלעזר: תרי קראי כתיבי בנותר, כתוב אחד אומר: +שמות יב+ לא תותירו ממנו עד בקר, וכתוב אחד אומר: +ויקרא ז+ לא יניח ממנו עד בקר, אם אינו ענין להניח, תנהו לענין מחשבת הינוח.

174 According to *Diqduqe Soferim*, bSanhedrin 61a and n. י and bZebaḥim 106a and n. ט. The mss. and early commentators all have "R. Elazar." See also the text witnesses for all these tractates in the Saul Lieberman Institute databases, which confirm this. The only exception is MS Paris H147A, which cites this *midrash* anonymously.

175 There may be some relationship between R. Elazar's *derashah* and pSanhedrin 7:1 (25c):

> אמר ר׳ תנחום בר יודן: אף על גב דרבי לעזר בי רבי שמעון אמר זיבח וקיטר ניסך בהעלם אחד אינו חייב אלא אח׳ מודה שאם עבדה בעבודת׳ בעבודת הגבוה בעבודת השתחויה שהוא חייב על כל אחת ואחת. מניין שאם עבדה בעבודתה בעבודת הגבוה בעבודת השתחויה שהוא חייב על כל אחת ואחת? ר׳ שמואל בשם ר׳ זעורה: ולא יזבחו עוד את זבחיהם לשעירים. אמר ליה: מטי תנה לקדשים.

176 שנאמר: סנהדרין: כ״י יד הרב הרצוג: דכת׳... דכת׳. וכ״ה בכ״י פירנצה 7–9 I II, קרלסרוהא רויכלין 2, ובכי״מ: דכ׳... דכת׳. אבל בדפוס ברקו רנ״ח: שנ׳... דכתי׳. ע״ז: כ״י ביה״מ לרבנים 15: ת״ל... דנפקא לי מאיכה. כי״מ: שנ׳... שנ׳. בכי״י פריז 731: שנ׳... דנפקא ליה מאיכה. בדפוס פיזרו רע״א: שנאמ׳... דכתיב. זבחים: וטיקן 118: שנ׳... ונפקא ליה מאיכה. וכ״ה בכ״י וטיקן 121: שנ׳... דנפקא ליה מואיכה, וכ״ה בכ״י פריז H147A, כי״מ: שנ׳... דנפקא לי׳ מואיכה , וכ״י קולומביה 141x893: שנ׳... דנפקא לי מואיכה. אך, בדפוס ונציה איתא: דכתיב... דכתי׳.

177 עי׳ מדרש תנאים, דברים יב, ל.

> written (דכתיב),[178] "... How do they (i.e., the nations) worship (their gods, that I may likewise serve them)?..." (Deut 12:30), apply it to atypical (forms of worshipping Mercury).

As we can readily see, this *midrash* considers the verse in Deut 12:30 the primary source for the prohibition on idolatrous worship carried out in its typical fashion. The Lev verse appears to repeat the same notion, thereby generating the אם אינו ענין. Accordingly, if all this is accurate, we have before us an amoraic אם אינו ענין *midrash*, and we may conclude that this form of אם אינו ענין is a third-generation Palestinian development. The issue, then, is whether all this is indeed accurate.

Here, as in some cases of the אם אינו ענין interpretations we have previously analyzed, there appears to be a gloss that interrupts the pure Hebrew of the *midrash* with an Aramaic rhetorical formula, דכתיב ("as it is written") or דנפקא ליה (לי) מואיכה ("he derives/I derive it"). This is supported by most manuscript traditions and early printed editions.[179]

Hence, it is likely that R. Elazar's *midrash* consisted only of its opening question, "Whence (do we know that) one who slaughters an animal to Mercury is culpable (for idolatry)?" and the prooftext, "... they shall no longer slaughter their offerings to the goat-demons...."[180] In this form, the meaning of the verse in R. Elazar's *midrash* would be as follows: Any act of slaughtering an animal for sacrificial purposes, which is what the Hebrew root ז-ב-ח used with the noun זבח implies,[181] would render the slaughterer culpable for idolatrous worship if he sacrificed to a "pseudo-deity."

178 Some mss. do not contain these different rhetorical introductions to a scriptural passage. Rather, they repeat שנאמר or דכתיב to introduce the biblical passages in this *midrash*. According to these readings, there are no glosses in this *midrash*. Based on the majority of mss., the discussion below accepts the idea that there is a gloss within this *midrash*. See *Midrash Tannaim, Deut.* 12:30, as the basis for culpability for idolatry performed in its regular mode.

179 As noted in the critical apparatus that appears in n. 176, the majority of the variants include Aramaic rhetorical introductions before the verse that produces the אם אינו ענין. The shift to Aramaic often indicates a post-amoraic interpolation. See Shamma Friedman, "על דרך חקר התלמוד," pp. 301–2, א-ב.

180 See the commentary of R. Ḥananel, b^cAvodah Zarah 51a:

> א"ר אלעזר מנין השוחט בהמה למרקוליס שחייב? ת"ל ולא יזבחו עוד את זבחיהם לשעירים וגו'.

> R. Elazar said: Whence (do we know that) one who slaughters an animal to Mercury is culpable (for idol worship). The Torah says, "They shall no longer sacrifice their sacrifices to the goat-demons, etc."

The term וגו' ("etc.") usually implies the completion of the verse. In this case that would mean the completion of Lev 17:7 rather than the completion of the *midrash* proposed by BT.

181 Ludwig Koehler and Walter Baumgartner, *Hebrew and Aramaic Lexicon of the Old Testament, CD-ROM Edition* (Leiden: Koniklijke Brill, 1994–2000), #2413:4.

bBekhorot 14b. In a discussion of the status of blemished animals that someone sanctified for sacrificial purposes,[182] R. Elazar takes the position that one who sacrificed them when private altars were permissible was culpable for violating the prohibition recorded in Deut 17:1 on sacrificing blemished animals. According to the talmudic passage, he created the following אם אינו ענין to substantiate his view:

> והשוחטן בחוץ פטור: רבי אלעזר מתני חייב ומוקי לה בבמת יחיד דאמר רבי אלעזר מנין לזובח בהמה בעלת מום בבמת יחיד בשעת היתר הבמות שהוא בלא תעשה שנאמר לא תזבח לה׳ אלהיך שור ושה אם אינו ענין לבמה גדולה דכתיב עורת או שבור וגו׳ תנהו ענין לבמת יחיד.[183]

> One who sacrifices them (blemished animals that have been dedicated as offerings) outside (of sanctified precincts) is exempt (from violating the law requiring sacrifice to take place in the sanctuary or other sacred precincts). R. Elazar taught: (He) is culpable. And he stated the case was one of (sacrifice of a blemished animal) at a private altar. As R. Elazar said: Whence (do we know that) one who sacrifices a blemished animal at a private altar during the era of permitted private altars violates a prohibition? As it says, "Do not sacrifice an ox or sheep (that is blemished) to the Eternal, your God" (Deut 17:1). If this verse has no application to a "great high place," as it is written (דכתיב): "Blind or lame" (Lev 22:25),[184] apply it to a private altar.

In this case, the *midrash* of R. Elazar superficially conforms to the tannaitic form of אם אינו ענין, but again the use of the Aramaic introduction דכתיב for the Leviticus verses suggests the presence of an addition into the original exposition. Therefore, we cannot be sure this *midrash* follows the formal patterns of the tannaitic אם אינו ענין.

In a certain sense, R. Elazar's *midrash* is a *non sequitur*. The central point

182 mBekhorot 2:2:

> כל הקדשים שקדם מום קבוע להקדשן, ונפדו, חיבים בבכורה ובמתנות, ויוצאין לחולין לגזז ולהעבד, וולדן וחלבן מתר לאחר פדיונן, והשוחטן בחוץ פטור, ...

> All sanctified animals whose permanent blemish precedes their sanctification, when redeemed, are subject (to the rules regarding) the firstborn and (other) priestly dues. But they are desacralized for the purposes of being shorn and worked. After their redemption, their progeny and milk are permitted, and the one who slaughters them outside the sanctuary precincts is (in all cases) exempt (from violating the prohibition of sacrificing outside of the area designated by the Torah), ...

183 There are no significant *variaes lectiones* in the major mss. and the ed. princ. Venice.

184 See Lev 22:20–25 for full context.

of the *mishnah* to which it is attached is that one who sacrifices a blemished animal dedicated as an offering does not violate any prohibition normally related to sacrifices. In sum, a blemished animal never becomes sanctified for sacrificial purposes. Thus, one cannot violate the prohibition on sacrificial slaughter outside of the sanctuary's precincts when one slaughters such an animal because the animal is, by definition, not a sacrificial beast. R. Elazar has a tannaitic tradition that says that, on the contrary, one is culpable for slaughtering this kind of animal outside the sanctuary. R. Elazar's *midrash*, however, does not address this matter. Rather, it addresses whether there was culpability for sacrificing a blemished animal at a private altar when private sacrifice was permitted, an issue that has nothing to do with the Mishnah's concerns. This suggests that R. Elazar's *midrash* originally had no direct connection to mBekhorot 2:2 but appears in relation to it due to the shared issues of blemished animals and culpability for sacrificing them. In fact, the connection, to the extent it exists, is the handiwork of the anonymous interlocutor who asserted that R. Elazar "stated the case (in mBekhorot 2:2) as one of (the sacrifice of a blemished animal) at a private altar." Therefore, we cannot know what purpose R. Elazar himself thought his *midrash* served.

Regarding the format of the *midrash* itself, I am tempted to approach it in the same manner as the previous case. The section including the אם אינו ענין may not be an integral part of the *midrash*, and the prooftext from Deuteronomy alone may serve all of R. Elazar's purposes. Two factors may have caused the addition of the אם אינו ענין section onto the original *midrash*: 1) it explains how the biblical citation refers to a private altar (במת יחיד); and 2) it deals with the Rabbis' perennial problem with repetition in the Pentateuch. In this case the problem of repetition emerges from the reiteration of the prohibition on sacrificing blemished animals (Lev 22:20–25, Deut 17:1). If indeed the אם אינו ענין is an addition onto his *midrash*, then R. Elazar's original *midrash* consists only of the following:

> אמר רבי אלעזר מנין לזובח בהמה בעלת מום בבמת יחיד בשעת היתר הבמות שהוא בלא תעשה שנאמר לא תזבח לה׳ אלהיך שור ושה....
>
> R. Elazar said: Whence (do we know that) one who sacrifices a blemished animal at a private altar during the era of permitted private altars violates a prohibition? As it says, "Do not sacrifice an ox or sheep (which is blemished) to the Eternal your God" (Deut 17:1). . . .

It is likely that the simple generality of this statement is enough to cover all cases, including the private altar. In that case, the *midrash*'s halakhic outcome is that blemished animals are never to be sacrificed to God under any circumstances. Doing so incurs culpability. Regarding Lev 22:20–25, one could make the argument that its realm of discussion, at least according to the rabbinic tradition, includes only sacrifices meant to be brought at the public altar of the communal sanctuary or במה גדולה.[185] But we need not claim that in order to understand R. Elazar's *midrash*.

If R. Elazar's original *midrash* lacks an אם אינו ענין component, we cannot conclude yet that a major change took place in the form of אם אינו ענין in the third amoraic generation. Further, even if his *midrash* includes such a factor, given the contamination of the original by a gloss, we have no way of knowing the nature of its original form.

bMe'ilah 12a. Finally we come to R. Elazar's *midrash* cited in bMe'ilah 12a. It seeks to prove that the ashes that the priest removes from the incense altar (מזבח הפנימי) should be placed next to the sacrificial altar in the outer court of the sanctuary. The talmudic passage is as follows:

> משנה: דישון מזבח הפנימי והמנורה לא נהנין ולא מועלין....
>
> גמרא: בשלמא מזבח החיצון דכתיב ביה ושמו אצל המזבח מזבח הפנימי מנלן אמר ר״א דאמר קרא והסיר את מוראתו בנוצתה[186] אם אינו ענין למזבח החיצון תנהו ענין למזבח הפנימי....[187]
>
> *Mishnah.* (The rule regarding) the ashes of the altar of incense (lit., "the inner altar") and of the candelabrum (is) that one may not have benefit from them, but one (is not culpable for) misappropriation (of a sanctified entity, Heb., מעילה)....
>
> *Gemara.* (That the ash from) the sacrificial altar (is removed and placed) next to it makes sense, as it is written of it, "(and he [the priest] shall remove the ash ...) and he shall place it next to the altar" (Lev 6:3).[188] Whence (do we know that a priest must remove and place) the ash from the altar

185 See *Sifra ᵓEmor*, par. 7.

186 והסיר את מורעתו בנוצתה: א״פ OPP. 726 (370), פריז כי״ח H 147A: וגו׳. וטיקן 120: והש׳ אותה אצל המזבח קדמ׳ אל מקו׳ הדשן. פירנצה II I 7–9: [והשלי׳ אותה ?א..?] כי״מ: והסיר את מוראתו בנוצת׳.

187 כל כי״י ודפוס ונציה הראשון מעידים על ה״אם אינו ענין״.

188 ולבש הכהן מדו בד ומכנסי בד יהיו על בשרו והרים את הדשן אשר תאכל האש את העלה על מזבח ושמו אצל המזבח.

> "And the priest shall put on a garment of linen and he shall have linen pants on his flesh; and he shall remove the ash that the fire created by consuming the burnt offering from the altar, and he shall place it next to the altar."

It is clear from the verse that the altar is the sacrificial altar and the placement of the ashes of the burnt offering takes place next to that altar. In rabbinic terminology, this is the "outer altar."

of incense (next to the sacrificial altar). R. Elazar said: As Scripture says, "... and he shall remove the crop with its feather(s) (and cast it next to the altar towards the east, at the place of the ash pile") [Lev 1:16] – if this has no relevance to the sacrificial altar, apply it to the altar of incense....

As Rashi explains this אם אינו ענין interpretation, Lev 1:16 is made redundant by Lev 6:3. That is, Lev 6:3 provides the information that the ash pile is at the side of the sacrificial altar. Thus when Lev 1:16 says that the priest should cast the crop of a sacrificial bird "next to the altar... at the place of the ash pile," it is rendered redundant by the latter verse. It thus becomes available for an אם אינו ענין teaching us about the removal of the ash from the altar of incense and its placement next to the sacrificial altar. The commentary attributed to R. Gershom (10th c.) concurs. The following citation from pYoma 2:2 (39d), however, undermines the idea that R. Elazar used אם אינו ענין to arrive at the conclusions attributed to him in the Babylonian *sugya*.

מניין לדישון המזבח הפנימי ר׳ פדת בשם ר׳ לעזר והשליך אותה אצל המזבח קדמה אל מקום הדשן אינו צריך אם לקבע לו מקום כבר כתיב אצל המזבח אם ללמדך שינתן במזרחו של כבש כבר כתיב קדמה אף הוא דרש אצל המזבח אצל המזבח מה כאן מזרחו של כבש אף כאן מזרחו של כבש....

Whence (do we know) that the ash from the altar of incense (must be removed and placed next to the sacrificial altar). R. Pedat said in the name of R. Lazar (= Elazar) "And he shall cast it (the crop of the bird offering) next to the altar towards the east, towards the place of the ash pile" (Lev 1:16). It (the phrase, "toward the place of the ash pile") is unnecessary.[189] If (it) exists in order to determine the place (where the priest places the crop of a sacrificial bird), it has already been written, "next to the altar" (Lev 6:3).[190]

If it is supposed to teach that (the crop is placed) eastward of the altar ramp, it has already been written, "eastward." And even in this manner did he (R. Lazar) interpret "next to the altar" (in Lev 1:16) and "next to the altar" (in Lev 6:3) – just as here (regarding the disposal of the bird's crop in Lev 1:16 "next to the altar" is defined as) towards the east of the sacrificial altar's ramp, so there (in Lev 6:3 "next to the altar" regarding the ashes of the sacrificial altar it means) towards the east of the sacrificial altar's ramp. (Therefore, since the superfluity of "towards the place of the ash pile" teaches nothing further about the ashes of the sacrificial altar, it must exist to teach that the priest clears away the ash of the

189 See *Pene Mosheh* and *Qorban ha-ᶜEdah*, s.v. אינו צריך.

190 In that verse, it was clear that the altar was the sacrificial altar. See n. 188.

altar of incense and places it on the ash pile at the eastern side of the sacrificial altar).

The hermeneutic actions in this *midrash* do amount to what we have seen happening in some PT and BT אם אינו ענין expositions we have already studied. Yet significantly, there is no mention of אם אינו ענין as the hermeneutic that R. Lazar = Elazar uses. PT uses this terminology elsewhere, but only in anonymous אם אינו ענין interpretations. I would suggest, therefore, that R. Elazar does not use this terminology because he does not consider this form of *midrash* to be an example of אם אינו ענין. Rather he created a *ribbui* by limiting the meanings of parts of verses Lev 1:16 and 6:3 until he produced an extraneous element that would address the issue of the placement of the ashes of the "inner altar."

Third-Generation 'Ulla's אם אינו ענין

bMaqqot 15a. We continue our investigation of the third amoraic generation's use of אם אינו ענין with an interpretation by 'Ulla. His אם אינו ענין *midrash* is of importance because as a traveller between the Land of Israel and Babylonia 'Ulla represents both traditions. Until now, we have only seen the אם אינו ענין traditions of the Land of Israel. Now we will see how someone who mediates both these traditions used אם אינו ענין.

'Ulla's *midrash* concerns a discussion about the type of commandment whose sanction is lashes. The discussion focuses on commandments in which a positive obligation precedes a prohibition. The case in point is in Deut 22:19. The rule there is that one who slanders his wife by claiming she is not a virgin at the time of his marriage (מוציא שם רע) must marry her permanently without recourse to divorce. In the same pericope, the same rule applies to one who rapes an unbetrothed virgin (Deut 22:28–29). The Talmud grapples with the question of the penalty of the slanderer or rapist who does divorce the woman that Torah law forced him to marry in perpetuity. Does he suffer the penalty of lashes, as is the case with one who actively violates a prohibition? Or because there is a positive, "thou shalt" element to the commandment – namely, marrying the victim, are these commandments not classified as true prohibitions? If the latter is the case, lashes would not be the punishment for the crime since there is the opportunity to avoid the prohibition by marrying the wronged woman.

'Ulla holds that the slanderer and rapist who divorce their wives are forced to remarry them as long as the Torah permits the remarriage. In that case, they avoid the punishment for violating the prohibition on divorcing their wives. If they may not legally remarry their wives – e.g., because the slanderer or rapist is a *kohen* (Aaronic priest), who according to the Torah (Lev 21:7) may not marry a divorcee – then they receive lashes. According to the Talmud, he derives this by use of אם אינו ענין. Here, as in the other cases of אם אינו ענין *midrashim* of the third amoraic generation, the form and methodology of the interpretation is, except for its heavier use of Aramaic, indistinguishable from that of the tannaitic אם אינו ענין derived by logic. The following is the text of the talmudic passage containing the אם אינו ענין *midrash*:

> תניא: אונס שגירש, אם ישראל הוא – מחזיר ואינו לוקה, אם כהן הוא – לוקה ואינו מחזיר; אם ישראל הוא מחזיר ואינו לוקה, אמאי? לא תעשה שקדמו עשה הוא, ולילקי! אמר עולא:[191] לא יאמר לו תהיה לאשה באונס וליגמר ממוציא שם רע, ומה מוציא שם רע שלא עשה מעשה-אמר רחמנא: +דברים כ״ב+ ולו תהיה לאשה, אונס לא כל שכן! (למה נאמר) אם אינו ענין לפניו – תנהו ענין לאחריו,[192] שאם גירש יחזיר.

It was taught (in a *baraita*): A rapist who divorces (the woman he raped), if he is an Israelite, he remarries her and does not receive lashes. If he is of priestly descent, he is lashed and may not remarry (his divorced wife).

"If he is an Israelite, he remarries her and does not receive lashes." Why is this so? It is a case of the violation of a prohibition preceded by a positive commandment, and (as such) he should receive lashes.[193] 'Ulla said: Let (Scripture) not say "and she shall be his wife" in the case of the rapist (Deut 22:19), and we would derive it from the case of the slanderer (by *a fortiori* reasoning):

The slanderer performed no action,[194] yet the Torah says, "she shall be his wife (he shall never send her away)," certainly the rapist who committed an act should be subject to this rule! Thus, if this verse (concerning the rapist) is superfluous (because it could be derived from the case of the slanderer and would teach that the rapist would have to marry and remain married to his victim forever), apply it to the situation of his having divorced his wife, and if he divorces her, he must take her back (a second time).

191 אמר עולא: כן איתא בכל כי״י ובדפוס ונציה בשינויים קטנים הנוגעים למלת „אמר".

192 ה„אם אינן ענין" איתא בכל כי״י ובדפוס ונציה. ברם, תוצאות ה„אם אינו ענין" שונות לפי כ״י יד הרב הרצוג שם איתא: אם אינו ענין למוציא שם רע, תניהו ענין לאונס. ואם אינו ענין לפניו, תנהו ענין לאחריו. ונראה שגירסא זו מושפעת מדפוסי לשון בהמשך הסוגיא. ובדפוס ונציה איתא: אם אינו ענין לאונס תניהו ענין למוציא שם רע שאם גירש יחזיר. ולפי הענין גירסא זו מוטעית כי הלימוד הוא ממוציא שם רע לאונס ולא ההפך.

193 See the opinion attributed to R. Johanan on bMakkot 14b.

194 Speech is not generally viewed as an action in rabbinic Jewish law unless the Torah says otherwise.

The logic of this *midrash* needs some explanation. According to it, the rapist's obligation to marry his victim for the first time is derived from the case of the slanderer by *a fortiori* reasoning. This reasoning equates the situation of the rapist, who has not married his victim yet, to that of the slanderer, who is a married man. At this point, this would mean that the rapist should marry his victim and maintain her as his wife forever. Nevertheless, the phrase describing this obligation ("and she shall be his wife," the same phrase that is found in Deut 22:19 regarding the slanderer) appears in Deut 22:29. This is obviously superfluous and facilitates the אם אינו ענין interpretation. In that interpretation the results move beyond the obligation to marry the woman for the first time to the matter of being obliged to remarry her if the rapist divorced her. The rule about obligatory remarriage does not have to be stated regarding the slanderer. Since he is married already, the future tense of the phrase "and she shall be his wife"[195] would be redundant since the woman he slandered already is his wife. Thus, the rule in Deut 22:19 is understood to mean that the slanderer must remarry her if he divorced her.

Again, the use of logic as the source for the interpretation takes place within a single chapter dealing with two situations in which the law requires certain categories of men who have dealt criminally with women to marry them permanently and disallows them to divorce. The logic of the new application section of the אם אינו ענין is also clear: the verses discuss marriages. If the discussion is not about first marriage, it must still be about some marriage. Hence, remarriage becomes the locus of the discussion. All of this conforms to tannaitic requirements for אם אינו ענין interpretations.

Despite this description of the workings of the passage in BT, there is evidence that the אם אינו ענין interpretation is an addition to 'Ulla's original midrashic interpretation. Again, R. Ḥananel is the source for an alternative version of the *midrash* as follows:

> ...ובא עולא לפרק כי זה לא תעשה שניתק לעשה הוא. דהאי ולו תהיה לאשה דכתב באונס אינו צריך לפניו, דגמר ממוציא שם רע. אלא לאחריו הוא דאתא שאם יגרש יחזיר ויקחנה ולו תהיה לאשה, לפיכך לא לקי. ודחי׳ (=ודחינן): להאי סברא הכי: אונס ממוציא שם רע לא גמר דאיכא למיפרך כו׳ (מה מוציא שם רע שלוקה ומשלם) אלא לא היה צריך למכתב ולו תהיה לאשה במוציא שם רע שהרי כבר אשתו היא. למה נאמר? ללמד שאם גירש מוציא שם רע אחרי שלקה ונענש, אינו לוקה אלא מחזירה בעל כורחו ודיו. וגמר אונס ממוציא שם רע שמחזיר ואינו לוקה. ודחי׳....

... and 'Ulla came to resolve (the question of why a rapist who divorces his victim does not receive lashes). (The reason is) because this (situation

195 More literally, "she shall become his wife."

is in the category of a) negative commandment that can be repaired by observing a related positive commandment. For the verse, "and she shall be his wife," which is written about the rapist (Deut 22:29), is unnecessary to teach (about his being obliged to marry his) victim the first time, for this is learned from the case of the slanderer (Deut 22:19). Therefore, (the mention of "and she shall be his wife" in regard to the rapist's victim) comes to teach about his second marriage. Namely, if he divorces his victim he must take her back and she shall be his wife. Therefore, he (the rapist) is not lashed (because he has repaired the violation of a prohibition on divorcing his victim by the performance of a positive commandment to remarry her).

But we rejected this reasoning (because it is possible to argue that the slanderer is worse than the rapist since he is punished with stripes and a fine, while the rapist is not punished in these ways at all). Rather (argue thus). It was not necessary to write "and she shall be his wife" in regard to the slanderer, for she is already his wife (at the time of the slander). Why then is it said? To teach that if he divorced his wife, after he was given stripes and fined (for defaming his wife as being a non-virgin when he married her, see Deut 22:18–19), he is not lashed (again). Rather, he takes her back against his will, and that is sufficient. And we learn (the rules regarding) the rapist from those applicable to the slanderer. But we rejected this reasoning. . . .

R. Ḥananel has reconstructed 'Ulla's *midrash* without recourse to an אם אינו ענין *derashah*. That is, according to him, the use of *a fortiori* reasoning based on the rules governing the slanderer is sufficient to teach the rules governing the rapist. Since the slanderer had slandered his wife immediately after he married her, the issue of a first marriage is gainsaid. Therefore, the rapist, who is worse than the slanderer, having committed an act, which is worse than just speaking, certainly must marry his victim. Therefore, stating "and she shall be his wife; he may not send her away" (Deut 22:29) regarding the rapist is unnecessary if it implies a first marriage. Since according to the midrashists no phrase in the Torah is regarded as meaningless, the phrase teaches that if the rapist divorces his wife, he must remarry her. If he does this, he avoids receiving lashes for violating "he may not send her away," because he corrected his violation by remarrying his victim.

This reasoning, however, is disputed because the slanderer, unlike the rapist, is required to receive lashes and pay a fine. This undermines the original *a fortiori* reasoning because the slanderer is now viewed as worse than the rapist. Because of this, R. Ḥananel says that 'Ulla took another tack. According to R. Ḥananel, 'Ulla argued that the Torah's phrase, "She shall be his wife" (Deut 22:19), was superfluous in regard to the slanderer because the slandered woman was already his wife. This superfluity informs us that if the slanderer divorces his wife, he must remarry her. If he does so, he does not receive stripes because he corrected his violation of "he may not send her away" by fulfilling the positive command of remarrying her.

By *a fortiori* reasoning, the same rules should apply to the rapist. However, according to R. Ḥananel's report of the Talmud's discussion, this reasoning was also dismissed because perhaps the rapist is worse than the slanderer because he committed an act, while the slanderer merely spoke. Consequently, the Torah might give the slanderer a chance to redeem himself while it would deny this opportunity to the rapist. Whatever the case, R. Ḥananel has shown us how 'Ulla's *derashah* could exist without dependency on אם אינו ענין.

Beyond this, the PT parallel of this *derashah* in pKetubot 3:5 (27d) indicates that the Palestinian tradition did not include an אם אינו ענין interpretation. Rather, it contained a גזירה שוה. Though 'Ulla is not the first tradent on the list of tradents, he is the second one, which might indicate that BT has an earlier version of 'Ulla's *midrash*. Further, the list of tradents contains R. Ishmael and R. Elazar, and perhaps, actually, R. Eliezer, which opens the possibility that the amoraic tradents in PT cite tannaitic interpreters. The following is PT's parallel to 'Ulla's interpretation in BT:

> ר׳ זעירא עולא בשם ר׳ ישמעאל בשם רבי אלעזר: לא יאמר ולו תהיה במוציא שם רע שאינו צריך. כבר היא תחת ידו. מה ת״ל ולו תהיה לאשה? מלמד הימנה לגזירה שוה. מתדרשה ולו תהיה ולו תהיה. מה תהיה שנא׳ להלן גירש אומר לו שיחזיר, אף לו תהיה האמור כאן גירש אומר לו שיחזיר. תני ר׳ חייה: אחד האונס ואחד המוציא שם רע שגירשו כופין אותו להחזיר. אם היו כהנים, סופגין את הארבעים.
>
> R. Ze'ira (cited) 'Ulla (who cited the tradition) in the name of R. Ishmael (who cited it) in the name of R. Elazar: Let (Scripture) not say "and she shall be his wife" in the case of the slanderer, (since) it is unnecessary for she is already his wife (lit., she is already in his possession). Why (then) does the Torah say, "she shall be his wife"? In order to teach a *gezerah shavah* from it. (The repeated phrase) "and she shall be his wife" is what is interpreted. Just as "she shall be" there (in the case of the slanderer means) if he divorces her, one says to him that he must take her back, so "she shall be" here (in the case of the rapist means) if he divorces her, one says to him that he must take her back. R. Hiyyah taught a tannaitic tradition: Whether the rapist or the slanderer divorced (their respective spouses),

we force them to take them back. If they were priests, they receive forty lashes.[196]

It is clear from the phrase "לא יאמר ולו תהיה לאשה...," which appears at the beginning of the argument in both BT and PT, that these midrashic interpretations are related. Both are attributed more or less directly to 'Ulla. Both begin with an *a fortiori* argument that creates superfluity. One, however, leads into an אם אינו ענין, unless we accept R. Ḥananel's version of the *sugya*, and the other into a גזירה שוה מופנה, a word comparison *midrash* based on a "free" linguistic element generated by superfluity.[197] In the continuation of the argument in BT there appears what is basically the opening argument in PT, namely, אלא לא יאמר לו תהיה לאשה במוציא שם רע שהרי אשתו היא, "Let (Scripture) not say 'And she shall be his wife' in the case of the slanderer, (since) it is unnecessary because she is already his wife...."

The overall picture is that 'Ulla's *derashah* did not require an אם אינו ענין element and may never have included one. Nevertheless, if we do posit the existence of an אם אינו ענין interpretation in his *midrash*, it does not deviate from the typical tannaitic form of this hermeneutic. Thus, an influential figure in Babylonian-Palestinian relations does not provide us with any insight into any changes in the form of אם אינו ענין in the third generation of the *amoraim*. The אם אינו ענין remains basically the same in this period of the *amoraim* as it was in the tannaitic period.

Fourth Generation, the אם אינו ענין *Midrash* of R. Jeremiah

Sanhedrin 84b. In a discussion of the definition of what constitutes an act that would make one capitally culpable for striking one's parents, the *sugya* demands that it be a blow that draws blood or causes a bruise to one's father or mother. This definition is predicated on various verses' use of the term נפש, "soul," in contexts that speak of striking an animal or person. The interpreters of those verses understand this term to imply the involvement of blood as a result of the striking, probably based on an intertextual reading of Deut 12:23, which maintains that "the blood is the soul (נפש)." R. Jeremiah objects that culpability in the case of an animal would not require causing bleeding or bruising. Therefore, the comparison between animal damages and human ones is useless for determining the definition of striking. He suggests that this should lead to a re-reading of Lev 24:21, which states, "One who strikes a human being shall die, and one who strikes an animal shall indemnify (for) it." The re-reading is accomplished by use of אם אינו ענין:

196 See tKetubot 3:7 for a *baraita* whose first clause parallels R. Ḥiyyah's *baraita*.

197 See Michael Chernick, לחקר מידת "גזירה שווה", pp. 39–40.

ואימא אף על גב דלא עביד ביה חבורה, אלמה תנן: המכה אביו ואמו – אינו חייב עד שיעשה בהן חבורה! – אמר קרא +ויקרא כ"ד+ מכה אדם ומכה בהמה, מה מכה בהמה[198] – עד דעביד בה חבורה דכתיב בה נפש, אף מכה אדם – עד דעביד חבורה. – מתקיף לה רב ירמיה:[199] אלא מעתה, הכחישה באבנים הכי נמי דלא מיחייב? אלא:[200] אם אינו ענין לנפש בהמה, דהא אי נמי הכחישה באבנים חייב – תניהו ענין לנפש אדם.

... I might say (one would be culpable for striking one's parent) even if one did not cause a wound. Then why is it taught, "one is not culpable until he causes a wound" (mSanhedrin 11:1)? (As) the Torah says, "One who strikes a human being... and one who strikes an animal" (Lev 24:21) – just as one who strikes an animal (is culpable only) when he causes a wound since it is written נפש, "soul," concerning the animal, so, too, one who strikes a human being (is culpable only) when he wounds (the person).[201]

R. Jeremiah attacked this (reasoning thus:) If this is so, (then when) someone ruins an animal by (loading it) with rocks, is he not culpable (for the damage)? Rather,[202] if the verse (Lev 24:21) is inapplicable to damaging the soul (i.e., causing a bleeding wound or bruise to an animal) since even damaging an animal with stones creates culpability, apply it (only) to the soul (i.e., the wounding) of a human being. (Hence, it is implicit that culpability in any case of striking a human being means that the struck person must suffer a bruise or wound.)[203]

R. Jeremiah's אם אינו ענין appears to conform to the tannaitic pattern of אם אינו ענין interpretations based on logic. He shows how an *halakhah* requiring indemnification from one who destroys an animal without wounding it or causing it to bleed contradicts the *midrash* of Lev 24:21. This leaves the verse without meaning. Since a meaningless verse is a theologically unacceptable

198 אמר קרא מכה אדם ומכה בהמה, מה מכה בהמה: כ"י יד הרב הרצוג: אמר קר' {נפש} בהמ' ישלמנה ומכה אדם יומת מקיש מכה בהמ' למכה אדם....

199 רב ירמיה: כ"י פירנצה II 9–7. ברוב כי"י: ר' ירמיה.

200 אלא אם אינו ענין: בשאילתות: אלא אמר ר' ירמיה אם אינו ענין.

201 This is a midrashic *heqesh*, which claims that juxtaposition of several legal rubrics in a single verse implies that the rules governing one matter also govern the other. In this case, since the striking of an animal must affect its נפש, i.e., it must bruise it or cause it to bleed, so too striking persons must bruise them or cause them to bleed. Cf. *Sifra ᵓEmor* 20:8.

202 Rather: Sheiltot: "R. Jeremiah said, Rather...." I am accepting the attribution of this אם אינו ענין to R. Jeremiah on the basis of the readings in the majority of mss. and the Berko imprint, and especially on the basis of the Sheiltot, which directly attributes the אם איני ענין to R. Jeremiah.

203 See שאילתות דר' אחאי גאון – ויקרא, ed. Mirsky (Jerusalem: Sura-Yeshiva University and Mossad Ha-Rav Kook, 1863), p. קצ and critical apparatus there, lines 24–25.

entity according to the majority of the Rabbis, Lev 24:21 is applied to a new subject. Usually this form of אם אינו ענין operates within a pericope that is the only one to discuss a particular subject. However, the Torah discusses humans damaging animals, animals damaging animals, and animals damaging humans, sometimes fatally, in pericopes other than the one under discussion. It also discusses harm to an animal caused by indirect human action, like digging a pit. Nevertheless, Leviticus 24 is the only pentateuchal chapter that speaks of human beings consciously harming animals without any profit motive in mind.[204] Consequently, we might be led to consider R. Jeremiah's אם אינו ענין *midrash* a tannaitic one in form and methodology. This, however, is not actually the case. No tannaitic אם אינו ענין interpretation contains an illogical or contradictory element based on a comparison between an *halakhah* and a pentateuchal verse or the *midrash* of one. Here, for the first time, we find a fourth-generation Palestinian *amora* clearly deviating from the tannaitic format of אם אינו ענין. Thus, the fourth amoraic generation in Babylonia seems to be the turning point in the development of a distinct amoraic form for אם אינו ענין.

Fourth Generation, Rava and Abbaye

We turn now to the אם אינו ענין interpretations attributed to Rava in order to determine what developments in this form of *midrash* took place in the fourth amoraic generation. Later we will turn to an example of אם אינו ענין attributed by Abbaye, viewed by the tradition as the other major figure among the fourth-generation Babylonian *amoraim*.

Rava

bYebamot 54b=bSanhedrin 55a. Ravina, Rava's student (5th amoraic generation, Babylonia), asked Rava several questions related to the matter of forbidden sexual relations. First he asked whether mere penetration in the case of a homosexual act was equivalent to the completed act of intercourse. Rava responded that it was. He based his view on the verse in Lev 18:22 which uses the term משכבי אשה, "the types of lying with a woman," in reference to homosexual acts. The plural, suggests Rava, implies both completed intercourse and mere penetration.

Ravina then asked the same question in regard to bestiality. Does mere penetration constitute the act? Rava says it does, based on an אם אינו ענין interpretation:

204 See Exod 21:37. The slaughter and or sale of a stolen ox or sheep is less a matter of damages than a matter of theft and the use of the stolen merchandise. In the case of damage, indemnification is equivalent to the loss. In the case of theft that includes slaughter or sale of a stolen animal, the repayment may be four or five times the worth of the stolen animal. This "fine" takes into con-

...בעא מיניה רבינא מרבא: המערה בזכור, מהו? בזכור משכבי אשה כתיבא! אלא המערה בבהמה, מהו? אמר ליה:[205] אם אינו ענין להעראה דכתיבא גבי אחות אב ואחות אם, דאתיא בהקישא מדרבי יונה,[206] תנהו ענין להעראה דבהמה.

> Ravina asked Rava: One who merely penetrates another male, what is (his law). It is written of the homosexual act, "(you shall not have homosexual intercourse with a male) in the manners of intercourse of a woman. . . ." But what of mere penetration of a beast?[207] He (Rava) responded: If the issue of penetration written regarding (the prohibition on relations with) the sister of (one's) father or mother (Lev 20:19) is not necessary, that having been established by R. Jonah's midrashic analogy, apply it to the act of penetration of a beast.[208]

Rava's interpretation is the first Babylonian example of a deviation from the typical tannaitic mode of applying אם אינו ענין. In the tannaitic *midrashim*, we find only one exceptional case in which the use of a midrashic interpretation creates superfluity.[209] Overwhelmingly, only biblical verses or logic can accomplish that among the *tannaim*. Here Rava alludes to R. Jonah's midrashic analogy in order to establish the superfluity that permits the application of the אם אינו ענין hermeneutic to Lev 20:19. Once, however, Rava takes that step,

---

sideration the profit motive a thief has. Such a motive may be absent in the case of one who damages a beast for no apparent reason.

205 ברוב כ״י של יבמות „אמר ליה״ ליתא וגם ליתא ברי״ף, רא״ש, רי״ד ומדרש הגדול, חוץ מדפוס פיזרו רס״ט ששם ישנה. ברם, בסנהדרין איתא בכל הנוסחאות ובראשונים שם וכן במובאה ביחוסי תנאים ואמוראים כ״י, ערך ר׳ ישמעאל. ע״ע ירוש׳ כתובות פ״א, ה״ג (כה ע״ב).

206 במקום „דאתיא בהקישא מדרבי יונה״ שביבמות, איתא ברוב נוסחאות של סנהדרין „דלא צריכא דהא איתקש להעראה דנדה.״

207 These two questions were also raised by R. Jose (fourth generation, Palestinian *amora*) in pKetubot 1:3 (25b). There is no answer to this question in PT.

208 The "analogy" of R. Jonah appears before the dialogue between Ravina and Rava in bYebamot 54b. It is a midrashic "analogy" in which a comprehensive biblical verse places all the distinct elements of a pericope into a single rubric. In the case of the prohibited relations, R. Jonah claims that this is what Lev 18:29 accomplishes. It states, "For anyone who commits any of these abominations, the souls who do (these things) shall be extirpated from among their people." R. Jonah interprets the verse as having connected all the prohibited relations to one another. Hence, whatever is forbidden in one case is forbidden in all. Since mere penetration is prohibited with a menstruant (Lev 20:18), it is prohibited for all the prohibited relationships. In the case of our אם אינו ענין, this analogy renders extraneous the verse in Lev 20:19, which mentions penetration in the prohibition of relations with the sister of one's father or mother.

In ||bSanhedrin 55a, the formulation does not simply allude to R. Jonah's *midrash*. Rather, it states straightforwardly, "If the case of penetration written in regard to the sister of one's father or mother is unnecessary because it has been derived by midrashic analogy from the menstruant, apply it to the act of penetration of a beast." What is eminently clear from the Talmud's discussion of the issue of penetration is that it does not know of the discussion of this issue in *Sifra*, *Qedoshim*, 12:2.

209 See, above, the אם אינו ענין *derashah* in *Sifre Num.* 78, pp. 164–70.

Lev 20:19 is extraneous in relationship to the verse that precedes it, Lev 20:18. This is the exact sequence we would expect if we were dealing with a tannaitic אם אינו ענין – i.e., the second verse is extraneous because the first has already covered the subject.

The choice of penetration of an animal as the appropriate new application of Lev 20:19 is literarily logical. Bestiality is *sui generis* among the prohibited sexual relations because it is the only one not performed with another human being. Whatever we might say by way of analogy regarding the other prohibitions might be denied in the case of bestiality: it is not analogous in a highly essential way. Hence, Rava had to resort to אם אינו ענין in order to include animals in the sanctions generated by the act of penetration. This form of new application applies the superfluous verse to a case within a single pericope where an aspect of that case needs clarification, and it is common in tannaitic אם אינו ענין interpretations. Apparently it carried over into the amoraic period.

Abbaye

bKeritot 26b–27a. I have claimed that Abbaye created an אם אינו ענין as a commentary on earlier tannaitic *midrashim*, but that is a matter of reasoned conjecture. bKeritot 26b presents an אם אינו ענין *midrash* attributed directly to Abbaye that does not reference any other midrashic sources. Therefore, it represents another fourth-generation Babylonian amoraic creation that illustrates the developments that took place in the application of אם אינו ענין.

The discussion in which the אם אינו ענין attributed to Abbaye appears focuses on a question that arises from a mishnaic law. The Mishnah requires those who became obligated to bring guilt and sin offerings prior to Yom Kippur to bring them even after the Day of Atonement. However, is one who was unaware prior to Yom Kippur of having committed a sin requiring either a guilt or sin offering obligated to bring that offering if he discovers his sin after Yom Kippur?

One could argue that Yom Kippur effects atonement for sins known only to God; and, indeed, one voice within the argument takes this position. If that is the case, the sin is "erased" and no sacrifice need be brought. The other side of the argument is that the Torah requires various offerings for sins known to the transgressor. Hence, awareness of the sin more than the sin itself obligates the transgressor to bring the required sacrifice. If this is so, then even after Yom Kippur the transgressor would have to bring the appropriate offering. Abbaye's אם אינו ענין supports the latter position:

אמר אביי, מהכא: מכדי מצות מצות ילפי מהדדי, כיון דילפי מהדדי, למה לי דכתיב שלש ידיעות גבי יחיד וגבי נשיא וגבי צבור? אם אינו ענין לגופיהן

דהא גמרי להן מצות מצות, תנהו ענין היכא דמתיידע ליה בתר יום הכיפורים הוא דמייתי חטאת.[210]

> Abbaye said: (Derive the rule that one who was not cognizant of a sin requiring an offering prior to Yom Kippur must bring that offering after Yom Kippur) from here: Because of (the midrashic analogy established by the use of the word comparison based on the word) *mizvot* (מצות מצות), we may learn them (i.e., individuals, communities, and the king) from one another.[211] (That being the case,) why are three "awarenesses" (הודע) written: (one) regarding the individual, (one) regarding the king, and (one) regarding the community? If they have no (useful) application to themselves (i.e., to teaching us the obligation of the individual, king, and community to bring a sin-offering, which was established by the word comparison of מצות מצות), apply them to the case of one who discovered after Yom Kippur that he had sinned (prior to Yom Kippur), (in which case) he must bring a sin-offering.

Abbaye's *midrash* does differ from a tannaitic אם אינו ענין interpretation. Though unnecessary repetition of an idea in several pericopes is consonant with tannaitic usage, Abbaye first refers to a word comparison *midrash* in order to render the use of the term "awareness, knowledge" (הודע) superfluous. That word comparison, מצות מצות, is merely a shorthand for a *midrash* that repeats itself several times in *Sifra*.[212] That superfluity then allows the use of the term for the purpose of deciding that one unaware of a sin prior to Yom Kippur must still bring the appropriate expiatory sacrifice after Yom Kippur, when he becomes aware of his sin. The *tannaim*, unlike Abbaye, would have

210 There are no significant *variaes lectiones* in mss. and incunabulae.

211 This refers to a talmudic passage on bHorayot 8a. There the individual, the king, and the community are analogized to one another by means of a word comparison based on the word מצות. The analogy requires any one of these parties to bring a *ḥattat* when he or it violates a prohibition whose punishment is *karet* when violated knowingly or the sacrifice of a sin-offering when it is violated unwittingly. This constitutes the first part of Abbaye's argument: Let us agree that these three parties' obligation to a sin-offering can be derived from the word comparison מצות מצות. This still does not tell us whether they have to bring this offering when they become aware of a sin they committed before Yom Kippur only after the holy day. The rest of his argument resolves that issue.

212 See *Sifra Ḥobah*, par. 4:11; ibid., 5:6; ibid., and 7:11. The kind of prohibition requiring a sin-offering mentioned in the case of the king, community, and individual begins with a definition found in the context of the high priest's violation of a prohibition. An extremely long and detailed discussion in *Sifra Ḥobah*, par. 1, chap. 1:4 finally determines that the type of sin intended is the violation of a prohibition deserving *karet* when committed knowingly and a sin-offering when committed unwittingly. In each of the *Sifra* passages cited above, the phrase מצות ה' generates the *midrash* linking community, king, and individual.

derived the extraneous element for an אם אינו ענין from the Torah's text itself rather than from a *midrash*.

The reapplication of the superfluous term "awareness" (הודע) is also consonant with the logic of reapplication used by the *tannaim*. The term implies that whenever one becomes aware of one's sin, one is required to bring the required expiatory sacrifices. This implication then leads to the clarification of a hard case – namely, the issue of bringing expiatory sacrifices for sins one was unaware of until after Yom Kippur.

The Generation of Change

Our review of the three cases of fourth-generation amoraic אם אינו ענין interpretations shows that it was that generation in which the application of this hermeneutic began to change in form. The characteristic change in general terms is that the amoraic sages of that generation use either a *halakhah* or a *midrash* rather than scriptural verses in finding, or perhaps better put, creating the superfluity that allows them to use אם אינו ענין. The use of extant law or existent or created *midrash* for this purpose indicates a new status for material generated by the rabbinic world. It becomes Torah in the same sense as the biblical text. In some respects this indicates that the full blossoming of a completely distinctive amoraic way of being did not take place until the fourth amoraic generation. The progressive acceptance of the Mishnah as the constitutional text of the rabbinic movement, combined with rabbinic Judaism's developing political and social success, began to direct rabbinic thought toward the idea that what Rabbis created was no less Torah than that which was revealed at Sinai. Deut 17:1–13 surely could be construed in that fashion, and PT, and perhaps the Mishnah as well held this view.[213] Once that idea was established as a typical mode of rabbinic thought, it became natural for midrashic sources and methods to be used as if they were biblical texts. We should also recognize that Rava and Abbaye both dealt with questions that were new. This suggests that אם אינו ענין *midrash* was still a force in the creation of *halakhah*, but only when confronting new situations. Settled matters were not overturned by the application of amoraic אם אינו ענין interpretations.

Scholars have recently noted how the third and fourth Babylonian amoraic generations are historically periods of transition and change.[214] Richard Kalmin notes the many ways in which transition expressed itself, beginning in the third Babylonian amoraic generation and increasing significantly in the

213 mSanhedrin 11:3; pBerakhot 1:4 (3b)=ᶜAvodah Zarah 2:7 (41c).

214 Isaiah Gafni, יהודי בבל בתקופת התלמוד (Jerusalem: The Zalman Shazar Center for Jewish History, 1990), pp. 190, 210–13; idem., "ישיבה ומתיבתא," *Zion* (1978), 43:31–37; David Goodblatt, *Rabbinic Instruction in Sasanian Babylonia* (Leiden: Brill, 1978), pp. 166–69 and 185–87.

fourth and onward.[215] Kalmin's views are helpful in explaining the changes in the אם אינו ענין hermeneutic and its application, especially his hypothesis that the middle-Babylonian amoraic generations, especially the fourth, may have been engaged in the first major editorial activity that led to the formation of BT. If indeed this is so, it would explain why Rava would grant R. Yonah's *midrash* the status of a biblical verse in the אם אינו ענין *midrash* that we analyzed above. The act of editorial collection and canonization of material would change its authoritative status for future generations, as indeed it does.[216] Also, the fact that examples of אם אינו ענין from the fourth Babylonian amoraic generation either deal with new or unresolved halakhic matter or support existent *halakhah* created by earlier *amoraim* is best explained by Kalmin's theory about middle-generation amoraic editing of material.

Fifth Generation, R. Phineas, son of R. Ami

One example of the application of אם אינו ענין by a fifth-generation *amora* appears in bZebaḥim 4a. The midrashic interpreter responsible for the *midrash* is R. Phineas, son of R. Ami (ר' פנחס בריה דר' אמי). The interpretation is part of a discussion about the role of intention in the sacrificial service. The early part of the talmudic discussion establishes that the officiants must have the specific type of sacrifice in mind when they perform each rite of the service: slaughter, receiving the blood, sprinkling it, and bringing the sacrificial portion to the altar. The next question to arise is whether the officiants must have the proper owners of the sacrifice in mind when they carry out the sacrificial rites. The אם אינו ענין attributed to R. Phineas, son of R. Ami, seeks to answer this question:

> ואשכחן שנוי קודש, שנוי בעלים מנלן? אמר רב פנחס בריה דרב אמי ,אמר קרא: +ויקרא ז+ ובשר זבח תודת שלמיו, שתהא זביחה לשם תודה, אם אינו ענין לשינוי קודש, דנפקא לן מהתם, תנהו ענין לשינוי בעלים.[217]

> We have established (the matter of not) changing (intentions regarding the type of) holy thing (i.e., a specific type of sacrifice), whence (do we know the same is true of) changing (intentions regarding the proper) owners? R. Phineas, son of R. Ami said: Scripture says: "... and the flesh of the sacrifice (זבח)[218] of his thank-*shelamim* offering" (Lev 7:15) –

215 Kalmin, *Sages, Stories*, chap. 9.

216 Op. cit., p. 172.

217 רוב כי"י משקפים את הטקסט דלעיל כדאיתא או בשינויים קטנים. ברם, בכ"י קולומביה T–141x893 איתא: ואשכחן שנוי קודש שנוי בעלים מנא לן סימן פש"ר דבב"ה אמ' רב פינחס בריה דרב אמי אמר קרא ובשר זבח תודת שלמיו שתהא זביחה לשם שלמיו. ע"כ. עי' רמב"ם, מעשה הקרבנות פ"ד, ה"י.

218 The term זבח, usually translated "sacrifice," also is related to "slaughter." In this *midrash* it has

(indicating) that slaughter should be for the sake of a thank offering. If, however, this has no application to (not) changing (one's intention regarding the type of) holy thing, we having derived that (matter) from there,[219] apply it to the matter of (not) changing (one's intention regarding the proper) owners.

This אם אינו ענין interpretation is in most ways like other amoraic אם אינו ענין interpretations we have noted, though in one respect it is different. Most of the examples we have seen have produced superfluity by using logic; here redundant repetition of an idea resurfaces as the source of superfluity. We also saw this phenomenon above in Rava's אם אינו ענין. This may signal a reappropriation of the full repertoire of tannaitic methods in the application of אם אינו ענין. Further, this אם אינו ענין uses a *midrash* as if it were a scriptural verse. This, too, is similar to Rava's use of R. Yonah's *midrash* in his אם אינו ענין interpretation. Thus, it would appear that developments that occurred in the fourth Babylonian amoraic generation continue into the fifth.

There is, however, the possibility that what I have described until now as the אם אינו ענין *midrash* of R. Phineas, son of R. Ami, may be an addition to his original *midrash*. This is a phenomenon we have seen before in our analysis of pre-fourth-generation Babylonian amoraic *derashot*. We raise this possibility because the אם אינו ענין includes an element of the *stam*, the anonymous stratum of the Talmud. As we noted in the Introduction, many academic Talmudic scholars categorize the *stam* as post-amoraic.[220]

On the surface, it seems that R. Phineas, son of R. Ami, responds only to the *stam*'s question, and that there is no other possible referent in the *sugya* to which he may respond. If, however, we follow MS Columbia 141 X 893-T, Rashi and Maimonides,[221] R.Phineas may have actually directed his midrashic

---

the latter meaning. In light of the *midrash* the translation's formulation would be: "... and the meat of the thing slaughtered as a thank-*shelamim* offering. ..."

219 I.e., from the *midrash* of Lev 3:1 at the beginning of bZebaḥim 4a:

> מנלן דבעינן זביחה לשמה? דאמר קרא: +ויקרא ג+ ואם זבח שלמים קרבנו, שתהא זביחה לשם [שלמים].
>
> Whence (do we know) that we require slaughter for the sake (of each specific sacrifice). As Scripture says, "If his offering is a *shelamim*-sacrifice (זבח שלמים)"– (this teaches that) its sacrificial slaughtering (זביחה) must be for the sake of a *shelamim* (and the same applies to all the other sacrifices).

220 See Introduction, pp. 25.

221 Rashi, s.v. שינוי בעלים מנלן and *Mishneh Torah*, Laws of the Sacrificial Rites, 4:10. Maimonides' *Mishneh Torah* states:

> כל הזבחים צריך העובד שתהיה מחשבתו לשם הזבח ולשם בעליו ... שנאמר: ובשר זבח תודת שלמיו – שתהיה זביחה עם שאר ארבע העבודות לשם שלמיו.

interpretation to mZebaḥim 4:6. The *mishnah* there includes among other requirements the obligation to slaughter a sacrificial offering in the name of the party who donates it. If that is the case, then his *midrash* would include only the following:

> אמר ר׳ פנחס בריה דרב אמי אמר קרא ובשר זבח תודת שלמיו שתהא זביחה לשם שלמיו. (נוסח כ״י קולומביה הנ״ל)
>
> R. Phineas, son of R. Ami, said: The Torah says, "... and the flesh of the sacrifice (זבח) of his thank-*shelamim* offering" (Lev 7:15) – (this means) that the slaughtering should be for the sake of his *shelamim*. (The translation follows MS Columbia 141 X 893-T.)

The emphasis in this *midrash* should be put on the possessive pronoun. Consequently, "his *shelamim*" or "his thank-*shelamim*" could midrashically imply that the one who slaughters the offering must do so with the donor in mind. Hence, it is uncertain whether the אם אינו ענין in the midrashic interpretation attributed to R. Phineas, son of R. Ami, is attributed properly. Whatever the case, the אם אינו ענין follows the late amoraic model, which means that the *sugya* may have accurately attributed this *midrash* to R. Phineas, or alternatively, it may be a post-amoraic addition onto R. Phineas's interpretation.

A Post-Amoraic אם אינו ענין *Midrash*

bḤullin 65b. bḤullin 65b presents an אם אינו ענין *midrash* attributed to R. Aḥai in the form פריך ר׳ אחאי, "R. Aḥai objected." Some medieval and modern talmudists hold that this formula introduces a dictum of R. Aḥai of Be Ḥatim, a post-amoraic Sage.[222] If this is so, we have an example of a post-amoraic אם אינו ענין that we may compare to its tannaitic and amoraic predecessors. As we shall see, the differences between these various types of אם אינו ענין are significant.

R. Aḥai's *midrash* appears in a discussion of the characteristics required of locusts to make them fit for consumption (כשר). A *midrash* introduced by *tanna de-be R. Ishmael*, which has its roots in the tannaitic or early amoraic

---

> (Regarding) all the sacrifices, the one who performs (the sacrificial rites) must intend (to slaughter the sacrifice) for the sake of the (particular) offering (being sacrificed) and for the sake of its owners ... as it says, "... and the flesh of the sacrifice (זבח) of his thank-*shelamim* offering"– (indicating) that the slaughter should be for the sake of his *shelamim*-offerings.

It should be noted that the next *halakhah* in Mishneh Torah is based on mZebaḥim 4:6. See *Mishneh Torah*, Laws of the Sacrificial Rites, 4:11. See כסף משנה ad loc.

222 Epistle of R. Sherira Gaon, ed. Lewin, p. 70, n. ב; E. Z. Melamed, פרקי מבוא לספרות התלמוד, p. 475.

period, precedes R. Aḥai's interpretation.[223] R. Aḥai finds this *midrash* flawed because it uses only examples of locusts without elongated heads to determine locusts' fitness for consumption. This implies that all locusts with elongated heads are unfit. According to R. Aḥai, however, that is not the case, and he supports his view with an אם אינו ענין *midrash*:

> פריך רב אחאי: מה להנך שכן אין ראשן ארוך!... אלא אמר רב אחאי: סלעם יתירא הוא; לא ליכתוב רחמנא סלעם ותיתי מארבה ומחרגול, דמאי פרכת – מה לארבה דאין לו גבחת-הרי חרגול דיש לו גבחת, מה לחרגול דיש לו זנב – הרי ארבה דאין לו זנב, סלעם דכתב רחמנא ל"ל? אם אינו ענין לגופו, תנהו ענין לראשו ארוך!
>
> R. Aḥai objected: What (about the fact that) all those (pentateuchal cases of locusts used to determine the requisite characteristics for fitness for consumption) do not (include) those with elongated heads? ...[224] But R. Aḥai said: *Sal'am* is extraneous. Let the Torah not write *sal'am*, and it could be derived from *arbeh* and *ḥargol*.[225] How might you have argued?[226] (*Sal'am* is unlike) *arbeh* that has no brow, (but it is similar to) *ḥargol* that has a brow. (*Sal'am* is unlike) *ḥargol* that has no tail, but (it is like) *arbeh* that has a tail.[227] Why then do I need *sal'am*, of which the Torah has written? If it (*sal'am*) is superfluous in relationship to itself, apply it to the case (of a variety of locust) whose head is elongated (so that it will be fit if it has the other four required characteristics).[228]

Several characteristics differentiate this post-amoraic אם אינו ענין *midrash* from its amoraic predecessors. 1) The amount of rich discourse present in this *midrash* is much higher than in typical amoraic אם אינו ענין expositions. This is generally true of late and post-amoraic *sugyot*.[229] 2) As was the case in the fourth amoraic generation's *midrashim*, R. Aḥai uses another form of *midrash* in order to generate the superfluity necessary for an אם אינו ענין interpretation. That *midrash* uses a hermeneutic called הצד השווה. This hermeneutic pro-

223 See bḤullin 65a–b.

224 Here I have eliminated a long anonymous gloss on R. Aḥai's question. R. Aḥai's comments continue with the phrase "But R. Aḥai said: . . ."

225 Two species of "kosher" locusts mentioned in Lev 11:22.

226 I.e., "How would the argument proceed?"

227 This form of midrashic argument is called הצד השווה. By creating analogies based on the characteristics of items or rubrics the Torah mentions, it derives the law regarding other items or rubrics that the Torah does not mention.

228 I have based my interpretation and translation of the *sugya* on Maimonides and Meiri. See *Mishneh Torah*, Laws of Forbidden Foods, 1:22 and *Bet ha-Beḥirah*, bḤullin 65b, s.v. וחזר והקשה.

229 Kalmin, *The Redaction of the Babylonian Talmud*, pp. 47–50 and 51–56. See also David Weiss Halivni, *Midrash, Mishnah, and Gemara* (Cambridge and London: Harvard University Press, 1986), pp. 77–79.

duces a midrashic analogy that employs the characteristics of rubrics X and Y, which are mentioned in the Torah, to define the law regarding Z, which is not. In our case, the characteristics of the varieties of acceptable locusts called *arbeh* and *ḥargol* could have been used to permit the variety called *sal'am* without the Torah explicitly mentioning it. The Torah did, however, mention the *sal'am* by name in its list of permitted locusts. Consequently, *sal'am* is superfluous and, according to R. Aḥai, useful for an אם אינו ענין interpretation.

R. Aḥai's *midrash*, like that of Rava's and Abbaye's in the fourth generation, has its roots in an existent tradition. After all, R. Aḥai is reacting to the *midrash* that precedes his own. He, however, has reworked the antecedent *midrash* in his own way, just as Rava and Abbaye did several generations before him. What differentiates R. Aḥai's *midrash* from the *midrashim* of Rava and Abbaye is that it exhibits a greater amount of discursiveness than is present in *derashot* of the fourth-generation Babylonian *amoraim*.

The אם אינו ענין *Midrashim* of the *Stam*

Until now we have analyzed those אם אינו ענין interpretations that have attributions or come from sources whose completion was clearly within the amoraic or early post-amoraic periods. Yet, the greater part of the Babylonian Talmud is anonymous. This anonymous stratum frequently connects amoraic statements into the running argument that characterizes most of the Talmud. Occasionally, the anonymous stratum operates independently, creating its own discourse without more than a tenuous connection to earlier tannaitic or amoraic sources.[230] The *stam* also contextualizes amoraic traditions and interpolates its view into them.[231] Many scholars hold that generally speaking this stratum of the Talmud is late.[232]

The application of אם אינו ענין in the anonymous stratum of the Talmud occurs at least sixteen times.[233] This represents the largest single contribution of

230 Abraham Weiss, מחקרים בתלמוד (Jerusalem: Mossad Ha-Rav Kook, 1975), pp. 213–14 and nn. 6–7.

231 Op cit., p. 70.

232 See, for example, Abraham Weiss, היצירה של הסבוראים (Jerusalem: 1952), pp. 17–18; Shamma Friedman, Introduction to "A Critical Study of *Yevamot X* with a Methodological Introduction," *Texts and Studies, Analecta Judaica*, v. 1 (Heb., Jerusalem and New York: Jewish Theological Seminary of America, 1977). David Weiss-Halivni, מקורות ומסורות – סדר מועד (Jerusalem: 1975), pp. 2–8, and most recently in his most detailed and definitive statement of his views in מקורות ומסורות – בבא מציעא, (Jerusalem: Hebrew University, 2007), pp. 1–51. For opposing views, see my Introduction, pp. 26–28.

233 bYoma 32b; Ketubot 35a; Nazir 18b; Qiddushin 42a; ibid. 43a; Baba Meẓiᶜaᵓ 88b; Sanhedrin 28a; Shabuᶜot 39b; Zebaḥim 7a; Ibid. 36a; Ḥullin 118a–b; Bekhorot 56a–b; Keritot 11a; Niddah 34b. There are a number of אם אינו ענין interpretations that we identified as additions onto *bona fide* amoraic *derashot*. These additions differ from the *stam*'s independent use of אם אינו ענין. The additions are shorter and less complex.

אם אינו ענין *midrashim* in the Babylonian Talmud. We will analyze a representative sample of these *midrashim*, noting others that follow similar forms, methods, or the logic of the transfer application of the superfluous verse.

Typical אם אינו ענין Forms in the Anonymous Stratum of the Talmud

As we determined earlier, the three most basic forms of אם אינו ענין interpretations are 1) those based on superfluity created by unnecessary repetition of the same legal data, usually in two pentateuchal pericopes; 2) those generated by the repetition of a single legal idea within a single pericope; and 3) those rooted in contradictions or logical discrepancies. The *stam* contains all three types of אם אינו ענין. Yet, it departs significantly from its predecessors in what it considers pentateuchal. That is, usually the "pentateuchal" element in a stammaitic אם אינו ענין exposition is not a verse from the Pentateuch. Rather, the "pentateuchal" elements are derived from a *midrash* of a pentateuchal verse or a tannaitic or amoraic source.[234] We will begin our survey of stammaitic אם אינו ענין *midrashim* with an example from bZebaḥim 36a.

bZebaḥim 36a. The passage in bZebaḥim 36a discusses a rule attributed to R. Judah that appears in mZebaḥim 3:6. He holds that if at the time of a sacrifice's slaughter one intends to leave the sacrificial elements reserved for the altar unused beyond their acceptable time limit, or if one intends to move these elements outside of the Temple court without making use of them, the sacrifice is invalid. The majority of Sages declare the sacrifice valid. The talmudic passage provides midrashic support for R. Judah's view:

> מ״ט דרבי יהודה אמר רבי אלעזר תרי קראי כתיבי בנותר כתוב אחד אומר {שמות יב} לא תותירו ממנו עד בקר וכתוב אחד אומר {ויקרא ז} לא יניח ממנו עד בקר אם אינו ענין להניח תנהו לענין מחשבת הינוח ורבי יהודה האי קרא להכי הוא דאתא האי מיבעי ליה לכדתניא {ויקרא ז} ובשר זבח תודת שלמיו למדנו לתודה שנאכלת ליום ולילה חליפין וולדות תמורות מנין ת״ל ובשר חטאת ואשם מנין ת״ל זבח ומנין לרבות שלמי נזיר ושלמי פסח ת״ל שלמיו לחמי תודה וחלות ורקיקים שבנזיר מנין ת״ל קרבנו כולן קורא אני בהן לא יניח א״כ לימא קרא לא תותירו מאי לא יניח אם אינו ענין להינוח תנהו ענין למחשבת הינוח....[235]

234 Out of the 16 citations mentioned in the previous note, only one departs from this generalization. The case I refer to is in bBaba Meẓiᶜaᵓ 88b. There the *stam*'s אם אינו ענין appears to be a totally independent support for the rule in mBaba Meẓiᶜaᵓ 7:2.

235 א״כ לימא קרא לא תותירו מאי לא יניח אם אינו ענין להינוח תנהו ענין למחשבת הינוח: כ״י וטיקן 118:
אם כן לימ׳ קרא לא תותירו מאי לא יניח אם אינו עניין לנותר תניהו עניין למחשבת נותר. כ״י וטיקן 121:
אם כן לימ׳ קרא לא יותירו מאי לא יניח ש״מ אם אינו עינין להינוח תניהו עינין למחשב׳ הינוח. כ״י פריז

What is R. Judah's rationale (for claiming that even an intention to leave the blood of the sacrifice and not to sprinkle it on the altar is enough to invalidate a sacrifice). R. Elazar said: There are two verses written about sacrificial elements left beyond their proper time for use. One verse says "You shall not leave any of it over until morning" (Exod 12:10), and another verse says, "You shall not leave any of it (i.e., thank-offering) until morning" (Lev 7:15). If the verse (in Leviticus is unnecessary for) the matter of (actually) leaving (the sacrifice without using it within its proper time), apply it to the intention to leave (the sacrifice without using it until beyond its proper time).

But does R. Judah (think) that this verse (in Leviticus) comes (to teach) this? (Rather,) this verse is needed for that which is taught in a *baraita*: "And the flesh of his thank-offering (shall be eaten on the day of its sacrifice, it shall not be left until morning)" (Lev 7:15) – this teaches us that the thank-offering may be eaten for a day and a night. Whence (do we know this applies to) replacements (for sacrifices) and the offspring of replacements? The Torah says, "and the flesh" (ibid.).[236] Whence (do we know this law applies to) *ḥattat*-offerings and guilt offerings? The Torah says, "sacrifice" (ibid.).[237] Whence (do we) include the *shelamim*-offering of the nazirite and the *shelamim*-offerings that accompany the Passover? The Torah says, "his *shelamim*-offerings" (ibid.). Whence (do we know these rules apply to) the loaves brought with the thank-offering and the wafers of the nazirite? The Torah says, "his sacrifice" (ibid.). I read "he shall not leave them, etc." in regard to all of them.

If that is so, let the Torah say לא תותירו ("you shall not leave over"). Why does it use the (odd terminology) לא יניח ("he shall not leave, abandon")? (In order to teach us that) if the phrase is inapplicable (because of redundancy) to (actually) leaving (sacrificial elements until a time beyond their being usable), apply it to the matter of an intention to leave (them until such a time).

This *sugya* begins with the third-generation *amora*, R. Elazar, creating an אם

כי"ח H147A: אם כן לימ' קרא לא תותירו מאי לא יניח ש"מ אם אינו עינין לנותר תניהו עיניין למחשבת נותר. כ"י קולומביה T-893x141: אם כן לימא קרא לא תותירו מאי לא יניח אם אינו ענין לנותר תניהו ענין למחשבת נותר. דפוס ונציה: א"כ לימא קרא לא תותירו מאי לא יניח אם אינו עניין להינוח תניהו עניין למחשבת הינוח.

236 The midrashist interprets the addition of the unnecessary ו ("and") in ובשר to mean an additional animal brought along with the original offering when a person designates a new animal in place of the original. See Lev 27:33.

237 By parsing the words of the verse in this fashion, the midrashist can use the word זבח, sacrifice, to mean any sacrifice that is eaten like the thank-offering.

אינו ענין *midrash* in support of the tannaitic view of R. Judah. The *midrash* conforms perfectly to tannaitic rubrics for a two pericope אם אינו ענין. As we have seen, this is common in אם אינו ענין interpretations until the third amoraic generation.

It is at this point that the *stam* enters the discussion. It challenges the idea that Lev 7:15 is redundant by claiming that the verse teaches that all edible sacrifices may be eaten only for a single day and night unless the Torah states otherwise. The *stam* responds to its own challenge and restores R. Elazar's support *midrash*, but it does so in a completely novel way: It claims that the odd usage of the Hebrew radical, י-נ-ח (in the form of יניח), instead of the root י-ת-ר, more commonly used in regard to improper "leaving over" of a sacrifice, signals that Lev 7:15 can generate an אם אינו ענין interpretation.[238] For the *stam*, the obvious redundancy of the rules in Exod 12:10 and Lev 7:15 by itself is apparently insufficient to create such a result. This phenomenon is completely new. What is even more significant, however, relates to the hermeneutic work of the *stam*. The center of this work is not the Torah itself; rather it is the resolution of what the *stam* views as a conflict between amoraic (R. Elazar) and tannaitic *midrashim* (|| *Sifra*, *Ẓav*, 12:1).[239] As we will see in other examples, the *stam* equates a great deal of early rabbinic *midrash* with pentateuchal law.

bYoma 32b. The passage in Yoma seeks the biblical source for the requirement that the high priest immerse five times (חמש טבילות) and wash his hands and feet ten times (עשרה קידושים) during the Yom Kippur service. Initially the Talmud cites three tannaitic midrashic sources to prove this point. Eventually, however, the *stam* raises questions about the need for so many tannaitic *midrashim* to teach a single point. Ultimately, it focuses on Rabbi's *midrash* and supports it with an אם אינו ענין of its own:

תלמוד בבלי מסכת יומא דף לב/עמוד ב

אמר רבי מנין לחמש טבילות ועשרה קידושין שטובל כהן גדול ומקדש בו ביום תלמוד לומר כתנת בד קדש ילבש הא למדת שכל המשנה מעבודה לעבודה

238 See Rashi, bZebaḥim 36a, s.v. ה"ג אם כן לימא קרא לא תותירו:

ה"ג א"כ לימא קרא לא תותירו – כדכתיב בכל שאר הנותרים לשון נותר.

This is our version: "Let Scripture say, "You shall not leave over (לא תותירו) – the same language of "leaving over" as is written in regard to all other cases of left over (sacrifices).

239 It is not necessary to propose that amoraic views must always be consistent with tannaitic ones. All the cases of רב תנא ופליג are testimony to this. Nevertheless, the traditional notion is that the *amoraim* never contradicted the dicta of the *tannaim*. See b^cErubin 50b; bKetubot 8a; bGittin 38b; bSanhedrin 83b. Other instances of this phenomenon have been noted by medieval commentators. For example, *Sefer Keritut* (see also pDemai 2:1 [22d]):

שטעון טבילה אשכחן מבגדי זהב לבגדי לבן מבגדי לבן לבגדי זהב מנין תנא דבי רבי ישמעאל קל וחומר מה בגדי לבן שאין כפרתן מרובה טעונין טבילה בגדי זהב שכפרתן מרובה אינו דין שטעונין טבילה איכא למפרך מה לבגדי לבן שכן נכנס בהן לפני ולפנים היינו דקתני ואומר בגדי קדש הם ורחץ את בשרו במים ולבשם וחמש עבודות הן תמיד של שחר בבגדי זהב עבודת היום בבגדי לבן אילו ואיל העם בבגדי זהב כף ומחתה בבגדי לבן תמיד של בין הערבים בבגדי זהב ומנין שכל טבילה וטבילה צריכה שני קידושין תלמוד לומר ופשט ורחץ ורחץ ולבש האי בטבילה כתיב אם אינו ענין לטבילה דנפקא ליה מבגדי קדש הם תנהו ענין לקידוש וליכתביה רחמנא בלשון קידוש הא קא משמע לן דטבילה כקידוש מה קידוש במקום קדוש אף טבילה במקום קדוש....[240]

. . . Rabbi said: Whence (do we know that there are) five immersions and ten sanctifications that the high priest performs on that day (Yom Kippur). As it says, "He shall wear a sanctified cloak of linen, (and there shall be linen pants on his flesh; he shall gird himself in a linen belt, and he shall wear a linen turban; he shall wash his flesh in water and don them)" (Lev 16:4) – from this you learn that anyone who shifts from one rite to another requires immersion. *We know this applies (to a change) from golden garments to linen ones; (how do we know it applies to a change) from linen garments to golden ones? The school of R. Ishmael taught: It is an a fortiori argument. The linen garments are not worn in the major rites of atonement, but they require immersion; (hence, change into) the golden garments that are worn during the major expiatory rites certainly require immersion.*

(Nevertheless,) it is possible to retort: the (change into) linen garments (requires the high priest to immerse) because the high priest enters into the holy of holies dressed in them.[241] That is why it is taught (in Rabbi's *midrash*).

מצינו בכמה דוכתין רב תנא ופליג, ר׳ יוחנן תנא ופליג, וכל שכן ר׳ חייא שהיה רבו. ומצינו ר׳ חייא תנא ופליג מהא דבבא מציעא (ה׳ עמ׳ א׳). ופשיטא שאינם תנאים שהרי לא הוזכרו לא במשנה ולא בברייתאת אלא רוצה לומר שהם חשובים כמו תנאים לחלוק על משנה ובריייתא. (ספר כריתותת לשון למודים, שער ג׳, אות קמ״א).

We have found in many places that "Rav is a *tanna* and may argue (against a tannaitic view)," "R. Johanan is a *tanna* and may argue (against a tannaitic view)." This is certainly so in regard to R. Ḥiyya who was his (i.e., R. Johanan's) teacher. And we have found that R. Ḥiyya is a *tanna* and may argue (against a tannaitic view) from that which is (stated) in Baba Meẓiᶜaᵓ (5a). "Are you citing a Mishnah against R. Ḥiyya? R. Ḥiyya is a *tanna* and may argue (against a tannaitic view)!" Certainly it is clear that they (the Rabbis named above) are not (true) *tannaim* because none of them are mentioned in a *mishnah* or *baraita*. They are, however, considered like *tannaim* because they can argue with a (dictum in a) *mishnah* or *baraita* (*Sefer Keritut, Leshon Lemudim*, section 3, #141).

240 אין כאן ש״נ משמעותיים חוץ מבכ״י בית המדרש לרבנים EMC (218270) שאין בו זכר ל״אם אינו ענין.״ אכן, נוסח זה כנראה לקוי בחסר ע״י ט״ס.

241 The italicized material does not appear in the original formulation of Rabbi's *midrash*. His *midrash* states:

"And (furthermore) the Torah says: 'They are sanctified garments, and he shall wash his flesh in water and don them' (Lev 16:4). And the five rites (of Yom Kippur) are: 1) the daily morning offering in golden clothing; 2) the rites peculiar to Yom Kippur in linen garments; 3) the (offering of) the priest's he-goat and the people's he-goat in golden garments; 4) the spoonful of incense and censer (brought into the holy of holies) in linen garments; and 5) the daily afternoon offering in golden garments. And whence (do we know that) each immersion requires two sanctifications? The Torah says, "He shall remove (his clothes) and wash . . . and he shall wash and dress. . . ." (see Lev 16:23–24).[242]

But this (verse used in Rabbi's *midrash*, i.e., Lev 16:24). is written in regard to immersion! If it is not applicable to immersion, which we derived from "They are sanctified garments (and he shall wash his flesh in water and don them)" (Lev 16:4), apply it to sanctification. Then let the Torah use the language of sanctification (קידוש)! (Rather,) this teaches us that immersion is like sanctification: Just as sanctification must be in the sanctuary precincts, so immersion (on Yom Kippur) must be in the sanctuary precincts. . . .

אמר רבי מנין לחמש טבילות ועשרה קידושין שטובל כהן גדול ומקדש בו ביום שנאמר כתנת בד קדש ילבש ומכנסי בד יהיו על בשרו ובאבנט בד יחגר ובמצנפת בד יצנף בגדי קדש הם ורחץ במים את בשרו ולבשם הא למדת שכל המשנה מעבודה לעבודה טעון טבילה ואומר בגדי קדש הם הוקשו כל הבגדים כולן זה לזה וחמש עבודות הן תמיד של שחר בבגדי זהב עבודת היום בבגדי לבן אילו ואיל העם בבגדי זהב כף ומחתה בבגדי לבן תמיד של בין הערבים בבגדי זהב ומנין שכל טבילה וטבילה צריכה שני קידושין תלמוד לומר ופשט ורחץ ורחץ ולבש.

Rabbi said: Whence (do we know that there are) five immersions and ten sanctifications that the high priest performs on that day? As it says, "He shall wear a sanctified cloak of linen, and there shall be linen pants on his flesh; he shall gird himself in a linen belt, and he shall wear a linen turban; he shall wash his flesh in water and don them" (Lev 16:4) – from this you learn that anyone who shifts from one rite to another requires immersion. "And (furthermore) the Torah says: 'They are sanctified garments, and he shall wash his flesh in water and don them' – all the garments are midrashically analogized to each other. The five rites (of Yom Kippur) are: 1) the daily morning offering in golden clothing; 2) the rites peculiar to Yom Kippur in linen garments; 3) the (offering of) the priest's he-goat and the people's he-goat in golden garments; 4) the spoonful of incense and censer (brought into the holy of holies) in linen garments; and 5) the daily afternoon offering in golden garments. (Since there are five shifts from one rite to another, there are five required immersions.) And whence (do we know that) each immersion requires two sanctifications? The Torah says, "He shall remove (his clothes) and wash. . . .and he shall wash and dress. . . ."

242 This "verse" does not actually exist. Rather, Rabbi uses the word ורחץ, "and he shall wash," which appears in Lev 16:24 retrospectively and prospectively. Midrashically interpreted in this way, it refers to the disrobing mentioned in Lev 16:23 and the dressing referred to in Lev 16:24. Thus, according to Rabbi's *midrash*, the sacramental washing of hands and feet must take place twice for each change of garments, i.e., ten times.

For the purposes of this study, the most significant argument in the citation is the claim that if Lev 16:24 is superfluous as a source for the rules of immersion, which were already derived from Lev 16:4, then we may apply Lev 16:24 to the issue of sanctification – i.e., the sacramental washing of hands and feet. The argument on behalf of the use of אם אינו ענין is not basically different from what is found in tannaitic אם אינו ענין discourse. The most important departure from the tannaitic and amoraic אם אינו ענין *midrashim* is that the *stam* finds a difficulty with Rabbi's tannaitic *midrash* and resolves it via the construction of its own midrashic commentary, based on the אם אינו ענין hermeneutic. In doing so, it uses what it considers a redundancy in Rabbi's *midrash*. Thus, it is not a redundancy of verses that is the generative source of the stammaitic אם אינו ענין, but the repetition of the same rule using two different midrashic derivations. Here, as in the Zebaḥim passage above, the *stam* regards *midrash* rather than a scriptural verse as Torah.

The logic of the reapplication section of this אם אינו ענין is not distant from that of its tannaitic and early amoraic forebears. Its new context is somewhat related to the original context of the verse as understood midrashically. In the present case, the *midrash* of Lev 16:24 understands ורחץ את בשרו במים, "he shall wash his flesh in water," as the immersion of the whole body within the precincts of the sanctuary.[243] The only other case of washing within the sanctuary is the sacramental hand and foot washing that Aaron and his sons performed in preparation for their priestly service. That is apparently why the sanctification of the high priest's hands and feet by washing becomes the targeted framework for the reapplication of the superfluous "verse" in the *stam*'s אם אינו ענין.

In sum, then, the *stam* discovers (creates?) a problem in an early rabbinic tradition and uses אם אינו ענין to resolve it. Here, as in other cases we have examined, the *stam* sees its task as one of solving a technical problem. This behavior is different from that of the *tannaim* and *amoraim*, whose midrashic praxis sought to create new legislation from the Written Torah's text or to ground existing legislation in the Torah's words. Thus, the focus of the *stam* shifts from the interpretation of the Written Torah for halakhic purposes to critical analysis, defense, and explanation of the words of the Sages. As we are beginning to see, this becomes the characteristic *leitmotif* of anonymous comment in the Babylonian Talmud.[244]

243 Obviously, ורחץ את בשרו במים might mean something other than immersion, but that was its meaning to most Second Commonwealth Jews. See E. P. Sanders, *Judaism: Practice and Belief, 63 BCE–66 CE* (London and Philadelphia: SCM Press and Trinity Press, 1992), pp. 222–29.

244 On the decrease in the creation of *halakhah* in the late amoraic period, see Richard Kalmin, *The Redaction of the Babylonian Talmud* (Cincinnati: Hebrew Union College Press), pp. 43–49 and 52–57; idem., *Sages, Stories, Authors and Editors*, p. 136.

An Anonymous אם אינו ענין Based on Logical Discrepancy

The *stam* also contains אם אינו ענין interpretations generated by logical discrepancies. bBekhorot 55b–56a presents such a case. The Talmud seeks the source of the mishnaic rule that states that an animal that is bought or received as a gift is exempt from the animal tithe. It discovers it in a confluence of verses in Exod 22:28–29. Those verses refer, however, to firstborns not tithes. That is where the anonyomous Talmud's אם אינו ענין becomes important:

תלמוד בבלי מסכת בכורות דף נה ב–נו א

משנה: הלוקח או שניתן לו במתנה פטור ממעשר בהמה: גמרא: מנא הני מילי אמר רב כהנא דאמר קרא בכור בניך תתן לי מה בניך אין בלקוח ובמתנה אף צאנך ובקרך אינו בלקוח ובמתנה והאי בבכור כתיב א״ק כן תעשה אם אינו ענין לבכור דלא איתיה בעשייה דברחם קדוש תנהו ענין למעשר בהמה....

Mishnah. One who buys or receives (an animal) as a present is exempt from the animal tithe:

Gemara. Whence (do we derive) these statements (of law). R. Kahana said: As Scripture says, "You shall give the firstborn of your children to Me" (Exod 22:28).[245] Just as your children (who) are not purchased or given (to you) as a gift (are subject to redemption), so your sheep and cattle not purchased or given as a gift (are subject to tithing).[246]

But isn't this (set of verses) written regarding firstlings (rather than tithes)?! Scripture says, "So shall you do (regarding your ox and sheep)" (Exod 22:29). If it is inapplicable to firstlings, which are not subject to "doing" (i.e., being sanctified) since they are sanctified from the womb, apply it to the animal tithe. . . .[247]

The *stam* understands the phrase "So shall you do/make (תעשה) regarding your ox or sheep" to mean that one sanctifies (i.e., makes holy) one's firstling animals. Sanctification by human action is impossible in regard to a firstborn animal because it is in a sanctified state from conception. This leaves the phrase "So shall you do/make (תעשה) regarding your ox or sheep," in contradiction to the Torah's norms regarding firstlings. Therefore, argues the *stam*, the verse cannot refer to firstlings and must refer to something else. The *stam* suggests that the verse refers to the animal tithe.

245 This is immediately followed by "so shall you do regarding your ox and sheep. . . ." (Exod 22:29).

246 By inference, those that are purchased or received as a gift do not require redemption.

247 Hence tithing applies only to animals that have not been bought or received as gifts.

As usual, the logic of the choice of the animal tithe in the place of the redemption of the firstborn animal needs inspection. The connection between the two rubrics is not difficult to establish since the Torah itself establishes it in Leviticus 27. There the issue of firstlings appears in Lev 27:26–27, and a discussion of the animal tithe appears a few sentences later in Lev 27:32. These two types of sanctified gifts also have another commonality: their sanctity is a matter of happenstance. The case of the firstborn is obvious. In the case of the animal tithe, animals are driven beneath a rod. The tenth one to pass beneath the rod is sanctified to God. It is not consciously dedicated to the altar, nor can it be replaced by a personal choice (Lev 27:33). So though the animal is not sacred from conception, its sanctity is not a matter of conscious decision or intent, and in this regard it is conceptually close to the firstborn. The combination of literary and conceptual similarity between the firstborn and tithe animal appears to direct the reapplication of Exod 22:29 toward the rubric of animal tithes.

The *stam*'s אם אינו ענין continues the basic formal and conceptual style of the tannaitic and early amoraic אם אינו ענין. Again, however, the generative source for the אם אינו ענין is not the Written Torah, but a problem with an amoraic dictum. The *stam* uses אם אינו ענין in the form of a "*midrash* on a *midrash*" to solve the problems that arise from R. Kahana's interpretation.

Independent Stammaitic אם אינו ענין Interpretations

The *stam*'s dependence on tannaitic or amoraic sources is not a universal phenomenon. In some cases of אם אינו ענין in PT, we found that what the *tannaim* considered a *ribbui*, the PT's interpreters considered an example of אם אינו ענין. This phenomenon also appears in the anonymous stratum of the Babylonian Talmud. An example from bBaba Meẓiᶜaᵓ 88b is paradigmatic for several other אם אינו ענין *midrashim* for which the *stam* is responsible.

bBaba Meẓiᶜaᵓ 88b. In an excursus, bBaba Meẓiᶜaᵓ 88b addresses the pentateuchal regulation that, during their work hours, harvesters may eat some of the produce they are harvesting. In trying to determine whether this permission extends to already harvested produce, the Talmud interprets Deut 23:26 using אם אינו ענין:

> אדם בתלוש מנלן קל וחומר משור ומה שור שאינו אוכל במחובר אוכל בתלוש אדם שאוכל במחובר אינו דין שאוכל בתלוש מה לשור שכן אתה מצווה על חסימתו תאמר באדם שאי אתה מצווה על חסימתו ויהא אדם מצווה על חסימתו מקל וחומר משור ומה שור שאי אתה מצווה להחיותו אתה מצווה על חסימתו אדם שאתה מצווה להחיותו אינו דין שאתה מצווה על חסימתו אמר קרא כנפשך

כנפשו של פועל[248] מה נפשו[249] אם חסמתו פטור אף פועל אם חסמתו פטור ואלא אדם בתלוש מנלן אמר קרא קמה קמה שתי פעמים אם אינו ענין לאדם במחובר תנהו ענין לאדם בתלוש.

Whence do we (derive that) a human being (who is working in a field may eat already) harvested produce? It is an *a fortiori* argument from (the rules governing) an ox: An ox, which may not eat from unharvested produce, may eat from harvested produce.[250] (Consequently,) a person who may eat unharvested produce may certainly eat from harvested produce.

(However, one might argue:) regarding an ox, one is commanded (not to) muzzle it. Shall you say that (the *a fortiori* argument works) regarding a human being whom you may muzzle (by a contractual agreement limiting or abolishing the worker's right to eat even unharvested produce)?[251]

248 בכתבי היד ישנן נוסחאות כאלו: „אמר קרא כנפשך – כנפשך כן נפשו של פועל" או „אמר קרא כנפשך כן נפשו של פועל" או „אמר קרא כנפשיך מה נפשיך אם חסמת פטור, אף פועל אם חסמת פטור." עי' כי"י אסקוריאל G–I 3, המבורג 135, וטיקן 115, כי"מ 95, פירנצה II I 9–7. נוסחי דפוס ונציה ודפוס ווילנה שווים הם.

249 לפי רוב הגירסאות צ"ל: נפשך.

250 See Deut 25:4. The term דיש refers to threshing, and threshing is carried out on harvested produce.

251 Compare this with pMa^{c}aserot 2:6 (50a):

כתיב לא תחסום שור בדישו אין לי אלא שור בתלוש ואדם במחובר אדם מהו שיאכל בתלוש. מה אם השור שאינו אוכל במחובר אוכל בתלוש אדם שאוכל במחובר אינו דין שיאכל בתלוש תלמוד לומר לא תחסום שור בדישו שור בלא תחסום ואין אדם בלא תחסום. שור מהו שיאכל במחובר מה אדם שאינו אוכל בתלוש אוכל במחובר שור שאוכל בתלוש אינו דין שיאכל במחובר או מה כאן בלא תחסום אף כאן בלא תחסום תלמוד לומר לא תחסום שור בדישו בדישו אין את חוסמו אבל חוסמו את במחובר לקרקע.

It is written, "You shall not muzzle an ox while it is threshing" (Deut 25:4) – I only know that an ox (may eat of) harvested (produce) and a human being (may eat of) unharvested (produce). What is the law regarding a human eating harvested (produce)? (I might deduce the rule from an *a fortiori* argument:) If an ox, which is not permitted to eat unharvested (produce), may eat harvested (produce), then a person, who may eat unharvested (produce), should certainly be permitted to eat harvested (produce). It is for this reason that the Torah says, "You shall not muzzle an ox while it is threshing." An ox is subsumed (under the prohibition) of "you shall not muzzle"; a man is not subsumed (under the prohibition of) "you shall not muzzle."

What is the law of an ox regarding eating unharvested (produce)? (I might deduce the rule from an *a fortiori* argument:) If a human being, who may not eat of harvested (produce), may eat of unharvested (produce), then an ox, which may eat of harvested produce, may certainly eat of unharvested (produce). Just as harvested (produce is permitted) because of "you shall not muzzle," so unharvested (produce is permitted) because of "you shall not muzzle." It is for this reason that the Torah says, "You shall not muzzle an ox while it is threshing"– while it is threshing (harvested) produce, you shall not muzzle it; but you may muzzle it when (it works in) unharvested (produce).

(One might retort from the case of the) ox (as follows:) Let a human being be commanded regarding the muzzling of a (fellow) human being by an *a fortiori* argument: You are not commanded to provide a living for an ox, yet you are commanded (not to) muzzle it. Therefore, regarding a human being, for whom you are commanded to provide a living, you are certainly commanded (not to) muzzle him (by any contractual restrictions on which produce he may eat).

(Therefore,) Scripture says, "as your soul (desires)" (Deut 23:25) – as is your soul, so is the soul of the worker. Just as regarding your own soul, if you muzzled it (i.e., if you fasted), you would be exempt, so, if you muzzled (i.e., you contractually limited or abolished the right of your worker to eat), you would be exempt.[252]

(Since the argument has taught us only that workers can be limited or prohibited from eating all kinds of food by contract), whence do we (derive) that a human being (may eat of) harvested produce (when he or she is a worker). Scripture says, "standing crops" (קמה) "standing crops" (קמה) twice (in Deut 23:26). If (the redundancy) is inapplicable to human beings (and their right to eat of) unharvested crops (which the Torah established in this verse), apply it to human beings (and their right to eat) harvested crops.

The אם אינו ענין *midrash* at the end of the talmudic passage departs from tannaitic and amoraic usage insofar as it interprets the repetition of the term "standing crops" (קמה) in the single verse, Deut 23:26. Redundancy within a single verse is one of the most classical forms of *ribbui* and would not generate an אם אינו ענין *midrash* among the *tannaim* or early *amoraim*.[253] While re-

It is clear that this PT source is parallel to the bBaba Meẓiᶜaᵓ material. Its conclusions about the right of a harvester to consume harvested produce are different from those of BT. Nevertheless, it seems that BT draws on a Palestinian tradition, though not necessarily PT, for its *sugya*.

252 This translation follows the text of the majority of Talmud mss.

253 Indeed, R. Yomtov b. Abraham of Seville (ריטב״א) seems to regard the repetition of the word קמה in Deut 23:26 as a simple *ribbui*. He writes in his novellae on the Talmud:

אתיא קמה קמה – לאו דוקא, אלא לומר דתרי קמה כתיבי, חד למחובר, וחד לתלוי.

"It (i.e., the right of a harvester to eat of) harvested (produce) is derived from "standing crops" "standing crops"– This is not exactly so (i.e., the word אתיא, which seems to have been part of the formulation of the Talmud that R. Yomtov possessed, implies a *midrash* based on a "comparison of words." R. Yomtov, however, does not think this is so.) Rather, (the Talmud means) to say that קמה ("standing crops") is written twice, once to indicate (the harvester's right to eat) unharvested (produce), and once (again) to indicate (the harvester's right to eat) harvested (produce).

R. Yomtov does not comment on the אם אינו ענין *midrash* or even make reference to it. This suggests the possibility that his version of the Talmud did not include the אם אינו ענין interpretation.

dundancies within a single pentateuchal pericope might generate an אם אינו ענין *midrash* in later Palestininan amoraic sources, redundancy within a single verse never does.[254] This phenomenon is peculiar to the *stam* of BT. This is one of the few instances in which the *stam* appears to have created its midrashic interpretation *de novo*.

The Rabbinic Tradition as Revealed Torah
The Tannaitic Period

Now that we have done a thorough study of the development of the אם אינו ענין hermeneutic, we should turn to the question of how various theologies of what constituted "Scripture" are reflected in those developments. In a more concentrated way, the question we are asking is, "Does the development of אם אינו ענין tell us anything about how the rabbinic tradition came to be viewed as a form of divine revelation?" Was this view about rabbinic sources subscribed to by rabbinic Judaism from the outset, or did it develop and gain general acceptance in rabbinic circles over time? I will endeavor to show that there is progressive acceptance of this idea in the formative rabbinic period. That is, there is little support for the idea among the *tannaim*, a mixed degree of support for it among the *amoraim*, and general support for it in the post-amoraic period.

In the entire tannaitic literary corpus, only three sources discuss the idea that God revealed the Oral Torah and the Written Torah to Israel. A source in *Sifra* states that "the midrashic interpretations, civil laws, and two Torahs, one Written and one Oral, were given to Israel."[255] Another source in *Sifre Deuteronomy* repeats *Sifra*'s conception of a Written and an Oral Torah and adds a

---

On the other hand, all the major mss. and imprints of the Talmud do include it.

254 For other examples of this phenomenon in BT, see bKetubot 35a, Qiddushin 43b, Sanhedrin 28a.

255 *Sifra Beḥuqotai*, 8:12:

אלה החוקים והמשפטים והתורות. החוקים אילו המדרשות. והמשפטים אילו הדינים. והתורות מלמד ששתי תורות ניתנו להם לישראל אחד בכתב ואחד בעל פה. אמר ר״ע וכי שתי תורות היו להם לישראל והלא תורות הרבה ניתנו להם לישראל. זאת תורת העולה. זאת תורת המנחה. זאת תורת האשם. זאת תורת זבח השלמים. זאת התורה אדם כי ימות באהל. אשר נתן ה׳ בינו ובין בני ישראל זכה משה ליעשות שליח בין ישראל לאביהם שבשמים. בהר סיני ביד משה. מלמד שניתנה התורה הלכותיה ודקדוקיה ופירושיה ע״י משה מסיני:

"These are the statutes, and the judgments, and the teachings" (Lev 26:46). "The statues"– these are the midrashic interpretations; "the judgments"– these are the civil laws; "and the teachings (Heb., *torot*)"– this teaches that two Torahs were given to Israel, one in writing and one orally. R. Akiba said, "Did Israel have (only) two Torahs? Were not many Torahs given to Israel? 'This is the *torah* of the burnt offering'; 'this is the *torah* of the meal offering'; 'this is the *torah* of the guilt offering'; 'this is the *torah* of the *shelamim*-sacrifice'; 'this is the *torah* of the person who dies in the tent.'" "That God gave (as a covenant) be-

story about an exchange between a Roman governor and Rabban Gamaliel that confirms this idea.[256] (However, there is no clear cut statement that God gave these *torot*.) Finally, ARN B attributes the concept of a Written and an Oral Torah to Shammai and Hillel.

Sifra's and *Sifre Deuteronomy*'s formulation of the concept of the Written and Oral Torahs states that they were given to Israel, but as regards the content of the Oral Torah, we receive no information. There are, however, references to a "rabbinic curriculum" that always include *miqra* and *mishnah*, though other elements change.[257] The juxtaposition of *miqra*, that which is read, to *mishnah*, that which appears to have been repeated orally, suggests that the idea of revealed Oral and Written Torahs at Sinai has it roots in the tannaitic period.[258] It is, however, one thing to categorize different elements of

---

tween Himself and the Israelites" (ibid.) – Moses merited to be made the messenger between Israel and their Father in Heaven. "At Mount Sinai by the hand of Moses" (ibid.) – this teaches that the Torah was given with its *halakhot*, fine points, and explanations by Moses from Sinai.

256 *Sifre Deut.* 351:

ותורתך לישראל. מלמד ששתי תורות ניתנו להם לישראל אחת על פה ואחת בכתב. שאל אגניטיס הגמון את רבן גמליאל אמר לו כמה תורות ניתנו לישראל אמר לו שתים אחת בכתב ואחת בעל פה:

"(They shall teach Your judgments to Jacob) and Your Torah (Heb., *toratkha*) to Israel"– this teaches that two Torahs were given to Israel, one orally and one in writing. Agnitos the governor asked Rabban Gamaliel, "How many Torahs were given to Israel? He responded, "Two. One orally and one in writing."

See, however, *Sifre Deut.*, ed. Finkelstein, p. 408–9, critical apparatus line 17 s.v. בה, נוסף. In *Midrash Hagadol*, a thirteenth- or possibly fourteenth-century Yemeni *yalqut* type *midrash* (see Strack and Stemberger, p. 354), Agnitos the governor asks R. Johanan b. Zakkai, "How many Torahs were given to you from Heaven (by God)?" R. Johanan b. Zakkai responded, "Two. One orally and one in writing." He (Agnitos) said to him, "Does it say, '(they shall teach) Your Torahs to Israel?' (It actually says, "They shall teach Your Torah to Israel [Deut 33:10]." The word "Torah" is in the singular nominal form. MC) He (R. Johanan b. Zakkai) replied, "Even so, (there are) two. As it says, '*torat* (which can be read as the plural *torot* if one accepts that the word is written *defectiva*) to Israel.'" Given its appearance in *Midrash ha-Gadol*, one should consider the possibility that this is a late formulation of the story, one in which there appears a more highly developed concept of the Written and Oral Torahs. In this telling of the tale, Agnitos is defeated, as he must be, but only by the flimsiest of proofs. His pointed question, based on the strength of Scripture alone, should have won the day. It is only R. Johanan b. Zakkai's midrashic reading that defeats him. This is the story's point – namely, one can only understand the Written Torah through the lens of rabbinic interpretation. See S. Fraade, *From Tradition to Commentary* (Albany: SUNY Press, 1991), pp. 87–89 and nn. 64 and 68.

257 *Sifre Deut.* 161, ed. Finkelstein, p. 212; ibid. 355, p. 418, lines 12–13; *Midrash Tannaim, Deut.* 32:13, ed. Hoffman, p. 193; ibid., *Deut.* 33:21, p. 219; tSotah 7:21, ed. Lieberman, p. 200, lines 207–10.

258 See S. Fraade, "Literary Composition and Oral Performance in Early *Midrashim*," *Oral Tradition* (Bloomington: Slavica Publishers, 1999) 14:1:33–51, especially pp. 42–45.

a curriculum (perhaps including traditional texts, lectures and lecture notes, and discussions and interpretations of the aforementioned literary compositions), to which the *tannaim* applied different study methods, and another to claim that these elements already formed a fully developed ideology of the Oral and Written Torahs.[259] Eventually, later rabbinic communities viewed the tannaitic and talmudic legacies as revealed Oral Torah. It does not seem, however, that the tannaitic world had completely accepted that view, as we will soon see.

ARN B contains the most developed theology of the Written and Oral Torahs, though like *Sifra* and *Sifre Deuteronomy*, it does not contain a description of what the Oral Torah encompasses. It does, however, state that the Oral Torah "was given from Heaven (i.e., by God)."[260] It is noteworthy, however, that this story does not appear in ARN A.

There is, however, a Babylonian *baraita* relating essentially the same story. It does not say that the Oral Torah "was given from Heaven," and in the form attested to by all the relevant manuscripts, it uses the same formulation re-

259 Martin Jaffee, "How Much 'Orality' in Oral Torah? New Perspectives on the Composition and Transmission of Early Rabbinic Tradition," *Shofar* 10(1992):2:55, 71 and 72, especially, "The self-evident ideological and jurisprudential *function* of the concept of the Oral Torah, therefore, is not to be confused with its origins. Rather, the conception emerges quite directly and uncontroversially out of the technology of rabbinic tradition as a *written* tradition. *The oral interpretive culture generated by the text is the primary referent of the term Oral Torah.* Quite naturally, it comes [eventually (MC)] to signify not only the discussion of the text, but the text which generates the discussion, i.e., the text of the rabbinic tradition, memorized and internalized, orally recited and transmitted – first the Mishnah and later, by assimilation, the entire collection of texts within which rabbinic culture transmitted its lore and values." Here Jaffee parts ways with Fraade. Fraade wishes to ascribe the view he presents as the one held universally among the Rabbis, especially those represented in "the earliest *midrashim*." Other views exist, some even within "the earliest *midrashim*."

260 ARN B, ed. Schechter

מעשה באחד שבא אצל שמאי הזקן. אמר לו: רבי, כמה תורות נתנו מן השמים? א״ל: אחת בכתב ואחת בפה. א״ל: אני מאמינך אלא זו שנתנה בכתב, אבל זו שנתנה בפה, איני מאמינך. [גער בו וסלקו בנזיפה. בא לפני הלל. א״ל: רבי, כמה תורות נתנו מן השמים? א״ל אחת בכתב ואחת בעל פה. א״ל אני מאמינך אלא זו שנתנה בכתב, אבל זו שנתנה בפה, איני מאמינך.]....

(There is) a story about someone who came to Shammai the Elder. He said to him, "How many Torahs were given from Heaven?" He (Shammai) replied, "One in writing and one orally." He (the inquirer) replied, "I believe you only (regarding) the one given in writing, but I do not believe you regarding the one given orally." [He (Shammai) yelled at him and got rid of him in anger. He came to Hillel. He said to him, "How many Torahs were given from Heaven?" He (Hillel) replied, "One in writing and one orally." He (the inquirer) replied, "I believe you only (regarding) the one given in writing, but I do not believe you regarding the one given orally."]....[ ] added by Schechter, see his edition of ARN, p. 62, n. לב to Version B.

garding the Written and Oral Torahs that *Sifra* and *Sifre Deuteronomy* do.[261] That being the case, I would explain the terms "in writing" and "orally" used in BT in the same manner as I explained those terms as they appear in *Sifra* and *Sifre Deuteronomy*.

If, however, we accept Schechter's position that the stories about Shammai and Hillel come from early sources from which BT drew,[262] then the Shammai-Hillel narrative is undoubtedly tannaitic. What is not clear is whether the Oral Torah "given from Heaven" to which the ARN B *baraita* refers is equivalent to the rabbinic traditions of the *tannaim* or to some other corpus. But to what corpus could the ARN B narrative refer if not to the traditions of the *tannaim*?

It is possible that the terms Written Torah and Oral Torah refer to material found in what today would be considered solely Written Torah. That is, the Pentateuch records that some of its material is written and some is oral. The most famous written communication is what presently most people call the Ten Commandments (Heb., עשרת הדברות, "ten words" or "ten communications"). Even the Ten Commandments begin their existence as a verbal communication (Exod 20:1–17), but later God reduces them to writing on stone (Exod 24:12; 31:18; 32:15–16). Nevertheless, the Pentateuch represents itself to be a "protocol" of many verbal communications, most of them from God to Moses.

261 bShabbat 31a contains the following parallel. It is presented as a *baraita* using the formula תנו רבנן to which all the text witnesses attest. Only the printed editions of BT, משפחת שונצינו ר״נ ואילך and Vilna, use תורה שבכתב and תורה שבעל פה in this passage. The story is as follows:

> תנו רבנן: מעש׳ בגוי אחד שבא לפני שמאי. אמ׳ לו: כמה תורות יש לכם? אמ׳ לו: שתים. אחת שבכתב ואחת שבעל פה. אמ׳ לו: שבכתב אני מאמינך. אבל שבעל פה איני מאמינך. גיירני עלמנת [צ״ל: על מנת] שתלמדני תורה שבכתב. גער בו והוציאו בנזיפהבא [צ״ל: נזיפה. בא] לפני הלל, גייריה. יומא קמא אמ׳ לו: אבג׳ד. למחר הפך ליה דגב׳א. אמ׳ ליה: והאלאו [צ״ל: והא לאו] איתמול אמרת לי הכי? אמ׳ ליה: והאיתמול [צ״ל: והא איתמול] לאו עלי דידי קא סמכת? על פה נמי סמוך עלי.
> (כ״י א״פ (OPP. ADD FOL. 23 (366)

> Our Rabbis taught (in a *baraita*): A gentile came before Shammai. He (the gentile) said, "How many Torahs do you have?" He (Shammai) replied, "Two. One in writing and one oral." He said to him, "I believe you regarding the one in writing, but I don't believe you regarding the oral one. Convert me on condition that you teach me (only) the Written Torah." Shammai yelled at him and threw him out in anger. He came before Hillel, who converted him. On the first day (after his conversion), he (Hillel) said to him (i.e., taught him), "*Aleph, bet, gimmel, dalet* (the first four letters of the Hebrew alphabet in their proper order)." The next day he reversed it (the order so that it was presented as) *dalet, gimmel, bet, aleph*. He said, "Yesterday didn't you say to me thus (*aleph, bet, gimmel, dalet*)?" He (Hillel) said, "Yesterday didn't you rely upon that which is mine (i.e., my tradition?) (Now,) rely on me also in regard to that which is oral. (based on MS Oxford OPP. ADD FOL. 23 (366)

262 אבות דרבי נתן, ed. Schechter, מבוא – פרק ז׳, p. xxvi. See, however, Menahem Kister, "מ-מות מילין," אבות דרבי נתו מהדורת ש"ז שכטר אקד (Jerusalem and New York: Jewish Theological Seminary, 1996), p. 35. Kister notes that sometimes BT influences ARN.

The Hebrew terms for these oral communications take several different forms, most prominently וידבר ה׳ ("God spoke") and ויאמר ה׳ (God said"). Frequently, God not only communicates verbally with Moses; He asks him to deliver His verbal message in oral form to the Israelites (דבר אל בני ישראל). Still there are instances in which God commands Moses to preserve some information in writing (Exod 17:14; Num 33:2). In other instances, the pentateuchal narrative states that Moses writes the "book of the Torah" on his own initiative (Exod 24:4; Deut 31:24). Hence, the view that Written and Oral Torahs "were given from Heaven," which receives expression in the *baraita* in ARN B, may refer to the material of what we know the *tannaim* considered divine revelation – namely, the Pentateuch.[263] The narrator of the ARN B story may be suggesting that the gentile who wanted to convert only on the basis of the study of the Written Torah sought to observe only that which was definitely written by God – for example, the Ten Commandments.[264] Shammai rejects this since both that which the Torah says God wrote and that which it says God spoke are incumbent upon Jews.

Whatever the meaning and concept of a Written and Oral Torah or tradition may be in some tannaitic sources, other sources attribute statements to various tannaitic figures that dispute the idea that "two Torahs were given to Israel, one in writing and one orally." *Sifra Beḥuqotai*, 8:12, one of the sources for the idea of a Written and Oral Torah, attributes a response to this notion to R. Akiba, who contests it:

> אמר ר״ע וכי שתי תורות היו להם לישראל והלא תורות הרבה ניתנו להם לישראל. זאת תורת העולה. זאת תורת המנחה. זאת תורת האשם. זאת תורת זבח השלמים. זאת התורה אדם כי ימות באהל.

263 Cf. S. Fraade, "Literary and Oral in *Midrashim*," *Oral Traditions* (1999), 14:1:42–45. Fraade suggests that the model of written and oral revelation of the Torah eventually becomes the model for the disciple-master relationship (exemplified by Moses and God) and for the "circularity" of learning (from text to oral performance and further development, which in turn becomes text again). When the author of the Shammai-Hillel story in ARN B suggests that "Heaven" gave two Torahs to Israel, one in writing and the other orally, he may be saying that the revelation at Sinai provided the model for rabbinic learning. This learning is what makes it possible for Israel to observe God's *mizvot* properly.

264 It is interesting to note that the *Talmudim* report that the Ten Commandments became a matter of polemical conflict between rabbis and *minim*. See pBerakhot 1:5 (3c)||bBerakhot 12a. The talmudic material should not, however, be read back into the ARN B story for several reasons: 1) there is nothing in the story that indicates even obliquely that the "Written Torah" mentioned therein means the Ten Commandments; and 2) if ARN B's story is tannaitic, then non-contemporary sources such as these talmudic amoraic ones do not necessarily shed light on the original meaning of the story.

> R. Akiba said, "Did Israel have (only) two Torahs? Were not many Torahs given to Israel? 'This is the *torah* of the burnt offering'; 'this is the *torah* of the meal offering'; 'this is the *torah* of the guilt offering'; 'this is the *torah* of the *shelamim*-sacrifice'; 'this is the *torah* of the person who dies in the tent."

R. Akiba's retort that "many *torot* were given to Israel" cites only pentateuchal verses without any midrashic adornment. All these passages begin with the formula, "This is the instruction (*torah*) regarding.... (וזאת תורת)." Thus, it seems that R. Akiba took a stand in favor of the idea that if indeed there were many *torot* given to Israel at Sinai, presently they all appear in the Written Torah.

Other tannaitic Sages also taught that the rabbinic tradition was not revealed at one moment at Sinai. Rather, they held it to be a continuously developing tradition. For example, tSotah 7:11 (ed. Lieberman, p. 194)[265] attributes the following to R. Elazar b. Azariah (*tanna*, third generation):

> ועוד אחרת דרש: דברי חכמים כדרבנות וכמסמרות נטועים ...[או אינן חסירין ולא יתירין תלמוד לומר נטועים,] מה נטיעה פרה ורבה אף דברי תורה פרין ורבין....

> "The words of the wise are like goads, like nails planted (in prodding sticks. They were given by one Shepherd") [Eccl 12:11] ... do they neither diminish nor increase? Scripture says, "planted" (נטועים) – just as a plant is fruitful and multiplies, so the words of Torah are fruitful and multiply....

According to this toseftan report, R. Joshua (*tanna*, second generation) heard R. Elazar b. Azariah's *midrash* and proclaimed, "The generation that has R. Elazar b. Azariah in it is not orphaned!" This would imply agreement with his views, thus adding yet another tannaitic voice to those in favor of the idea that the rabbinic tradition is a developing one rather than one revealed *in toto* at Sinai.[266]

265 tSotah 7:9–11||bḤagigah 3a–b.

266 Martin Jaffee also notes that tannaitic sources are mixed in their view of whether rabbinic teachings are part of the Sinaitic revelation. He finds that the Mishnah and Tosefta are virtually silent on this issue. The tannaitic *midrashim*, on the other hand, make more of an effort to equate the various sorts of divine communications and laws with various forms of rabbinic teachings – for example, *aggadot*, *gezerot*, and *halakhot*. Yet when the issue of the Oral Torah arises, it is not clear to what it refers. Nor does everyone mentioned in the tannaitic *midrashim* agree that "two Torahs" were given at Sinai. See Martin Jaffee, *Torah in the Mouth*, pp. 84–92 and 97–99.

Summary

To summarize, it is likely that the roots of the idea that the Oral Torah was revealed at Sinai are tannaitic.[267] Those *tannaim* who began to develop the concept of a Torah that was given orally did little to define what that Torah encompassed. Therefore, there is no basis for a claim that there is a unified tannaitic view regarding the equivalency between the term "two Torot . . . one given orally" and the contents of the tannaitic rabbinic tradition.[268]

What is certain is that the *tannaim* agreed that God had revealed the Written Torah. Hence, the application of אם אינו ענין and other hermeneutics to

267 See n. 259. Even mʾAvot 1:1 does not state explicitly that the Oral Torah was revealed at Sinai. All it says is משה קבל תורה מסיני, "Moses received the Torah at Sinai." It is possible that this was directed against those who denied that "Torah was from Heaven" (see mSanhedrin 10:1, *Sifre Deut.* 102) as much as it is possible that it is a rabbinic "chain of tradition" statement supporting the concept of the Oral Torah. As we have seen, there is no truly firm notion of the Oral Torah in the tannaitic period also because there is little use of that terminology in tannaitic literature and its meaning there is not well defined. For further thoughts on this issue, though in a different direction, see Martin Jaffee, *Torah in the Mouth*, p. 98 and idem., "The Oral Cultural Context of the Talmud Yerushalmi," in *The Talmud Yerushalmi and Graeco-Roman Culture I* (Tübingen: Mohr Siebeck, 1997), pp. 57–58.

268 See n. 266 above. We should compare *Sifra Beḥuqotai*, 8:12, which appears to equate the Oral Torah and the rabbinic tradition, to *Mek.*, *ʿAmalek*, 2, s.v. כי יהיה; ibid., s.v. והזהרת אתהם; *Sifra*, *Shemini*, par. 1:9; *Aḥare*, par. 9:9; *Sifre Deut.* 58 and 59; *Midrash Tannaim*, *Deut.* 11:32; 12:1; and 26:16. In all those cases, the tannaitic *midrashim* interpret the biblical term חקים (*ḥuqqim*, "statutes") as *midrashot*; and in all those cases, human beings either deliver the *midrashot* or God asks them to "make" them. *Sifra Beḥuqotai* 8:12 stands alone insofar as its context implies that God revealed *midrashot* at Sinai.

It appears that the dictum is the product of automatic interpretation of *ḥuqqim* as *midrashot*. See Ch. Albeck, מבוא התלמודים, p. 87 and E. Z. Melamed, פרקי מבוא לספרות התלמוד, pp. 185–86, regarding the automatic repetition of midrashic interpretations wherever their generative biblical word or phrase appears. Once we have established that an automatic repetition of a midrashic interpretation has occurred, we need not assume that a high degree of editorial thoughtfulness informs the *derashah* where the repetition occurs. This is especially so when the *derashah* is contextually problematic.

The *midrash* of the terms *ḥuqqim* and *mishpatim* in *Sifra Beḥuqotai*, 8:12, is a good case in point. There is no use in interpreting these terms as *midrashot* and civil laws if they are aspects of the Written or Oral Torah referred to in *Sifra*'s dictum. That is, if they are not part of those Torahs, then the rabbinic tradition of *midrash* is not part of the Oral Torah. In terms of the verse it interprets, however, *Sifra* implies that *midrashot* were part of the Sinaitic revelation. Are there then *midrashot* that are not part of the rabbinic tradition? Similarly, if *mishpatim* in Lev 26:46 are civil laws, as the *Sifra* seems to interpret, those are generally thought of as being part of the Written Torah. Why do they have to be mentioned as a separate category of revealed laws? The problems caused by the midrashic interpretations of these two biblical terms are so many in the context of *Sifra Beḥuqotai* that they are best explained by the phenomenon of automatic repetition of midrashic interpretations of particular biblical words or phrases wherever those words or phrases appear.

the Pentateuch was taken for granted. Since it appears that the idea of the Oral Torah, the definition of the term, and the status of whatever it encompassed as a form of divine revelation were only in the beginning stages of their development,[269] it is not surprising that we do not find the *tannaim* applying the hermeneutics they used to their own teachings.

The Rabbinic Tradition as Revealed Torah
The Amoraic Period

Once we enter the amoraic period, we see an increase of clarity on the part of some *amoraim* about the Oral Torah being equivalent to the rabbinic tradition. The claim that it was given at Sinai now grants the authority of revelation to rabbinic teachings, especially to those of the *tannaim*. Examples of the claim that the Oral Torah and rabbinic teachings are equivalent appear in the two Talmuds and the early aggadic *midrashim*. The first-generation *amora*, R. Joshua b. Levi, held the following view:

תלמוד ירושלמי מסכת פיאה פרק ב דף יז עמוד א/ה"

רבי יהושע בן לוי אמר עליהם ועליהם כל ככל דברים הדברים מקרא משנה תלמוד ואגדה אפילו מה שתלמיד וותיק עתיד להורות לפני רבו כבר נאמר למשה בסיני מה טעם יש דבר שיאמ׳ ראה זה חדש הוא וגו׳ משיבו חבירו ואומר לו כבר היה לעולמים.

R. Joshua b. Levi said: "on them" "*and* on them" (Deut 9:10). "all" "*according to* all"; "words" "*the* words"[270] (these unnecessary additions teach)

269 Jaffee, *Torah in the Mouth*, pp. 98–99; Steven Fraade, "Oral and Literary in Midrashim, *Oral Tradition*, 14:1:37–39; 43–46.

270 Deut 9:10 states:

ויתן ה׳ אלי את שני לוחת האבנים כתבים באצבע אלהים ועליהם ככל הדברים אשר דבר ידוד עמכם בהר מתוך האש ביום הקהל:

And the Eternal gave to me (Moses) the two tablets of stone, written by the finger of God; and upon them (was) according to all the words the Eternal spoke with you at the mountain from the midst of the fire on the day of the assembly.

The Hebrew text and its translated counterpart, which I have translated more literally than idiomatically, would read much better if the ו in the word ועליהם ("and upon them"), the כ in ככל ("according to all"), and the ה in הדברים ("the words") were absent. Then the translation would be: "And the Eternal gave to me (Moses) the two tablets of stone, written by the finger of God; upon them (was) everything the Eternal spoke with you at the mountain from the midst of the fire on the day of the assembly." R. Joshua b. Levi viewed these excess prefixes as extraneous. Therefore, in typical rabbinic fashion, he held that they generated special meaning. The meaning he finds in them is that the entire tradition was given at Sinai. It is interesting to note that J. N. Ep-

> that the Scriptures, Mishnah, *talmud*,[271] and even that which a seasoned student will in the future teach before his master was already said to Moses at Sinai. What (then) is the meaning (of the verse), "There is a thing of which it is said, 'Behold, this is new. . . .'" (Eccl 1:10)? (The rest of the verse teaches that) his fellow should answer him thus, "It has already existed forever (from before us)" (ibid.). (pPe'ah 2:4, 17a)[272]

This dictum certainly views the entire rabbinic tradition as part of the Sinaitic revelation and may reflect zealous support of Rabbi Judah the Prince's Mishnah, a position that not all early *amoraim* espoused. For example, the view that the entire rabbinic tradition was not revealed at Sinai finds further support in the words of R. Yannai:[273]

---

stein in his מבוא לנוסח משנה, pp. 166–352, does not include R. Joshua b. Levi among the *amoraim* who participate significantly in the criticism or reformulation of R. Judah ha-Nasi's Mishnah.

271 It is clear that this term does not refer to the *Talmudim* as we know them. It may mean interpretations or extensions of tannaitic law by the use of logic.

272 Cf. bBerakhot 5a:

> ואמר רבי לוי בר חמא אמר רבי שמעון בן לקיש: מאי דכתיב „ואתנה לך את לחות האבן והתורה והמצוה אשר כתבתי להורותם" (שמות כד, יב)? „לחות" – אלו עשרת הדברות. „תורה" – זה מקרא. „והמצוה" – זו משנה. „אשר כתבתי" – אלו נביאים וכתובים. „להורותם" – זה תלמוד. מלמד שכולם ניתנו למשה מסיני.

> And R. Levi b. Hama said that R. Simeon b. Laqish said: What (is the meaning of) that which is written, "And I (God) will give to you (Moses) the tablets of stone and the Torah and commandment that I have written to instruct them (Israel)?" "Tablets" (implies) the Ten Commandments; "Torah" (implies) Pentateuch (lit., Scripture). "the commandment" (implies) the Mishnah; "that I have written" (implies) the Prophets and Writings' "to instruct them" implies *talmud* (probably meaning reasoning using written and oral traditions). This teaches that all of these were given at Sinai.

The text witnesses have significant differences in formulation from the Vilna edition cited above, but the basic message remains the same. The tradents that BT cites are a third-generation Palestinian *amora* citing a second-generation Palestinian *amora*. The most significant alternative version of this citation is in MS Paris 671 and MS Munich 95, presenting this teaching as tannaitic with the introductory תאנא or תנא. Those manuscripts credit the citation of this tradition primarily to R. Levi b. Ḥama (Laḥma) but continue to say "and some say Resh Laqish said. . . ."

273 The fact that other members of the "bridge generation" between the *tannaim* and *amoraim* chose to create alternative collections of *mishnayyot* testifies to this position. As we shall discuss further on in this chapter, in the first few generations after the Mishnah's publication, its rulings were often contested. Yet, as the dictum of R. Joshua b. Levi indicates, there were strong supporters of what was destined to become the primary source of law for talmudic rabbinic Judaism. R. Johanan has also been depicted as a major supporter of the Mishnah on the basis of the many rules for deciding the law from the Mishnah attributed to him indicate. See Ch. Albeck, מבוא לתלמודים, p. 184. See, however, Abraham Goldberg, "גישותיהן השונות של ר' יוחנן ושל ריש לקיש לשאלת יחסה של המשנה אל התוספתא והברייתא," *Proceedings of the Seventh World Congress of Jewish Studies* (1980), 3:109–16.

תלמוד ירושלמי מסכת סנהדרין פרק ד דף כב עמוד א

> אמר רבי ינאי אילו ניתנה התורה חתוכה לא היתה לרגל עמידה מה טעם וידבר יי׳ אל משה אמ׳ לפניו רבונו של עולם הודיעיני היאך היא ההלכ׳ אמר לו אחרי רבים להטות רבו המזכין זכו רבו המחייבין חייבו כדי שתהא התור׳ נדרשת מ״ט פנים טמא ומ״ט פנים טהור

> R. Yannai said, "If the Torah had been given fully determined (regarding the disposition of the law for every case), no one would have been able to survive. What then is the meaning of, "And God spoke to Moses"? Moses spoke (thus) in the presence of God: "Tell me what is the (final disposition of) the law." God said, "You shall incline after the majority" (Exod 23:2) – if those who exonerate (a criminal) are in the majority, they have exonerated; if they condemn, they have condemned. (I have arranged it thus) in order for the Torah to be interpreted forty-nine ways (inclining) towards impurity and forty-nine ways (inclining) towards purity. . . . (pSanhedrin 4:2 [22a])

R. Yannai's *aggadah* certainly denies that the Torah given at Sinai was fully determined. God's words to Moses were general and open to interpretation. The final disposition of the law was, in his view, something accomplished by human reasoning and majority rule. Hence, the entire rabbinic tradition is not divinely revealed, but rather evolves through the interpretive endeavors of the Sages.

BT attributes a debate to R. Elazar b. Pedat and R. Johanan, two second-generation Palestinian *amoraim*. It claims that R. Elazar held that the majority of the Torah revealed at Sinai was written;[274] R. Johanan purportedly holds

---

There were two Palestinian *amoraim* by the name of R. Yannai, one in the first amoraic generation, the other in the third. It is difficult to determine who authored the *memra* under discussion. I am arbitrarily linking the R. Yannai to whom this *memra* is attributed to R. Joshua b. Levi. If he is the first generation R. Yannai, then his teaching represents a first-generation amoraic counterpoint to R. Joshua b. Levi's view.

274 Compare, however, the *memra* attributed to R. Elazar in pPeah 2:4 (17a)=pḤagigah 1:8 (76d). There R. Elazar seems to admit that the greater part of the Torah is oral, but the Written Torah provides the basis for a greater amount of *midrash*:

> ר׳ זעירא בשם ר׳ לעזר אכתוב לכם רובי תורתי וכי רובה של תורה נכתבה אלא מרובין הן הדברים הנדרשים מן הכתב מן הדברים הנדרשים מן הפה.

> R. Zeira said in the name of R. Lezar (Elazar). "If I would write for him (Israel) the greater part of My Torah, they would be considered as a stranger" (Hosea 8:12). But is the majority of the Torah written? Rather, there are more things derived by *midrash* from that which is in writing than there are things derived by *midrash* from that which is oral.

It is possible, however, that R. Elazar is only saying that the amount of what is considered *torah*

that the greater part of the Torah was delivered orally:[275]

תלמוד בבלי מסכת גיטין דף ס עמוד ב

א"ר אלעזר: תורה – רוב בכתב ומיעוט על פה, שנא': +הושע ח'+ אכתוב לו רובי תורתי כמו זר נחשבו; ור' יוחנן אמר: רוב על פה ומיעוט בכתב, שנא': +שמות ל"ד+ כי על פי הדברים האלה.

R. Elazar said: (regarding) Torah – the greater part (of it) is in writing, and the lesser part is oral. As it says, "I shall write for you (Israel) the greater parts of my Torah, (lest) they be considered a stranger" (Hos 8:12).[276] But R. Johanan said: the greater part (of the Torah) is oral and the lesser part is written. As it says, ". . . for on the basis of these words (have I established covenant with you (Moses) and with Israel)" (Exod 34:27).[277]

These statements in BT have no true parallels in coeval rabbinic sources, especially PT. Nevertheless, the issue of the relative importance of one type of Torah over the other appears to have exercised the Palestinian *amoraim* of the first through fourth generations. In the major PT *sugya* that discusses this issue, pPeah 2:4 (17a) = pḤagigah 1:8 (76d), most of the *amoraim* represented agree that that which was "by the mouth (presumably of the Sages)" is an expression of divine revelation. In that *sugya*, however, R. Johanan, who agrees that there is a body of revealed Oral Law, limits its scope. The *memra* attributed to him says that there are "*halakhot* that were spoken to Moses at Sinai."[278] These, according to the citation in R. Johanan's name, comprise a relatively lim-

---

in rabbinic circles is greater than the amount of what comprises the (written) Torah. Then his statement could mean that the midrashic derivations from the Written Torah vastly outnumber midrashic derivations based on rabbinic *torah*. This suggests that R. Elazar may have been aware of interpretations of mishnaic and *baraita* sources that used hermeneutics. See, for example, the interpretations of R. Johanan and R. Simeon b. Laqish above. Such interpretations are indeed few in comparison to the midrashic interpretations based on scriptural sources.

275 There is no equivalent *memra* in PT. BT's representation of R. Johanan's view seems to conflict with the position ascribed to him by R. Zeira in PT. See pPeah 2:4 (17a)=pḤagigah 1:8 (76d).

276 Translated in accord with BT's *midrash* of the verse.

277 The Hebrew states: כי על פי הדברים האלה. The literal translation is, "for on the mouth of these words." Even the Hebrew word דברים in the phrase can be interpreted as "these spoken words" because the Hebrew radical from which דברים is derived is ד-ב-ר normally meaning "to speak." See the *memra* of R. Ḥaggai in the name of R. Samuel b. Naḥman in pPeah 2:4 (17a)=pḤagigah 1:8 (76d). It is not uncommon for BT to attribute Palestinian traditions to R. Johanan even though PT does not. See Abraham Weiss, על היצירה הספרותית של האמוראים, pp. 247, n. 84 and 310, n. 2.

278 For a thorough contemporary discussion of "*halakhah le-Moshe mi-Sinai*," see Christine Hayes, "*Halakhah le-Moshe mi-Sinai* in Rabbinic Sources: A Methodological Case Study" in *The Synoptic Problem in Rabbinic Literature*, ed. Shaye J. D. Cohen, Brown Judaic Series 326 (Rhode Island: Brown Judaic Studies, 2000). See especially pp. 111–14.

ited corpus included within the Mishnah as part of that work but not its sum total. Thus, BT and PT, despite problematic issues of attributions, both agree that the second amoraic generation debated how much of that which is now called Oral Torah or Oral Law is divine.

Only two other dicta directly attributed to *amoraim* state that the rabbinic tradition was part of the Sinaitic revelation. One is attributed to R. Aḥa, citing R. Jose b. R. Ḥanina – that is, a fourth-generation Palestinian *amora* citing a second-generation Palestinian *amora*. The other is attributed to R. Judah b. Shalom, a fifth-generation Palestinian *amora*. The first source appears in in *Pesiqta de-Rav Kahanah*:[279]

> ר׳ אחא בשם ר׳ יוסי בר׳ חנינה בשעה שעלה משה לשמי מרום שמע קולו של הקב״ה יושב ועוסק בפרשת פרה ואומ׳ הלכה משם אומרה, ר׳ אליעזר או׳ עגלה בת שנתה ופרה בת שתים. אמ׳ משה לפני הקב״ה, רבון העולמים העליונים והתחתונים ברשותך ואת יושב ואו׳ הלכה משמו של בשר ודם. אמ׳ לו הקב״ה, משה, צדיק אחד עתיד לעמוד בעולמי ועתיד לפתוח בפרשת פרה תחילה, ר׳ אליעזר אומ׳ עגלה בת שנתה ופרה בת שתים. אמ׳ לפניו רבון העולמים יהי רצון שיהי מחלציי, א׳ לו חייך שהוא מחלציך.

> R. Aḥa said citing R. Jose b. R. Ḥanina (said). When Moses ascended to the highest heavens (to receive the Torah), he heard God sitting and studying the biblical section about the red heifer (Num 19:1–22), and He was reciting the law in the name of its author, "R. Eliezer says, 'a calf (עגלה) is one year old; a heifer is two years old.'" Moses said in the Holy Blessed One's presence, "Sovereign of the Universe! You have the heavenly and earthly beings at your disposal, and you sit and recite the law in the name of a human being (lit., flesh and blood)?!" The Holy Blessed One responded, "Moses, there is a righteous person who will arise in My world in the future, and he will be the first to open (the discussion of) the section of the red heifer. (He will recite his tradition thus:) "R. Eliezer says, 'a calf (עגלה) is one year old; a heifer is two years old.'" He (Moses) responded, "Sovereign of the Universe! May it be Your will that he be from (among) my descendents. He (God) responded to him, "By your life, he is one of your descendents!" (*Pesiqta de-R. Kahana*, ed. Mandelbaum, 4:7)[280]

279 For a thorough discussion of the date of *Pesiqta de-Rav Kahana*, see H. L. Strack and Günther Stemberger, *Introduction to the Talmud and Midrash*, pp. 295–96. Stemberger states that internal evidence indicates that the core of this work is of fifth century provenance (295).

280 Compare this material to bGittin 6b and bBaba Meẓiᶜaᵓ 86a. According to mss. Vatican 130, Vatican 140, Munich 95, and the Vilna imprint of the Talmud, Abbaye told the story about R. Eviatar that appears in bGittin 6b. This story is of a similar literary genre as the *Pesiqta de-R Kahana* material. The story about Rabbah b. Naḥmani in bBaba Meẓiᶜaᵓ 86a is somewhat more distant in form from the material in *Pesiqta de-R Kahana* and bGittin. Nevertheless, the story intimates

Though the central issue in this passage is the incomprehensible nature of the rite of the red heifer, it also contains a section on the greatness of certain Sages. In the passage, R. Aḥa praises R. Akiba first, then he cites R. Jose b. R. Ḥanina's praise of R. Eliezer. The implication of the *aggadah* attributed to R. Jose b. R. Ḥanina is that R. Eliezer's words were already communicated by God to Moses when he went to receive the Torah. Whether R. Jose b. R. Ḥanina actually believed this or not cannot be determined beyond a shadow of a doubt. Obviously, his remarks are in story form and do not address the issue of the rabbinic tradition and revelation directly. Yet, to argue that R. Jose b. Ḥanina did not subscribe to this view argues against the most obvious meaning of his story.

It is interesting that within the same *Pesiqta* pericope, R. Aḥa,[281] who cited R. Jose b. Ḥanina, has this to say about R. Akiba: דא׳ ר׳ אחא דברים שלא ניגלו למשה בסיני ניגלו לר׳ עקיב׳ וחביריו. וכל יקר ראתה עינו (איוב כח, י)׳ – זה ר׳ עקיב׳, "[S]aid R. Aḥa, 'Matters that were not revealed to Moses at Sinai were revealed to R. Akiba and his colleagues. (As it says,) 'His eye beheld every precious thing' (Job 28:10) – this (refers to) R. Akiba'" (*Pesiqta de-Rav Kahana*, ed. Mandelbaum, 4:7).[282] Consequently, we would have to place R. Aḥa himself in the school that did not hold that the entire rabbinic tradition was part of the divine revelation at Sinai. This means that the debate about the divinely revealed status of rabbinic teachings still continued into the fourth amoraic generation in Palestine.

The final source indicating a view that the rabbinic tradition was divinely revealed at Sinai appears in *Pesiqta Rabbati*.[283] It states:

---

that God knows rabbinic *halakhah* and supports it with His authority. Most mss. agree that R. Kahana is the narrator of that story. Only MS Florence II I 9–7 attributes the story to Rabina.

281 The mss. of *Pesiqta de-Rav Kahana* are unanimous in attributing this statement to R. Aḥa. Similarly, *Tanḥuma, Ḥuqqat* 24, ed. Buber (reprinted Jerusalem: 1964), p. נט, n. רמה; *Yalqut Shim'oni, Ḥuqqat* #756, ed. Mossad ha-Rav Kook (Jerusalem: Mossad ha-Rav Kook, 1986), p. 378, lines 74–75; *Yalqut Shim'oni, Isaiah* #454, ed. Vilna (1878), p. 794, s.v. והולכתי. Other midrashic complilations contain the statement about R. Akiva and his colleague, but not in R. Aḥa's name. See *Midrash Tanḥuma, Ḥuqqat* 8, ed. Vilna (1831, reprinted Jerusalem: Levin-Epstein, 1970), p. 99 and *Bemidbar Rabbah* (Jerusalem: Makhon ha-Midrash ha-Mevoar, 1996), pp. רנה–רנו.

282 Mandelbaum understands this to mean that R. Akiba discovered and understood matters in the Torah that the other Sages did not. *Pesiqta de-Rav Kahana*, ed. Mandelbaum, 4:7, p. 72, commentary to line 11. This interpretation is not consonant with the plain sense of this *aggadah*. It seems to me that Mandelbaum's comment reflects an unwillingness to accept that R. Akiba was privy to more of God's revelation than Moses was.

283 Regarding the various opinions about the dating of *Pesiqta Rabbati*, see H. L. Strack and Günther Stemberger, *Introduction to the Talmud and Midrash*, pp. 299–302. Because of the nature of this work, exact dating is extremely difficult. The source appears in *Pesiqta Rabbati* 5, ed. Friedmann, 14b. See Marc Bregman, "Mishnah and LXX as Mystery: An Example of Jewish-Christian Polemic in the Byzantine Period," in *Continuity and Renewal in Byzantine-Christian Palestine*, ed. Lee I.

> אמר רבי יהודה ברבי שלום ביקש משה שתהא המשנה בכתב וצפה הקדוש ברוך הוא שהאומות עתידין לתרגם את התורה ולהיות קוראים בה יונית ואומרים אין הם ישראל אמר לו הקדוש ברוך הוא הא משה עתידין האומות להיות אומרים אנו הם ישראל אנו הם בניו של מקום וישראל אומרים אנו הם בניו של מקום, ועכשיו המאזניים מעויין, אמר הקדוש ברוך הוא לאומות מה אתם אומרים שאתם בניי איני יודע אלא מי שמסטירין שלי בידו הוא בני אמרו לו ומה הם מסטירין שלך אמר להם זו המשנה, והכל היאך לדרוש אלא אמר רבי יהודה הלוי בי רבי שלום אמר הקדוש ברוך הוא למשה מה אתה מבקש שתהא המשנה בכתב ומה בין ישראל לאומות מניין (כך) [שכך] הוא אומר אכתוב לך רובי תורתי (הושע ח׳ י״ב) ואם כן כמו זר נחשבו (שם /הושע ח׳/).
>
> R. Judah b. Shalom said: Moses sought to have the Mishnah in writing. But the Holy Blessed One foresaw that the nations would translate the Torah, read it in Greek, and say, "They (the Jews) are not Israel." (So,) the Holy Blessed One said to Moses, "Behold, Moses, in the future the nations will claim, 'We are Israel. We are the children of God.' Israel will also say, 'We are the children of God.' The scales will then be balanced (i.e., both claims will seem equal). God will (then) say to the nations, "You say you are My children. Perhaps. But the one who possesses my mysteries, he is My child." They (the nations) will say to Him, "And what are your mysteries?" He (God) will reply, "The Mishnah." And where is all this derived from? Rather, R. Judah Halevi b. R. Shalom (actually) said: The Holy Blessed said to Moses, "Why do you seek to have the Mishnah in writing? What (then will be the) difference between Israel and the nations?" Whence do we know this? (The verse) says, "If I will write for you (Moses) the majority of My Torah" (Hos 8:12), then "they (Israel) shall be considered like a stranger" (ibid.)

This passage's main thrust appears to be a polemic against Christian claims that Jewry had been superseded by Christians as God's chosen.[284] Incidentally, however, R. Judah b. Shalom suggests that the Mishnah was revealed at Sinai, and at that time Moses begged God to write it as He had written the Written Torah. God refused, in order to protect Israel's status as His chosen. The

---

Levine (Jerusalem: Hebrew University-Dinur Center for the Study of Jewish History, Yad Ben Zvi Press, and Jewish Theological Seminary, 2004), p. 333, n. 3 regarding the attribution of this *aggadah* to R. Judah ben-R. Shalom.

284 For a full discussion of this aggadic statement of R. Judah b. Shalom, see op. cit., pp. 333–42. Bregman equates the Mishnah and the Oral Law; see pp. 333 and n. 4; 334, n. 6; 335 and n. 12 there; 338 and n. 23 there. This may or may not be the meaning of "the Mishnah" with the definite article. Whatever the case, R. Judah b. Shalom's *aggadah* does imply that the major work of the tannaitic rabbinic tradition and the source of its continued development was revealed at Sinai.

Mishnah, which contained God's "secret mysteries,"[285] belonged only to them. Therefore, they could use it to prove their right to be called God's elect.

Amoraic Attitudes toward the Accuracy and Authority of Tannaitic Rabbinic Traditions

In the Babylonian Talmud, we find that *amoraim* dismiss tannaitic traditions by declaring them erroneous or only the view of an individual. The terms used for this activity are משבשתא היא, "it is erroneous," and יחידאה היא, "it is an individual opinion." Those who questioned the accuracy or authority of tannaitic traditions are not likely to have considered these traditions divine. We find statements attributed to *amoraim* that question or negate the accuracy of a tradition in the following sources: bShabbat 121b (R. Jeremiah, third generation, Babylonia). Pesaḥim 100a (Mar Zutra, seventh generation, Babylonia). Qiddushin 47b (Rava, fourth generation, Babylonia). Ḥullin 141b (R. Zera, third generation, Babylonia and Palestine).[286]

We find that BT attributes dicta to *amoraim* who dismiss traditions as the views of individuals and, therefore, as not authoritative. These appear in bShabbat 140a (R. Yannai, first generation, Palestine). Sukkah 19b (R. Josef, third generation, Babylonia). Mo'ed Qatan 12b (R. Ḥuna, second generation, Babylonia). ibid. 20a (Rava). Yebamot 104a (Samuel, first generation, Babylonia). Baba Qama 28a (R. Naḥman, third generation, Babylonia). Baba Batra 79b (Rava). One such dismissal appears in Beẓah 31a without attribution.[287] Thus, with one exception, all the claims that a tannaitic teaching is an individual opinion and, consequently, not authoratative are attributed to *amoraim*. Denying authority to these traditions by showing them to be the views of individuals implies that they are not products of divine revelation. If they were, their authoritative status could not be dismissed just because they were individual opinions.

Finally, the many cases where PT recognizes variant versions in the Mishnah and *baraitot* suggests that even most Palestinian Sages viewed the rabbinic tradition as human even though they regarded it as sacred. The rhetorical formula indicating this recognition is אית תניי תני ... ואית תניי תני, "there are those *tannaim* who teach (the mishnaic or *baraita* tradition thus)[288]..., and there are

285 See Saul Lieberman, *Hellenism in Jewish Palestine* (New York: 1962), pp. 207–8 for an informative discussion of the Jewish "mysteries." See also Bregman as indicated in the previous note.

286 The attributions to these *amoraim* is unanimous in the text witnesses. The only exception is that the attribution to Rava is missing in MS Munich 95, but the entire dictum seems truncated there.

287 This would be the only instance of this claim by the *stam*. The formulation מתני' יחידאה היא and the attributions in the listed sources are well attested in all the published text witnesses.

288 *Tannaim* in this context are not the Sages of the mishnaic period, but individuals who committed tannaitic traditions to memory.

those *tannaim* who teach (the mishnaic or *baraita* tradition thus) . . . ," and it appears nearly 390 times in PT. Though some of these may be likened to *qeri* and *ketib* variants in Scripture, a text that the *amoraim* certainly considered divinely revealed, there are textual variations as wide as "fit" (כשר) and "unfit" (פסול) in texts discussing a single subject. Most people would not expect to find such variations in divinely revealed texts, nor would most people accept the divinity of such texts.

Summary

As this section of our study shows, the amoraic era was rich in opinions about the Written and Oral Torahs and their origins. Some of the *amoraim*'s views about these Torahs were stated explicitly; other amoraic views were stated implicitly. On occasion a statement that seemed tangential to the issue of the origins of the "two Torahs" nevertheless provided insight into an *amora*'s views on this matter. Those *amoraim* who had a major stake in all or some of the early rabbinic teachings as significant constitutional, curricular, or covenantal matters for Jewry sought to strengthen these teachings' authority by asserting that they had been revealed at Sinai. It is hard to assess whether the *amoraim* who reputedly held these views were propagandizing or stating what they considered to be historical fact.[289]

Not surprisingly, given the nature of rabbinic and talmudic literature, other *amoraim* disagreed with this view. Hence, we find statements reflecting a rejection of the divinely revealed status of all or some rabbinic teachings in some of the *aggadot* of the *amoraim*. We have also seen that there is a willingness on the part of some *amoraim* to reject the authority of certain rabbinic teachings due to their being either in error or individual opinions. Amoraic acceptance of variations – some of them major – in the formulation of rabbinic sources suggests that some *amoraim* viewed the rabbinic tradition as sacred but not necessarily divinely revealed. Therefore, it is to be expected that some of the *amoraim* would preserve the method of the *tannaim* in their application of אם אינו ענין and other hermeneutics – i.e., they would use them only on legal passages from the Pentateuch. Other *amoraim* would extend their use of אם אינו ענין and other hermeneutics beyond the Pentateuch to the Prophets, Writings, and rabbinic teachings.

289 See Martin Jaffee, "The Oral Cultural Context of the Talmud Yerushalmi," pp. 57–60 and 61. Jaffee's conception of Oral Torah as an ideological (propagandistic?) matter is useful in celebrating and institutionalizing the necessity of the disciple-Sage relationship within the rabbinic community. My view, which does not necessarily exclude Jaffee's, is that what may also have been at stake was the authority of the Mishnah and other collections and forms of rabbinic dicta as constitution and curriculum for the rabbinic community, and later, as a boundary marker between the (rabbinic) Jewish community and Christians.

The Divinity of the Rabbinic Tradition: The Anonymous Stratum of the Talmud

To the best of my knowledge there are no anonymous aggadic traditions that deal directly or tangentially with the divinity of the rabbinic tradition. This means that we must adduce evidence about this question from the behavior of the *stam* in regard to the rabbinic tradition. I propose that if we find 1) that the *stam* frequently applies hermeneutics usually used in the interpretation of scriptural texts to rabbinic teachings; and 2) that the *stam*'s interpretation of rabbinic material is midrashic rather than commentative, then we have a basis for believing that the *stam* regards the rabbinic tradition as a form of scripture. The definition of "midrashic" in this context is 1) that the *stam* extracts a point from a halakhic source that is somewhat at a remove from the source's simple meaning; or 2) that the *stam* extends or limits the law in a tannaitic or amoraic halakahic source. To be "midrashic," the *stam* must use an hermeneutical method used in the *midrash* of Scripture.

The Stam's Textual Methodology and the Divinity of the Rabbinic Tradition

The *stam*'s method of interpreting the rabbinic tradition it received indicates a mindset that views that tradition as divine. A few examples of the *stam*'s interpretational methods that demonstrate this view are phenomena like משנה יתירה, midrashic interpretations of redundancies and repetitive phrases in the Mishnah, and לאתויי, midrashic interpretations of inclusive terms like כל, "all" in rabbinic sources. These add to the specific cases we found in stammaitic אם אינו ענין *midrashim* in which the redundant or illogical "verse" was in most cases a rabbinic interpretation or *halakhah*. Let us investigate some examples of these other stammaitic methods.

Redundancies within a Tannaitic Text

There is a body of gaonic opinion that considers the first *sugya* in bBaba Meẓiʿaʾ a late anonymous addition onto the rather small amoraic core of the *sugya*.[290] Within that passage there is a claim that what the *sugya*'s author considers unnecessary repetition teaches more law than the first *mishnah* in Baba Meẓiʿaʾ appears to contain.[291] In that *mishnah* we find the case of two parties clutching at a garment they found. The *mishnah* formulates their claims thus: "This one

290 *Oẓar ha-Geaonim, Baba Meẓiʿaʾ*, ed. Lewin, p. 4 of the commentaries section, continuation of #ג.

291 The repetitive phrasing of mBaba Meẓiʿaʾ 1:1 is based on the typical formulation of claims and counterclaims of litigants. See Kings I, 3:22–23. At least one early commentator recognized this. See *Shittah Mequbezet*, bBaba Meẓiʿaʾ 2a:

says, 'I found it'; and that one says, 'I found it.' This one says, 'It is all mine'; and that one says, 'It is all mine.'" The *mishnah* rules that they must take an oath related to their claims and divide the garment. The *stam* claims that this is unnecessarily repetitive. Would we not have known from a claim of "I found it" that the person was claiming the entire garment? Why state, "It is all mine"? After considerable discussion of this matter, the *stam* comes to the conclusion that a statement about finding an object without a statement of complete ownership would give the incorrect impression that acquisition might be accomplished by sighting alone. The additional and actually unnecessary claim of "It is all mine" creates a משנה יתירה, a redundancy in the *mishnah* that teaches us that wherever the radical מ-צ-א ("to find" or any of its declensions) appears in the Mishnah it means the object is acquired only by possession, not by simple sighting. Obviously, a simple reading of the *mishnah* would not lead us to any conclusions about what the exact meaning of מ-צ-א (find) is.

The *stam* also addresses the repetitiveness in the formulation "This one says.... That one says. This one says... That one says...." (זה אומר....וזה אומר. זה אומר....וזה אומר). It claims that this extends the rules of the Mishnah from finds to business transactions. While this explanation seems to be supported by an amoraic tradition, that tradition most likely is older than the stammaitic material in which it is now embedded.[292] Rather than proving the *stam*'s point, the amoraic tradition may be a shorthand orientation to Tractate Baba Meẓiᶜaᵓ, which begins with the laws of finds and concludes with laws governing business dealings.

Here, too, the *stam* has interpreted mBaba Meẓiᶜaᵓ 1:1 in a way that is not consonant with its explicit meaning. The *mishnah* discusses no other issue besides finds; business matters are completely beyond its purview. Nevertheless, because the *stam* treats the Mishnah's text as the earlier Sages treated the Torah, it interprets redundancies and repetitiveness as implying something above and beyond the Mishnah's surface meaning. The *stam* seems to assume that what the Mishnah contains is omnisignificant in the same way the Torah is.[293]

חדא קתני זה אומר אני מצאתיה וכולה שלי וכו׳ ואם תאמר כל אריכות זה למה מאחר שתירץ דחדא קתני הא משתמע שפיר. ותו קשה היכי אפשר לומר דחדא קתני דנהי דזה וזה לא משמע ליה לחלק הרי הפסיק בזה אומר אני מצאתיה, ובשלמא אי תרתי קתני שפיר אבל אי חדא קתני איך הפסיק באמצע טענתו של ראשון במקצת טענה של שני. ויש לומר דחדא מיתרצא חברתה דהיינו שהוצרך להאריך ולומר זה אומר אני מצאתיה וכולה שלי שזו היא טענתו וחדא קתני והתנא סדר הדברים כפי דרך הטוענים דלא שבקיה לסיומי למילתיה עד דאמר אידך אני הוא שמצאתיה ומעשים בכל יום בין הטוענים כזה:

292 That amoraic tradition states ,אמר ר׳ פפא ואיתמא ר׳ שימי בר אשי ואמרי לה כדי:רישא במציאה וסיפא במקח וממכר, "R. Papa said, and some say R. Shimi b. Ashi said, and there are those who recite this tradition without attribution: The beginning speaks of finds, and the end speaks of business transactions." See n. 290 above regarding this material.

293 See Yaakov Elman on omnisignificance as it has been applied to biblical and rabbinic sources in

Examples of לאתויי

The term לאתויי, roughly translated "to include," is usually a response to the query, ?לאתויי מאי, "to include what?" The *stam* usually poses this question about an undefined, inclusive clause in a *mishnah*, *baraita*, or *memra*. The response provides an example that gives the clause greater definition. Beginning in the fourth generation of Babylonian *amoraim*, there are amoraic dicta that include the term לאתויי, sometimes preceded by ?לאתויי מאי.[294] In these amoraic sources, the example provided by the dictum is always consonant with the plain meaning of the tradition it clarifies. This cannot always be said to be true for stammaitic cases of לאתויי. Further, many amoraic examples of לאתויי explain clauses in a *mishnah* or *baraita* that need a higher degree of definition, whether or not the source contains an inclusive word or phrase. The following amoraic dicta will demonstrate how the amoraic לאתויי functions.

bḤagigah 4a. In bḤagigah 4a we find the following *baraita* accompanied by Rava's clarifying example:

"Progressive *Derash* and Retrospective *Peshat*," in *Modern Scholarship and the Study of Torah*, pp. 229–40.

294 There are two exceptions. There is a *memra* attributed to Rav Judah, a second-generation Babylonian *amora*, which uses לאתויי in its formulation. The *memra* appears in bSanhedrin 36b=Niddah 49b and bYebamot 22a. Its original source is in bSanhedrin as is proved by its parallel in PT, where it functions as a defining comment to mSanhedrin 4:2. The formulation in PT, which indicates that there is no need for לאתויי, states: הכל כשירין לדון דיני ממונו׳ ר׳ יהוד׳, אומ׳ אפי׳ ממזירין "'Everyone is fit to judge a monetary case'— R. Judah says, 'Even *mamzerin* (i.e., offspring of incestuous or adulterous relations)'" (pSanhedrin 4:7 [22b]). See also MS Florence II I 9–7, Sanhedrin 36b, where the formula וה[ו]ינן בה, a sign of intervention by the *stam*, appears before לאתויי מאי. This formulation appears in all Niddah mss. that include bNiddah 49b. In view of the לאתויי מאי formulation of the question, R. Judah's *memra* would naturally include ... לאתויי. bYebamot 22a makes "secondary use" of R. Judah's *memra*. That is, the anonymous redactors made use of R. Judah's *memra* to explain a section of mYebamot 2:5. The attribution to R. Judah does not appear in MS Oxford HEB. D. (2675), though it does appear in all the other relevant mss. and in דפוס פיזרו רס"ט.

Other *memrot* using לאתויי are attributed to Rabbah bar 'Ulla (Babylonia, fourth amoraic generation) Rav Josef, (Babylonia, third amoraic generation) and Abbaye (Babylonia, fourth amoraic generation). All these *amoraim* appear in bNiddah 63b. This is true, however, only for MS Vatican 111, דפוס שונצינו רמ"ט, and the Vilna edition of BT. In MS Munich 95 the only *amora* cited who uses the term לאתויי is Abbaye. In MS Vatican 113, R. Josef does not appear.

These early amoraic uses of לאתויי tend to introduce explanations of unclear formulations in the Mishnah. For example, who is included in the rule, "All who are fit to judge are fit to be witnesses; but there are those who are fit to witness but not to judge"? Or, what is included in the phrase "and everything like these" (mNiddah 9:8), which follows a list of symptoms that indicates the onset of menses. These are not examples of a midrashic use of לאתויי as I have defined it above. These examples may be added to the phenomenon we will discuss in the main text of our work.

והחיגר והסומא וחולה והזקן. תנו רבנן: +שמות כ"ג+ רגלים – פרט לבעלי קבין. דבר אחר: רגלים – פרט לחיגר. ולחולה, ולסומא, ולזקן, ולשאינו יכול לעלות ברגליו. – ושאינו יכול לעלות ברגליו לאתויי מאי? – אמר רבא: לאתויי מפנקי דכתיב +ישעיהו א'+ כי תבאו לראות פני מי בקש זאת מידכם רמס חצרי.

> (Mishnah citation:) "and the halt, the blind, the sick and the old (are exempt from the obligation of appearing in the Temple during the pilgrimage festivals)": The Rabbis taught (in a *baraita*): "pilgrimage festivals" (lit., רגלים, feet) – this excludes those who use canes. Another interpretation: "pilgrimage festivals" (lit., רגלים, feet) – this excludes the halt, the sick, the blind, the old, and the one who cannot go up (to the Temple) on his feet.
>
> "And the one who cannot go up (to the Temple) on his feet"– includes whom? Rava said, "It includes the delicate, as it is written, "When you come to appear before Me, who has requested this of you, that you trample My courtyards?" (Isa 1:12).

Rava's interpretation is generated by the need to define the rather vague "one who cannot go up on his feet." This phrase is all the more problematic because it appears in an explicit list of parties who are exempt from appearance in the Temple on the pilgrimage festivals because their age or health prevents them from making the climb on foot. What more could be meant by the clause "and the one who cannot go up (to the Temple) on his feet"? Rava answers that the clause includes those who, unlike the others, have the basic physical capability to climb up the Temple mount, but who cannot do so barefoot, as required by the *halakhah*, because their feet are too tender. This person is literally "one who cannot go up the Temple mount on his (bare) feet." Hence, according to Rava's interpretation, the *baraita*'s clause adds to the list those who are prevented from making the appearance in the Temple for extrinsic rather than intrinsic physical reasons.

bTemurah 31b. In bTemurah 31b we find Rabina's comment on a clause in mTemurah 7:2: הקדש בדק הבית חל על הכל, "dedication of (a thing) for the upkeep of the Temple is effective in regard to everything." That is, if one dedicates something for the upkeep of the Temple, whether the thing or its value will be used, it may be used only for the purpose of maintaining the Temple. "Everything," however, is highly inclusive. What is included in this unspecific generality? Rabina, a sixth-generation Babylonian *amora*, suggests the following examples: the sawdust from sawing down a dedicated tree or the leaves that fall from it. Even the monetary worth of these must go to the Temple's upkeep.

Rabina's comment does not exhaust all the possible meanings of "everything," but it does provide an example of how far that term's provisions extend when an object has been dedicated for the Temple's upkeep. No aspect or part of the object, whether or not it can be used directly for the maintenance of the Temple, can be used for any other purpose. This is exactly what the mishnaic passage, "dedication of (a thing) for the upkeep of the Temple is effective in regard to everything" means in its most literal sense. Rabina merely provides a concrete example of this rule.

Stammaitic Examples of לאתויי

We should not be surprised that there are stammaitic examples of the use of לאתויי like those of the *amoraim*. Once a certain rhetorical or logical formula exists, later generations generally make use of it. In its use of לאתויי, the *stam*, however, goes beyond the plain meaning orientation that characterized the amoraic לאתויי phenomenon. It apparently understands לאתויי as the Aramaic equivalent of the tannaitic midrashic term להביא, "this includes," which always generates a rule that exceeds the explicit meaning of a scriptural text. This is what I meant when I spoke of the midrashic application of scriptural hermeneutics to the rabbinic tradition.

Let us analyze three examples of the stammaitic use of לאתויי. One example comes from Jacob E. Ephrathi's work, *The Sevoraic Period and its Literature*.[295] In that work's second section, Ephrathi analyzes *sugyot* in which the phrase זה הכלל לאתויי מאי? appears. זה הכלל, "This is the general rule," usually sums up in a single generalization all the rules appearing in a *mishnah* or *baraita*. The question, "'This is the general rule'– includes what?" is, therefore, either a rhetorical ploy or a misunderstanding of the implications of a general rule clause in a *mishnah* or *baraita*. Whatever the case, the *stam* interprets the phrase זה הכלל, "This is the general rule," in midrashic fashion and "derives" some application beyond the plain meaning of the clause. In some cases the application does not even conform properly to the general rule stated in the זה הכלל clause. Ephrathi analyzes mMegillah 2:5–6 and the *gemara* on it. The *mishnah* states:

> משנה ה. כל היום כשר לקריאת המגילה ולקריאת ההלל ולתקיעת שופר ולנטילת לולב ולתפלת המוספין ולמוספין ולוידוי הפרים ולוידוי המעשר ולוידוי יום הכפורים לסמיכה לשחיטה לתנופה להגשה לקמיצה ולהקטרה למליקה ולקבלה ולהזייה ולהשקיית סוטה ולעריפת העגלה ולטהרת המצורע:
>
> משנה ו. כל הלילה כשר לקצירת העומר ולהקטר חלבים ואיברים זה הכלל דבר שמצותו ביום כשר כל היום דבר שמצותו בלילה כשר כל הלילה:
>
> *Mishnah 5*. The entire day is fit for reading the Scroll (of Esther on Purim), reading the *Hallel* (i.e., Ps 113–119 on the festivals), blowing the *sho-*

295 Jacob E. Ephrati, תקופת הסבוראים וספרותה (*The Sevoraic Period and its Literature in Babylonia and in Eretz Yisrael*) (Petah Tiqvah: Hotza'at Agudat Benei Asher, 1973).

far (i.e., the ram's horn blown on Rosh ha-Shanah), taking the *lulav* (i.e., the palm branch, myrtle, willow and citron waved on Sukkot), the additional prayer (recited on holy days), the additional offerings (offered on holy days), the confession made over the bullocks (see Lev 4:3 and 14), the declaration regarding tithes (see Deut 26:13), the Yom Kippur confession, laying on of hands (on the heads of sacrificial animals), slaughtering (offerings), waving (of parts of the sacrificial offering or the *ᶜomer* measure of barley on the day after Passover), bringing (the flour-offerings to the altar), taking a handful (of a flour-offering), burning (the flour-offering), pinching off the head (of bird-offerings), receiving sacrificial blood, sprinkling sacrificial blood, causing the suspected adulteress to drink (the bitter waters, see Numbers 5), decapitating the heifer (see Deut 21:1–9), and the purification of the leper.

Mishnah 6. The entire night is fit for cutting the *ᶜomer* of wheat (to be waved on the day after Passover) and burning the fats and limbs (left over from a day's sacrificial victims). This is the general rule: A matter whose obligation is during the day, the entire day is fit (for its performance). A matter whose obligation is at night, the entire night is fit (for its performance).

It is clear that the general rule clause of these *mishnayyot* merely sums up all the particulars that precede it. It adds nothing *per se*, though there are other obligations whose proper time is day – for example, circumcision.[296] Yet, these are not what the *stam* chooses to include using the formula, "לאתויי מאי? לאתויי x." Rather, as the *gemara* of this *mishnah* shows, the *stam* includes the arrangement of the incense jars on the showbread table and their removal:

תלמוד בבלי מסכת מגילה דף כא עמוד א

זה הכלל: דבר שמצותו ביום כשר כל היום, זה הכלל לאתויי מאי? - לאתויי סידור בזיכין וסלוק בזיכין, וכרבי יוסי. דתניא, רבי יוסי אומר: סילק את הישנה שחרית וסידר את החדשה ערבית - אין בכך כלום. ומה אני מקיים (לפני ה׳ תמיד) +מסורת הש״ס: [לפני תמיד (שמות כ״ה)]+ - שלא יהא שולחן בלא לחם.

"This is the general rule: A matter whose obligation is during the day, (its performance) is fit the entire day"– what does this include? It includes the arrangement of the incense jars and the removal of the incense jars (from the showbread table), in accordance with (the view of) R. Jose. As it is taught: R. Jose said: If one removed the old loaves (from the showbread table) during the morning, and arranged the new ones in the evening, there is no (problem). But how, then, do I fulfill "(and you shall

296 See tMegillah, ed. Lieberman, 2:10, where circumcision is included in the general rule.

> place showbread on the table to be) before Me always" (Exod 25:30)? (By not allowing) the table to be without bread (for an entire day).[297]

As Ephrathi notes, beyond the midrashic handling of the general clause, the result of the *midrash* that claims that the arrangement of incense jars and the removal of showbread is intended is quite distant from the plain meaning of the mishnaic text. Why are these activities more worthy of inclusion than others? In fact, insofar as R. Jose's rule governing the removal of the showbread is an individual and disputed opinion, it deserves less of a place than others. Moreover, as Ephrathi notes, the "prooftext" for this inclusion does not even discuss the removal and arrangement of the incense jars, but the removal and replacement of the showbread. While the incense jars and the showbread are connected issues, it would have made more sense simply to claim that זה הכלל included the placement and removal of the showbread loaves alone.[298] All these complications make it clear that the *stam* dealt with the general rule clause of mMegillah 2:5–6 in a fully midrashic fashion, ignoring the *mishnah*'s plain sense. The use of the Mishnah as a source for midrashic interpretation indicates that the *stam* believed that it was basically equivalent to the Scriptures.[299]

297 The Sages require that as one removes the old showbread one replaces it simultaneously with new loaves.

298 See חידושי הריטב"א – מגילה, ed. Stern (Jerusalem: Mossad ha-Rav Kook, 3d printing, 1983), p. קנא, s.v. זה הכלל. RITbA explains in detail the connection between the showbread and the incense jars. He also provides a reason why the arranging of the incense jars received preference over the arranging of the showbread in terms of being the matter included by the midrash of זה הכלל. A similar explanatory route is taken in פסקי הרי"ד, ed. מכון התלמוד הישראלי השלם (Jerusalem: Makhon ha-Talmud ha-Yisraeli ha-Shalem, 1992), p. רנט, s.v. מתני'. There R. Isaiah di Trani explains the preference for the inclusion of the arrangement of the incense jars on the basis of the fact that the contents of the incense jars are burned as a "remembrance of the bread, a fire offering before the Eternal" (Lev 24:7). The showbread is not given to God but to the priests. See also Rashi to Lev 24:7, s.v. ללחם לאזכרה. Therefore, the incense is more significant than the showbread.

299 Ephrati's discussion does not ultimately explain why the *stam*'s *midrash* of זה הכלל led him to add the arrangement of the incense jars to the Mishnah's list of actions permitted to be performed throughout an entire day. I myself cannot provide any convincing reason. Among the medieval commentators RITbA (ריטב"א) provides some insight into this matter. He explains that the amoraic *sugya* in bMenaḥot 99b seems to indicate that R. Jose won the debate that the Talmud says took place between him and the Sages. In that debate, the Sages held that when the old showbread loaves were removed on the Sabbath, the new ones had to be put in place simultaneously. R. Jose held that the new loaves could be replaced anytime on the Sabbath and this would still fulfill "and on the table you shall place the showbread, to be before Me always" (Exod 25:30). Other *memrot* in that *sugya* view actions performed at different times during the day as continuous. R. Ammi states that it is from R. Jose's view that we learn this principle. Hence, the Talmud seems to declare that the law is in accordance with R. Jose. Since the arrangement of the showbread and the incense jars are linked, the law accords with R. Jose in both instances. For RITbA's full discussion, see the source cited in the previous note.

bSukkah 56a. mSukkah 5:7 discusses the role of the priests during the pilgrimage festivals. In some respects all the 24 priestly contingents that served twice annually in the Temple were equal during these festivals. In other ways, the contingent whose week to serve fell during the festival had special obligations and privileges. The *mishnah* sets forth these rules as follows:

> בשלשה פרקים בשנה היו כל משמרות שוות באמורי הרגלים ובחלוק לחם הפנים בעצרת אומרים לו הילך מצה הילך חמץ משמר שזמנו קבוע הוא מקריב תמידין נדרים ונדבות ושאר קרבנות צבור ומקריב את הכל....
>
> During the three pilgrimage festivals during the year all the priestly contigents were equal (in terms of the distribution of) the priestly gifts from the festival offerings and in regard to the distribution of the showbread. On Shabu^cot they would say to him (a priest), "Here is *maẓẓah* for you; here is leavened bread for you."[300] The priestly contingent whose time was set (to serve, and the time fell out during a pilgrimage festival) offers the daily offerings, votive offerings, donated offerings, and other communal offerings, and it offers everything. . . .

The last two phrases are quite general and, therefore, inclusive. What are the "other communal offerings" to which the *mishnah* refers? What does the *mishnah* mean when it says that the priestly contingent whose assignment fell during the festival week "offers everything (הכל)"? The anonymous *stam* responds:

תלמוד בבלי מסכת סוכה דף נו עמוד א

> משמר שזמנו קבוע [וכו'] ושאר קרבנות צבור. לאתויי מאי? – לאתויי פר העלם דבר של צבור, ושעירי עבודה זרה. והוא מקריב את הכל לאתויי מאי? – לאתויי קייץ המזבח.
>
> "The priestly contingent whose time is set, etc. . . . and all the other communal offerings": What does this include? It includes the bull brought

---

If RITbA is correct, then the list of actions in mMegillah 1:9 is missing at least one item. Therefore, when the Mishnah summed up the general principle guiding the choice of particulars in its list, it did so in order to include any item it may have missed. In this case, that item was the allowance for the showbread's replacement to take place throughout all the daytime hours of the Sabbath in accordance with R. Jose's *halakhah*.

See also the discussions of the following *aḥaronim*: R. Judah Najar, מועדי ה' in ספר מצות גדול – הלכות מגילה (Lakewood: Mishnat Aharon, 1999), קכז; R. Zvi Pesach Frank, "מוקף בן יומו ופרוץ בן יומו, וגדריהן," כרם ציון (Jerusalem: Midrash Benei Zion, 1948), 10:כז and his reference to Aryeh Leib Ginzburg, שאגת אריה החדש והמלא, ed. Metzger (Jerusalem: Makhon Sha'ar ha-Mishpat, 2004), p. עד.

300 On Shabu^cot leavened bread was part of the offerings (Lev 23:17). Consistent with the prohibition on offering leavened products on the altar (Lev 2:11), the leavened loaves were distributed to the priests.

for a communal sin committed in error[301] or for (communal) idolatry.[302] "And it (i.e., the appointed priestly contingent) offers everything": What does this include? It includes the fueling of the altar with burnt offerings when it was otherwise unoccupied (קייץ המזבח).[303]

If we compare these stammaitic definitions of the general clauses in mSukkah to the Tosefta, it becomes apparent to what degree the *stam*'s definitions actually limit rather than extend what is implicit in "the other communal offerings" and "everything." The Tosefta actually includes "everything:"

תוספתא מסכת סוכה (ליברמן) פרק ד הלכה יט

התמידין והנדרים והנדבות והבכורות והמעשרות ומוספי שבת חטאות צבור ועולותיהן ועולת חובה של יחיד עבודתן ואכילתן במשמר הקבוע.

Daily offerings, vowed offerings, donated offerings, firstborns, and (animal) tithe offerings, the additional offerings of the Sabbath, communal sin offerings and their (i.e., the communal) burnt offerings, and the individual's obligatory burnt-offerings – their rites and consumption (where applicable, are carried out by) the priestly contingent appointed (for the week in which the festival falls).[304]

We may conclude from this analysis that the *stam* applied the *ribbui* hermeneutic to interpret the general and undefined clauses in mSukkah 5:7. Perhaps the plural form קרבנות, "offerings," in the clause "and other communal offerings" caused him to "uncover" a minimum of two communal sacrifices. Accordingly, the term "everything" (הכל), because it was in the singular form, included, according to the *stam*, only one thing: fueling the altar with burnt offerings to keep it from being unoccupied. The latter "inclusion" is extremely distant from the expected and plain meaning of the *mishnah*; the former is too limited to conform to the *mishnah*'s plain sense.

bḤullin 54a. The *sugya* in bḤullin 54a discusses a clause in mḤullin 3:1. The

301 See Lev 4:13–21. According to the rabbinic tradition, the community offers a bull when it sins unwittingly by following an erroneous judgment of the Sanhedrin.

302 The rabbinic interpretation of Num 16:22–26 claims that that pericope discusses the sin of idolatry and the sacrifice needed to atone for it. See *Sifre Num.* 111, ed. Horovitz, p. 116.

303 The burnt offerings for this purpose were supplied out of either the excess funds donated for supplying sheep for the daily sacrifice or from the proceeds of dedicated animals that could not be sacrificed for some reason but nevertheless had to be replaced.

304 The Tosafists also recognized that the *stam* failed to account for the full breadth of what was implied in mSukkah 5:7. See Tosafot, bSukkah 55b, s.v. ובחילוק לחם הפנים.

mishnah lists various fatal defects in animals that render their meat טרפה (*terefah*, "torn") and, therefore, unfit for consumption according to Torah law.[305] In summing up this list, the *mishnah* states: זה הכלל: כל שאין כמוה חיה טרפה "This is the general principle (underlying the *mishnah*'s list): any animal (afflicted with a condition from which) it will not survive is a *terefah*." This summary suggests that the mishnaic list is not exhaustive and other conditions may also constitute prohibited defects (טרפות).

The Mishnah's generalization provides the *stam* with an opportunity to question what else might be included under this general rule. Accordingly, they state: זה הכלל. לאתויי מאי? לאתויי שב שמעתתא, "'This is the general rule': What does this include? It includes the 'seven traditions.'" The "seven traditions" to which the Talmud refers are seven amoraic traditions about prohibited defects in addition to those recorded in the Mishnah.[306] Yet, in bḤullin 54a there are two cases in which R. Judah b. Betera ruled that it was prohibited to add to the list of defects created by the mishnaic Sages. The *stam* seems to be reacting to this idea in its interpretation of the זה הכלל clause. By claiming that the *mishnah*'s general clause implies the inclusion of the "seven traditions," the *stam* obviates the problem of amoraic additions to the Mishnah's list. That is, for the *stam*, the amoraic traditions are already implicit in the Mishnah. Hence, they are not truly additions.

It should be apparent that the *stam*'s interpretation of the general clause in mḤullin 3:1 is a *midrash*-like interpretation of the *mishnah*. It certainly is not the *mishnah*'s plain sense. If anything, the general clause might extend well beyond the "seven traditions," a notion implicit in the questions put to R. Judah b. Betera by two different trappers, R. Joseph and R. Pappa b. Abba. Indeed, Maimonides in one of his responsa adds another prohibited defect beyond the mishnaic list and amoraic traditions – namely, the loss of the animal's palate and nostrils, on the basis of the general rule, "any animal (afflicted with a condition from which) it will not survive is a *terefah*."[307] This addition shows that despite R. Judah b. Betera's resistance to adding to that which the Sages had enumerated, the general clause in mḤullin 3:1 opened the way to additions that were consonant with the mishnaic definition of a *terefah*. All this shows to what degree the stammaitic interpretation of the Mishnah is often no different from the tannaitic treatment of the Torah's text. Implicitly, this is due to a stammaitic view of the rabbinic tradition as a form of divinely revealed Torah.

305 See Exod 22:30: ואנשי קדש תהיון לי ובשר בשדה טרפה לא תאכלו לכלב תשלכון אתו; "Holy people shall you be to Me, therefore you shall not eat meat (found) torn in the field; you shall cast it to the dog(s)."

306 See bḤullin 42b.

307 Responsa of Maimonides, פאר הדור, ed. David Yosef (Jerusalem: 1984), pp. פה-פו and n. 23 there.

Conclusions

There is an interplay between conceptions of the rabbinic tradition and its status as a form of divine revelation and the forms that אם אינו ענין interpretation took. There is little evidence that the *tannaim* viewed their own efforts as divinely revealed Torah. Indeed, most evidence suggests that for the *tannaim* the Written Torah was the primary if not exclusive source of divine revelation.[308] It is therefore not surprising that almost all the cases of tannaitic אם אינו ענין *midrashim* are based on the Pentateuch and generate results derived exclusively from within the Pentateuch.[309] All examples of אם אינו ענין in tannaitic sources appear in the tannaitic halakhic *midrashim*, whose primary function was to interpret the Written Torah's text. Not one example appears in the Mishnah or Tosefta. Within the halakhic *midrashim*, the overwhelming majority of אם אינו ענין interpretations generate new *halakhot*. Only rarely do they support existent law.

In the amoraic period we find some continuation of what is basically the tannaitic use of אם אינו ענין, though with some changes in the idea of how redundancy between two scriptural verses occurs. The *amoraim* did create a somewhat new use for אם אינו ענין by using it to derive pentateuchal support for *halakhot* that are admitted to be of rabbinic origin. The practice of supporting rabbinic legislation using *midrash* was, however, not new. We find it in use by the *tannaim*, though they did not use אם אינו ענין or any other standardly formulated hermeneutic method like *gezerah shavah* or *binyan av* to accomplish this. Generally, the favored method for this sort of support among the *tannaim* was close reading of the pentateuchal text. The use of the Pentateuch to support rabbinic law, whether by the *tannaim* or the *amoraim*, had the effect of diminishing the appearance of rabbinic tampering with the Torah's system of *mizvot* by implicitly suggesting that rabbinic enactments had already been embedded in or licensed by the Torah itself.

Yet, PT has two examples of the use of אם אינו ענין that go even further than the support of rabbinic law using אם אינו ענין. In them, אם אינו ענין is applied to the exegesis of purely rabbinic texts, one a *mishnah* and the other a *baraita*. In both cases there are indications within the sources themselves

308 In tannaitic literature only a few *halakhot* are assigned to the category of הלכה למשה מסיני, "laws (given) to Moses at Sinai," See mPe'ah 2:6; m'Eduyyot 8:7; mYadaim 4:3; tSukkah, ed. Lieberman, 3:1; tYadaim, ed. Zuckermandel, 2:16; *Sifra*, Ẓaw, 11:6. R. Judah ha-Nasi described the tradition of thirty-nine main classes of Sabbath work prohibitions as "delivered to them (i.e., Israel) orally by Moses" (Mekhilta, Shabbata, par. 1, s.v. ויאמר אליהם אלה הדברים) This is the sum total of what extant tannaitic material assigns to the Sinaitic oral tradition. See also Christine Hayes, pp. 67–77.

309 See pp. 115–19 for the single exception and our discussion of it.

that the meanings that אם אינו ענין "discloses" are already close to the surface and most likely the proper readings of the material. Nevertheless, the application of אם אינו ענין removes any doubts that the interpreters, R. Simeon b. Laqish and R. Johanan, may have had about their understanding of the mishnaic and toseftan material they analyze. In these cases, אם אינו ענין functions more as a means for determining the correct reading of tannaitic sources than as a means of creating or supporting *halakhot*, which is the classical aim of *midrash* and the application of midrashic hermeneutics. In all other cases in PT and BT, *amoraim* apply אם אינו ענין only to rabbinic sources that contain a scriptural verse.

During the period of the anonymous Talmud (*stam*) there is a marked shift. The *stam* used אם אינו ענין almost exclusively to support existent rabbinic law, sometimes interpreting biblical material and frequently using rabbinic sources themselves as the source of the אם אינו ענין *midrash*. While the אם אינו ענין interpretations of the *tannaim* and *amoraim* are relatively concise, those of the *stam* are characterized by lengthy argumentation and intricate reasoning, a common characteristic of the *stam*'s contribution to the talmudic *sugya*.[310] The shift to exclusively "support *midrash*" as opposed to generative *midrash*, and to the use of rabbinic traditions and texts as the source for אם אינו ענין *midrash* appears to derive from a stammaitic sense of awe in regard to the tannaitic and amoraic traditions. The *stam* appears to deal with these traditions as divinely revealed *torah*. Again, we see that the ideological perspective held by the interpreter about the material he interpreted intersects with the direction and form his interpretation takes. In sum, rabbinic theology, ideology, and human judgment as to how a divinely revealed or inspired text should be read or intepreted go hand in hand with the interpretational activity manifest in midrashic praxis. This is true whether this praxis is found in *midrash halakhah* or in the *midrash* of *halakhah*.

310 David Weiss Halivni, מקורות ומסורות – שבת, pp. 7–9; idem., *Midrash, Mishnah, and Gemara*, p. 79.

4

"Two Scriptural Passages That Teach a Single Principle" and "Two Restrictions"

Among the hermeneutics the Talmud claims the Sages used for interpreting the Torah, there is one called שני כתובים הבאים כאחד אין מלמדין, "two scriptural passages that come (to teach) a single principle, do not teach (anything)." In a certain sense, this midrashic method functions differently from all the others we have examined in that it foils attempts to create or determine *halakhah* from Scripture. According to this hermeneutic principle, when "two scriptural passages come (to teach) a single principle" they prevent extrapolation or analogy from those passages. The logic of those who use this hermeneutic seems to be that if the Torah, which now includes even rabbinic Torah, presents a principle of law one time, it might then constitute a precedent for other cases. If, however, the Torah (again, broadly understood) must repeat a legal principle more than once, it indicates thereby that it is judging each case independently and not creating any sort of general rule for use in an analogy.[1]

This hermeneutic represents a major shift in thinking about the Torah's repetitions, which in earlier generations expanded the purview of the law. The developments we discussed in the last chapter – namely, the progressive acceptance of the idea that even rabbinic law was divine – provide a context for the development of a hermeneutic that would thwart changes in the existent halakhic tradition. It is therefore significant that this restrictive hermeneutic appears about 25 times, usually in the late amoraic and post-amoraic strata of the Babylonian Talmud, but it does not appear anywhere in Palestinian tannaitic or pre-fourth generation amoraic literature. This points to its wide acceptance only at a late date in the Talmud's development.[2] Its rather late provenance is important because despite the conservative tendency it supports, it shows that the creation of hermeneutics continued even into the late talmudic

1 A case can be made for an alternate view. Namely, if the Torah repeats a rule several times, it intends to communicate strongly that the law must be carried out in a specific fashion. This view may inform the position of those who, according to the Talmud, reject the notion that "two verses that come (to teach) a single principle, teach nothing." Nevertheless, the Talmud claims that everyone agreed that "three verses that come (to teach) a single principle, teach nothing."

2 See Shamma Friedman, "A Critical Study of Yebamot X with a Methodological Introduction," *Texts and Studies*, pp. 283–301.

era. Though in general this late period is one of less use of *midrash* among the talmudic Rabbis, once rabbinic *torah* was conceived of as a form of divinely revealed Torah, *midrash* that firmly maintained the received rabbinic tradition was welcomed by those who accepted this view. They, for the most part, were the majority in the latest moments of the Talmud's evolution. The hermeneutic we will now examine is one of their primary midrashic tools.

Gittin 76a. Though I have given a general description of the "two scriptural passages that teach a single principle" hermeneutic and the theory behind it, an example of its function within a talmudic discussion will greatly clarify how it operates. Let us then begin by analyzing the first example of it that appears in BT – namely, a passage in bGittin 76a. The issue the Talmud deals with there is conditional stipulations (Heb., sing., תנאי, plur., תנאים).

Biblical cases tend to indicate that all conditional stipulations had to be "doubled" (Heb., כפול) – that is, stated in both positive and negative form. Hence, the legal form of any stipulation should be, "If you do A, then B will occur; but if you fail to do A, then B will not occur." From the Talmud's perspective, the classical example of a legal condition is the one Moses stipulated with the tribes who sought pasture land in the Transjordan (Num 32:29–30):

> (כט) ויאמר משה אלהם אם יעברו בני גד ובני ראובן אתכם את הירדן כל חלוץ למלחמה לפני ה׳ ונכבשה הארץ לפניכם ונתתם להם את ארץ הגלעד לאחזה:
> (ל) ואם לא יעברו חלוצים אתכם ונאחזו בתככם בארץ כנען:

> And Moses said to them, "If the Gadites and Reubenites pass over the Jordan with you, all the warriors in the Eternal's presence, and the land is conquered by you, then you shall give them the land of the Gilead as a portion. But if they do not pass over as warriors with you, then they shall inherit among you in the land of Canaan.

This material impacts on an argument about the meaning of a view of R. Simeon b. Gamaliel that appears in a *baraita* in bGittin 76a:

> ת״ר: הרי זה גיטך על מנת שתשמשי את אבא שתי שנים, ועל מנת שתניקי את בני שתי שנים, אע״פ שלא נתקיים התנאי – הרי זה גט, לפי שלא אמר לה אם תשמשי אם לא תשמשי, אם תניקי ואם לא תניקי, דברי רבי מאיר; וחכ״א: נתקיים התנאי – ה״ז גט, ואם לאו – אינו גט; רשב״ג אומר: אין לך תנאי בכתובים שאינו כפול.

> Our Rabbis taught (in a *baraita*): This is your bill of divorce on condition that you serve my father for two years, or on condition that you nurse my son for two years: even though the condition is not fulfilled, this is a (valid) bill of divorce because he (i.e., the husband) did not say to her

(i.e., the wife), "If you serve . . . , but if you do not serve. . . ." (or) "If you nurse . . . , but if you do not nurse. . . ." These are the words of R. Meir. But the Sages say: If the condition is fulfilled, it is a (valid) bill of divorce; if not, it is not a (valid) bill of divorce. R. Simeon b. Gamaliel says: There is no conditional stipulation in Scripture that is not "doubled."

The anonymous *gemara* on this *baraita* discusses whether R. Simeon b. Gamaliel's comment refers to R. Meir's or the Sages' view. The *gemara* offers differing interpretations, which, given the ambiguity and almost *non sequitur* quality of R. Simeon b. Gamaliel's statement, is not surprising:

איכא דאמרי: לר׳ מאיר קאמר ליה, ואיכא דאמרי: לרבנן קאמר להו. איכא דאמרי לר׳ מאיר קאמר ליה, והכי קאמר ליה: אין לך תנאי בכתובים שאינו כפול, והוו להו שני כתובים הבאין כאחד, וכל שני כתובים הבאין כאחד אין מלמדין. איכא דאמרי לרבנן קאמר להו, והכי קאמר להו: אין לך תנאי בכתובים שאינו כפול, וגמרינן מינייהו.

There are those who say that (R. Simeon b. Gamaliel) said (his rule to contradict) R. Meir; and there are those who say he said (his rule to contradict) the Sages.

There are those who say that (R. Simeon b. Gamaliel) said (his rule to contradict) R. Meir, and thus he said to him: There is no conditional stipulation in Scripture that is not "doubled." Therefore, (each restatement of this rule constitutes) two passages that come (to teach) the same principle, and two passages that come (to teach) the same principle, do not teach (anything).[3]

There are those who say he said (his rule to contradict) the Sages, and thus he said to them: There are no conditional stipulations in Scripture that are not "doubled," and we extrapolate from them (to all conditional stipulations).[4]

The translated formulation, "thus he (R. Simeon b. Gamaliel) said to him," gives the impression that R. Simeon b. Gamaliel is speaking. The statement is, however, a mixture of a Hebrew citation of R. Simeon b. Gamaliel's opinion plus an Aramaic commentary on it. Thus it is not actually a statement made by R. Simeon b. Gamaliel himself, but rather an argument supplied by the anonymous tal-

3 Hence, no general rule can be established about the form conditional stipulations should take. That being the case, there is no specific form that a husband who is divorcing his wife must use to state any conditions that might affect the divorce's validity.

4 That is, we use the formulas for conditions found in the Bible as the basis for formulating all conditions. As Rashi notes in his commentary to this *sugya*, some examples of this type of formulation can be found in Gen 24:41, Num 5:19, and Isa 1:19.

mudic voice (*stam*) to explain R. Simeon b. Gamaliel's debate with either R. Meir or the Sages.[5]

From this passage one can see how "two scriptural passages that come (to teach) a single principle" operates. The first position of the Talmud is that R. Simeon b. Gamaliel opposes R. Meir. If so, then R. Simeon's statement that "all scriptural conditional formulas are doubled" means that in scriptural repetitions of doubled conditional formulas, each case of conditional stipulations is *sui generis* and case specific. Since there is no specific scriptural rule that requires a husband to "double" the conditions he sets for his wife's divorce, any formula he uses to state these conditions is effective. Therefore, his wife is required to fulfill his conditions in order to obtain her divorce. R. Meir disagrees and requires the husband to state the conditions for his wife's divorce in the scriptural "doubled" form. If he fails to do so, his stipulations are void. and his wife will receive her divorce even if she never fulfills her husband's demands.

Some Examples of the "Two Scriptural Passages" Hermeneutic: bQiddushin 34b–35a

One of the richest collections of "two scriptural passages" examples appears in bQiddushin 34b–35a. The central point of this rather extended, mostly anonymous *sugya* is to offer biblical support for the rule that women are exempt from time-oriented positive commandments.[6] As the discussion shows, there are almost as many exceptions to this rule as there are cases that conform to it. That being so, the *sugya* argues that the exceptions are not paradigmatic, but the cases that conform to the rule are. One can envision how useful a notion like "two scriptural passages that come (to teach) a single principle, do not teach (anything)" might be in this argument. I will cite only as much of the *sugya* as is necessary to provide a sense of how this hermeneutic operates.

5 See תוספתא כפשוטה – גיטין, ed. Lieberman (New York: Jewish Theological Seminary, 1973), p. 266, lines 39–40, and comments on lines 37 and 39.

6 A "time-oriented positive commandment" is one that calls for a commanded action to be carried out at a specific time. For example, *haqhel* is a time-oriented positive commandment because it requires all Israelites to congregate at the national sanctuary once in seven years, at the Festival of Sukkot, to hear the Torah read. See Deut 31:10–13. The example of *haqhel* is an exception to the rule of women's exemption from such *mizvot*. A *baraita* in bQiddushin 34a lists *tefillin* as a "time-oriented positive commandment." The *Mekhilta* supports this view on the basis of *derashot* of Exod 13:10 that limit the wearing of *tefillin* only to the daytime or to days that are not holy days. See *Mekhilta*, *Pisḥa*, 17, ed. Horovitz-Rabin, pp. 68–69. The presupposition that *tefillin* is a "time-oriented positive commandment" and the possibility of connecting its laws with the laws of *mezuzah* will be important for our analysis of material on bQiddushin 34b.

Mazzah and *Haqhel*

As the *sugya* opens, it tries to use the obligation of putting on *tefillin* as a paradigm for women's exemption from time-oriented positive commandments. The claim put forth is that women are exempt from *tefillin*, just as they are from Torah study. The two matters share a common rule, according to the Talmud, because they are proximate in both Deut 6:7–8 and 11:18–19. This form of interpretation is what I call a midrashic analogy as opposed to a truly logical one. This is what the *tannaim* called *semukhim*.

After some give-and-take about other possible *mizvot* as paradigms, the Talmud then argues from an incontrovertible case of a time-oriented positive commandment that the Torah itself states is incumbent on women: *haqhel*. This event, described in Deut 31:10–13, calls for gathering the entire Israelite nation – men, women and children – to hear the reading of the Torah once every seven years on Sukkot following the sabbatical year. The following is the Talmud's discussion of this point:

> ונילף מהקהל! משום דהוה מצה והקהל שני כתובים הבאים כאחד, וכל שני כתובים הבאין כאחד אין מלמדים.

> Learn (women's obligation to all time-oriented positive commandments) from *haqhel*! (We cannot allow that because) *mazzah* and *haqhel* are two scriptural passages that come (to teach) a single principle, and all cases of two scriptural passages that come (to teach) a single principle, do not teach (anything). (Hence, we cannot extrapolate from these cases to other time-oriented positive commandments).

Thus, the counter-argument to deriving women's obligation from *haqhel* is based on the "two scriptural passages" hermeneutic. Since the Talmud holds that *mazzah* must be eaten on the first night of Passover by women as well as men (bPesaḥim 43b),[7] *mazzah* constitutes another time-oriented positive commandment incumbent on women. Thus, the Torah contains "two scriptural passages"– that is, two cases, teaching a single principle – that, according to the "two scriptural passages" hermeneutic, bars extrapolation from either case to any other case. Thus, according to this section of the *sugya*, we cannot make the generalization that women must observe time-oriented positive commandments beyond the two that are explicitly designated, namely, *haqhel* and *mazzah*.

7 The Talmud argues that "all who are restricted from eating *ḥamez* (roughly translated as "leaven"), are required to eat *mazzah*." This is based on the juxtaposition within a single verse of the prohibition on *ḥamez* and the requirement to eat *mazzah*. Though this is a midrashic interpretation, this *sugya* regards the midrashic "proof" as having biblical status.

Tefillin and the Pilgrimage Obligation

The argument in bQiddushin continues with a challenge to the use of *tefillin* as a paradigm for women's exemptions from time-oriented positive commandments:

אי הכי, תפילין וראיה נמי שני כתובים הבאים כאחד, ואין מלמדים!

> If so, (then) *tefillin* and the pilgrimage obligation are also "two scriptural passages that come (to teach) a single principle, and (therefore) teach (nothing)."

This argument claims that *tefillin* is one scriptural case that joins with another, the obligation of all males to appear at the Sanctuary thrice annually, to create a case of "two scriptural passages that come (to teach) a single principle, teach (nothing)." This is the obverse of the *maẓẓah-haqhel* argument. Women's exemption from *tefillin*, like their obligation to consume *maẓẓah*, is not based on any straightforward biblical statement, but on rabbinic *midrash*. Here, as in the case of *maẓẓah*, the *midrash* is granted the status of biblical proof.[8] The exemption of women from the pilgrimages at Passover, Shabuᶜot, and Sukkot, or at least the restriction of the obligation to males, like their obligation to *haqhel*, is explicitly stated in the Pentateuch (Exod 23:17; ibid. 34:23; and Deut 16:16). The result is that *tefillin* and the pilgrimage obligation, both of which are viewed as time-oriented positive commandments, combine to form "two scriptural passages that come (to teach) a single principle, (and therefore) do not teach (anything)." At this juncture, the *sugya* is at a stalemate: there is no firm biblical support for women's obligation to or exemption from time-oriented positive commandments. Each case seems to be *sui generis*. To prove that women are exempted from this class of commandments, the *sugya* will look elsewhere.

Undermining the Restrictiveness of the "Two Scriptural Passages" Hermeneutic: צריכא, The Necessity of Each Passage

It is clear that the *sugya* we are analyzing cannot allow the last example of the "two verses" hermeneutic to stand. If it does, we are left without any biblical-midrashic support for the exemption of women from time-oriented positive commandments. The Mishnah states this exemption as a general rule, and even though the Talmud cites R. Johanan in order to deny its general application (bQiddushin 34a), the mishnaic view prevails in this *sugya*. What strategy does the Talmud employ to avoid *tefillin* and pilgrimage obligations from being

8 See the previous note.

viewed as "two scriptural passages that come (to teach) a single principle, (and therefore) do not teach (anything)" in order for the Mishnah to prevail? The following citation shows the "escape route" that the *sugya* took:

> אי הכי, תפילין וראיה נמי שני כתובים הבאים כאחד, ואין מלמדים! צריכי, דאי כתב רחמנא תפילין ולא כתב ראיה, הוה אמינא נילף ראיה ראיה מהקהל; ואי כתב רחמנא ראיה ולא כתב תפילין, הוה אמינא אקיש תפילין למזוזה, צריכא.
>
> If so, *tefillin* and pilgrimage obligations also constitute two verses that come (to teach) a single principle, and (therefore) do not teach (anything).[9] (Not so, because) both verses are needed (to teach something beyond the single principle of women's exemption from time-oriented positive commandments). For if the Merciful One had written (only the commandment of) *tefillin*, but not the commandment of the pilgrimage obligation, I might have said, "Let us learn the pilgrimage obligation from (the commandment of) *haqhel* (and require women to make the pilgrimage)."[10] And if the Merciful One had written (only) the (exemption from the) pilgrimage obligation, but not (the law of) *tefillin*, I might have said, "Analogize *tefillin* to *mezuzah* (and require women to put on *tefillin*)."[11] (Therefore, each passage is) necessary (to undermine these incorrect analogies).

According to the *sugya*'s conclusion, we "need" the passages concerning *tefillin* and the pilgrimage obligation in order to prevent incorrect analogies. This "need" provides these passages with a function other than teaching a single principle. They are, therefore, no longer "two scriptural passages that come (to

9 Hence, neither *tefillin* nor the pilgrimage obligation can serve as a paradigm for the exemption of women from time-bound, positive commandments. In fact, no other pentateuchal or *midrash*-based exemptions of women from this type of commandment can serve as sources for analogies or extrapolations since they will all form "two scriptural passages coming (to teach) a single principle" with either *tefillin* or the pilgrimage obligation.

10 Rashi notes that Deut 31:11, which introduces the commandment of *haqhel*, contains language that is also used to describe the pilgrimage. Compare Deut 31:11: לראות את פני ה׳ אלהיך במקום אשר יבחר to Deut 16:16: יראה... את פני ה׳ אלהיך במקום אשר יבחר. *Haqhel* occurs at Sukkot, one of the pilgrimage festivals. Hence, if we had only the pentateuchal law of *haqhel*, we might have extrapolated from it to all the pilgrimage festivals and included women in the obligation to observe them. The explicit exemption of women from the pilgrimage observance (Exod 23:17 and 34:23, Deut 16:16) must therefore be stated if women are to be freed from this commandment.

11 A midrashic analogy between *tefillin* and *mezuzah* could be created on the basis of the proximity of these two *miẓvot* in Deut 6:8–9. The Mishnah (Berakhot 3:3) uses *mezuzah* as an example of a commandment that both men and women must perform. The analogy the Talmud suggests here might lead one to the conclusion that the commandment of *tefillin* is obligatory for women. The Talmud prevents this outcome, however, by saying that the paradigm of the pilgrimage obliga-

teach) a single principle, and (therefore) do not teach (anything)." Rather, the two scriptural passages now can be used in analogies and extrapolations. Thus, either of these commandments may serve as the biblical or midrashic basis for the exemption of women from time-oriented positive commandments.

The attempt to provide a specific "need" for the scriptural passages or cases in situations where the application of the "two scriptural passages" hermeneutic might damage biblical-midrashic support for accepted *halakhah* is used throughout this extended *sugya*. It is a classical tactic for undermining the restrictions that the "two verses" hermeneutic imposes. Therefore, this strategy also appears in bPesaḥim 45a and Qiddushin 24b and 37b.

Rejection of the Limitations Imposed by the "Two Scriptural Passages" Hermeneutic

According to the Talmud, not all Sages accepted the limitations imposed by the "two verses" hermeneutic. According to Rashi, the *sugya* that is the primary source for its rejection appears in bSanhedrin 67b. There, R. Zechariah, possibly a fourth-generation Palestinian *amora* (c. 340 C.E.), claims that one must conclude that R. Judah (fourth-generation *tanna*, c. 150–185 C.E.) rejects the notion that "two scriptural passages that come (to teach) a single principle do not teach (anything)." Rather, he holds that one can extrapolate and create analogies from such sources. The typical formulation of the argument against the "two scriptural passages" hermeneutic is הניחא למאן דאמר אין מלמדין, אלא למאן דאמר מלמדין, מאי איכא למימר?, "This (argument) is acceptable according to those who say ('two scriptural passages that come to teach a single principle) do not teach (anything),' but according to those who say ('two verses that come to teach a single principle) teach (something),' what is there to say (i.e., argue)?" When the anonymous Talmud raises this argument, it is asking how halakhic matters supposedly settled by the "two scriptural passages" hermeneutic's prevention of extensions of the law can be maintained according to the view of those who do not accept that hermeneutic.[12]

bSanhedrin 67b. Since Rashi identified bSanhedrin 67b as the source of the argument against the "two scriptural passages" hermeneutic in all the other talmudic passages in which it appears, let us analyze that *sugya* first. Interestingly

tion, a time-bound, positive commandment, exists primarily (i.e., "is needed") to thwart this proposed midrashic analogy. This leaves *tefillin* open for a midrashic analogy only with Torah study (see Deut 6:7–8 and bQiddushin 34a). According to that analogy, women are exempt from *tefillin* just as they are from Torah study. For the exemption of women from Torah study, see bQiddushin 29b.

12 The argument against the "two scriptural passages" hermeneutic appears in Pesaḥim 26a || Yoma

enough, it does not contain any of the typical rhetorical formulas for rejecting the "two verses" hermeneutic:

> תנו רבנן: מכשפה – אחד האיש ואחד האשה. אם כן מה תלמוד לומר מכשפה – מפני שרוב נשים מצויות בכשפים. מיתתן במה? רבי יוסי הגלילי אומר: נאמר כאן +שמות כ״ב+ מכשפה לא תחיה, ונאמר להלן +דברים כ׳+ לא תחיה כל נשמה, מה להלן בסייף – אף כאן בסייף. רבי עקיבא אומר: נאמר כאן מכשפה לא תחיה ונאמר להלן +שמות י״ט+ אם בהמה אם איש לא יחיה, מה להלן בסקילה – אף כאן בסקילה. אמר לו רבי יוסי: אני דנתי לא תחיה מלא תחיה ואתה דנת לא תחיה מלא יחיה! – אמר לו רבי עקיבא: אני דנתי ישראל מישראל, שריבה בהן הכתוב מיתות הרבה, ואתה דנת ישראל מנכרים, שלא ריבה בהן הכתוב אלא מיתה אחת. בן עזאי אומר: נאמר +שמות כ״ב+ מכשפה לא תחיה, ונאמר +שמות כ״ב+ כל שכב עם בהמה מות יומת, סמכו ענין לו; מה שוכב עם בהמה בסקילה – אף מכשף בסקילה. אמר לו רבי יהודה: וכי מפני שסמכו ענין לו נוציא לזה בסקילה? אלא, אוב וידעוני בכלל מכשפים היו, ולמה יצאו – להקיש עליהן ולומר לך: מה אוב וידעוני בסקילה – אף מכשף בסקילה. לרבי יהודה נמי, ליהוו אוב וידעוני שני כתובים הבאים כאחד, וכל שני כתובין הבאין כאחד אין מלמדין! – אמר רבי זכריה:[13] עדא אמרה: קסבר רבי יהודה שני כתובין הבאין כאחד מלמדין.

> Our Rabbis taught (in a *baraita*): . . . Ben Azzai said: It says, "A witch you shall not preserve alive." It says (in the next verse), "Anyone who lies with a beast shall surely be put to death." (The Torah) juxtaposes this matter to the other (to teach:) Just as bestiality is punished by stoning, so those who practice witchcraft are punished by stoning.
>
> R. Judah said to him, "Because (the Torah) juxtaposed this matter (of bestiality) to it (witchcraft), we should bring this one (i.e., the practitioner of witchcraft) forth for stoning? Rather, אוב and ידעוני (two forms of witchcraft prohibited under penalty of death in Lev 20:27)[14] were originally subsumed under the general prohibition of witchcraft. Why were they then treated independently? In order to function as paradigms for an analogy: Just as אוב and ידעוני (are punished) by stoning,[15] so (any) practitioner of witchcraft (is punished) by stoning."

60a||Zebaḥim 46a||Ḥullin 117||Keritot 6a, bQiddushin 34b, 35b, and 58a; ᶜArakhin 14b, though sometimes in different formulations than הניחא למאן דאמר אין מלמדין, אלא למאן דאמר מלמדין, מאי איכא למימר?.

13 ליתא בילקוט שמעוני, משפטים, סי׳ שמ״ז. מ״אמר ר׳ זכריה״ עד סוף המימרא נתוסף בכ״י קרלסרוהא רויכלין שאר עדי הנוסח מקיימים את גירסת דפוס ווילנה. כי״מ גורס „הדא״ במקום „עדא״.

14 אוב is a form of necromancy where the voice of the dead seems to emanate from between the joints of the necromancer's fingers or from his wrists. ידעוני is a form of witchcraft in which the bone of a hyena is placed in the practitioner's mouth and appears to speak automatically. See mSanhedrin 7:7 and tSanhedrin 10:6.

15 Lev 20:27: ואיש או אשה כי יהיה בהם אוב או ידעני מות יומתו באבן ירגמו אתם דמיהם בם. "A man

> But also (according to) R. Judah (there should be some difficulty insofar as) אוב and ידעוני should be (considered) "two scriptural passages that come (to teach) a single principle and (therefore) do not teach (anything)." R. Zechariah said: "This implies that R. Judah holds that "two scriptural passages that come (to teach) a single principle teach (something)."

We might summarize this *sugya* thus: Four tannaitic Sages argue about which form of punishment a practitioner of witchcraft should suffer. Three of the four (R. Akiba, Ben 'Azzai, and R. Judah) hold that the punishment for witchcraft is death by stoning. R. Jose held that death by the sword (decapitation) was warranted.

R. Judah negated Ben Azzai's interpretation on the grounds that the mere proximity of two verses is too flimsy a basis for assigning the harshest form of death penalty – stoning – to the practitioner of witchcraft. He therefore based his *midrash* on one of the thirteen classical hermeneutics that tradition assigns to R. Ishmael:[16] "Any matter that was included in a general rubric, then was discussed and defined independently (by the Torah), teaches something not only about itself, but about the general rubric as well."[17]

In this case, the Torah discussed and defined independently the forms of witchcraft called אוב and ידעוני. Until the Torah discussed them as separate categories in Lev 20:27, they were generally understood as subsumed under the rubric of "witchcraft." However, once the Torah discussed them as separate entities and declared that those who practiced either of them should suffer the penalty of stoning, they became paradigmatic. Therefore, according to R. Judah, all those who practice any form of witchcraft receive the penalty of stoning.[18]

The Talmud argues that R. Judah's *midrash* should fail to provide paradigms for analogy to the entire rubric of witchcraft because אוב and ידעוני constitute "two scriptural passages (rubrics) that come (to teach) a single principle and (therefore) do not teach (anything)." According to the standard edition of the Talmud and most manuscripts and incunabula, R. Zechariah saves R. Judah's *midrash* by declaring that it simply proves that R. Judah rejected the notion that "two scriptural passages teaching a single principle do not teach

---

or woman who practices (the practices associated with) אוב or ידעני shall surely be put to death. They shall stone them with stones. Their blood shall be upon them."

16 See Azzan Yadin, *Scripture as Logos*, pp. 99–106 and Gary Porton, *The Traditions of Rabbi Ishmael* (Leiden: E. J. Brill, 1982), 4:201–5 and idem., "Rabbi Ishmael and his Thirteen Middot," *New Perspectives on Ancient Judaism*, eds. J. Neusner, P. Borgen, E. S. Frerichs, and R. Horsley (Lanham: University Press of America, 1987), 1:3–18.

17 כל דבר שהיה בכלל, ויצא מן הכלל ללמד, לא ללמד על עצמו יצא, אלא ללמד על הכלל כולו יצא.

18 See n. 15.

(anything)." According to the reading of this *sugya* in *Yalqut Shim'oni*, the anonymous Talmud saves R. Judah's *midrash*.

This passage suggests the likelihood that as early as the time of R. Zechariah, the "two scriptural passages" hermeneutic was in existence.[19] It also implies that the preponderance of talmudic Sages who knew of the hermeneutic held that most of the *tannaim* accepted it. This suggests that the hermeneutic had to have been in existence long enough for it to gain recognition as a legitimate interpretive method at least among some of the later *amoraim*, including not only R. Zechariah, but also Rava,[20] Abbaye,[21] R. Aḥa b. de-R. Avia, and R. Ashi.[22] Since no earlier *amoraim* make mention of either the positive or negative formulation of this hermeneutic, there is only sufficient data to date the beginnings of these "two scriptural passages" hermeneutics to the fourth amoraic generation. This, however, depends on whether R. Zechariah's statement is one of fact or conjectural deduction. Thus, the central question is, "Did R. Judah actually know of the 'two scriptural passages' hermeneutic and reject it or was his supposed knowledge of it a retrojection on R. Zechariah's part?" As we will see, it appears that neither R. Judah nor his fellow *tannaim* knew of this hermeneutic.

The "Two Scriptural Passages" Hermeneutic and the Tannaitic Midrashists

We stated at the outset of this study that the "two scriptural verses" hermeneutic appears explicitly only in BT. This is *prima facie* evidence of it being

19 This depends on whether the version of the *sugya* in *Yalqut Shim'oni* is correct. I have researched the other talmudic sources that use the phrase עדא אמרה, "that implies," which begins R. Zechariah's dictum. It is a specifically Palestinian idiom, which appears in the form הדא אמרה in PT almost 500 times. It appears in BT in the dicta of named Palestinian *amoraim*. See bBaba Meẓiᶜaᵓ 60a; bBaba Batraᶜ 158b; bSanhedrin 67b (our *sugya*); and bBekhorot 45b. Therefore, the likelihood is that the dictum beginning עדא אמרה in bSanhedrin is R. Zechariah's dictum and not the anonymous Talmud's words. The *Yalqut Shim'oni*'s version is less likely to be the complete one.

20 bQiddushin 43a. Rava (רבא) appears in all text witnesses to mQiddushin 43a. It should be noted that according to the Talmud, R. Zechariah and Rava only testify that "two scriptural passages teaching a single principle teach (something)." They do not make any explicit reference to the "two scriptural passages teaching a single principle do not teach (anything)" hermeneutic. The Talmud cites only Abbaye R. Ashi and R. Aḥa b. R. Avia as *amoraim* who made explicit use of the latter hermeneutic. See nn. 21 and 22. Nevertheless, R. Zechariah's and Rava's support for "two scriptural passages teaching a single principle teach (something)" implies that there is an alternative view that negates the application of this hermeneutic.

21 bZebaḥim 57a.

22 For R. Ashi and R. Aḥa b. R. Avia, see bPesaḥim 44b–45a||Nazir 37b. In bPesaḥim the overwhelming majority of text witnesses agree that R. Aḥa b. R. Avia questions R. Ashi, who responds using

a purely Babylonian hermeneutic, and, given those named Sages connected with it, a fairly late development.[23] Nevertheless, the Talmud assigns acceptance of this hermeneutic to figures like R. Akiba and rejection of it to R. Judah. Hence, the Talmud clearly claims that the *tannaim* knew of this hermeneutic and allowed it to inform their *midrashim* if they accepted it.

Mek. de-RSBY, Exod 21:27. Do any of the interpretations in the classical tannaitic halakhic *midrashim* support this? I believe the following sources suggest not. Let us begin with *Mek. de-RSBY*, Exod 21:27, which discusses the injuries that entitle a slave to freedom.

ואם שן עבדו או שן אמתו יפיל יכול כיון שהכהו על שנו יהא יוצא בן חורין ת״ל יפיל יכול עד שעה שיפילנה לארץ מנין אתה אומר הכהו על שנו ונדנדה ואינו יכול להשתמש בה יהא יוצא בן חורין ת״ל עין ושן מה עין ששחת אף שן ששחת. יכול אפלו הפיל שנו שלחלב ת״ל שן ועין מה עין שאינה חוזרת אף שן שאינה חוזרת. . . .

"If one (i.e., a slave owner) causes the tooth of his male or female slave to fall (out)" (Exod 21:27) – (Without this verse) I might have thought that if he struck him on his tooth, he (i.e, the slave) would go free. Therefore the Torah says, "(If) one causes (his slave's tooth) to fall out." (On that basis,) I might have thought (that the slave's freedom would not be granted) until he caused it (i.e., the tooth) to fall to the ground.[24] Whence would you say (that if) he struck him on his tooth and loosened it (to the point where) he cannot use it that he goes free? The Torah says, "eye" and "tooth"[25] – just as (the slave goes free for a) ruined eye, so (he goes free for) a ruined tooth. I might have thought (the slave went free) even if he (i.e.,

the hermeneutical principle "Two verses that teach the same principle do not teach (anything)." Columbia X 893T 141, however, has R. Aḥa b. R. Ḥiyya and Vatican 109 has R. Aḥa b. deRava. The same question and response pattern appears in bNazir 37b. Only in Vatican 110 do we find an anonymous response to R. Aḥa b. R. Avia's query.

23 Even though R. Zechariah's comments suggest that a Palestinian *amora* knew of the "two scriptural passages" hermeneutic, this does not mean that it originated in Palestine. Babylonia and Palestine did share traditions. The fact that the PT does not mention this hermeneutic suggests that its amoraic rabbinic Sages did not accept it. R. Zechariah does not necessarily say anything different than that. He suggests that at least one *tanna*, and perhaps all of them, did not accept the limitations imposed by the "two scriptural passages" hermeneutic. This would allow us to assume that the Palestinian *amoraim* as a group rejected it as well.

24 This possibility arises because the verb יפיל means "he shall cause to fall." A hyperliteral reading would yield the *midrash*'s conclusion.

25 Exod 21:26 speaks of a slave owner who destroys his slave's eye. The same rule applies to such a case: the slave goes free as compensation for his injury.

> the master) caused an immature tooth to fall out. Therefore the Torah says "tooth" and "eye"– just as an eye does not return (to its original state after injury), so the tooth (mentioned in our verse) must be one that does not return (after injury). . . .

Note that the *midrash* uses the cases of a destroyed eye and a destroyed tooth in analogical fashion as it works through what sorts of damage to a slave's tooth will grant him or her freedom. There is nothing in this *midrash* that calls a halt to this process and says, "But 'eye' and 'tooth' constitute two scriptural passages that come (to teach) a single principle and (therefore) do not teach (anything)." Though the anonymous Talmud views this as a problem regarding another analogy based on "tooth" and "eye" mentioned in bQiddushin 24a, its solution only makes reference to a distinction that may be drawn between immature teeth and an eye. It does nothing to solve the problems that should have been raised by the other rules found in *Mek. de-RSBY*, all of which are based on the analogy between a destroyed eye and a destroyed tooth. The totality of those rules in *Mek. de-RSBY* should be invalid if we apply the hermeneutic principle that "two scriptural passages that come (to teach) a single principle, do not teach (anything)" because it makes analogies and extrapolations impossible. But *Mek. de-RSBY*'s *midrash* neither refers to this hermeneutic principle nor seems to be at all aware of its existence to the extent that it might have to argue against it.

Sifra, Nedabah, par. 4:9–10. A *midrash* in *Sifra* seeks to provide the biblical source for the practice of tossing sacrificial blood twice on the diagonal corners of the altar in order to surround the altar with the blood. The requirement of surrounding the altar with blood appears in Lev 1:5 and other sources that use the term סביב meaning, "around, all around, surrounding."

> (ט) וזרקו יכול זריקה אחת תלמוד לומר סביב אי סביב יכול יקיפנו בחוט[26] תלמוד לומר וזרקו הא כיצד שתי מתנות שהן ארבע. (י) רבי ישמעאל אומר נאמר כאן סביב ונאמר להלן סביב מה סביב האמור להלן הפסק[27] ארבע מתנות אף סביב האמור כאן הפסק ארבע מתנות.

> ". . . and they (i.e., the sons of Aaron) shall toss (the sacrificial blood)"– I might think (this implies only) one toss; therefore the Torah says, "סביב, around (the altar)." If (the Torah says) סביב, I might think he (i.e., the priest) should surround it with one continuous line (of blood). But the

26 בבבלי זבחים נג ב׳ ובפירש״י לויקרא א, ה: כחוט.

27 בספרא אחרי: הפסיק; בבבלי שם: פיסוק וארבע מתנות.

> Torah says, "and they shall toss."[28] How (then are all the stipulations of Scripture to be accomplished)? (By) two applications (of blood) that are (equal to) four. R. Ishmael said: It says here (Lev 1:5) סביב ("around") and it says there (Lev 8:15) סביב ("around").[29] Just as סביב there means an interrupted four applications, so here, too, סביב means an interrupted four applications.

These two midrashic interpretations regarding the application of sacrificial blood to the Sanctuary's altar arrive at their conclusions in different ways. The first one points out the physical impossibility of surrounding the altar with a line of sacrificial blood with a single toss. It therefore concludes that the only possible way to toss the blood and also surround the altar with it is to toss it twice at diagonal corners of the altar.

R. Ishmael's interpretation is more intertextually midrashic. Rather than concentrating on the practical problems raised by the first midrash, he sets as his goal the defining of the word סביב ("all around") in the context of the application of sacrificial blood to the altar. For him, once that definition was a settled matter, then how the blood should be applied would become clear.

He noted that in several places in Leviticus the Hebrew root זרק, "to throw, toss, or splash," is used in its various verb forms in reference to sacrificial blood and its application to the altar. But exactly how was one to perform this rite?

In order to resolve this question he used a highly descriptive verse in which the Torah tells us that the application of the blood to all the corners of the altar, which thus surrounded it with blood (סביב), did not occur by splashing. Rather Lev 8:15, which describes the dedication of the Sanctuary and its appurtenances, tells us that when Moses had sacrificed the dedicatory *ḥattat*-offering he took its blood and applied it to each corner of the altar with his finger, thereby surrounding it. Inevitably if Moses used his finger to apply the blood to the altar's corners, he touched the altar four times. Hence R. Ishmael concludes that the way one arrives at סביב, the surrounding of the altar with sacrificial blood, is by making separate and distinct manual applications of the blood to the altar's four corners, not by dashing the blood on its diagonal sides. According to this definition, whenever the Torah uses the term סביב, even if a verse mentions some variation of the Hebrew root זרק, "to throw, toss, or splash," the

28 A single toss of blood from one side of the four-cornered altar cannot physically surround it with a continuous line of sacrificial blood.

29 In Lev 1:5 it simply says that the priest should toss the blood "around the altar," על המזבח סביב. Lev 8:15 provides a much more detailed description of the application of sacrificial blood to the altar. That description will become a crucial part of a *midrash* by R. Ishmael, which we will discuss thoroughly in the body of this chapter.

"throwing" is done by four separate manual applications of blood to the altar's four corners.

What is problematic is that bZebaḥim 57a claims that סביב written regarding the burnt-offering and the *ḥattat*-offering constitutes "two verses that come (to teach) a single principle, and (therefore) do not teach (anything)." Rashi explains this as follows:

> סביב בחטאת – במילואים ובעולה מסביב שמעינן ביה ד׳ מתנות שסובב בדמה רוחות המזבח.
>
> "סביב, all around" regarding the *ḥattat*":[30] (is written in the pericope of) the priests' investiture (מילואים).[31] Regarding the burnt offering (עולה), we learn from סביב four applications that surround the sides of the altar with its blood.

That is, סביב as it applies to the *ḥattat*-offering implies applications of blood on all four sides of the altar, and סביב as it applies to the burnt offering implies the same thing. Thus סביב in both cases generates a "two scriptural passages teaching a single principle" situation. According to Rashi, the result is that the verses cannot generate either a logical analogy (בנין אב) or an analogy based on a comparison of words.[32] If Rashi is correct, we must wonder how the word comparison *midrash* of R. Ishmael came into existence. It seems to be based on "two passages" or, perhaps, even more cases of the use of סביב, which according to the Talmud everyone agrees prevents extrapolations and analogies.[33] Yet, R. Ishmael proceeds with his *midrash* nevertheless.

30 Usually translated "sin offering," it probably means "clearing away offering" or "transition offering." It appears that individuals or the community bring *ḥattat*-offerings at moments of clearing away one status or season and entering another. Thus, a woman brings a *ḥattat* after childbirth; the community offers the *ḥattat* at each new moon and festival season. The connection to sin in these cases is tenuous at best. The Rabbis, who did understand the *ḥattat* as an offering for the expiation of sin, tried to explain why these seasons or events required a *ḥattat*. A penitent would bring a *ḥattat* to signal the transition from being a sinner to one who had repented.

31 Rashi holds that the *ḥattat* involved is the one mentioned in Lev 8:15.

32 אין מלמדין – ואע״ג דהכא לאו בבנין אב אנו באין ללמוד אשמעינן אביי דשני כתובין הבאין כאחד אין מלמדין אפי׳ בג״ש אותו דבר שנכתב בשניהן.

33 See the end of the *sugya* in bZebaḥim 57a, which concludes:

> ניחא למ״ד אין מלמדין, אלא למ״ד מלמדין מאי איכא למימר? הוי אשם שלשה, ושלשה ודאי אין מלמדין.
>
> This is correct according to those who accept (that "two passages") do not teach (anything). According to those who say that ("two passages") teach (something), what is your argument? The (repetition of סביב in the pericope that discusses) the guilt-offering (אשם)

It would appear that R. Ishmael knew nothing of the "two scriptural passages" or "three scriptural passages" hermeneutics. I would go further and suggest that none of the tannaitic midrashists knew of them either. Certainly, there is no internal evidence of these limiting hermeneutic principles in any of the tannaitic halakhic *midrashim*. They are not mentioned, used, or refuted.

"Two Limitations"

Discussed earlier, R. Zechariah's conclusion that R. Judah, a fourth-generation *tanna*, held that "two scriptural passages that come (to teach) a single principle, do teach (something)." Though it is likely that R. Judah never heard of the "two passages" hermeneutic, as we demonstrated above, the later *amoraim* and anonymous Talmud sometimes argue according to R. Zechariah's view. Therefore, at times the Talmud will take the stance that, given the circumstances of the *sugya*, two scriptural passages or rubrics can be used in analogies and for the purposes of extrapolation. Where this jeopardizes the halakhic *status quo* – for example, the view of a highly authoritative source like the Mishnah or a unanimous view – the *sugya* "discovers" the presence of limitations (Aram., מיעוטי, *mi*ᶜ*uti*) in each of the passages. According to the Talmud, these limitations prevent the passages and the legal rubrics they represent from being used as sources for analogies or extrapolations, especially halakhically destabilizing ones. Though this hermeneutic appears in six *sugyot*, five cases are parallels and only one other is a new instance of "two limitations (תרי מיעוטי)."

*Mi*ᶜ*utim*, words or phrases that imply a limitation or exclusion, are among the hermeneutical tools of the tannaitic midrashists. Sometimes they are words with essentially limiting or exclusive meanings. For example, רק, "only," is an essentially limiting term. It always implies "only this, but not that."

Contextual limitation is somewhat more complicated, though an example from the halakhic *midrashim* should shed some light on how this form of *mi*ᶜ*ut* operates. So, for example, Lev 1:2 serves as the source for a *Sifra* interpretation. It says, דבר אל בני ישראל ואמרת אלהם אדם כי יקריב מכם קרבן לה׳, מן הבהמה מן הבקר ומן הצאן תקריבו את קרבנכם, "Speak to the Israelites and say to them: a person from among you who offers a sacrifice to the Eternal from among the (domesticated) animals, from cattle or from sheep shall (each of) you bring your sacrifice." *Sifra* proceeds to atomize this verse, thereby generating considerable halakhic refinement of the biblical law. We will present one *Sifra* interpretation of the verse's opening clause:

---

constitutes "three passages," and according to everyone three passages certainly do not teach (anything).

ספרא ויקרא – דבורא דנדבה פרשה ב

(ג) אדם, לרבות את הגרים, מכם, להוציא את המשומדים ומה ראית לומר כן אמור אדם לרבות המשומדים, מכם להוציא את הגרים, אחר שריבה הכתוב מיעט תלמוד לומר בני ישראל מה בני ישראל מקבלי ברית, אף הגרים מקבלי ברית, יצאו המשומדים שאינן מקבלי ברית, אי מה ישראל בני מקבלי ברית אף המשומדים בני מקבלי ברית יצאו הגרים שאינם בני מקבלי ברית תלמוד לומר מכם, ועכשו הא אל תאמר אלא מה ישראל מקבלי ברית אף הגרים מקבלי ברית יצאו המשומדים שאינן (בני) [מקבלי] ברית שהרי הפרו ברית....

"... A person"– this includes converts (in the law of sacrifices).[34] "From among you"– this excludes apostates. But what forced you to say this? (Rather,) say: "a person"– to include apostates; "from among you"– to exclude converts. (Not so, because) after Scripture includes, it excludes by saying, "Israelites" (בני ישראל). Just as Israelites accept the covenant, so converts accept the covenant. This would exclude apostates who do not accept the covenant. However (one might argue that) just as בני ישראל (lit., the children of Israel) are the descendants of those who accept the covenant, so apostates are the descendants of those who accept the covenant. This would exclude converts who are not the descendants of those who accept the covenant. Therefore, the Torah says, "from among you (but not all of you)." Conclude therefore, that just as Israelites accept the covenant, so converts accept the covenant, and exclude apostates who do not accept the covenant, for they have broken the covenant....
(*Sifra*, *Nedabah*, par. 2:3)

This give-and-take finally settles on observant Israelites and converts as parties who may offer sacrifices. Apostate Israelites, for all their possible claims of biological "belonging" to the Israelite group, may not offer sacrifices until they recant their apostasy. Philosophically, it is clear what is going on: allegiance to the Torah makes one a member of the community; disloyalty to it puts one beyond it. Blood is not thicker than ideology. But how can the rabbinic community state that as a matter rooted in the Torah itself? *Sifra*'s response is the use of *ribbui* and *mi*ᶜ*ut*, a process of inclusion and exclusion based on biblical terms or phrases that, at least according to *Sifra*'s midrashist, suggest extensions and limitations of definitions. "A person" is totally extensive in this view; "from among you" limits "a person" to some people, but not all. Placed

34 In context, of course, אדם מכם means "a person from among you," i.e., any one part of the (Israelite) group. This might include all biological Israelites, even apostates, and "naturalized" Israelites, like converts. מכם is being read as if its מ"ם was partitive: "some of you, but not all of you (Israelites)." Thus, it functions as a *mi*ᶜ*ut* here. We will soon see that בני ישראל, "Israelites," will also be forced to function as a limiting or exclusive term.

in this context, "Israelite" becomes a *miᶜut*, a term that excludes anyone who does not share the characteristic essence of an Israelite. It remains only to determine what that essence is. Once *Sifra* determines that Israelites are those who accept the covenant, it is easy to exclude apostates from access to the sacrificial cult. "Israelites" is a contextual *miᶜut*.[35]

Our short analysis of *miᶜutim* shows that these limitations tend to work within a single biblical pericope, but they do not preclude or impede extrapolations from one pericope's rubric to another. This, however, is exactly what the talmudic "two limitations" hermeneutic does. Thus, "two limitations" is just another version of "two scriptural passages" in terms of function. Its fully Aramaic title, תרי מיעוטי, suggests it is a later development than the "two scriptural passages" hermeneutic, whose function is still described in Hebrew.

Some Examples of the "Two Limitations" Hermeneutic

At this point I will present a few examples of how the "two limitations" hermeneutic's use of *miᶜutim* differs from that of the tannaitic *midrashim*. A classical example of the "two limitations" hermeneutic appears in bPesaḥim 26a and five other *sugyot*.[36] The *sugya* is attached to different amoraic dicta in different tractates, but its essence remains the same in each case: it argues that whenever a sacred item's commanded use has been completed, it is no longer subject to *me'ilah*, ritual misappropriation. This principle needs protection because there are situations that contradict it. For example, even after the ashes of the altar have been collected, thereby completing the commanded use of these ashes, one can still ritually misappropriate them by using them as fertilizer.

The rhetorical response of the *sugya* is to take the exceptional case and join it with other cases in order to create "two scriptural passages that come (to teach) a single principle." This strategy fails several times until the *sugya* finally declares the collected altar ash (תרומת הדשן, Lev 6:3) and the beheaded heifer (עגלה ערופה, Deut 21:6) "two scriptural passages that come (to teach) a single principle."[37] This saves the rule that "*me'ilah* does not apply to items whose *mizvah* has been performed."

Though this protects the principle that in general "sacred items whose *mizvah* has been performed are not subject to ritual misappropriation," this

35 For a detailed definitions of *ribbui* and *miᶜut*, see Michael Chernick, לחקר המידות „כלל ופרט וכלל", pp. 79–80.

36 bYoma 60a; Zebaḥim 46a; Ḥullin 117a; Keritot 6a; and Me'ilah 11b.

37 The midrashic interpretations of verses connected with these two issues conclude that the altar ashes and the beheaded heifer must be disposed of in the places the Torah dictates, the first "next to the altar," the second "there, in an inarable wadi." The *sugya* assumes that the Torah requires disposal of these items in order to prevent ritual misappropriation of them, even though their respective *mizvot* have been performed. Since both verses' midrashic interpretations es-

is true only according to those who accept that "two scriptural passages that teach a single principle do not teach (anything)." What of those who hold that two passages do provide useful material for analogies and extrapolations? How would they protect the principle the *sugya* has worked so hard to preserve? The answer the *sugya* provides is that these Sages would declare that there are "two limitations attached to phrases in the verses discussing the altar ashes and the beheaded heifer." These limitations would cause each verse's rubric to be deemed *sui generis*. The argument runs as follows:

> הניחא למאן דאמר אין מלמדין, אלא למאן דאמר מלמדין, מאי איכא למימר? – תרי מיעוטי כתיבי, כתיב ושמו, וכתיב +דברים כא+ הערופה.

> . . . All this (prior argumentation) is acceptable according to those who say ("two verses which come [to teach] a single principle) do not teach (anything)." But what is there to say (i.e., argue) according to those who say "(they do) teach (something)?"[38] (We might argue thus:) there are two limitations written (in regard to our two contrary cases). (Regarding the altar ashes) it is written, "he shall place *it*" (Lev 6:3). (Regarding the beheaded heifer) it is written, "*the* beheaded (heifer)."[39]

---

tablish the same rule for each case, the *sugya* concludes that they are "two passages that come (to teach) one principle." Because of this status, these passages (cases) are not capable of creating analogies to other similar situations. Hence, ritual misappropriation does not apply to any other items whose *miẓvot* have been completed save the altar ashes and the beheaded heifer.

The *sugya*, however, is seriously flawed. It shifts the paradigm from sanctified items subject to ritual misappropriation (*me'ilah*) to a case of a non-sacred item subject to a prohibition on benefit (*ah'issur hana'*). The case I refer to is the beheaded heifer, which has no sanctity and, therefore, no possibility of being ritually misappropriated. In view of this shift, the *sugya* seems to propound the following argument: Since both the altar ash and the heifer must be disposed of in a designated place, and their use is prohibited even after their respective *miẓvot* have been performed, they represent "two passages that teach one principle." This prevents extrapolation from either of these cases to any other legal rubric. Since altar ash is a case of a sacred item, prevention of extrapolation from it to any other sacred item generates important legal consequences for our *sugya*. The most important of these is that, in general, sacred items whose *miẓvah* has been completed is not to be assumed to share the same rules as the ashes of the altar – i.e., it is not assumed to be subject to ritual misappropriation.

See Rashi ad loc. for the explanation of the *sugya* that informs our comments here. Meiri ad loc. notes that the beheaded heifer is not subject to *me'ilah*, and therefore is not congruent with the altar's ashes, but he does not suggest that this is a logical flaw in the *sugya*'s argument.

38 According to those who allow extrapolations from "two scriptural passages," how can we prevent the subversion of the principle of "sacred items whose *miẓvah* has been performed are not subject to ritual misappropriation"? After all, the "two passages" regarding the altar ashes and beheaded heifer are examples that contradict this principle.

39 The formulation of this argument in Keritot 6a presents a clearer statement of the "two limitations" argument:

Regarding the "limitations" (*mi^c^utim*), the *sugya* indicates that the suffix ו' ("it") in ושמו ("he shall place *it*," i.e., the collected altar ash, next to the altar) and the indicative ה' in הערופה ("*the* beheaded [heifer]") are the verses' *mi^c^utim*. "It" is understood to limit the rules governing the altar ash to "it, and it alone." "The" is understood as directed solely to its subject, the beheaded heifer, and to exclude all other subjects. Hence, the rules of the heifer apply to it and to nothing else.

It should be noted that the tannaitic halakhic *midrashim* did not treat these *mi^c^utim* as the *sugya* did. That is, they did not claim that the presence of these *mi^c^utim* eliminated the possibility of their respective scriptural rubrics from being used in analogies or extrapolations. Indeed, they did not necessarily consider these elements *mi^c^utim* at all. For example, *Sifra* interprets ושמו ("he shall place *it*," i.e., the collected altar ash) in this way: ושמו בנחת, ושמו כולו, ושמו שלא יפזר, "'he shall place it'– gently; 'he shall place it'– all of it; 'he shall place it'– (this implies) that he should not disperse it" (*Sifra*, *Ẓav*, 2:4). If anything, the suffix ו' ("it") serves as a *ribbui*, an inclusive and extensive particle, rather than a *mi^c^ut*, in this *Sifra* passage. That is, due to its lack of definition, the pronoun "it" suggests "all of it (i.e., the ash)" to *Sifra*'s midrashic interpreter.

Regarding the beheaded heifer, the tannaitic halakhic *midrashim* do not use the indicative ה' in the adjective הערופה ("beheaded") in any way. Rather, *Midrash Tannaim* on Deut 21:6 interprets it in this manner: "הערופה בנחל" – שתהא עריפתה בנחל, "'(the elders of the city shall wash their hands on the heifer) beheaded in the wadi'– (this teaches) that its beheading should take place in the wadi." Clearly, the indicative ה' plays no role whatsoever in this interpretation. It is certainly not a *mi^c^ut*, and there is no suggestion that anything would preclude using the case of the beheaded heifer in legal analogies or extrapolations.

bḤullin 113a–b. We find another *sugya* employing the "two limitations" hermeneutic in bḤullin 113a–b. The *sugya* seeks to provide a biblical basis for considering all mammals subject to three prohibitions: 1) cooking their meat and dairy products together; 2) eating the product of such cooking; and 3)

בתרומת הדשן כתיב ושמו – הדין אין, מידי אחרינא לא, גבי עגלה ערופה כתיב הערופה – ערופה אין, מידי אחרינא לא.

Regarding the altar ashes its is written, "he shall place *it*"– yes, (he shall place) this item (i.e, the ashes, at the altar's side for disposal), but no, (one shall not place) anything else (at the place where its *mizvah* of disposal is performed). Regarding the beheaded heifer it is written, "*the* beheaded (heifer)"– yes, the beheaded heifer (should be disposed of in the place where it is beheaded); but no, nothing else should (be disposed of where its *mizvah* is performed).

enjoying any beneficial use from the results of mammalian meat and dairy products that were cooked together. The Torah's wording does not immediately lead to this conclusion because it only says, "You shall not seethe a kid (גדי) in its mother's milk." The *sugya* tries to prove that the noun means the young of any mammal, not just that of a goat:

מנא הני מילי? א״ר אלעזר, אמר קרא: +בראשית ל״ח+ וישלח יהודה את גדי העזים כאן – גדי עזים, הא כל מקום שנאמר גדי סתם – אפילו פרה ורחל במשמע; ולילף מיניה! כתיב קרא אחרינא: +בראשית כ״ז+ ואת עורות גדיי העזים, כאן גדיי העזים, הא כל מקום שנאמר גדי סתם – אפילו פרה ורחל במשמע: ולילף מיניה! הוו להו שני כתובין הבאין כאחד, וכל שני כתובים הבאים כאחד אין מלמדין הניחא למ״ד אין מלמדין, אלא למ״ד מלמדין, מאי איכא למימר? תרי מיעוטי כתיבי עזים העזים....[40]

Whence do we learn these things (i.e., that all mammals are subject to the milk and meat prohibition)? R. Elazar said: The Torah says, "And Judah sent a kid of the goats" (Gen 38:20)[41] Here it says "a kid of the goats," (implying) that wherever it says just "kid,"[42] even a heifer or lamb is included. (But why not) extrapolate from this (the phrase "kid of the goats" to the kid mentioned in the meat and dairy prohibition, and claim that it refers to goat kids only)?[43] (But) there is another scriptural verse: "and (she dressed him) in the skins of the kids of the goats" (Gen 27:16).[44] Here it says "kids of the goats," (implying) that wherever it just says "kid," even a heifer or lamb is included. (But why not) extrapolate from this (use of "kid of the goats" to the kid mentioned in the meat and dairy prohibition, and claim that perhaps it, too, refers only to goat kids)? (No. Such extrapolation is impossible because these verses) constitute two scriptural passages that come (to teach) a single principle, and two scriptural passages that come (to teach) a single principle, do not teach (anything).[45]

40 כל כתבי היד והדפוסים שווים בעצם חוץ משינויים קטנים הנראים בלתי-משמעותים.

41 The reference is to the Judah-Tamar incident. Judah mistakes his veiled daughter-in-law for a prostitute. Having had intercourse with her, but no payment on hand, he returns to his flocks and sends her a kid described in the Torah as "a kid of the goats" (גדי העזים).

42 As in the case of the meat and dairy prohibition where it says only לא תבשל גדי בחלב אמו, "you shall not seethe a kid גדי (without any reference to being the young of a goat) in its mother's milk."

43 Rashi suggests that the extrapolation should take the form of a word comparison (גזירה שוה). This would mean that the term גדי should be compared to the word גדי in the phrase גדי העזים, "the kid of a goat," thereby deriving that the meat and dairy prohibition would apply only to goat kids.

44 The reference is to Jacob's theft of his father's blessing from Esau. Rebecca dressed Jacob in "the skins of the kids of the goats" in order to simulate Esau's hairiness.

45 That is, we cannot learn anything from these passages containing the term "kid of the goats" about

> This is true (that any "kid" is implied in the meat and dairy prohibition) according to those who say that "two passages do not teach (anything)," but what is there to say (i.e., argue) according to those who say "two scriptural passages that come (to teach) a single principle, do teach (something)"? (We may argue that there) are two limitations written (in each of the verses), (and they are) "*the* goats" (rather than) "goats."

As in the last example, this *sugya* views the indicative 'ה added to the noun "goats" as indicating only its subject and excluding all others. Hence, the "kid of the goats" referred to in the narratives about Tamar and Jacob are *sui generis*. Thus, they, and they alone, refer to goat kids. "Kid" in other contexts, however, may refer to other kinds of mammalian young.

Because the verses that the Talmud interprets are in narrative sections of Genesis, there is no tannaitic halakhic *midrash* available to which we can compare the interpretations in our *sugya*. Nevertheless, we have shown in Chapter Two that the *tannaim* do not derive any *halakhah* from narrative and poetic scriptural passages. Our *sugya* basically relies on the dictum of R. Elazar (third-generation Palestinian *amora*, Babylonian emigre) for its midrashic foundations. It is, however, the anonymous Talmud (*stam*) that is responsible for the creation of the "two scriptural passages" and "two limitations" *midrashim* in this *sugya*. This and the problematic logic[46] and general artificiality of the *sugya* point to a late provenance for both of these forms of interpretations.

Summation

The "two verses" and "two limitations" hermeneutics serve the conservatism of the later *amoraim* and post-amoraic anonymous Sages regarding the halakhic system they inherited: they limit analogies and extrapolations that

the kid meant in the meat and dairy prohibitions. Thus, any "kid" of any mammalian animal is subject to the prohibition connected to the cooking of meat and dairy together.

46 According to the Talmud's formulation of the argument, even the principle "that wherever it says just 'kid,' even a heifer or lamb are included" is repeated twice, once in the *midrash* of גדי העזים in the Tamar narrative and once again in the *midrash* of גדיי העזים in the Jacob story. This would make it a case of "two passages," which should prevent using this principle beyond the cases in Gen 27 and 38. Of course, this would totally undermine the idea that mammals other than goat kids are subject to the milk and meat prohibitions. The only thing that prevents us from reading the Talmud's argument this way is R. Gershom's and Rashi's post-talmudic commentaries. See the previous note. The somewhat improved formulation of bḤullin 113a–b in *Yalqut Shim'oni*, Gen. #115 and Exod. #359 appears to be an attempt to have us focus only on the phrases גדי העזים and גדיי העזים as the clauses that generate the "two verses" hermeneutic. This reading is informed by the same logic found in R. Gershom's and Rashi's comments. The Talmud as is, however, uses very forced reasoning.

might change the halakhic *status quo*. Ironically, in the case of the "two limitations" hermenteutic, those who would have declared themselves "dust under the feet" of their tannaitic predecessors extend the restrictiveness of tannaitic *mi^cutim* well beyond anything the *tannaim* would have recognized. This conservatism points to a desire to strengthen and determine norms based on the inherited tannaitic and early amoraic traditions. Thus, for the late *amoraim* and those who followed them, the tannaitic and early amoraic *torah* became Torah in almost the fullest sense of the word. They felt constrained "not to add thereto or subtract therefrom"[47] in order to begin the work of consolidating the normative law. This explains why the largest number (17) of "two passages" and "two limitations" interpretations preserve a single halakhic norm that appears in a *mishnah*, *baraita*, or early amoraic (pre-fourth generation) *memra*.

Despite the conservatism inherent in these hermeneutics' results, we must recognize the ironic reality that there was a hermeneutical renaissance in the late amoraic and post-amoraic periods. One would have imagined that the Sages of these eras would have resisted any development of new halakhic midrashic techniques and deferred to their predecessors in the matter of hermeneutics as they did in matters of the legal tradition. As we have shown, they did not refrain from creating new midrashic hermeneutics even though their purpose was to prevent new *midrash* from wreaking havoc with the received and accepted tradition. I believe they did this because they were convinced that for the most part their predecessors did not legislate without pentateuchal or other biblical support for their legislation. This was even more the case when the law was normative.

The second greatest number of "two verses" interpretations (5) explain the view of one party to a tannaitic dispute. This supports the worth, though not necessarily the normative status, of the opinion. Again, I would suggest that the reason that these "two passages" interpretations support only tannaitic disputes is because the late *amoraim* and post-amoraic teachers assumed that most disputes among the *tannaim* were based either on different interpretations of Scripture or on different logical arguments (*sevara*). The use of the "two verses" hermeneutic implies that the tannaitic debate is scripturally based.

In two cases, "two scriptural passages" interpretations function as "straw

47 See Christine Hayes, "Halakahah le-Moshe mi-Sinai in Rabbinic Sources," *The Synoptic Problem in Rabbinic Literature*, especially pp. 82 (second paragraph) and 116–17. Hayes recognizes that the later strata of the Babylonian Talmud use the concept of "law given to Moses at Sinai" to maintain or determine norms by equating this type of law's authority with scriptural authority. The concept, she notes, is not used to bolster the authority of exceptional, disputed, or unstable traditions. . . ." Again, we see a late talmudic trend toward strengthening the authority of legal traditions that are received as matters of general consensus or at least as well-preserved formulated dicta.

men." They are used as arguments against elements of tannaitic midrashic interpretations in order to prove the ultimate inevitability of those interpretations. In both cases there is no attempt to undermine the "two passages" interpretation by raising the possibility that the tannaitic *midrash* is the product of "those who say that 'two passages' teach something." Rather, the "two passages" hermeneutic, which in both cases appears in a presumably late anonymous discussion, is viewed as absolutely authoritative and normative. This implies that this hermeneutic became more accepted over time. Indeed, in bSanhedrin 76b, the "two scriptural passages" hermeneutic functions as the main rationale for the necessity of a tannaitic *midrash*, and no voice raises the counter argument, "That is all well according to those who say, 'two passages do not teach (anything)'; but according to those who say, 'two passage do teach (something), what would you argue?'" We should not dismiss this as merely the result of editorial satisfaction ("The argument has been clinched. Why go further?") because other *sugyot* do go the "extra mile." Rather, here we have indications that the "two passages" hermeneutic has become the means by which the anonymous Talmud tests the strength of various *halakhot* and halakhic *midrashim*. This, in turn, indicates the increased interest in proclaiming certain ideas so absolutely correct that they must be normative and authoritative.

The data points to a tendency on the part of the late talmudic teachers to turn away from the open-ended and indeterminate style of their predecessors and toward decided, normative law. This activity of late talmudic Sages represents the second wave of determining halakhic norms. The early Palestinian and Babylonian *amoraim* were among the first to declare which position in the tannaitic disputes was normative. Those most prominent in this activity were the Palestinian teachers R. Joshua b. Levi (first-second generation, approximately 30 decisions) and R. Johanan (second generation, approximately 65 decisions). Among the Babylonian *amoraim*, Rav (second generation, approximately 80 decisions), Samuel (first-second generation, approximately 100 decisions), and their student R. Ḥuna (second generation; approximately 15 decisions) are the most frequently mentioned decisors. The third generation of *amoraim* has not one major figure that produces more than ten decisions except R. Naḥman, who has approximately 15 decisions attributed to him. Between all the major figures of this generation (R. Elazar, R. Naḥman, and 'Ulla) there is a total of approximately 34 decisions. Of all the major *amoraim* of the fourth generation, only Rava (Babylonia) receives credit for approximately 10 halakhic decisions. The number of such decisions on the part of all the other Palestinian and Babylonian *amoraim* of that generation is negligible. That is, the largest number of decisions tends to be about 5 for any single *amora*.

Most often, the number of such decisions is between one and three. In the fifth through seventh amoraic generations, including to the extent possible both Palestinian and Babylonian *amoraim*, we find no significant number of halakhic decisions (not even 2–5) for any of the major *amoraim* of this period including R. Jose b. Abin (fifth generation, Palestine), R. Ashi, the two Ravinas, and Mar b. R. Ashi. For example, R. Ashi has no halakhic decisions credited to him. The same is true for Ravina, though it is impossible to tell to which Ravina the Talmud refers. Mar b. R. Ashi has one halakhic decision attributed to him.[48] Yet, halakhic decisions indicated by the Aramaic (ו)הלכתא ("[and] the law is") appear about 250 times in the anonymous, late, mostly post-amoraic stratum of the Talmud. Indeed, some of these have been identified as being geonic additions to the basic talmudic text, making them even later.[49] Hence, we may reasonably posit a decline in halakhic decision-making that starts in the third amoraic generation. Despite Rava's somewhat higher percentage of decisions relative to the majority of third-generation amoraic figures, were it not for his significance as an amoraic Sage, I would not have counted his contribution of approximately 10 decisions. Following this last extremely minor "burst" of decision-making by Rava, there is a period in which there is only the scantest record of any halakhic decision-making whatsoever. It is only in the post-amoraic stratum of the Talmud that halakhic decision-making reaches its apogee. In that stratum, there are almost as many records of halakahic decisions as there are for the entire first and second amoraic generations. Hermeneutic developments like "two scriptural passages do not teach (anything)" and "two limitations," which inhibit continued halakhic development, stabilize the traditional sources of *halakhah* and serve the agenda of formulating normative rabbinic law very well.

Conclusions

In this chapter we have analyzed what we have called "the two scriptural passages" and "two limitations" hermeneutics, both of which limit the expan-

48 I have only counted those *amoraim* responsible for 15 or more decisions. Nevertheless, a drop from 80–180 halakhic decisions by significant first- and second-generation amoraic figures to between 1–10 such decisions by significant third- through seventh-generation *amoraim*, and often 0–2 among the fifth- through seventh-generation amoraic Sages, is a striking phenomenon. This shows that as we move later into the amoraic period, argumentation and interpretation increase and the attempt to state or establish norms decreases. The middle and late *amoraim* are thus in a trajectory that leads from halakhic decision and creativity to interpretation of and argument built around earlier rabbinic traditions. For a more detailed study of these phenomena, see Kraemer, *The Mind of the Talmud*, pp. 30–41. For the phenomenology of the contributions of the crucial fourth through final generations of the *amoraim*, see Kalmin, *The Redaction of the Babylonian Talmud*, pp. 52–55.

49 B. M. Lewin, רבנן סבוראי ותלמודם, pp. 47–53; E. Z. Melamed, פרקי מבוא לספרות התלמוד, p. 478.

sion of *halakhah* beyond its traditional boundaries. We have also analyzed the hermeneutic that declares two scriptural passages independently necessary (צריכי) and thereby frees them from the limitations imposed by "the two scriptural passages" hermeneutic. One would imagine that by doing so, the צריכי hermeneutic would allow for renewed halakhic development. This, however, is not the case. Rather, צריכי, like the other hermeneutics, only supports existent tannaitic and early amoraic halakhic traditions or late undisputed ones.

These hermeneutics have much in common with the late לא קשיא and אם אינו ענין. They too largely maintained and supported tannaitic and pre-fourth-generation amoraic traditions. Also, their approach to the earlier material was that it was to be handled in the same way as Scripture. Thus, the late לא קשיא mimicked the behavior of "the two contradictory hermeneutic." The late אם אינו ענין did the same using early rabbinic sources, especially midrashic ones, to create the necessary superfluity or logical problem that traditionally generated an אם אינו ענין interpretation. The use of older *midrashim* and *halakhot* as if they were pentateuchal material indicates exactly what the status of that material was in the minds of the creators of the late אם אינו ענין.

What is notable about the midrashic work of the hermeneutics analyzed in this chapter is that they all seek to assign scriptural status to what are rabbinic *halakhot*. It is hard to point to the *sugya* of the "doubled" condition (bGittin 76a) because in that *sugya* the "two scriptural passages" hermeneutic is first portrayed as a rule that R. Simeon b. Gamaliel accepts and then as one he rejects. However, according to the view that R. Simeon b. Gamaliel accepts the "two scriptural passages" hermeneutic, the view of the Sages who say that a husband may stipulate conditions for giving his wife a divorce in any form he wishes would have scriptural warrant. Similarly, the rule that women are exempted from the performance of positive, time-oriented biblical commandments appears in the Mishnah without a claim that it is a scriptural principle. It is also possible that the principle is the view of a single individual at the outset,[50] and there is little unanimity about which *mizvot* are included among the positive, time-oriented ones.[51] One is hard pressed to consider this exemption for women to be a Torah law. Yet, by the time the *sugya* in Qiddushin 34a–35a completes its work, that is its status. This is also true for the principle, apparently first enunciated by R. Papa (bPesaḥim 26a), that sanctified things, whether animal sacrifices or sacred objects, are no longer subject to misappropriation once all the commandments related to them have been fulfilled. There is nothing in the Torah that directly states this to be the case. However, by using the "two scriptural passages" or "two limitations" hermeneutic, this

50 *Sifre Num.*, 115, ed. Horovitz, p. 124, where the rule that women are exempt from positive time-oriented *mizvot* is attributed to R. Simeon and to him alone.

51 *Sifre Num.*, 115, ed. Horovitz, p. 124 (*ẓiẓit* are excluded from the category) and b^c^Eruvin 96b (*tefil-*

undisputed mishnaic principle receives scriptural status.

What emerges is a pattern that suggests that the later generations of the *amoraim* and the *stam* – when it behaves in the same manner as the late *amoraim* – viewed various rabbinic principles as essentially scriptural ones. These rabbinic principles are mostly, but not always, undisputed.[52] Thus, it appears that the latest generations of *amoraim* and those who followed their hermeneutic practices held that rabbinic traditions were essentially Torah law.

---

lin) are excluded from the category by some. *Tefillin*, however, is the paradigmatic case of a positive, time-oriented commandment in Qiddushin 35a–b!).

52 In bQiddushin 24b, the *stam* adamantly argues that a law derived by the use of *midrash*, including צריכא and others, is Torah law though it is *midrash ḥakhamim*. For a late but probably accurate reading of the essence of the *stam*'s position, see *Tosafot ha-RID* ad loc., s.v. הואיל ומדרש חכמים; חידושי הרשב״א ad loc., s.v. אלא הואיל ומדרש חכמים הוא. Note, all the parties to the discussion of whether a non-Jewish slave goes free if his owner damages one of the tips of 24 "limbs" agree that it is a universally held view. There is only debate about whether the master must give him a document of manumission.

Conclusions

The main thrust of this work has been to document the Rabbis' continuous extension of the canon of sources they used for the development of *halakhah*. Each chapter of this study has taken us further on this journey of canonization. In the first chapter we concluded that the *tannaim* used only the Pentateuch as solid proof for their *halakhot* while the *amoraim* accepted even the *midrash* of pentateuchal narratives and non-pentateuchal sources as proofs. The latter view extended the canon from the Pentateuch alone to the entire *TaNaKh*. As we noted, this change was due to the different theologies of revelation between the *tannaim* and *amoraim*. The former seem to have held that the Mosaic revelation was complete and that no other revelation could produce anything new. The latter held that anything a prophet would prophesy in the future was already incorporated in the Sinaitic revelation. Hence, the *tannaim* considered the Pentateuch their sole source of authority for *halakhah*, while the *amoraim* considered the entire *TaNaKh* as a source for their legislation. The canon of divinely revealed sources available for the making of law had grown.

In the second chapter we saw how the *tannaim* dealt with contradictions in the Pentateuch. It was clear that they had no tolerance for them. This resistance to the reality of scriptural contradictions seems unquestionably rooted in the notion of "Torah from Heaven." How could a contradiction exist in a document created by God? Hence, contradictions had to be apparent but not real, and each instance of apparent contradiction demanded that the midrashist find a resolution that either resided in Scripture itself or in the Rabbis' ability to interpret the Pentateuch.

On the basis of the above, we can understand that the Pentateuch, the prime scriptural source of law, should be contradiction free. This should not necessarily be the case regarding rabbinic sources of law like *mishnayyot* and *baraitot* or conflicting amoraic *memrot*. After all, we might argue, these are the works of human beings. And, indeed, that seems to be the view of the early *amoraim*. Confronted with what appear to be contradictions between various sorts of tannaitic teachings, the early first- through third-generation *amoraim* assign the conflicting views to rabbinic disputants. In short, there is no early amoraic indication that obviously human works should not be in conflict, especially in a society so open to debate as that of the early Rabbis.

However, this approach changes over time. Once we enter the age of the later amoraic generations and that of the anonymous commentators, conflicts and contradictions between rabbinic sources are responded to with לא קשיא, "there is no contradiction." This response is not like the לא קשיא response of the early *amoraim* described above. Rather, it is an attempt to obliterate contradiction in the same way that the *tannaim* attempted to obliterate every semblance of contradiction in the Torah. This is a massive late application of a form of "two contradictory verses" hermeneutic to the rabbinic canon, which now seems to have become a divinely revealed legacy unto itself. Rather than claiming that a human debate is responsible for conflicting or contradictory halakhic rules, the late לא קשיא applies one part of the contradiction to one situation or case and the other to another. This form of לא קשיא mimics the tannaitic "two contradictory verses" resolution, using reason when a scriptural verse resolving the contradiction does not exist. Such a solution, whether between verses in Scripture or between halakhic views, not only resolves the contradiction, but also preserves the verses and opinions that are in tension as part of the canon. This act of conservation is another indication of the sanctity with which the canon was regarded and of its divine status. After all, how could a pious (late rabbinic) Jew imagine ejecting a verse from Scripture or a law from what he believed was the divinely revealed collection of (early) rabbinic teachings?

The longest of our chapters involved the study of a hermeneutic that transfers the rules of scriptural topic A to scriptural topic B. The midrashist takes this action in response to a redundancy that arises out of two scriptural pericopae repeating the same law or in response to a logical problem that arises within a single pericope. In Hebrew the hermeneutic is called אם אינו ענין ל... תנהו ענין ל... – that is, "if the verse is not useful or meaningful in relation to A, apply it to B." Here, too, issues of what might be called the rabbinic theology of Scripture play a role in the development of this midrashic hermeneutic. For the Rabbis who used this midrashic method, redundancy and illogic, like contradiction, were not consonant with their understanding of divine revelation by a God whom they viewed as perfect, at least in His role as legislator.

The length of the chapter can be explained by the fact that the *tannaim*, *amoraim*, and the *stam* all used this hermeneutic without changing its name. This does not mean, however, that it did not change in form. The *tannaim*, as to be expected, used it only on pentateuchal sources, with the exception of one case in which a midrash of a pentateuchal verse and a verse from Ezekiel provide the scriptural basis for the אם אינו ענין *midrash*.

As we turn to the amoraic אם אינו ענין, we find quite a few formal changes, but they are not significant in terms of our present discussion. In several instances in PT, אם אינו ענין *midrashim* appear to be attempts to reconstruct vaguely remembered tannaitic *midrashim* based on various forms of superfluity or inclusive language called *ribuyyim*. What is striking in at least one of these reconstructions is the ease with which the midrashist makes use of a verse in Joshua. This would tally with the amoraic view of the entire *TaNaKh* as a source for the generation of *halakhah*.

We also find that PT uses אם אינו ענין support *midrash* for what it identifies as purely rabbinic *halakhah*. This, however, is not particularly surprising since the *tannaim* also support rabbinic enactments using the pentateuchal text. Tannaitic support *midrash* for rabbinic *halakhot*, however, tends to be based on close and direct readings of the pentateuchal text rather than on formal hermeneutics like אם אינו ענין. Nevertheless, there is a difference between these two methods of support for rabbinic enactments besides one of form. The tannaitic method of support responds to the discomfort that the Rabbis appear to have had with enacting beyond and occasionally against what the Torah appears to require. Therefore, they try to find a license for their enactments within the Torah's text itself.

The *amoraim*, on the other hand, were already heirs to a considerable amount of purely rabbinic legislation, much of it tannaitic. Their question is, at most, an academic and retrospective one: What principles or interpretive methods did our tannaitic predecessors use to undergird their enactments? The response can be anything from a legal theory to a midrashic support. In one case in pShebi[c]it 1:1 (3a), we have a retrospective claim that an אם אינו ענין interpretation provides the basis for the purely rabbinic rule that planting must stop even before the sabbatical year arrives, a point already made in the mShebi[c]it 1:1. Hence, this use of אם אינו ענין is not significantly different from the *amoraim*'s characteristic use of *midrash* to show how Scripture generated the teachings of the *tannaim*. All this behavior indicates is that the *amoraim* believed that *tannaim* would not legislate anything without it having a basis in the Torah. This is not particularly distant from what the *tannaim* seemed to believe about themselves. This, however, is not a claim that the *torah* of the *tannaim* is Torah in the sense of divine revelation.

Yet the presence in PT of two applications of אם אינו ענין to tannaitic sources seems to move us closer to the view that the teachings of the *tannaim* are indeed divinely revealed. As I concluded in a rather detailed discussion of this important development, it is not at all clear that those who used אם אינו ענין on a *baraita* and a *mishnah* respectively – namely R. Johanan and Resh Laqish – did so because they thought they were dealing with a form of "Scripture." These Rabbis' way of handling tannaitica – declaring some of it mistaken and frequently referring to varying formulations of the same material – do not give the impression that they thought that this material was the product of divine revelation. Therefore, though they applied אם אינו ענין to rabbinic sources, they did so more as a form of clarifying comment than as *midrash*. That is, their use of אם אינו ענין confirmed that a rule that was fairly clear and implicit in a *baraita* or *mishnah* was, in fact, undoubtedly and explicitly the rule. This is different from true *midrash*, which uncovers what the text on its own does not imply, especially in the case of a hermeneutic like אם אינו ענין, which transfers the rules of one rubric to another.

A chronological study of אם אינו ענין in BT showed that until the third amoraic generation there was little change in the form and midrashic methodology of אם אינו ענין. Any irregularities in the tannaitic or early amoraic *midrashim* containing אם אינו ענין are indicative of late interpolations and commentaries that use it to explain or clarify those early midrashic sources.

This picture changes starting with the fourth amoraic generation. In that generation we find many changes in the content of אם אינו ענין *derashot* that indicate a change in amoraic and post-amoraic perceptions of rabbinic sources. For example, BT attributes an אם אינו ענין *derashah* to R. Jeremiah, a fourth-generation Palestinian *amora*. In the formation of his אם אינו ענין interpretation, R. Jeremiah used one verse from the Pentateuch and one rabbinic rule. In two אם אינו ענין interpretations attributed respectively to Rava and Abbaye, one element in each *derashah* is based on *midrash*. Rava uses a *midrash* attributed to R. Yonah, a fourth-generation Palestinian, and Abbaye uses a *midrash* based on *Sifra* to create the elements of his אם אינו ענין interpretation. This pattern continues into the post-amoraic generation of R. Ahai and is prevalent in the *stam*'s formulations of אם אינו ענין interpretations, which in the richness of their discourse are similar in form to R. Ahai's *midrash*.

The *stam*'s אם אינו ענין interpretations always support the teachings of a *tanna* or *amora*, responding to problems that arise and challenge these teachings. The *midrashim* of these *tannaim* and *amoraim* provide the "verses" for the *stam*'s אם אינו ענין. Thus, for the *stam* it is obvious that the status of rabbinic *torah* as it is expressed in tannaitic and amoraic *midrashim* is that of Torah.

This attitude of the *stam* also extends to some instances of the tannaitic non-*midrash* halakhic heritage as well, as can be gleaned from the four cases of independent stammaitic אם אינו ענין interpretations that differ completely, in both form and content, from any others we have seen. These interpretations are based on the doubling of a single word, usually within a single verse, that would be viewed as a *ribbui* in tannaitic midrashic praxis. The *stam*, however, interprets these cases using אם אינו ענין. Every case of this form of אם אינו ענין supports a tannaitic or amoraic halakhic rule, most of them not based on a *midrash*.[1] This activity of support of even late rabbinic legislation with *midrash* is not surprising since it has precedents in the tannaitic and amoraic eras. Significantly, it forms a very small portion of the *stam*'s use of *midrash* on rabbinic sources. Even so, it assumes that such legal sources are rooted in

1 See bKetubot 35a, Qiddushin 43b, Baba Meẓiᶜaᵓ 88b, Sanhedrin 28a.

the Torah's text and inextricably bound up in it. This might suggest that we are dealing with what I have called "pentateuchal *halakhah*" in my discussion of tannaitic *midrash*. Yet, if we consider the vast majority of stammaitic midrashic approaches to rabbinic texts – the application of ריבוי ומיעוט and לא קשיא interpretations to *mishnayyot* and *baraitot*, or the use of early midrashic material as the "scriptural" basis for אם אינו ענין – it is reasonably clear that the *stam* views the legacy of the *tannaim* and the *amoraim* as no less canonical and revealed than the Torah itself.

In our final chapter, which covers several late midrashic phenomena, it became clear that the overriding intention of midrashic interpreters beginning in the fourth amoraic generation was to maintain the halakhic *status quo*. Several hermeneutics that are not part of the repertoire of the *tannaim* or early *amoraim* develop in this period. Among these are שני כתובים הבאים כאחד אין מלמדין ("two scriptural passages that teach a single principle do not teach anything"),[2] תרי מיעוטי ("two limitations"), and צריכי ("they are necessary").

The first hermeneutic did not permit the growth or extension of an *halakhah* if two scriptural passages taught a single idea. For example, let us say that two scriptural passages dealing with conditional statements formulated them in both a positive and negative form ("If you do X, then Y will occur; but if you do not do X, Y will not occur. . . ."). According to the "two scriptural passages" hermeneutic, we would not be able to extrapolate from these cases to any others. Similarly, where there were "two limitations" in a scriptural text,[3] we would face the same limitation on interpretation as in the "two scriptural passages" hermeneutic. צריכי, however, opens the lock that the "two scriptural passages" and "two limitations" hermeneutics place on interpretation. It does so, however, only when those hermeneutics fail to give adequate support to received tannaitic and amoraic traditions. In that case, it provides the necessary support.

An interesting characteristic of the interpretations based on the abovementioned hermeneutics is that one never finds a scriptural citation in them. Rather, rabbinic rubric titles drawn from or based on scriptural passages function in the place of actual verses or passages from the *TaNaKh*. For example, in a long discussion in bQiddushin about women's obligations to and

2 There is a view that says that "two scriptural passages that teach a single principle do teach something." In order to compensate for this view when necessary, the view emerged that "everyone agrees that three scriptural passages teaching a single principle taught nothing," שלשה כתובים הבאים כאחד לדברי הכל אין מלמדין.

3 A limitation usually meant a word that was traditionally viewed as a מיעוט, i.e., a word or even a particle that is limiting in meaning. Some examples that appear in these forms of *midrash* are the use of the possessive pronoun ו understood as "it, and none other"; or the definite article ה' understood as "the (specific thing)," but no other one.

exemptions from various commandments, the *sugya* makes use of terms like *mazzah*, by which it means the obligation to eat unleavened bread on Passover night; *haqhel*, by which it means the requirement that the entire Israelite community hear the reading of the Torah on the Sukkot after the sabbatical year; and *tefillin*, by which it means the obligation to don phylacteries. This last term does not appear in Scripture at all.

In actuality, many cases of these highly conceptualized "pentateuchal" terms do not include the unvarnished legal implications of the Bible. Rather, what these disembodied terms imply are what the *tannaim* or *amoraim* have understood them to imply. For example, *mazzah* as used in the Qiddushin *sugya* refers to the Rabbis' understanding of the Torah's requirements regarding eating unleavened bread on Passover. That obligation is, from their perspective, to eat *mazzah* on the first night of the holy day. According to the Rabbis, no further obligation to eat *mazzah* exists during Passover. Further, according to the Rabbis, women are required to eat *mazzah* on the first night of Passover. None of these requirements or exemptions are apparent from the Pentateuch's references to Passover and *mazzah*. Reading the Torah, one would get the impression that Jews are required to eat *mazzah* for the full week or six days of Passover.[4] Further, there is no reference in the Torah to women being either obligated to or exempted from eating *mazzah* on Passover.[5] Both ideas, namely, that one must eat *mazzah* only on the first night and that women share this requirement with men, are purely rabbinic.[6] Hence, *mazzah* here is neither a scriptural verse nor even a truly scriptural reference. It is a rabbinic construction of a scriptural commandment.

Similarly, *tefillin*, which the Qiddushin *sugya* uses as part of its "two scriptural passages" and צריכי arguments, is a thoroughly rabbinic construction. The idea of *tefillin* as actual objects to be put on one's body is derived from the rabbinic understanding of several pentateuchal passages that include a commandment to place or tie something on one's hand as a sign and to place something as a memorial or *totefet*, a word whose meaning is uncertain, between one's eyes.[7] That this "something" is *tefillin* is certainly not spelled out in the verses, and even the Rabbis themselves say that most of the the rules regarding the

4 See Exod 12:14–19; 23:15; 34:18; Deut 16:8.

5 See the previous note. Also see Exod 23:17; 34:23; and Deut 16:16, where the obligation to make pilgrimage and observe Passover, Shabu^c^ot, and Sukkot involves only males.

6 See *Mek.*, Pisḥa, 8, ed. Horovitz-Rabin, p. 27, lines 1–11 and tPisḥa 2:22. In tPisḥa 2:22, women are exempted from *mazzah* consumption except on a voluntary basis. See, however, tPisḥa 8:10 and more significantly bPesaḥim 91a and Maimonides' Code, Laws of *Ḥamez* and *Mazzah*, 6:1 and 6:10 and *Shulḥan 'Arukh*, *'Oraḥ Ḥayyim*, 475:1 and 472:14.

7 Exod 13:9 and 16; Deut 6:8 and 11:18. Even some medieval rabbinic Jewish commentators wrote that these verses could be understood symbolically rather than as references to the objects called *tefillin*. See, for example, Rashbam on Exod 13:9 and Ibn Ezra on the same verse. Ibn Ezra hints

construction of *tefillin* are *halakhah le-Moshe mi-Sinai*, oral laws given to Moses at Sinai.[8] Finally, even if *tefillin* were undoubtedly what Scripture meant and commanded in the verses the Rabbis cite, there is nothing in any of these verses that indicates that women are exempt from *tefillin*. In fact, this seems to be a matter of argument: bʿErubin 96b suggests that not all the Sages thought that *tefillin* was an example of a positive, time-oriented commandment, a view that is central to the discussion in Qiddushin.

In the *sugya*, the "two scriptural passages," "two limitations," and צריכי midrashic methods use the rubric names created by the Rabbis. As we have noted, most of these rubric names are based on pentateuchal usage – for example, *maẓẓah* and *haqhel*. They are also defined in term of rabbinic *halakhot*, some of which are subject to debate,[9] yet the *sugya* does not distinguish between them and what it views as pentateuchal "positive commandments with (or without) time-orientation." Furthermore, the above-mentioned hermeneutics use these terms as their "verses" or "scriptural passages," which shows once more how the rabbinic has become synonymous with the pentateuchally revealed. Thus, the fourth-generation *amoraim*, their fifth- through seventh-generation amoraic successors, and the *stam* appear to view the legacy of their forebears as divinely revealed Torah containing the word and will of God.

The major conclusion of this work is that, according to the Rabbis and the Torah itself, at Sinai the people had heard the great voice of God speak to them. The rabbinic mission was to make sure that that voice did not cease to speak. There was no rabbinic generation that did not possess what it considered a divinely-revealed canonical work that it believed itself to be licensed and obligated to interpret.[10] It was the content of that canon that changed. The most radical change in rabbinic thinking took place when the conception of a divinely revealed canon moved past the borders of Scripture and began to encompass and include the rabbinic legacy. Our study shows this to have happened starting with the fourth amoraic generation, and it becomes

---

that there are those who actually subscribe to this view in practice. Most likely his reference is to Karaitic commentators and rank-and-file Karaites, who did not observe *tefillin* and understood the scriptural verses cited above as metaphors.

8 bShabbat 28b=Menaḥot 35a; ibid. 62a; ibid. 79b=bMenaḥot 32a; bʿErubin 97a=Menaḥot 35a; bMakkot 11a; and Menaḥot 35a. It is clear that *tefillin* is not only a rabbinic practice. *Tefillin* were also discovered at Qumran, which means that the Rabbis and at least the Qumran sect agreed on the interpretation of the scriptural passages cited in n. 7 or that both groups borrowed the idea of *tefillin* from the same external source. See Y. Yadin, *Tefillin from Qumran* (Jerusalem: Israel Exploration Society and Shrine of the Book, 1969), XQ Phyl 1–4.

9 For example, not everyone holds that *tefillin* is a "positive commandment with time-orientation." See bᶜErubin 96b. This is particularly ironic in a *sugya* that considers *tefillin* the paradigm for all the "positive commandments with time-orientation."

10 Deut 17:8–11.

an increasingly entrenched idea as time went on at the end of the talmudic period. In that period, the later Sages certainly continued to hear the great voice speak in Scripture. But for them it continued to speak in the now "scriptural" Mishnah, *baraitot*, and pre-fourth generation amoraic teachings.

Theology, Canon, and *Midrash*

We have reached a very important point in our work – namely, we have provided at least one major reason for the changes in the sources and methods of rabbinic halakhic, and occasionally aggadic, *midrash*. That reason appears to be that the rabbinic theology that defined canonicity shifted from time to time. When the definition of what was canonical changed, Rabbis shifted their midrashic activities to new texts or collections of traditions.

What all the rabbinic theologies that defined canonicity seem to have in common is that "canonical" means divinely revealed, and divinely revealed means that whatever is now so defined could or should be subjected to midrashic interpretation. But interpretation of a canonical text is not a given. What may have been the Rabbis' motivation for interpreting that which they deemed canonical?

It seems that when we ask this question in reference to halakhic *midrash*, two answers present themselves, based on the evidence of this work and the data of other midrashic methods. First, whatever is a canonical legal source becomes a basis for the observance of what Jews, and in our case specifically rabbinic Jews, hold to be God's commandments. To the extent that the canon contains statements that are unclear or overly general according to the understanding of its human recipients, it requires the employment of some interpretational method by someone with authority that will provide the clarity and specificity that a Jew needs to fulfill the commandments. Second, once interpretive work on the canon begins, its human interpreter inevitably confronts the problematic linguistic or literary aspects of what he believes to be the canonical, divinely revealed text or tradition he interprets. Contradictions, syntactical and grammatical oddities, stylistic difficulties, and the like must be seen as apparent rather than real in a divine text or they must encode more information.[11] As it turns out, dealing with these problematic elements often supports the work of clarification and specification of the canon for the purposes of observance. Thus, the resolution of a contradiction may extend the law to more situations than one would have imagined at first glance, or the smooth-

11 Harris, *How Do We Know This?*, pp. 7–9. For a useful alternative view, see David Stern, *Midrash and Theory*, pp. 27–29. Stern's reasoning from a single aggadic midrashic source may negatively affect his conclusions. With this caveat in mind, his theory, and particularly its formulation, is useful for elucidating the characteristic behaviors of *midrash* and why they may occur.

ing of a stylistic "bump" may define even more clearly and particularly for the interpreter and his pious followers what the law requires of them both. Apparently, as long as there was the possibility of human misunderstanding of or confusion about the divine word on one hand, and a requirement to lead life in consonance with God's laws and expectations on the other, the Rabbis were impelled to "do *midrash*."

The Fourth Amoraic Generation and its Successors

Our work has pointed out the significance of the fourth amoraic generation and those who followed them. In three out of four cases, that generation represents a turning point in midrashic method. Frequently, midrashic styles with new patterns of argument and source usage that develop for the first time in the fourth generation only become more entrenched and extended in later generations.[12] To paraphrase the Haggadah, "Why is this generation (and its successors) different from all other generations?"

For the time being, the answers, to the extent that they exist, are guesses at best. Richard Kalmin suggests the possibility that the changes that take place in amoraic institutions may account for the developments that begin in the fourth amoraic generation. However, he expends more effort trying to explain the phenomenon by theorizing about the middle *amoraim* being among the editors of the Talmud.[13] After all is said and done, Kalmin admits that there is much more to know before we can explain why the fourth generation is the turning point it is. As he writes, "Systematic examination of the role of the fourth-generation Amoraim in Talmudic discussions is necessary before firm conclusions can be reached."[14] In part, my work has been an attempt to create a chronology of rabbinic midrashic praxis. As it has turned out, it has uncovered something "of the role of the fourth-generation Amoraim in the Talmudic discussions," but conclusions about why that generation's discourse begins to have its own distinct character, one that will shape the discourse that comes after, is still not completely within reach.

Nevertheless, the לא קשיא "hermeneutic" of BT and its PT counterpart, לא פליגי, suggest a certain pattern, one that emerges from some of the other

12 The special and different character of the fourth amoraic generation, its distinction from its predecessors, and its impact on the subsequent amoraic generations have been noted by Kraemer, *The Mind of the Talmud*, pp. 37–41; Yaakov Elman, "An Argument for the Sake of Heaven: The Mind of the Talmud: An Intellectual History of the Babylonian Talmud," *Jewish Quarterly Review* 84 (1993–94): 267; and Kalmin, *Sages, Stories, Authors, and Editors*, pp. 169–70.

13 Kalmin, p. 170, n. 3 and pp. 170–73.

14 Kalmin, p. 173.

hermeneutics we have analyzed in the past as well. That pattern is the unwillingness to accept contradiction and dispute in the area of halakhic differences. This is also true of developments that took place in the forms of כלל ופרט וכלל, ריבוי ומיעוט, „גזירה שווה "פשוטה" and „גזירה שווה "מופנה". Each one of these midrashic hermeneutics began as a distinct and favored methodology of a specific midrashic school. As their continued use in the amoraic strata of PT and BT indicates, over time their specific forms drew closer to one another. By BT's end stages of development, they were basically indistinguishable in form and, to some extent, even in methodology.[15] These movements toward unity and convergence begin in the fourth amoraic generation.[16] What is this need for unity about?

At this stage of our knowledge, this question cannot be answered with certainty. Yet today we are further ahead in our understanding of this period's history than we have been at any previous time. Therefore, what follows is a very provisional hypothesis about why the fourth Babylonian amoraic generation is a transitional one.

It seems that what we are looking at is a reaction to a force or forces, internal or external, that seems to have required the Babylonian rabbinic community to take a firmer stance in regard to its essential unity. If Richard Kalmin is correct, the Babylonian rabbinic community may have had enough in common and have been large enough to be a recognizable entity, but it was a decentralized community in Babylonia.[17] Its decentralized nature may have created a force that called for greater unity, lest the movement atomize or lose what power it had over the community. In order to preserve this decentralized rabbinic movement more effectively, processes of gathering in the movement's disparate legacies and incorporating its various traditions into a rabbinic "comity" in which differences were both preserved and minimized might have drawn the movement together. This greater unity had the potential to extend the rabbinic movement's authority and control beyond its own already committed adherents.[18]

If the following portrayals of life that emerge from Rava's Mahoza are true,

15 Michael Chernick, לחקר המידות „כלל ופרט וכלל" ו„ריבוי ומיעוט" במדרשים ובתלמודים, pp. 114, 126, and 128 and לחקר מידת „גזירה שווה": צורותיה במדרשים ובתלמודים, pp. 229–30.

16 For example, the amoraic מיעוט אחר מיעוט לרבות hermeneutic, which is the "mirror image" of the tannaitic ריבוי אחר ריבוי למעט hermeneutic, has its origins in the fourth Palestinian amoraic generation.

17 Kalmin, *Sages, Stories, Authors, and Editors*, pp. 213–14.

18 See Daniel Boyarin, "A Tale of Two Synods: Nicaea, Yavneh, and Rabbinic Ecclesiology," in "*Turn It Again*": *Jewish Medieval Studies and Literary Theory*, ed. Sheila Delany (Asheville: Pegasus Press, 2004), pp. 20–58. Boyarin claims that just as the "history" of the Nicean council that determined the Church's orthodoxies is a re-imagination of that Council, so Yavneh, where rabbinic "orthodoxy" is supposed to have begun, is a late Babylonian talmudic re-imagination of the Yavnian

or even if they are fictitious and only portray rabbinic attitudes rather than realities, they provide some support for our attempt to explain why the fourth Babylonian amoraic generation behaves as it does, creating, to a degree, the template of the future. In an important article, Yaakov Elman points to several sources that may shed light on why the fourth Babylonian amoraic generation is as significant as it is.[19]

Portrayals of Rava's Relationship with the Jewish Laity

bMakkot 22b

אמר רבא: כמה טפשאי שאר אינשי דקיימי מקמי ספר תורה ולא קיימי מקמי גברא רבא, דאילו בספר תורה כתיב „ארבעים" ואתו רבנן ובצרו חדא.

Rava said: How foolish are most people who rise before a Torah scroll but not before a rabbinic scholar. For in the Torah it is written, "forty [lashes shall you give him and not more]" (Deut 25:3), and the Rabbis came and reduced it by one!

Here Rava's complaint is that "his" Jews are prepared to show reverence to the Torah scroll, perhaps an icon for Written Torah, but they do not show deference to the Rabbis, whose authority over the written word is, in their own circles, virtually absolute. Obviously, in this complaint there is a sense of distance between "most people" and the Rabbis and between the respect "most

---

"synod." The "orthodoxy" that Boyarin speaks of is supposed to have supported what Boyarin says is rabbinic Judaism's interest in the preservation of debate, its heteroglossia and orthodox "heterodoxy." My study questions whether this depiction of the Talmud's later legacy is actually correct. Perhaps for the rabbinic movement's tannaitic and early amoraic periods the interest in debate and its preservation is a fact, but a more unified view of law and other forms of rabbinic expression begins to characterize the Talmud from the fourth amoraic generation on. What is significant about Boyarin's article for our work is his sense that the imaginary recreation of Yavneh in the fourth-fifth century is part of a rabbinic attempt to use its power – namely, the power of knowledge and the authority it had over the interpretation of Torah, to control the lives and behaviors of rank and file Jews. Given my understanding of the later amoraic period, is it possible that echoes of Nicaea resounded in rabbinic circles, especially in cosmopolitan and religiously diverse Maḥoza? For the situation in Palestine, see Lee I. Levine, *The Rabbinic Class in Roman Palestine* (Jerusalem and New York: Yad Yitzchak Ben-Zvi and Jewish Theological Seminary, 1989), pp. 173–76; 185; 193–95. More recently, see Alyssa Gray, *A Talmud in Exile*, pp. 201–3. The details of how or if the developments in Palestine affected the historical development of the Babylonian rabbinic community have yet to be explored.

19 I refer to Yaakov Elman, "Middle Persian Culture and Babylonian Sages: Accommodation and Resistance in the Shaping of Rabbinic Legal Tradition," *Cambridge Companion to the Talmud and Rabbinic Literature* (Cambridge: Cambridge University Press, 2007), eds. Charlotte Fonrobert and Martin Jaffee.

people" have for the Written Scroll and the lack thereof for those who view themselves as the Scroll's sole authorized interpreters.

bSanhedrin 99b–100a

אפיקורוס כגון מאן?... רבא אמר: כגון הני דבי בנימין אסיא דאמרי: מאי אהני לן רבנן? מעולם לא שרו לן עורבא, ולא אסרו לן יונה. רבא כי הוו מייתי טריפתא דבי בנימין קמיה, כי הוה חזי בה טעמא להיתירא אמר להו: תחזו, דקא שרינא לכו עורבא. כי הוה חזי בה טעמא לאיסורא, אמר להו: תחזו, דקא אסרנא לכו יונה.

(Who is a) heretic?... Rava said: (People) like those members of the household of Benjamin the Physician, who say, "What use are the Rabbis to us? They have never permitted the raven [which the Torah forbids], nor have they prohibited the dove [which the Torah permits].

When members of the household of Benjamin the Physician would bring a (question regarding the permissibility of an animal) with a fatal organ defect (which therefore might not be *kasher*) before Rava, if he saw a reason to be lenient, he [Rava] would say to them, "See, I have permitted the raven to you!" When he saw a reason to be stringent, he would say to them, "See, I have forbidden the dove to you!"

Heretics, according to Rava's definition, are those who come to Rabbis with *kashrut* questions but nevertheless question the level of their authority when compared with that of Scripture. Rava is quite vocal in letting these "heretics" know how dependent they are on the religious knowledge of the Rabbis and their power to interpret the Torah for its practical observance by the Jewish community. Yet, there is nothing in this true or fictional report that indicates that the attitude of the house of Benjamin the Physician changed because of Rava's views.

Further, Elman points to the low opinion that some Jews had of the rabbinic courts compared to those of the Sasanian Persians. For example, one report states that a Mahozan Jew preferred to litigate before the Resh Galuta, who judged according to Persian law rather than before a rabbinic court. Only when he lost there did he think he would be better off in a rabbinic court (bBaba Qamaʾ 53b). Similarly, a woman who did not like Rava's judgment harassed him (bBaba Batraʾ 153a). While Rava's behavior was less than exemplary in the denouement of the case, the fact that the woman would behave in this fashion indicates her low esteem for the rabbinic judge – in this case, Rava. Elman also postulates that some changes in Jewish law may have been the result of Jewish courts and judges trying to compete for Jewish loyalty in the face of challenges from Persian law (see, for example, bBaba Batraʾ 148b).

If these attitudes actually existed in the fourth amoraic generation, or even if they are the fourth rabbinic generation's expression of how they saw the problem of their generation vis-à-vis "their fellow rabbinic Jews," the need for a higher degree of rabbinic unity would be understandable. I am suggesting, and only very tentatively, that the fourth Babylonian amoraic generation's most prominent members began the process of organizing the rabbinic "movement" by adopting methods of study that would allow that movement to claim that its traditions and interpretive methods were essentially unified. Perhaps it was their hope that if this effort met with success, their rabbinic world and that of their successors would be able to exercise more control and influence over rank and file Jews and gain the respect they felt the Rabbis and their movement deserved.

All this is conjecture at best, based on too few sources and insights into the world of the Jews in the late Sasanian period. I offer it only as a starting point and a goad to thinking about why the fourth Babylonian amoraic generation stands out as it does. Perhaps emerging studies of this period in Sasanian Babylonia will provide a firmer understanding of the yet mysterious reasons for the distinct developments that mark the fourth Babylonian amoraic generation.

Asmakhta-Methodology and the Late Talmudic Period

In the chapter dealing with אף על פי שאין ראיה לדבר, זכר לדבר, "though there is no proof for the matter, there is a prooftext for it," I dealt with Maimonides' contention that *asmakhta*, which also means "support," was the same as זכר, "mnemonic."[20] Inspection of the twenty-seven cases of the phrase מדרבנן וקרא אסמכתא בעלמא, "(the rule) is of rabbinic (origin) and the verse (that was cited) is a mere support," showed that אסמכתא (*asmakhta*) differed from זכר (*zekher*).

In the case of *asmakhta*, an older *midrash* of a scriptural verse, usually from the Pentateuch,[21] presents an impediment to the present understanding of the law. At one time tannaitic or amoraic Sages held that the *midrash* produced pentateuchal *halakhah*. At a later stage of the Talmud's development, however, the regnant rabbinic opinion was that the law was a rabbinic enactment or "traditional" law.[22] Wherever *asmakhta* appears, it closes the gap between these two points of view.

In many ways *asmakhta* functions as לא קשיא, the "there is no contradiction"

20 *Mamonides' Introduction to his Commenatry on the Mishnah*, ed. Kapah, p. י and Mishnah Commentary, mShabbat 9:2.

21 There are two exceptions to this general rule, one in bNedarim 49a, where the verse that is cited is from 2 Chron 35:13, and bḤullin 17b, where the verse is from 1 Sam 14:34.

22 "Traditional" law is a translation of הלכתא גמירי לה. Later commentators hold that this term refers to laws given orally to Moses that have no true basis in Scripture. Hence, Scripture is, at most, a support. See הליכות עולם, שער ב׳, ed. Warsaw (1883), p. 14; Rashi, bPesaḥim 17b, s.v. הלכתא; and שו״ת חוות יאיר, סי׳ קצב, צט א׳.

methodology. In this case, instead of recognizing conflict between sources, it recognizes the lack of congruence between an older view and a present one. Instead of assigning one aspect of this conflict to one case and the other aspect of the conflict to a different case, *asmakhta* reduces what was "pentateuchal" to what is now rabbinic. This act is very significant because it makes a strong rabbinic claim for authority over the interpretation of Scripture. The *asmakhta* method places in rabbinic hands the right to declare which rabbinic interpretations of Scripture should be viewed as true *derashot*, which produce "pentateuchal" *halakhot*, and which interpretations are mere props for independent rabbinic legislation.

It is hard to say with certainty that this method of resolving contradictions is late. The only named *amora* who used it was R. Ashi, a sixth-generation Babylonian (c. 375–425 C.E.). All other examples of the use of *asmakhta* are anonymous, but these would have to be carefully analyzed in order to verify whether they are actually all from the late amoraic or post-amoraic period. Nevertheless, the method itself initially recognizes, even as it finally denies, "early" and "late" understandings of *derashot*. Though the *asmakhta* method clearly distinguishes between scriptural and rabbinic levels of authority, it does not necessarily relegate rabbinic legislation to the status of "not revealed." In fact, it may indicate that those who use this method arrogate to themselves a very strong position of authority. By stating that a law is rabbinic and Scripture is a "mere support," the parties involved may be saying that rabbinic legislation has its own independent authority, but the ability to find scriptural backing for it shows that it is part of the divine revelation called Torah. If this is the correct interpretation of this method's "back story," then if it is late, it is similar to other late phenomena we have seen. That is, *asmakhta* suggests an attempt on the part of the late talmudic Sages to claim that rabbinic law and rabbinic scriptural interpretational authority should have the final word regarding the way Jews conduct their lives.

Where Now?

Though it is my hope that this work has answered some questions about the various eras within the larger era of the formation of the Talmud, it is clear that many questions remain unanswered. What I have done is to try to answer, at least for myself and only provisionally, the question, "If the rabbinic theology of canon and revelation changed, what made that happen?" In order to answer that question with more certainty, we must know much more about the social, religious, and historical context in which these changes took place. That means, to the extent that is possible, we must have even more reliable histories of the rabbinic Jewish movement in Palestine and Babylonia than we possess today. If anything, that is a challenge to go beyond the sources of rabbinic literature itself and make use of pagan and Christian Roman sources that may shed more light on the religious and social realities of Palestine. Regarding Babylonian Jewry, we will have to look to Sasanian sources and traditions to uncover the story of Babylonia's Jews and among them the Rabbis.

Each study of talmudic methods – modes of thought, midrashic interpretation, rules of decision-making, and the like – moves us a bit closer to understanding PT and BT and how they came to be. These studies are significant because they help those modern Jews who seek the wisdom of what has emerged as "the tradition" to gain better access to it and to make better sense of the works that are its souces. The *Talmudim* and the literatures that flow from them still remain sources for what I will call "Jewish ideas." These ideas may be expressed differently in Jewish life today, and some may be more useful than others in today's world; but a "Jewish idea" still opens a door to what were and may still be Jewish values. These values can enrich the content of individual and communal Jewish life and provide a glimpse of important Jewish ideas to people of other traditions.

And for us "antiquarians" who find in the *Talmudim* a world of tantalizing thoughts and historical questions regarding these works' development, redaction, teachers, heroes, villains, values, beliefs and culture, there is always the echo of "a great voice that does not cease," urging us to know more. And, no doubt, we will.

Appendix A
A Critique of Robert Brody's Views Regarding the *Stam*

In Robert Brody's presentation at the Jewish Theological Seminary (2005), he cited R. Huna's statement in bKetubot 70b: אמר ר' הונא: באומר כל הזן אינו מפסיד, "R. Huna said, This speaks of the case where he (the husband) said 'Anyone who feeds (my wife) will not lose (thereby).'" Brody understands this *memra* to respond to an anonymous question raised in reference to mKetubot 7:1, which speaks of a husband putting his wife under a vow that prohibits her from benefiting from him. If the vow is for a thirty-day period, the Mishnah says he must arrange for someone to be responsible for her food allotment. The *stam* inquires: But doesn't the provider of her food allotment act as his agent? (And since an agent is viewed as the legal equivalent of the one who appointed him, isn't the wife essentially benefiting from her husband in violation of the vow?). Supposedly, R. Huna responds to the *stam* saying that this is a case in which there is no direct appointment of the agent, only a general statement, "Anyone who provides (for my wife) will not lose." If, however, we remove the *stam*'s question, we might view R. Huna's statement as a direct comment on the Mishnah, as follows:

> *Mishnah.* One who puts his wife under a vow not to have benefit from him for thirty days must appoint a provider (for her).
>
> *Gemara.* R. Huna said, "(In reference to appointing a provider, the Mishnah) is applicable when he (the husband) says, 'One who provides (for my wife) will not lose (thereby).'"

R. Huna may simply be defining the appropriate language the husband must use to appoint his wife's provider. Anonymous questions may have been added at a later time in order to explain more clearly the connection between an amoraic comment and a *mishnah* or *baraita*. In this case, the *stam*'s question may be trying to explain to the reader why R. Huna made his remark, but that does not mean that R. Huna originally responded to that question. Opening questions that introduce an *amora*'s remarks may therefore not be good examples.

There are also cases where there is more of what Brody calls "substantive discussion" that is anonymous. In some cases of this kind of discussion, it appears that an *amora* responds to an extended talmudic give-and-take. He cites the mostly anonymous *sugya* in bKetubot 70b that ends with R. Ashi's statement,

"This is a case where she has sufficient for major needs and insufficient for minor ones." Brody views this as R. Ashi's (MS Vatican 130: R. Sheshet) response to the problems raised by the *stam* – namely: 1) How can a husband take a vow against his obligatory responsibilities – in this case, providing food for his wife? 2) If you say that he gave up his rights to her earnings and had her use them for her food, then why does the husband have to appoint a provider? The wife is taking care of herself. 3) If you say the husband must appoint a provider because his wife's earnings are insufficient to cover her food allotment, then we are back to question 1. Then, according to Brody, R. Ashi (Sheshet) responds, "This (the appointment of a provider) is (required) in a case where she has sufficient (earnings) for major needs and insufficient (earnings) for minor ones."

An alternative to Brody's understanding is to assume that R. Ashi's statement is a direct comment on the *mishnah* that is at the center of the discussion, namely, mKetubot 7:1: "If one puts his wife under a vow not to have benefit from him for thirty days, he must appoint a provider. . . ." If we assume that R. Ashi's comment was the *gemara* to this *mishnah*, then the passage might look like this:

> *Mishnah.* If one puts his wife under a vow not to have benefit from him for thirty days, he must appoint a provider. . . .
>
> *Gemara.* "R. Ashi said, 'This (mishnaic rule) obtains when she (the wife) has sufficient for major needs but insufficient for minor ones.'"

That is, the husband may vow and appoint a provider only when most of her food needs are guaranteed and a small amount will have to be covered by the husband's administrator. If, however, this is not the situation – for example, when she has sufficient for her needs – then the husband may make his vow but not impose an administrator on his wife.[1] Alternatively, if she does not have sufficient wherewithal for her major needs, he may not vow and appoint an administrator for his wife because under those conditions the husband has taken a vow that undermines his *ketubah* obligations to her.[2] Therefore, the only case in which he may take the vow and appoint a provider as described in mKetubot 7:1 is "when she (the wife) has sufficient for her major needs but insufficient for her minor ones."[3]

1 See Maimonides' *Mishneh Torah*, Laws of Marriage, 12:23.

2 See *Tosafot R. Akiba Eiger*, #69, mKetubot 7:1.

3 Pinḥas Kehati, *Mishnah Mevoʾeret* – Ketubot (Jerusalem: Heikhal Shelomoh, 9th reprint, 1977), p. רטז, s.v. המדיר וכו׳ and עד שלשים וכו׳. Kehati explains the Mishnah assuming that R. Ashi's comment addresses it directly.

Appendix B
A Midrashic Oddity in *Mekhilta*, *Pisḥa* 5

Midrash proceeds on the principle that no word of Scripture is meaningless. This is especially true in the case of R. Akiba. Nevertheless, in *Mek.*, *Pisḥa* 5, R. Akiba uses the "two contradictory verses" hermeneutic (שני כתובים המכחישים זה את זה) to resolve a scriptural contradiction. His interpretation leaves a scriptural verse with no meaning. Given the rarity of this phenomenon, I feel obliged to try to account for this midrashic oddity.

It is possible that we may understand the view attributed to R. Akiba as the same as others expressed in *Pisḥa* 5. The majority of midrashists represented there resolved the contradiction between Exodus's requirement that flock animals be used for the paschal offering and Deuteronomy's permission to use herd animals for that purpose. Their solution was to require flock animals for the paschal offering and permitting the use of herd offerings for the pilgrimage offering (חגיגה), which according to rabbinic *halakhah* accompanied the paschal offering. That interpretation of R. Akiba's *derashah*, however, constitutes an argument from silence, since R. Akiba does not use the word "cattle" in his *midrash*.[1]

Perhaps it is possible to understand the point R. Akiba's "two contradictory verses" interpretation is trying to make by comparing it with the following *derashah* in *Mek. de-RSBY*, Exod 13:5:

> ועבדת את העבודה [הזאת בחדש הזה מכלל שנא׳ וזבחת פ]סח לייי אלהיך צאן ובקר (דב׳ טז ב) [יכול יה]א פסח דורות בא מן הצאן ומן הבקר ת״ל ועבדת את העבוד׳ הזאת בחדש הזה מה פסח מצ׳ לא בא אלא מן הכבשים ומן העזים אף פסח דורות אינו בא אלא מן הכבשים ומן העזים

> "And you shall perform this service in this month"– since it says, "And you shall sacrifice a Passover offering to the Eternal, your God, flock and

1 A *midrash* attributed to Hillel in pPesaḥim 4:1 (33a) is similar to the one attributed to R. Akiba in the *Mekhilta*. That midrashic interpretation actually resolves the contradiction between the Exod and Deut verses by assigning the flock animals for the Passover sacrifice and "cattle" for the *ḥagigah*. *Yalqut Shim'oni* preserves a similar resolution in its formulation of R. Akiba's *midrash*, but it is too late a source to rely on, and it is the only one that contains a resolution of the "two contradictory verses" identified in the *midrash* attributed to R. Akiba. The fact that pPesaḥim attributes a similar, more elegant *midrash* to Hillel rather than to R. Akiba raises some questions about the accuracy of the attribution of this *midrash* to R. Akiba, though it is possible that Akiba had not heard of Hillel's *midrash*. It is also quite possible that the *midrash* attributed to Hillel is a refinement of R. Akiba's *midrash* attributed pseudepigraphically to Hillel. It is just such a quandary that forces us to use phrases like "attributed to Hillel" or "attributed to R. Akiba."

> cattle. . . ." I might have thought that the Passover offering of the (future) generations might come from flock (animals) or cattle. Therefore, the Torah says, "You shall perform this service in this month" (Exod 13:5) – just as the Passover offering in Egypt came only from sheep and goats, so the Passover offering of the generations must come from sheep and goats.

This *midrash* seeks to undo the impression that the passage in Deut 15:2 makes when it mentions cattle in the context of the paschal offering. Insofar as Deuteronomy portrays a temporal context right before Moses' death and the Israelites' entry into the Land of Israel, the reference clearly speaks of the rules for the Passover sacrifice that should be observed for all future generations. This opens the possibility that the rules for the paschal offering to be observed at the central sanctuary differed from those of the original Passover in Egypt. By citing Exod 13:5, *Mek. de-RSBY* concludes that God's command is that the future generations observe "this service"– that is, the same one in regard to sacrifice as was observed in Egypt. This would exclude cattle as acceptable animals for the paschal offering. Here, as in R. Akiba's "two contradictory verses" *midrash*, there is no attempt to account for the role cattle play in the Passover offering. No doubt there is some role for them, but the *midrash*'s agenda is to maintain the equivalency between the animals used for the paschal offering of the "Egyptian Passover" and those that should be used for that purpose in the future observance of Passover.

The *Mekhilta*'s *midrash* attributed to R. Akiba may serve a similar purpose. It is not interested in determining what the place of cattle is in the observance of the Passover sacrifices. Rather, its function is to define clearly what constitutes acceptable animals for the paschal offering. As in *Mek. de-RSBY*, the problem is the contradiction between the rules established at the time of the Egyptian Passover and the rule mentioned in Deuteronomy. The central point of the *midrash* is that the rules for acceptable animals for the paschal offering have not changed. According to the "two contradictory verses" *midrash*, this can be proved by the preponderance of scriptural references to the paschal offering and the types or species of animals commanded for use in it. This Akiban *midrash* does not view the halakhic application for the term "cattle" as necessary to its agenda. Like its counterpart in *Mek. de-RSBY*, its only agenda seems to be to establish what animals are fit for the paschal offering. These rules, the *midrash* tells us, are the same for the future Passover as they were for the "Egyptian Passover."

Appendix C
Random Examples of לא קשיא in Early and Late Amoraic and *Stam* Sources

Pesaḥim

Early Amoraic

תלמוד בבלי מסכת פסחים דף מט עמוד א

משנה. ההולך לשחוט את פסחו ולמול את בנו, ולאכול סעודת אירוסין בבית חמיו, ונזכר שיש לו חמץ בתוך ביתו. אם יכול לחזור ולבער ולחזור למצותו – יחזור ויבער, ואם לאו – מבטלו בלבו. גמרא. ורמינהו: ההולך לאכול סעודת אירוסין בבית חמיו ולשבות שביתת הרשות – יחזור מיד! אמר רבי יוחנן: לא קשיא; הא – רבי יהודה, הא – רבי יוסי. דתניא: סעודת אירוסין – רשות, דברי רבי יהודה. רבי יוסי אומר: מצוה.

תלמוד בבלי מסכת פסחים דף נה עמוד א

משנה. וחכמים אומרים: ביהודה היו עושין מלאכה בערבי פסחים עד חצות, ובגליל לא היו עושין כל עיקר. הלילה, בית שמאי אוסרים, ובית הלל מתירין עד הנץ החמה.

גמרא. מעיקרא תנא מנהגא, ולבסוף תנא איסורא! – אמר רבי יוחנן: לא קשיא; הא – רבי מאיר, הא – רבי יהודה. דתניא, אמר רבי יהודה: ביהודה היו עושין מלאכה בערבי פסחים עד חצות, ובגליל אינן עושין כל עיקר. אמר לו רבי מאיר: מה ראייה יהודה וגליל לכאן? אלא, מקום שנהגו לעשות מלאכה – עושין, מקום שנהגו שלא לעשות – אין עושין.

These are the only cases of early amoraic uses of לא קשיא in Pesaḥim.

Late Amoraic – Post-third Generation

תלמוד בבלי מסכת פסחים דף ט עמוד א

משנה. אין חוששין שמא גיררה חולדה מבית לבית וממקום למקום, דאם כן מחצר לחצר ומעיר לעיר – אין לדבר סוף.

גמרא. טעמא – דלא חזינא דשקל, הא חזינא דשקל – חיישינן, ובעי בדיקה. ואמאי? נימא אכלתיה! מי לא תנן: מדורות הנכרים טמאים. וכמה ישהה במדור ויהא המדור צריך בדיקה – ארבעים יום, ואף על פי שאין לו אשה. וכל מקום שחולדה

וחזיר יכולין להלוך – אין צריך בדיקה! – אמר רבי זירא:[1] לא קשיא; הא – בבשר, והא – בלחם. בבשר – לא משיירא, בלחם – משיירא. אמר רבא: האי מאי? בשלמא התם – אימור הוה אימור לא הוה, ואם תמצא לומר הוה – אימור אכלתיה. אבל הכא – דודאי דחזינא דשקל – מי יימר דאכלתיה? הוי ספק וודאי, ואין ספק מוציא מידי ודאי.

תלמוד בבלי מסכת פסחים דף פא עמוד ב–פב עמוד א

משנה. נטמא שלם או רובו שורפין אותו לפני הבירה מעצי המערכה נטמא מיעוטו והנותר שורפין אותו בחצרותיהן או על גגותיהן מעצי עצמן הציקנין שורפין אותו לפני הבירה בשביל ליהנות מעצי המערכה.

גמרא. מאי טעמא אמר רבי יוסי בר חנינא כדי לביישן נטמא מיעוטו וכו׳ ורמינהו וכן מי שיצא מירושלים ונזכר שיש בידו בשר קדש אם עבר צופים שורפו במקומו ואם לאו חוזר ושורפו לפני הבירה מעצי המערכה אמר רב חמא בר עוקבא[2] לא קשיא כאן באכסנאי כאן בבעל הבית רב פפא אמר הא והא באכסנאי[3] כאן שהחזיק בדרך כאן שלא החזיק בדרך.

These are the only cases of late amoraic uses of לא קשיא in Pesaḥim.

Stam

In Pesaḥim there are approximately 50 anonymous uses of לא קשיא. Most are formulated similarly to the following two examples:

1 It is difficult to determine the identity of R. Zera because there are two *amoraim* by that name, one a third-generation Palestinian and the other a fourth-generation Babylonian. The proximity of his comment to that of Rava (a fourth-generation Babylonian *amora* whose name is attested to in this *sugya* by all the text witnesses) adds weight to the likelihood that R. Zera in this context is the fourth-generation *amora*. See how Rashi connects Rava's statement to that of R. Zera in Rashi, ad loc., s.v. מאי האי.

2 Most mss. have אמר רב חמא בר עוקבא אמר ר׳ יוסי בר חנינא. R. Ḥama b. ʿUqba is a third-generation Palestinian *amora* and R. Jose b. R. Ḥanina is a second-generation Palestinian *amora*. His or their use of לא קשיא may be an exception to the rule that this form of usage is found only starting with the fourth-generation *amoraim*. There are, however, some indications that he may not have been the party who used לא קשיא here. PT resolves the contradiction by distinguishing between an אכסניי, a visitor and others just as BT does. PT's response is anonymous. R. Ḥananel also records the לא קשיא in anonymous form. While we cannot discount the virtual unanimity of the BT text witnesses, we should note that PT's *sugya* begins with an attribution to R. Ḥama b. ʿUqba citing R. Jose b. R. Ḥanina. This attribution may have been misunderstood by the Babylonian recipients of PT's *sugya* or a source similar to it as applying to the complete contents of the Palestinian material. If so, what was an independent tradition in PT mistakenly became the opinion of R. Ḥama b. ʿUqba (and R. Jose b. Ḥanina). In that case, R. Ḥama b. ʿUqba is not actually responsible for the לא קשיא attributed to him. Certainly, R. Papa's response is consonant with our findings.

3 The following mss. have the reading הא והא באכסנאי (באכסניי, באכסני) ולא קשיא: Munich 95, New York-JTS Rab. 1623/2 EMC 21, ColumbiaX893 T141, Oxford Opp. Add. fol. 23, Vatican 109, Vatican 125.

תלמוד בבלי מסכת פסחים דף ח עמוד א

כל מקום שאין מכניסין וכו' [בו חמץ, אין צריך בדיקה].

כל מקום לאתויי מאי? – לאתויי הא דתנו רבנן: חורי בית העליונים והתחתונים, וגג היציע, וגג המגדל, ורפת בקר, ולולין, ומתבן, ואוצרות יין, ואוצרות שמן – אין צריכין בדיקה. רבן שמעון בן גמליאל אומר: מטה החולקת בתוך הבית ומפסקת – צריכה בדיקה. ורמינהו: חור שבין אדם לחבירו – זה בודק עד מקום שידו מגעת, וזה בודק עד מקום שידו מגעת, והשאר מבטלו בלבו. רבן שמעון בן גמליאל אומר: מטה החולקת בתוך הבית, ועצים ואבנים סדורים תחתיה, ומפסקת – אינה צריכה בדיקה. קשיא מטה אמטה, קשיא חורין אחורין! – חורין אחורין לא קשיא; הא – בעילאי ובתתאי, והא – במיצעי. מטה אמטה לא קשיא; הא – דמידליא, הא – דמיתתאי.

תלמוד בבלי מסכת פסחים דף ח עמוד א

אמר רב חסדא: בי דגים אין צריך בדיקה. והתניא: צריכין בדיקה! – לא קשיא; הא – ברברבי, הא – בזוטרי.

There is a single example in Pesaḥim where the *stam* uses an early amoraic form of לא קשיא:

תלמוד בבלי מסכת פסחים דף כו עמוד ב

תנו רבנן תנור שהסיקו בקליפי ערלה או בקשין של כלאי הכרם חדש יותץ ישן יוצן אפה בו את הפת רבי אומר הפת אסורה וחכמים אומרים הפת מותרת בישלה על גבי גחלים דברי הכל מותר והא תניא בין חדש ובין ישן יוצן לא קשיא הא רבי והא רבנן אימור דשמעת ליה לרבי משום דיש שבח עצים בפת זה וזה גורם מי שמעת ליה אלא לא קשיא הא רבי אליעזר הא רבנן.[4]

Sotah

All the cases of לא קשיא in Sotah are *stam*. They all follow the late amoraic/*stam* usage.

Nedarim

Early Amoraic Use of לא קשיא

תלמוד בבלי מסכת נדרים דף יח עמוד ב

מתני'. סתם נדרים להחמיר, ופירושם להקל. גמ'. והתנן: ספק נזירות להקל! אמר ר' זירא, לא קשיא: הא ר' אליעזר, הא רבנן; דתניא: המקדיש חייתו ובהמתו – הקדיש את הכוי, ר' אליעזר אומר: לא הקדיש את הכוי.

4 There are several examples of a reversion to the early amoraic לא קשיא in the anonymous stratum of bBerakhot. See 16a and 37a. These are negligible compared to the approximately 60 cases of the more typical stammaitic לא קשיא.

תלמוד בבלי מסכת נדרים דף פג עמוד ב

משנה...קונם כהנים לוים נהנים לי – יטלו על כרחו, כהנים אלו ולוים אלו נהנים לי – יטלו אחרים.

גמרא. כהנים ולוים נהנין לי – יטלו כו'. אלמא טובת הנאה אינה ממון, אימא סיפא: כהנים אלו ולוים אלו נהנין לי – יטלו אחרים, אבל להני לא, אלמא טובת הנאה ממון! אמר רב הושעיא, לא קשיא: הא רבי, והא ר' יוסי ב"ר יהודה; דתניא: הגונב טבלו של חבירו ואכלו – משלם לו דמי טבלו, דברי רבי, רבי יוסי בר"י אומר: אינו משלם אלא דמי חולין שבו.

These are the only cases of early amoraic לא קשיא in Nedarim.

Late Amoraic לא קשיא

תלמוד בבלי מסכת נדרים דף יד עמוד ב

תניא. הנודר בתורה – לא אמר כלום, במה שכתוב בה – דבריו קיימין. בה ובמה שכתוב בה – דבריו קיימין. קתני: במה שכתוב בה – דבריו קיימין, בה ובמה שכתוב בה צריך למימר? אמר רב נחמן,[5] לא קשיא: הא דמחתא אורייתא ארעא, הא דנקיט לה בידיה, מחתא על ארעא – דעתיה אגווילי, נקט לה בידיה – דעתיה על האזכרות שבה.

All other cases of לא קשיא are anonymous and follow the form of the late amoraic and *stam* usage. For example:

תלמוד בבלי מסכת נדרים דף פו עמוד ב–פז עמוד א

משנה. נדרה אשתו וסבור שנדרה בתו, נדרה בתו וסבור שנדרה אשתו, נדרה בנזיר וסבור שנדרה בקרבן, נדרה בקרבן וסבור שנדרה בנזיר, נדרה מתאנים וסבור שנדרה מן הענבים, נדרה מן הענבים וסבור שנדרה מן התאנים – הרי זה יחזור ויפר.

גמרא. למימרא, דיניא אותה דוקא הוא והא גבי קרעים דכתיב על על, דכתיב: +שמואל ב א+ על שאול ועל יהונתן בנו, ותניא: אמרו לו מת אביו וקרע, ואחר כך נמצא בנו – יצא ידי קריעה! אמרי, לא קשיא: הא בסתם, והא במפרש התניא: אמרו לו מת אביו וקרע, ואחר כך נמצא בנו – לא יצא ידי קריעה, אמרו לו מת לו מת, וכסבור אביו הוא וקרע, ואחר כך נמצא בנו – יצא ידי קריעה.

These examples taken randomly from both so-called regular tractates and from "different" tractates like Nedarim indicate that, generally speaking, the

5 The identification of R. Nahman in this *sugya* is problematic. There is a third-generation Babylonian *amora* and a fifth-generation Palestinian *amora* by that name. If he is the fifth-generation *amora*, this use of לא קשיא is completely appropriate. There may, however, be some occasional usage of this form of לא קשיא among third-generation *amoraim*, though it is most commonly associated with the late *amoraim*. See n. 4.

earlier *amoraim* tended to resolve contradictions between rabbinic sources by claiming they were debates. Later *amoraim* and the *stam* generally resolved contradictions by assigning each of the conflicting elements to separate situations. There is the possibility that early *amoraim* occasionally used the לא קשיא methodology that characterizes the late *amoraim* and the *stam*. The reverse is also true. The *stam* in particular occasionally reverts to using the early form of לא קשיא.

I have also checked tractates Baba Meẓiᶜaᵓ (about 60 examples, only one late amoraic, the rest *stam*); ᶜAvodah Zarah (about 16 examples, including two early amoraic uses of לא קשיא; two late uses, one typical, and one similar to the early amoraic usage; and the rest *stam*); Horayot (one typical late amoraic לא קשיא; no others); Tamid (one typical late amoraic application of לא קשיא). and Zebaḥim (27 examples: one possible typical early amoraic case of לא קשיא and one definite typical early amoraic use of לא קשיא; an early amoraic לא קשיא that uses the late form and contains the attribution formula "R. Ami cites R. Johanan," attested to by all text witnesses; a late amoraic לא קשיא that uses the early form; one *stam* that uses the early amoraic form of לא קשיא; all the rest are *stam* and typical.

Selected Bibliography

Albeck, Chanoch. *Untersuchungen über die Halakischen Midraschim* (Berlin: Akademie Verlag, 1927).

———. מחקרים בברייתא ובתוספתא (Jerusalem: Mossad Ha-Rav Kook, 1969).

———. מבוא התלמודים (Tel Aviv: Dvir, 1969).

———. ששה סדרי משנה – מפורשים ומנוקדים, סדר מועד (Jerusalem and Tel Aviv: Bialik Institute and Dvir, 6th printing, 1987).

Alter, Robert. *The Art of Biblical Narrative* (New York: Basic Books, Inc., 1981).

Benowitz, Moshe. תלמוד בבלי מסכת שבועות – פרק שבועות שתים בתרא (Jerusalem: Jewish Theological Seminary, 2003), pp. 8–11.

Botterweck, G. Johannes, Helmer Ringgen, and Heinz-Josef Fabry, eds., trans. Douglas W. Stott, *Theological Dictionary of the Old Testament* (Grand Rapids: William B. Eerdmans Publishing Company, 2003).

Boyarin, Daniel. "A Tale of Two Synods: Nicaea, Yavneh, and Rabbinic Ecclesiology." In *"Turn It Again": Jewish Medieval Studies and Literary Theory*, ed. Sheila Delany (Asheville: Pegasus Press, 2004), pp. 20–58.

Bregman, Marc. "Mishnah and LXX as Mystery: An Example of Jewish Christian Polemic in the Byzantine Period." In *Continuity and Renewal in Byzantine-Christian Palestine*, ed. Lee Levine (Jerusalem: Dinur and Jewish Theological Seminary of America, 2004), pp. 333–42. The Hebrew version, "משנה כמסטרין" appears in מחקרי תלמוד, ed. Yaakov Zussman and David Rosenthal (Jerusalem: Magnes Press, 2005), pp. 101–9.

Chernick, Michael. לחקר המידות „כלל ופרט וכלל" ו„ריבוי ומיעוט" במדרשים ובתלמודים (Lod: Habermann Institute for Literary Research, 1984).

———. מידת גזירה שווה: צורותיה במדרשים ובתלמודים (Lod: Habermann Institute for Literary Research, 1994).

Cohen, Avinoam. "על מיקום הבלתי-כרונולוגי של דברי מר בר רב אשי," *Sidra* 2 (1986): 65–66.

Dünner, Joseph Zvi Hirsch. *Die Theorien über Wesen und Ursprung der Tosephta* (Amsterdam, 1874).

Elman, Yaakov. *Authority and Tradition* (New York: Yeshiva University Press, 1994).

———. "Prospective *Derash* and Retrospective *Peshat*." In *Modern Scholarship in the Study of Torah*, ed. Shalom Carmy (New York: Jason Aronson, 1996), pp. 229–40.

———. "Middle Persian Culture and Babylonian Sages: Accommodation and Resistance in the Shaping of Rabbinic Legal Tradition." In *Cambridge Companion to the Talmud and Rabbinic Literature*, eds. Charlotte Fonrobert and Martin Jaffee (Cambridge: Cambridge University Press, 2007).

Ephrati, Jacob E. תקופת הסבוראים וספרותה (*The Sevoraic Period and its Literature in Babylonia and in Eretz Yisrael*) (Petah Tiqvah: Hotza'at Agudat Benei Asher, 1973).

Epstein, J. N. מבואות לספרות התנאים (Jerusalem and Tel Aviv: Magnes Press and Dvir Press, 1957; second edition, 1978).

———. מבואות לספרות האמוראים (Jerusalem and Tel Aviv: Magnes Press and Dvir Press, 1962).

———. מבוא לנוסח המשנה (Jerusalem and Tel Aviv: Magnes Press and Dvir Press, 1948, 2nd ed. 1964).

Finkelstein, Louis. "הערות ותיקוני-נוסח בתורת כהנים." In *Louis Ginzberg Jubilee Volume on the Occasion of his Seventieth Birthday*, eds. Saul Lieberman, Alexander Marx, Shalom Spiegel, and Solomon Zeitlin (New York: Jewish Theological Seminary, 1945).

Fischel, Henry A. *Rabbinic Literature and Greco-Roman Philosophy* (Leiden: Brill, 1973).

Fraade, Steven. "Literary Composition and Oral Perfromance in Early Midrashim," *Oral Tradition* 14 (1999): 33–51.

Frankel, Yonah. מדרש ואגדה, vol. 2 (Tel Aviv: Everyman's University, 1997).

Frankel, Zacharias. מבוא הירושלמי (Breslau: Schletter, 1870 reprinted, Jerusalem: n.p. 1967).

Friedman, Shamma. "על דרך חקר הסוגיא." In מחקרים ומקורות. (New York: Jewish Theological Seminary, 1977), pp. 283–300.

———. "על דרך חקר הסוגיא." In *Introduction to Texts and Studies: Analecta Judaica*, ed. H. Z. Dimitrovsky (New York: Jewish Theological Seminary, 1977).

———. "הברייתות בתלמוד הבבלי ויחסן למקבילותיהן שבתוספתא," עטרה לחיים (Jerusalem, 2000).

———. "Uncovering Literary Dependencies in the Talmudic Literary Corpus." In *The Synoptic Problem in Rabbinic Literature*, ed. Shaye J. D. Cohen (Providence: Brown Judaic Studies, 2000), pp. 35–57.

Gafni, Isaiah. "ישיבה ומתיבתא," *Zion* 43 (1978): 31–37.

———. יהודי בבל בתקופת התלמוד (Jerusalem: The Zalman Shazar Center for Jewish History, 1990.

Ginzberg, Louis. *A Commentary on the Palestinian Talmud* (New York: Jewish Theological Seminary, 1971), Hebrew Introduction.

Goldberg, Abraham. פירוש למשנה – מסכת שבת (Jerusalem: Jewish Theological Seminary of America, 1976.

———. "גישותיהן השונות של ר׳ יוחנן ושל ריש לקיש לשאלת של המשנה אל התוספתא והברייתא," *Proceedings of the Seventh World Congress of Jewish Studies* 3 (1980): 109–16.

———. "דבי ר׳ עקיבא ור׳ ישמעאל בספרי דברים פיס׳ א-נד." In תעודה (Ramat Aviv: Tel Aviv University, 1983).

———. פירוש למשנת שבת (Jerusalem: Jewish Theological Seminary of America, 1986).

Goodblatt, David. *Rabbinic Instruction in Sasanian Babylonia* (Leiden: Brill, 1978).

———. "Toward the Rehabilitation of Talmudic History." In *History of Judaism – The Next Ten Years*, ed. Baruch Bokser, Brown Judaic Studies 21 (Chico: Scholars Press, 1980)

———. "Babylonian Talmud." In *The Study of Ancient Judaism*, ed. Jacob Neusner (New York: Ktav, 1981).

Gray, Alyssa. *A Talmud in Exile: The Influence of Yerushalmi Avodah Zarah on the Formation of Bavli Avodah Zarah* (Providence, RI: Brown Judaic Studies, 2005).

Green, W. S. "What's in a Name? The Problematic of Rabbinic 'Biography.'" In *Approaches to Ancient Judaism: Theory and Practice* (Missoula: Scholars Press, 1978).

Halevi, Yitzchak Eizik. דורות הראשונים (Frankfurt a.M.: M. Slobotzky, 1901).

Harris, Jay. *How Do We Know This?* (Albany: State University of New York Press, 1995).

Hauptman, Judith. *Development of the Talmudic Sugya: Relationship Between Tannaitic and Amoraic Sources* (Lanham, New York, and London: University Press of America, 1988).

Hayes, Christine. "*Halakhah le-Moshe mi-Sinai* in Rabbinic Sources: A Methodological Case Study." In *The Synoptic Problem in Rabbinic Literature*, ed. Shaye J. D. Cohen (Rhode Island: Brown Judaic Studies, 2000).

Higger, Michael. אוצר הברייתות (New York: De-be Rabbanan, 1939).

Hoffman, D. Z. "לחקר מדרש התנאים" (German, *Zur Einleitung in die halachischen Midraschim*), trans. A. S. Rabinowitz (Tel-Aviv: n.p., 1928, reprinted Jerusalem: Carmiel, 1970).

Horovitz, H. S. "Einleitung." In ספרי דבי רב (Leipzig, Gustav Fock, G.m.b.H, 1917).

R. Isaiah di Trani. פסקי הרי"ד (Jerusalem: Makhon ha-Talmud ha-Yisraeli, 1964).

Jacobs, Louis. "Are There Fictitious Baraitot in the Babylonian Talmud?" *HUCA* 42 (1971): 185–96.

Jaffee, Martin. "How Much 'Orality' in Oral Torah? New Perspectives on the Composition of Early Rabbinic Tradition," *Shofar* 10,2 (1972): 70.

———. "The Oral Cultural Context of the Talmud Yerushalmi." In *The Talmud Yerushalmi and Graeco-Roman Culture I* (Tübingen: Mohr Siebeck, 1997).

———. *Torah in the Mouth: Writing and Oral Tradition in Palestinian Judaism* (New York: Oxford University Press, 2001).

Kahana, Menahem. "The Tannaitic Midrashim." In *The Cambridge Genizah Collections, Their Content and Significance*, ed. Stefen Reif (Cambridge, Cambridge University Press, 2002).

———. ספרי זוטא דברים (Jerusalem: Magnes Press, 2002).

Kalmin, Richard. *The Redaction of the Babylonian Talmud: Amoraic or Saboraic?* (Cincinnati: Hebrew Union College Press, 1989).

———. *Sages, Stories, Authors and Editors in Rabbinic Babylonia*. Brown Judaic Studies 300 (Atlanta: Scholars Press, 1994).

Kister, Menahem. "אקדמות מילין." In אבות דרבי נתן מהדורת ש"ז שכטר (Jerusalem and New York: Jewish Theological Seminary, 1996).

Koehler, Ludwig and Walter Baumgartner. *Hebrew and Aramaic Lexicon of the Old Testament. CD-ROM Edition* (Leiden: Koniklijke Brill, 1994–2000).

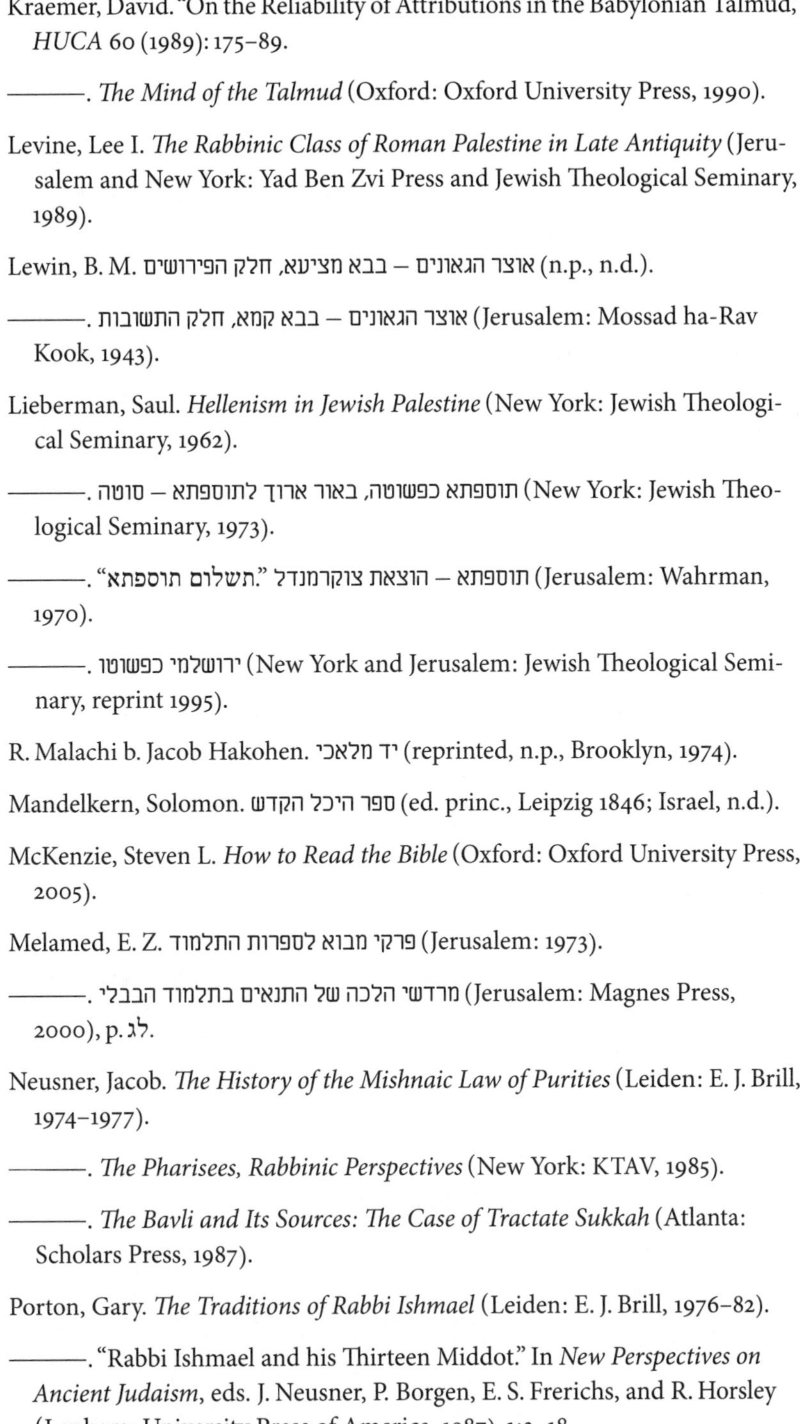

Kraemer, David. "On the Reliability of Attributions in the Babylonian Talmud," *HUCA* 60 (1989): 175–89.

———. *The Mind of the Talmud* (Oxford: Oxford University Press, 1990).

Levine, Lee I. *The Rabbinic Class of Roman Palestine in Late Antiquity* (Jerusalem and New York: Yad Ben Zvi Press and Jewish Theological Seminary, 1989).

Lewin, B. M. אוצר הגאונים – בבא מציעא, חלק הפירושים (n.p., n.d.).

———. אוצר הגאונים – בבא קמא, חלק התשובות (Jerusalem: Mossad ha-Rav Kook, 1943).

Lieberman, Saul. *Hellenism in Jewish Palestine* (New York: Jewish Theological Seminary, 1962).

———. תוספתא כפשוטה, באור ארוך לתוספתא – סוטה (New York: Jewish Theological Seminary, 1973).

———. "תוספתא – הוצאת צוקרמנדל. "תשלום תוספתא (Jerusalem: Wahrman, 1970).

———. ירושלמי כפשוטו (New York and Jerusalem: Jewish Theological Seminary, reprint 1995).

R. Malachi b. Jacob Hakohen. יד מלאכי (reprinted, n.p., Brooklyn, 1974).

Mandelkern, Solomon. ספר היכל הקדש (ed. princ., Leipzig 1846; Israel, n.d.).

McKenzie, Steven L. *How to Read the Bible* (Oxford: Oxford University Press, 2005).

Melamed, E. Z. פרקי מבוא לספרות התלמוד (Jerusalem: 1973).

———. מדרשי הלכה של התנאים בתלמוד הבבלי (Jerusalem: Magnes Press, 2000), p. לג.

Neusner, Jacob. *The History of the Mishnaic Law of Purities* (Leiden: E. J. Brill, 1974–1977).

———. *The Pharisees, Rabbinic Perspectives* (New York: KTAV, 1985).

———. *The Bavli and Its Sources: The Case of Tractate Sukkah* (Atlanta: Scholars Press, 1987).

Porton, Gary. *The Traditions of Rabbi Ishmael* (Leiden: E. J. Brill, 1976–82).

———. "Rabbi Ishmael and his Thirteen Middot." In *New Perspectives on Ancient Judaism*, eds. J. Neusner, P. Borgen, E. S. Frerichs, and R. Horsley (Lanham: University Press of America, 1987), 1:3–18.

Quintillian, *Institutio Oratoria*, trans. John Watson (Cambridge and London: Loeb Classics, 1922).

Rabinovitz, Zeev Wolf. שערי תורת ארץ ישראל (Jerusalem: I. Rabinovitz, 1940).

Rosenthal, David. "פירקא דאביי," *Tarbiz* 46 (1977): 97–109.

———. "מסורות ארץ-ישראליות ודרכן לבבל" (English title: "The Transformation of Eretz Israel Traditions in Babylonia"), *Cathedra* 92 (Jerusalem: Yad Izhak Ben-Zvi Press, 1999).

Rubenstein, Jeffrey. *Talmudic Stories: Narrative Art, Composition, and Culture* (Baltimore: Johns Hopkins University Press, 1999).

———. *The Culture of the Babylonian Talmud* (Baltimore and London: Johns Hopkins University Press, 2003).

R. Samson of Chinon, ספר הכריתות (Warsaw: 1885).

Sanders, E. P. *Judaism: Practice and Belief 63* B.C.E.*–66* C.E. (London and Philadelphia: SCM and Trinity, 1992).

Spanier, Arthur. *Die Toseftaperiode in der tannaitischen Literatur* (Berlin: C. A. Schwetschke, 1922; reprinted, Schocken, 1936).

Stern, David. *Midrash and Theory* (Evanston: Northwestern University Press, 1996).

Stern, S. "Attribution and Authorship in the Babylonian Talmud," *Journal of Jewish Studies* 45 (1994): 28–51.

Strack, H. L. and Günther Stemberger, *Introduction to the Talmud and Midrash* (Minneapolis: Fortress Press, 1996).

———. "ושוב לירושלמי נזיקין." In *Meḥqerei Talmud* 1, eds. D. Rosenthal and Y. Zussman (1990): 109–15.

Towner, W. S. *The Rabbinic "Enumeration of Scriptural Examples"* (Leiden: E. J. Brill, 1973).

Weiss, Abraham. היצירה של הסבוראים (Jerusalem: 1952).

———. לחקר התלמוד (New York: Feldheim, 1954).

———. על היצירה הספרותית של האמוראים (New York: Horeb-Yeshiva University, 1962).

———. מחקרים בתלמוד (Jerusalem: Mossad Ha-Rav Kook, 1975).

Weiss, I. H. דור ודור ודורשיו (Jerusalem and Tel Aviv: reprinted, Ziv, n.d.), (Vilna: n.p., 1871–1873 ; reprinted, Vilna 1904 ; reprinted, Jerusalem and Tel Aviv: Ziv Publishers, n.d.).

———. דור דור ודורשיו (Jerusalem: Dor, 1910, reprinted most recently in Jerusalem and Tel Aviv: Ziv, 1963).

Weiss-Halivni, David. מקורות ומסורות – נשים (Tel Aviv: Dvir, 1968).

———. מקורות ומסורות – שבת (Jerusalem: Jewish Theological Seminary, 1982) p. רסו; מקורות ומסורות – עירובין-פסחים (Jerusalem: Jewish Theological Seminary, 1982), p. כט, n. 11; מקורות ומסורות – מועד (Jerusalem: Jewish Theological Seminary, 1975).

———. *Midrash, Mishnah, and Gemara* (Cambridge and London: Harvard University Press, 1986).

———. מקורות ומסורות – בבא מציעא (Jerusalem: Hebrew University, 2007).

Yadin, Azzan. *Scripture as Logos: Rabbi Ishmael and the Origins of Midrash* (Philadelphia: University of Pennsylvania Press, 2004).

Zucker, Moshe. "לבעית פתרון ל״ב מדות ו,משנת ר׳ אליעזר׳," *PAAJR* 23 (December 1954): א-לט.

Zussman, Y. סוגיות בבליות לסדרים זרעים וטהרות (Hebrew University, 1969).

Index of Passages Cited

Bible

Genesis

Exodus

Leviticus

Numbers

Deuteronomy

Joshua

Mishnah

Tosefta

Palestinian Talmud

Babylonian Talmud

Nazir

Sotah

Gittin

Qiddushin

Baba Qama

Baba Meẓi'a

Baba Batra

Sanhedrin

Makkot

Shevu'ot

'Avodah Zarah

Zebaḥim

Menaḥot

Ḥullin

Bekhorot

'Arakhin

Temurah

Keritot

Me'ilah

Niddah

Mekhilta of Rabbi Ishmael

Mekhilta de Rabbi Simeon Bar Yoḥai on Exodus

Sifra

Sifre Numbers

Sifre Zuta to Numbers

Sifre Deuteronomy

Midrash Tanna'im on Deuteronomy

Pesiqta de-Rav Kahana

Pesiqta Rabbati

Avot de-Rabbi Natan Version B

Shittah Mequbeẓet on b.Baba Meẓi'a

Midrash ha-Gadol

Tosafot

bSukkah

Penei Moshe

Qorban ha-'Edah

Index of Authorities Cited

Subject Index